Praise for Always in God's Hands

I gladly commend this tremendous collection of devotions. A bit of Scripture, a bit of Edwards, and a bit of meditation—a powerful combination.

TIM CHALLIES
Author and blogger at challies.com

Jonathan Edwards held an unshakable faith in the sovereignty and active providence of God. The center of this faith was absolute confidence in the goodness of God and His loving relationships with His creation—especially His human creatures. Edwards was a man of unparalleled devotion and an unrivaled mind. The passage of three centuries has not dimmed his words or diminished his monumental contribution to Christian thought. This new devotional by Owen Strachan is a welcome introduction to Edwards's piety and theological insights. Strachan gives us the best of Edwards's theologically rich, warmhearted worship of the Savior he loved.

R. ALBERT MOHLER JR.
President of Southern Baptist Theological Seminary

I must confess, I really like daily devotional books. Luther, Lloyd-Jones, the Puritans, the church fathers, and, of course, Spurgeon, among others, are constant companions of mine in this format. Now I have another one to add. Dr. Owen Strachan, a noted Jonathan Edwards scholar, has put together a wonderful collection of quoted material penned by Edwards, with accompanying reflections and Scripture, for every day of the year. This is an excellent way to be introduced to and benefit from Jonathan Edwards if you've never really read him. (Your high school or college American Lit course reading of "Sinners in the Hands of an Angry God" doesn't count.) Even if you've read a lot of Edwards's works, you'll enjoy approaching them devotionally here. *Always in God's Hands* will give you beautifully and powerfully stated biblical truth from the writings of Edwards—providing you with plenty to think about profitably and to pray over personally.

LIGON DUNCAN
Chancellor and CEO of Reformed Theological Seminary

always in God's hands

✝

DAY BY DAY IN THE COMPANY OF

Jonathan Edwards

OWEN STRACHAN

TYNDALE
MOMENTUM®

The nonfiction imprint of
Tyndale House Publishers, Inc.

Visit Tyndale online at www.tyndale.com.

Visit Tyndale Momentum online at www.tyndalemomentum.com.

TYNDALE, Tyndale Momentum, and Tyndale's quill logo are registered trademarks of Tyndale House Publishers, Inc. The Tyndale Momentum logo is a trademark of Tyndale House Publishers, Inc. Tyndale Momentum is the nonfiction imprint of Tyndale House Publishers, Inc., Carol Stream, Illinois.

Always in God's Hands: Day by Day in the Company of Jonathan Edwards

Designed by Mark Anthony Lane II

Published in association with the literary agency of Wolgemuth & Associates, Inc.

For information about special discounts for bulk purchases, please contact Tyndale House Publishers at csresponse@tyndale.com, or call 1-800-323-9400.

ISBN 978-1-4964-2485-3

Printed in the United States of America

24	23	22	21	20	19	18
7	6	5	4	3	2	1

To Jason Allen

"They will be grateful that,
at the threatened nightfall,
the blood of their fathers ran strong."

WILLIAM F. BUCKLEY, JR.

Introduction

JONATHAN EDWARDS IS WELL-KNOWN—in many cases *exclusively* so—for his sermon "Sinners in the Hands of an Angry God," read in many high school English classes. There, students learn to fear Edwards, and to look askance at his God.

Edwards did not shy away from preaching the whole counsel of God, and neither should any pastor. He knew that God's justice and mercy do not clash, but together drive the needy sinner to repentance and faith. Only by seeing the depths of our sin will we hunger to taste the great grace offered us through Christ's death and resurrection. But having noted his sound commitment to preaching the whole Bible, we can see that Edwards also preached a great deal on heaven. Moving beyond the caricatures, this book seeks to recapture the true Jonathan Edwards. He was a faithful pastor who believed that humankind was not made for small pleasures, but Godward ones. Today, as ever, we need to recover this vision for our daily lives.

The title *Always in God's Hands* emerges from some of the letters Edwards wrote. For example, writing to his daughter Esther in 1753, Edwards reminded her that he could not perfectly guide her and guard her, but God would. This comforting perspective, coming from a doting father to his beloved child, goes to the very heart of the Christian faith. It is a fearsome thing to fall into the hands of a justly angered God, but it is a wonderful thing—impossible beyond words, beyond finite human reckoning—to be secure in the hands of a loving Savior.

This devotional will bring you into close contact with the soaring theology, comforting spirituality, and invigorating exhortation of one of history's most faithful and gifted pastors. You will see that I quote from all sorts of Edwards's materials—letters to his friends, sermons on many biblical themes, philosophical works, and more. As you read materials that, in many cases, very few have studied in a devotional way, you will get a sense for just how prolific Edwards's pen—and mind—were. This is intentional. If you have little familiarity with Edwards, I hope you will enjoy reading a range of his writings. And if all you've ever read from Edwards are the excerpts presented in this book, you will have read roughly 30,000 words from his pen—a lot more of his work than most people on the planet have ever read.

We follow a simple format. Each day begins with a selection from Edwards's writings, usually just a paragraph in length, and then offers brief commentary and a suggestion for application. A verse concludes the day's offering, inviting you to delve more deeply into the Scriptures that Edwards gave his life to herald. We have also spliced in numerous historical selections. These give context and showcase Edwards's endeavors, struggles, and faith. He was a sinner like us, and we lament his shortcomings. But as with every redeemed sinner, we can learn much from him. Outside of Christ, God has not left us to emulate perfect human guides, only imperfect ones (1 Corinthians 11:1; 2 Corinthians 4:5-7).

I pray that this devotional approach to the writings of Jonathan Edwards will help to strengthen your faith, hope, and spiritual practice. Discouragement is so close at hand in our day, but we can be certain that God is closer still. We see this theme throughout Edwards's writing.

At Midwestern Seminary, I teach classes on Edwards and on theology more broadly. I am confident that no writer in the great Christian tradition gives more attention to the hope of heaven than Edwards does. No theologian directs readers more insistently to think about everlasting life as an actual reality. We need this focus as human beings; in our hyperconnected age, we *especially* need to think about eternity. We will profit greatly from spending less time on all that is misfiring in our world, and more time concentrating on the glories of God. We need to be so heavenly minded, we could say, that we are of some earthly good.

It is remarkable that the church only now gains a daily devotional from Edwards's voluminous writings. As you will see, he is an inspiring motivator, counselor, and guide into the wonders of the God-made world. Two hundred sixty years after his death, Jonathan Edwards still speaks.

We who love the Word of God he preached are still listening.

January

†

January 1

Of all kinds of knowledge that we can ever obtain, the knowledge of God, and the knowledge of ourselves, are the most important. As religion is the great business, for which we are created, and on which our happiness depends; and as religion consists in an intercourse between ourselves and our Maker; and so has its foundation in God's nature and ours, and in the relation that God and we stand in to each other; therefore a true knowledge of both must be needful in order to [understand] true religion.

THE FREEDOM OF THE WILL, 1754

WHAT'S THE NUTRITIONAL CONTENT of that granola bar? What SPF is that sunscreen? Can you get a weird disease by using an old microwave?

We're encouraged to gain knowledge about many things today. Scarcely does a question pop up in conversation before we have our smartphone out, Google at the ready. We crave information—and yet the more facts we learn, the less interest we tend to have in the bigger picture. This is true spiritually as well. Details crowd in; eternity gets crowded out.

Jonathan Edwards corrects this tendency of our distractible hearts. He reminds us that there is nothing more needful in a stressed-out society than the knowledge of God. This is the "great business" for which mankind exists: not simply to store up facts about the Almighty, but to draw near to our Creator in a living, loving union. Sure, we need to troubleshoot all sorts of situations in our daily lives; but we were made for something more. We were made to know God, to experience the delight of a life centered around him. In worshiping God, we discover our true purpose, gaining "knowledge of ourselves" through a biblical prism. Life isn't supposed to be self-driven; it's supposed to be God-defined.

Today, and every day, let us make it our pursuit to know God as his Word reveals him. In an age of superficial distractions and concerns, let us lose ourselves in our Creator, studying him, communing with him, worshiping him.

Do not be conformed to this world, but be transformed by the renewal of your mind, that by testing you may discern what is the will of God, what is good and acceptable and perfect. ROMANS 12:2

January 2

The infinitely holy God, who always used to be esteemed by God's people, not only virtuous, but a being in whom is all possible virtue, and every virtue in the most absolute purity and perfection, and in infinitely greater brightness and amiableness than in any creature; the most perfect pattern of virtue, and the fountain from whom all others' virtue is but as beams from the sun; and who has been supposed to be, on the account of his virtue and holiness, infinitely more worthy to be esteemed, loved, honored, admired, commended, extolled and praised, than any creature . . . these things in God are good.

THE FREEDOM OF THE WILL, 1754

WE ALL HAVE BENEFITED from random acts of kindness on our behalf. For example, when I was in seminary, a man from my church in Washington, DC, bought me a computer. Forget the Corvette or the fancy clothes—a computer was just what a paper-writing student needed! It was a simple gift, but that laptop meant the world to me. We all have our memories of such acts of grace.

Typically, a kind deed will encourage us, but the boost to our spirits fades as time wears on. In his discussion of virtue—by which he means pure goodness exercised toward others—Jonathan Edwards points us beyond a momentary warming of the soul. When someone helps us in an unexpected way, we catch a glimpse of the glory and character of God. Virtue does not simply *exist*. It doesn't emerge out of cosmic blackness. It comes from the Lord, the "fountain" of all goodness and graciousness in this realm.

Random acts of kindness might seem to come out of nowhere. But we do not live in a void. We inhabit a God-made world, and every last beam of light ultimately comes from a being of total virtue. How helpful this is to remember today. In experiencing and extending kindness, we feel warmth on our faces. We have many challenges to handle, but through it all our God is good, inestimably good.

The Rock, his work is perfect, for all his ways are justice. A God of faithfulness and without iniquity, just and upright is he.

DEUTERONOMY 32:4

January 3

Resolved, that I will do whatsoever I think to be most to God's glory, and my own good, profit and pleasure, in the whole of my duration, without any consideration of the time, whether now, or never so many myriads of ages hence. Resolved to do whatever I think to be my duty, and most for the good and advantage of mankind in general. Resolved to do this, whatever difficulties I meet with, how many and how great soever.
LETTERS AND PERSONAL WRITINGS

ONE OF THE ICONIC EVENTS of my twentysomething years was the release of a new Apple product. In the Steve Jobs era, the debut of a new iPod or iPhone unleashed cultural chaos. People camped outside of retail stores for days. They stood in line for hours. They schemed and strategized to acquire the latest Apple device.

Those tech-savvy folks—displaying impressive patience—are just like us. They worked to obtain what they wanted most. If we desire season tickets for the local sports team, we scrape and scrap and find a way to buy them. If we want to present a flawless image, we put in the time to make sure that every last photo we post online looks perfect. We all devote ourselves to what we value most highly.

When Jonathan Edwards was a young man of eighteen, he resolved to live wholeheartedly for God's glory. This became his personal credo. He valued God above all and wanted to live for him. He saw no conflict between a doxological (glory-centered) lifestyle and his "own good, profit and pleasure." He believed that whatever brought glory and honor to God would also bring happiness to himself. Edwards's intentional example encourages us to approach all our days with a similar clarity. What can we do today that will glorify God—that will please him and show his greatness to others? Smartphones are great; but what words can we say, what deeds can we perform, what biblical truths can we share to magnify the Lord?

Everyone seeks out the things they love most. For followers of Jesus, joy comes not through a single event, a momentary splash, but through every moment we faithfully serve our King.

We exhorted each one of you and encouraged you and charged you to walk in a manner worthy of God, who calls you into his own kingdom and glory. I THESSALONIANS 2:12

January 4

The same thing is evident from all the promises which God made to the Messiah, of his future glory, kingdom and success, in his office and character of a mediator: which glory could not have been obtained, if his holiness had failed, and he had been guilty of sin. God's absolute promise of any things makes the things promised necessary, *and their failing to take place absolutely* impossible: *and in like manner it makes those things necessary, on which the thing promised depends, and without which it can't take effect.*

THE FREEDOM OF THE WILL, 1754

THERE IS NO DISAPPOINTMENT quite like failing to honor your word to beloved children. We tell that energetic little boy we'll play soccer with him tomorrow, but we end up being swept along by the obligations of the hour. We set up a tea party date with the six-year-old hostess, and the dolls are all in their places; but at the appointed time we're not sipping watery tea. We sometimes struggle to remember—and keep—promises we made minutes ago, let alone days, let alone years.

Here is the wondrous truth about God the Father: Unlike you and me, he has never failed to keep a commitment. As Jonathan Edwards beautifully teaches, God's character stands behind every promise he makes. His promises are *absolute*; ours are, at best, hopeful and provisional. If the Lord tells us he will do something, it is "absolutely impossible" it will not come to pass. His perfections, ten thousand of them, stand behind every word he utters.

What a cheering word this is. The Lord does not only keep his calendar consistently; he provides for our greatest need—a Messiah who saves our souls. We may sense our inadequacy and feel that our future is uncertain, but the Word of God assures us that the Lord is leading history to its rightful conclusion in Christ (Revelation 21–22). He is in charge. He will keep his word. His purposes will not fail. Though at times we may struggle to honor our promises, we have tremendous comfort in knowing that the Lord always keeps his.

God is not man, that he should lie, or a son of man, that he should change his mind. Has he said, and will he not do it? Or has he spoken, and will he not fulfill it? NUMBERS 23:19

January 5

All the promises that were made to the church of God under the old testament, of the great enlargement of the church, and advancement of her glory, in the days of the gospel, after the coming of the Messiah: the increase of her light, liberty, holiness, joy, triumph over her enemies, etc., of which so great a part of the Old Testament consists; which are repeated so often, are so variously exhibited, so frequently introduced with great pomp and solemnity, and are so abundantly sealed with typical and symbolical representations; I say, all these promises imply, that the Messiah should perfect the work of redemption; and this implies, that he should persevere in the work which the Father had appointed him, being in all things conformed to his will.

THE FREEDOM OF THE WILL, 1754

IT COMES NATURALLY TO us to make resolutions. Granted, some people resolve not to make them; but others among us set goals we swear we will keep. Fewer cookies in the new year. A spin class every Tuesday and Thursday. Whatever the precise commitment, it is not hard to make a resolution. Resolutions are not the problem. Perseverance is. (It's when those freshly baked chocolate chip cookies come out of the oven that our resolve begins to waver.)

Thankfully, the Christian life relentlessly reminds us that we are not the standard. Jesus is. On matters both great and small. Jesus came into the world to fulfill his Father's will. He came not merely to encourage us, but chiefly to "perfect the work of redemption," as Jonathan Edwards notes. Jesus kept his word. He honored the one who sent him. He shows us a better way.

Jesus is not an indifferent Redeemer. His mission took great effort. He "learned obedience from the things he suffered" (Hebrews 5:8, NLT). His example empowers and instructs us today: Whether we join the spin class or not, we are called to persevere in the faith. There are, after all, no accidental Christians in heaven. Praise God, we are not on our own. The Holy Spirit is powerful. By the Spirit's indwelling power, we have the strength we need to push through hardship, persevere through trials, and be "in all things conformed" to the Father's will, just as Jesus was.

Therefore, since we are surrounded by so great a cloud of witnesses, let us also lay aside every weight, and sin which clings so closely, and let us run with endurance the race that is set before us. HEBREWS 12:1

January 6

The saints of old trusted on the promises of a future redemption to be wrought out and completed by the Messiah, and built their comfort upon it: Abraham saw Christ's day and rejoiced; and he and the other patriarchs died in the faith of the promise of it (Hebrews 11:13). . . . But if Christ's virtue might fail, he was mistaken: his great comfort was not built so sure, as he thought it was.

THE FREEDOM OF THE WILL, 1754

EVERY ONCE IN A WHILE, we have an airline flight that reminds us of our lack of control. I had one recently—on a plane hurtling into my destination like roller coaster cars careening down the track. Times like this open our eyes to how much we have staked on someone else. Our very existence depends on a couple of pilots in the cockpit we've never met.

In a much greater sense than any airline flight, our eternal destiny rests on one man. It has always been this way. God has always called his people to trust the great promise of a serpent-crushing, sin-destroying Savior (Genesis 3:15). Jesus fulfilled this promise. Jesus is the one who did the work we could not do, and would not have wanted to do if we knew of it. God put everything on his back. Jesus did not falter or fail.

Today, we may face discouragement. We may feel as if we are hurtling through life at breakneck speed. We might be afraid of death. But we are not the final word on the matter. Our feelings are not determinative. Jesus is our hope—not we ourselves. We have "built [our] comfort" upon him, as Edwards says Abraham did. This comfort will not fail. Let us think often of this: Whatever comes our way, Christ will hold us fast. Uncertain as this life is, we know this for certain: He will bring us home.

> These all died in faith, not having received the things promised,
> but having seen them and greeted them from afar, and having
> acknowledged that they were strangers and exiles on the earth.
> HEBREWS 11:13

January 7

From a vigorous, affectionate, and fervent love to God, will necessarily arise other religious affections: hence will arise an intense hatred and abhorrence of sin, fear of sin, and a dread of God's displeasure, gratitude to God for his goodness, complacence and joy in God when God is graciously and sensibly present, and grief when he is absent, and a joyful hope when a future enjoyment of God is expected, and fervent zeal for the glory of God.
RELIGIOUS AFFECTIONS, 1746

IT'S ALWAYS FUN to caravan together on a road trip. The snacks are packed, spirits are high, and the road stretches off into the distance. Soon, it's your turn to take the lead, and so you do. You direct the group to a pit stop, only to wind up at a dead end. Enjoyment gives way to embarrassment. In the heat of the moment, we don't have time for excuses or explanations. We have to find a way back to the freeway.

So it is with our sin. In his magnificent kindness, the Lord has enabled us to repent and trust Jesus as our sin-cleansing Redeemer. But though we are redeemed, we are not sinless. We must continually fight our flesh. Yet we must take care: We cannot drive into a dead end of discouragement. At times, our sin may seem so big that God seems small. But Jonathan Edwards calls us back to the bigness and greatness of God. We head back to the Bible. There, we find the Spirit stirring up in us a "vigorous, affectionate, and fervent love [for] God" as we meditate on God's works and his will.

The way out of our spiritual dilemmas, and the shame and embarrassment they cause, is not self-fixation. We confront our sin, to be sure. But in seeking its defeat, we concentrate on God. We return to him. We savor our hope, our eternal destiny, and our forgiver. Soon, we're on our way once more, the narrow path stretching out before us like the open road.

You shall love the LORD your God with all your heart and with all your soul and with all your might. DEUTERONOMY 6:5

January 8

The deceitfulness of the heart of man appears in no one thing so much, as this of spiritual pride and self-righteousness. The subtlety of Satan appears in its height in his managing of persons with respect to this sin. And perhaps one reason may be, that here he has most experience: he knows the way of its coming in; he is acquainted with the secret springs of it; it was his own sin.
RELIGIOUS AFFECTIONS, 1746

MOST PEOPLE DO NOT HAVE a hard time finding the energy within themselves to sin. It's a sad reality, but an honest one. When was the last time you heard someone say, "I don't know what is wrong with my temper. I want to get really mad, but I just can't!" Usually we feel sins such as pride, envy, and anger welling up in us uninvited. They sometimes seem to come from nowhere, like a sudden storm that lowers the outdoor temperature by twenty degrees.

Jonathan Edwards's observation compels us to take stock of our hearts. His words are aimed squarely at us. Do we have spiritual pride over our accomplishments? Having rejected the world, have we fallen into a posture of self-righteousness? If so, we have fallen into one of the hardest traps to spot. It seems as if we're serving the Lord, when in truth we're serving ourselves.

Satan, the tempter, wants to nudge us off track. He is the author of such unrighteousness, of puffing up self in order to make us forget God. Today, let us be shrewder than the devil. Let us be zealous for good works, but let us also examine our hearts, and root out any pride we feel about our Christian lives. Those who avoid deceit are less like a shocking thunderstorm and much more like a pleasing rain of refreshment.

When pride comes, then comes disgrace, but with the humble is wisdom. PROVERBS 11:2

January 9

THE FUTURE MRS. SARAH EDWARDS, Jonathan's wife, was born on this day in 1710 to James Pierpont, a Congregationalist minister in New Haven, and his wife, Mary. James Pierpont was a widely respected minister who helped found the Connecticut Collegiate School, later known as Yale University. Mary Pierpont trained her daughter in godly femininity, and from a young age she garnered the reputation of having exceptional social skills, knowledge, and beauty. Samuel Hopkins described Sarah's demeanor as a "peculiar loveliness of expression, the combined result of goodness and intelligence."[1]

Sarah first met Jonathan at her father's church when she was thirteen and he was twenty. Jonathan, to put it simply, was transfixed. He wrote the following to himself:

> They say there is a young lady in [New Haven] who is beloved of that Great Being, who made and rules the world, and that there are certain seasons in which this Great Being, in some way or other invisible, comes to her and fills her mind with exceeding sweet delight; and that she hardly cares for any thing, except to meditate on him—that she expects after a while to be received up where he is, to be raised up out of the world and caught up into heaven; being assured that he loves her too well to let her remain at a distance from Him always. There she is to dwell with him, and to be ravished with his love and delight forever. . . . She has a strange sweetness in her mind, and singular purity in her affections; is most just and conscientious in all her conduct; and you could not persuade her to do any thing wrong or sinful, if you would give her all the world, lest she should offend this Great Being. She is of a wonderful sweetness, calmness and universal benevolence of mind; especially after this Great God has manifested himself to her mind. . . . She loves to be alone, walking in the fields and groves, and seems to have someone invisible always conversing with her."[2]

After four years of courtship, Jonathan and Sarah were married on July 28, 1727. Their union lasted until Jonathan's death in March 1758, and Sarah's own death came just seven months later. Marriage for the couple was not always easy; Jonathan was very busy, and Sarah had a great deal to manage as a wife and mother. Yet their love never faded. Instead, it served as a testament to scores of their peers of the beauty and power of a Christian marriage. This happy union reminds us today to do what we can to strengthen godly marriages, and to never forget the gospel of which they testify (Ephesians 5:22-33).

January 10

That is the nature of true grace and spiritual light, that it opens to a person's view the infinite reason there is that he should be holy in a high degree. And the more grace he has, the more this is opened to view, the greater sense he has of the infinite excellency and glory of the Divine Being, and of the infinite dignity of the person of Christ, and the boundless length and breadth, and depth and height, of the love of Christ to sinners. . . . And so the more he apprehends, the more the smallness of his grace and love appears strange and wonderful: and therefore is more ready to think that others are beyond him.
RELIGIOUS AFFECTIONS, 1746

I'M ALWAYS AMAZED by the capacity of the human heart to create competition. One minute, we're swimming lazily in a lake; the next minute, we're having a contest to see who can make the biggest splash jumping off the dock. More than we might admit, we have competitive hearts, whether seen at the lake, in the classroom, or even in our friendships. It is natural to compete.

The truth of the Christian life is this: We are not fundamentally in competition with one another. As believers, we live theocentric (God-centered) lives. We're not playing a zero-sum game in which only one person wins. As believers, we worship God *and* we seek to build one another up. It's not that faith kills our competitive instincts in our daily endeavors. But as followers of Christ, our focus is no longer on ourselves, nor on triumphing over our peers. It's on "the infinite excellency and glory of the Divine Being."

Jonathan Edwards is quite right in saying that the more we take in of God, the less we are consumed with ourselves. Where once we felt dissatisfaction, now we gain peace. This transformation affects our relationships, as well. Where once we were driven to look better than others, now we readily see ways "that others are beyond [us]." Being God-centered creates humility, and humility creates love. Instead of fighting, now we dwell together in peace. We may still (happily) splash into the lake, but we're freed from the need to best others for our own glory.

Everyone who exalts himself will be humbled, and he who humbles himself will be exalted. LUKE 14:11

January 11

No wonder that a love to holiness, for holiness' sake, inclines persons to practice holiness, and to practice everything that is holy. Seeing holiness is the main thing that excites, draws and governs all gracious affections, no wonder that all such affections tend to holiness. That which men love, they desire to have and to be united to, and possessed of. That beauty which men delight in, they desire to be adorned with. Those acts which men delight in, they necessarily incline to do.

RELIGIOUS AFFECTIONS, 1746

JONATHAN EDWARDS USES the word *affections* quite often, as we shall see. Though we don't use the word much today, we can think of "affections" as the soul's strongest inclinations. Affections are closely connected to our will. What we feel drawn toward, what we make our highest priority, reveals what our affections most want. This shows us what is most important to us.

Many people, for example, say they love God. But though they may respect him, attend church at times, and read the Bible sporadically, they do not treasure him. In truth, their affections, their deepest longings, are not for God. What they hunger and seek after are the things of the world.

For Edwards, being a Christian does not mean having a vague inclination to follow God. God is not a passing fancy for true believers. The born-again man or woman sees *beauty* in God that draws us to *delight* in him. God's holiness is dazzling to believers. We cannot get enough of it. We are like tourists ushered into a glorious cathedral who end up sitting for hours, dazzled. This is what the holiness of God does for all who have eyes to see it—it grips us, takes hold of us, refuses to release us. We delight in it. This delight in the divine is not a distraction; it is a way of life for us, today and every day.

As obedient children, do not be conformed to the passions of your former ignorance, but as he who called you is holy, you also be holy in all your conduct, since it is written, "You shall be holy, for I am holy."

I PETER 1:14-16

January 12

The saints are said to live by Christ living in them (Galatians 2:20). Christ by his Spirit not only is in them, but lives in them; and so that they live by his life; so is his Spirit united to them, as a principle of life in them; they don't only drink living water, but this living water becomes a well or fountain of water, in the soul, springing up into spiritual and everlasting life (John 4:14), and thus becomes a principle of life in them.
RELIGIOUS AFFECTIONS, 1746

IT IS NO SMALL THING to think of everlasting refreshment. Many of us scheme and strategize to get water in the midst of our daily commitments. There's a reason why "the water cooler" is still symbolic of the hub of a workplace. Everyone needs refreshment. Because we guzzle liquids almost constantly, we can scarcely comprehend how nice an unending stream would be—and how much small talk would magically disappear along with the water cooler.

In today's passage, Jonathan Edwards alludes to the Samaritan woman's struggle to comprehend the concept of "living water" (John 4:10-15). She is astonished by the prospect of continual bodily refreshment and has no category for something even greater. But this *something greater* is precisely what Christ offers her—and us. He promises to send the Holy Spirit to dwell in every born-again believer, uniting us with Christ. Not that we now have a spiritual landlord clumping around in our brains, but that we may now partake of the goodness of Christ at all times, without interruption, without cessation.

This news is so good that we, like the Samaritan woman, struggle to believe it. But it is real and true. We may yet face dryness, and the world at times may feel like a desert. But the Spirit is a "principle of life" in us, "springing up into spiritual and everlasting life." Christ is not a trickle of grace. He is an overflowing fountain of love—both now and forever.

I have been crucified with Christ. It is no longer I who live, but Christ who lives in me. And the life I now live in the flesh I live by faith in the Son of God, who loved me and gave himself for me. GALATIANS 2:20

January 13

What chiefly makes a man, or any creature lovely, is his excellency; and so what chiefly renders God lovely, and must undoubtedly be the chief ground of true love, is his excellency. God's nature, or the divinity, is infinitely excellent; yea 'tis infinite beauty, brightness, and glory itself.
RELIGIOUS AFFECTIONS, 1746

WE'VE ALL HEARD what could be called the perennial youth group question: *Will heaven be boring?* We don't dismiss the question out of hand. After all, we'll have to experience the afterlife to fully comprehend it.

But we need to think hard about what is behind this question. For the converted Christian, God is not merely the means to heaven, the preselected entry point. God is the *purpose* of heaven. He is the reason there is a realm of pure glory and undiluted light. Heaven exists to display his perfections, perfections that no space or place can contain. God is "infinitely excellent," as Edwards points out. He uses the term *excellent* to denote the joining of every wonderful element of life. If you are infinitely excellent, you have the fullest possible goodness. You are perfect in every way. You blow the standards out of the water.

This is what makes heaven great: Our infinitely excellent God is there. This is why we embrace the Christian life: It gives us God. This is what makes us want to know God: He is pure "beauty, brightness, and glory itself." Will living with God for eternity in the new heavens and new earth be boring? Not a chance. He has captivated us here amid our sin and distraction; in the life to come, all our sin will fall away. We will see God as he is. What has begun already for the believer will intensify to a wondrous degree, and being with God will never be boring.

One thing have I asked of the LORD, that will I seek after: that I may dwell in the house of the LORD all the days of my life, to gaze upon the beauty of the LORD and to inquire in his temple. PSALM 27:4

January 14

The first foundation of the delight a true saint has in God, is his own perfection; . . . the way of salvation by Christ, is a delightful way to him, for the sweet and admirable manifestations of the divine perfections in it; the holy doctrines of the gospel, by which God is exalted and man abased, holiness honored and promoted, and sin greatly disgraced and discouraged, and free and sovereign love manifested.

RELIGIOUS AFFECTIONS, 1746

WE MAY WELL REMEMBER the path of salvation we once schemed for ourselves. We would be okay eternally, we reasoned, because we played by the rules. We had never done anything awful, and God grades on a curve, right? Perhaps we even lashed out at those who dared challenge our self-directed doctrine of salvation.

When God strikes, however, he upends our beliefs. Like the items on a money changer's table in a once-quiet temple, the pat sayings and self-serving reassurances end up in a heap. By God's divine grace, we discover "the way of salvation by Christ." Conversion leads to a grand embarrassment, a glorious stripping away. How silly our thinking was. How misguided our views. How silly was our scheme to save ourselves and justify our behavior.

This recognition happens for every Christian. Once saved, we never stop marveling at how "sweet and admirable" the good news of Christ is in contrast to our ideas. All our good works and tidy truisms end up "greatly disgraced." In the light of saving faith, God is utterly *exalted*. This is true not merely of the moment of first repentance; it is the pattern of our redeemed lives, now and always. We are brought low and humbled; God is lifted high and treasured.

You make known to me the path of life; in your presence there is fullness of joy; at your right hand are pleasures forevermore.

PSALM 16:11

January 15

A true saint, when in the enjoyment of true discoveries of the sweet glory of God and Christ, has his mind too much captivated and engaged by what he views without himself, to stand at that time to view himself, and his own attainments: it would be a diversion and loss which he could not bear, to take his eye off from the ravishing object of his contemplation, to survey his own experience, and to spend time in thinking with himself.
RELIGIOUS AFFECTIONS, 1746

I DON'T KNOW WHETHER you've heard of narcissistic personality disorder, but it's a thing. An increasingly common reality, it seems. Psychologists use the term to refer to individuals who simply cannot stop talking and thinking about themselves. For such a person, life is not about serving others; it is squarely and solely about *me*. *Me* is what I talk about, think about, and live to promote.

In salvation, Christ rescues us from ourselves. Regeneration—the miracle of being made alive by the Spirit—is not only a change of heart. It is a change of focus. Before, we could scarcely stop concentrating on our own consuming concerns. Now, being released from sin, Satan, death, and hell, we can scarcely bear to take our eyes off the glorious God who has made us his own. We would have to be dragged away from God, so hungry is our heart for him.

Jonathan Edwards is speaking here in ideal terms. We all—every one of us—take our eyes off of God, and we must repent daily. Yet Edwards reminds us of our true identity. The work of Christ has broken the power of sin's spell. We need not live for our own glory. We are gloriously ruined by God, and now he is the one we want to talk about, think about, and promote. In today's world, this may sound like an obligation, a burden; but it is not. In truth, it is a rescue, and we may freshly savor it now, in this day God has given us.

He must increase, but I must decrease. JOHN 3:30

January 16

A true love to God must begin with a delight in his holiness, and not with a delight in any other attribute; for no other attribute is truly lovely without this. . . . They that don't see the glory of God's holiness, can't see anything of the true glory of his mercy and grace.
RELIGIOUS AFFECTIONS, 1746

NO ONE EVER OBJECTS to the idea of a loving God. We all like the idea that the so-called man upstairs has our back. And he is love at his very core, right? Because of this, the thinking goes, there's no need to lose ourselves in the rigors of organized religion. We're good to go.

But here's the truth: Though many people understand that God is transcendent, very few see that he is all-consumingly holy. Transcendence is fine, but divine holiness makes folks uneasy. If God is holy, we sinners have a problem—a holiness problem. We know, even without the Spirit renewing us, that we are not holy as God is holy.

In God's kindness, the story does not end here. The Christian faith presents us with a God who is both holy *and* loving. As we study the all-surpassing righteousness of God, the "true glory of his mercy and grace" dawns on us. In the miracle of miracles, the Holy One of Israel gave us Christ for our salvation. Today, as believers, we rejoice in a God who is totally good, perfectly just, and incomparably loving. God did not relax his standards in order to save us; in Christ, the God-man, all God's standards are fulfilled. Grace abounds. We are free to be holy and loving because we worship a holy and loving God.

> Who will not fear, O Lord, and glorify your name? For you alone are holy. All nations will come and worship you, for your righteous acts have been revealed. REVELATION 15:4

January 17

The end of the word of God is to teach and instruct us. If persons therefore carelessly lose that knowledge and instruction they received, they may be said to have let the word of God slip. The word of God is to help us against our ignorance and errors. If persons don't lay up the instruction they have received, but though they seem to get knowledge by it in the time of it, yet when they go, think no more of it, and divert their minds wholly from it, and spend their thoughts about other things . . . they may be said to lose what they have heard.

SERMONS AND DISCOURSES, 1734-1738

EVERY FATHER OR MOTHER knows how challenging it is to make our children *listen* to us.

"Yes, I said to pick up in the playroom," we sigh, "but I also said to make sure the swords were in the sword box." (The swords, alas, did not end up in the sword box.)

But how easy it is for us as adults to be just like a half-hearing child. We receive instruction from the Lord, clear as a bell at midday, yet we so often divert our minds and forget what we have heard. The Word is not misleading; it is clear. It hacks away at the underbrush of our hearts, overwhelming the "ignorance and errors" common to creatures like us. Yet, to use the language of Jonathan Edwards, we are careless, easily diverted creatures.

The good news is that we have the power to fight our diversions. One helpful practice is to meditate on the teaching and instruction we receive from the Word of God. It's not a bad thing to listen to some soothing music on our commute, or to catch up on the latest news, but we can also use that time to reflect on Scriptures we have read. Whatever our precise practice, we have been given gold by God—pure wisdom. Let us pick up "the sword of the Spirit, which is the word of God" (Ephesians 6:17). Let us not lose what we have heard.

Blessed is the man who walks not in the counsel of the wicked, nor stands in the way of sinners, nor sits in the seat of scoffers; but his delight is in the law of the Lord, and on his law he meditates day and night. PSALM 1:1-2

January 18

Resolved, never to lose one moment of time; but improve it the most profitable way I possibly can.
LETTERS AND PERSONAL WRITINGS

"I DIDN'T HAVE TIME." If Guinness World Records were somehow able to track excuses, this one might hold the all-time number one spot. We've all said it at some point; and we've certainly all felt it. Yet when we step back and think about how we've used the moments that were given to us, the fervor of our self-defense may fade.

Sheepishly, we might admit that we *had* the time, but we didn't make good use of it. Every person on earth has 168 hours in a week, and 8,760 hours in a year. That's a lot of time. Jonathan Edwards realized this from a young age, and he wished to grab hold of the clock and squeeze it for all he could. He did not want to "lose" precious hours, but to "improve" them, to use them profitably for a divine purpose.

Some might wonder whether such a mentality breeds exhaustion and eventual frustration. After all, none of us can redeem our days the way we might wish. Nonetheless, the church is on a mission for Christ Jesus. We rest in God, and steward our bodies well. But we are not a movement of leisure, fundamentally; we are a movement of action. We seek to take the gospel to the ends of the earth (Acts 1:8), and to be salt and light wherever we are (Matthew 5:13-16). We want to love God with all our heart, soul, mind, and strength, and our neighbor as ourselves (Mark 12:30-31). These callings do not merely take a little of our day—they call for whole-soul investment. We should not be time wasters; we should be time *improvers*, using our days for divine purpose.

> For everything there is a season, and a time for every matter under heaven: a time to be born, and a time to die; a time to plant, and a time to pluck up what is planted. ECCLESIASTES 3:1-2

January 19

It shows a wicked contempt in a child, when he is no way careful to retain the counsels and admonitions given him by a father. How much more when men thus treat the infinitely great God, when he in a solemn manner directs himself to us, and gives us his holy counsels and instructions.

SERMONS AND DISCOURSES, 1734-1738

ONE OF THE MOST STARTLING events of my life happened on a calm walk in California. My wife and I were enjoying a stroll when we spotted a little boy dancing in an unpredictable way, as children do. This was a bad place for a jig, though; the boy was nearly out in the road. I could hear a car approaching, and I looked to see whether the boy's father would corral him. He did not, and the situation looked dire until a passerby shouted "STOP!" The boy halted, and the car drove by, roughly one foot from where the boy stood frozen. It was a sobering moment.

It is not hard to wander away from our heavenly Father. It is easy to slip into an undisciplined or even out-of-control life. How kind of God that we have been given clear guidance and "holy counsels" from the Lord. He has, in a serious and seriously loving way, given us his perfect direction. We need not carve our own path; we need not blunder in the dark. God's way is best, and it is laid out for us in the Bible.

As followers of Jesus, we cannot neglect our Father's counsel. Yet, we may glimpse flickers of "wicked contempt" in our hearts for our Father's wisdom in Scripture. Jonathan Edwards exhorts us to root out such foolish disdain for divine instruction. The way of God is sure; the way of sin is dangerous. Let us not spin out of control; let us not live foolishly. Let us listen to our Father's voice.

We also thank God constantly for this, that when you received the word of God, which you heard from us, you accepted it not as the word of men but as what it really is, the word of God, which is at work in you believers. I THESSALONIANS 2:13

January 20

It may be observed that among a backsliding and degenerating people, a zeal for positive duties and outward forms of worship is generally held up much longer than of moral duties, though moral duties are much more essential. So it was among the Jews in Christ's time. They were a great deal more zealous of tithing mint, and anise, and cumin, than they were of judgment, mercy, and peace.

SERMONS AND DISCOURSES, 1734-1738

IT IS ALWAYS EASIER TO just get the family to church than it is to actually love your family. I have learned this over the years as a husband and father. Most of us can pull ourselves together enough to practice what Jonathan Edwards calls the "outward forms of worship." We can smile, respond cheerfully to questions from friends, and sing songs in church. But it is harder to fake the faith in quieter moments, when our character is truly on display.

No Christian lives with perfect spiritual consistency. We all must regularly examine our hearts to see whether inward realities are fueling outward forms, or whether we are using outward forms to mask inward realities. In other words, does our public worship overflow from our true spiritual lives? Or is our public worship—or our charitable deeds—a cover for a lack of spiritual vitality? It is a very good thing to give money to the church; but it is a greater thing to love mercy.

In Edwards's Massachusetts congregation, he sensed that numerous church members were merely playing at Christianity. This is a temptation we all must avoid. We must continually press in to Christ, and pursue him with heart, soul, mind, and strength. We want the real thing; we crave the whole Christ. The truth is, he is ours, and we may worship him now in spirit and in truth.

Woe to you, scribes and Pharisees, hypocrites! For you are like whitewashed tombs, which outwardly appear beautiful, but within are full of dead people's bones and all uncleanness.

MATTHEW 23:27

January 21

The humble, sensible Christian is most ready to complain of himself. He is ready to cry out of his own badness, is ready to say that he has been the chief of sinners, and has been the most undeserving. His thoughts turn chiefly on what he has done, the hand he has had in provoking God, and bringing down his judgments.

SERMONS AND DISCOURSES, 1734-1738

YOU MAY HAVE OBSERVED the cultural phenomenon I call the "Hollywood apology." When a celebrity is caught in a transgression and the time comes for a public statement, instead of expressing full sorrow, he or she often seeks to soften the wrongdoing with a conditional apology: "I apologize—*if* I offended you," or, "*If* anyone's feelings were hurt, I'm sorry." At its core, the Hollywood apology is no apology at all.

The truth of the matter is that we all—famous or obscure—naturally *want* to let ourselves off the hook. We would much rather shift the blame. The problem isn't *us*; it's our circumstances, or another person, or the cosmos itself. One of the most explosive aspects of biblical Christianity is this: It frees us to be honest. When God saves us, he convicts us of the "bad news" about our unrighteousness and God's judgment, which makes the "good news" of Christ's cleansing work on the cross and life-giving resurrection ten thousand times sweeter.

Everyone wants a miracle, a sign, that Christianity is true. Here is one of the greatest miracles on earth: sinners who once made excuses to cover themselves now confessing that they are "chief of sinners," as Jonathan Edwards says. We don't have to construct elaborate explanations for our ungodly behavior. In Christ, we are free to be honest about our failings; in Christ, we are free to humbly apologize and repent.

> The tax collector, standing far off, would not even lift up his eyes to heaven, but beat his breast, saying, "God, be merciful to me, a sinner!"
> LUKE 18:13

January 22

'Tis certain that a religious and holy life has the greatest excellency to recommend it. 'Tis fit in itself that you should embrace [it] for the excellency of it; for 'tis that that makes persons heavenly, and confirms them to God.
SERMONS AND DISCOURSES, 1734-1738

THE CHRISTIAN FAITH is a mystical faith. It introduces us to God, who is spirit, and enables us to continually partake of his goodness. As believers in God, we are made to be *otherworldly*, with our true citizenship in another realm.

Yet we sometimes go to great lengths to show people around us that we're not awkward zealots for Christ. We emphasize how similar we are to everyone else. When we go out to eat, we pray the world's fastest prayer over our meal, eager for the moment to pass, nervous that someone might actually see us communing directly with God. When someone asks us a question about biblical teaching, we clam up, afraid of saying the wrong thing and driving our friend away.

Jonathan Edwards's terse words embolden us to embrace the beauty of Christianity. Being a Christian is not silly; it is the most naturally excellent way to live. Everything coheres in a biblical perspective and makes sense out of our living faith. We were not created to be worldly. We were made to be *heavenly* and to be known by God. This does not condemn our everyday lives. But it means that, as spiritual pilgrims, we do not apologize for the gospel of grace. We celebrate it, share it, and praise God that it is making us heavenly.

By faith Abraham obeyed when he was called to go out to a place that he was to receive as an inheritance. And he went out . . . looking forward to the city that has foundations, whose designer and builder is God. HEBREWS 11:8, 10

January 23

God is wont to be using many and great means with many wicked men to bring them to forsake their sins, and continues using means with them for a long time. He commands them to forsake their sins, and uses the authority of a lord and sovereign.

SERMONS AND DISCOURSES, 1734-1738

ONE OF THE MOST POWERFUL cinematic scenes I've witnessed takes place in *The Lord of the Rings: The Two Towers*, based on the book by J. R. R. Tolkien. The good wizard Gandalf seeks to cast out evil influences from the enslaved mind of Théoden, king of Rohan. Long before, Théoden had allowed a wicked ruler to overtake his mind. With Gandalf on the scene, a battle ensues, and Gandalf overthrows the forces that have long ruled Théoden. The king and his kingdom are saved.

This fictional story reminds us of our own spiritual deliverance. We are claimed by the King through faith in his name. But despite this wondrous reality, it is tempting to become lazy with our besetting sins. Without knowing it, we can slip into what might be called a sin-management plan. In other words, we don't focus on destroying ungodliness (as we're exhorted to do in Colossians 3:1-11). Instead, we trim the unruly hedges of our sins, making sure they don't get too big or too embarrassing. In such instances, we conveniently forget the reality of God's sovereign rule over our lives. He does not merely *suggest* that we put sin to death, root and branch; he *commands* us to do so.

It is easy to try to domesticate God; to make him seem small. But he is not a small God, and his Word is not a collection of suggestions. Likewise, when we hear God call us to holiness, we should not imagine that he is speaking in a whisper. We should picture a lion, mighty in power, roaring over his creation. Here is what he tells us: Sin is defeated in Christ, and the enemy is overthrown. We can claim this evil-defeating power today, and every day.

Say to them, As I live, declares the Lord GOD, I have no pleasure in the death of the wicked, but that the wicked turn from his way and live; turn back, turn back from your evil ways, for why will you die, O house of Israel? EZEKIEL 33:11

January 24

He [Satan] counsels men to sin under pretense of duty. When Satan would tempt men to sin, this is a stratagem he oftentimes makes use, [namely], to persuade men that 'Tis their duty. Thus oftentimes when he counsels men to a violent pursuit after the world, he suggests to them that 'Tis more than their duty. . . . He calls their anxiousness and eagerness after the world a prudent care.

SERMONS AND DISCOURSES, 1734-1738

IN POPULAR CULTURE, our spiritual foe is often portrayed in outsized, almost gleeful, terms. Satan is depicted as a cartoon figure, in a weird shade of red and holding a pitchfork. But this does not fit the biblical portrait of our enemy. Satan is more like a smooth operator, a peerless mover-and-shaker. He glides through life, and many fall under his spell.

But not us. We are children of God. We are freed from the power of sin by the cross of Christ (Romans 6:6-7). This means that Satan has no hold over us. Yet he tries to convince us that he indeed still rules over us. He attempts to rule our behavior, to make us think we owe allegiance to our temptations and snares. In the chilling words of Jonathan Edwards, the devil wants nothing less than to incite "a violent pursuit after the world" in our hearts.

Scripture tells us not to fear the devil, but rather to fear God (Ecclesiastes 12:13). God holds the ultimate sway over us, not Satan. We must make this truth operational in our hour-by-hour existence. We do not owe our smartphone an addiction. We do not have any bond with pornography. We are not in chains when it comes to loneliness or our marital struggles. Christ is victorious over darkness, and we are presently being made new by the Holy Spirit. The enemy is unmasked—not only unmasked, but defeated.

Satan disguises himself as an angel of light.   2 CORINTHIANS 11:14

January 25

The devil is "a roaring lion, going about, seeking whom he may devour" (1 Peter 5:8). But men would beware of him, if he appeared in such a shape. . . . If there should come a lion, or bear, or some such wild beast into town, how would all the town be raised, and be up in arms against him! But the devil is a wolf in sheep's clothing. He is a roaring lion, but looks as harmless to men as a lamb. Hence men are bold with him, have a great deal to do with him, and think no harm, are no way upon their watch or guard against him.
SERMONS AND DISCOURSES, 1734-1738

THE NEW ENGLAND WILDERNESS is beautiful to behold, but it is not a tame place. If like Jonathan Edwards you enjoy a long walk in the woods, your coat wrapped tightly against the evening chill, you know to savor your surroundings but not ignore them. At any moment, you could come across a "wild beast," perhaps a Maine black bear. No doubt the bear would be as surprised to see you as you are to see it, but the odds in such an encounter do not tilt in your favor.

Edwards, who loved a nice stroll in the wilderness, is right. If Satan appeared to us as a vengeful, teeth-baring animal, we would take him far more seriously than we do. Yet in the mystery of God's creation, Satan is invisible to us. His *greatest* feat, however, is how he makes himself seem insignificant. In our culture, we laugh at the idea of Satan. We joke about him. We even tune in to songs that cheekily express "sympathy for the devil." (Here's a life principle: Do not feel warmly toward those who crave your undoing.)

Christians are in no way obsessed with the devil. We are focused on God, not on his blaspheming adversary. God, not Satan, rules the cosmos. Yet we must always stay alert as Christians. We walk through the wilderness, following the path of righteousness, aware at all times of the foes who watch us. The enemy is hungry. Many think of him as a harmless house cat. But we know who he is. We always stay close to God, we fear him alone, and we remember that we will not be devoured by, but delivered from, this present evil age.

Be sober-minded; be watchful. Your adversary the devil prowls around like a roaring lion, seeking someone to devour.   1 PETER 5:8

January 26

Make much use of prayer, seeing you have such a subtle and cruel enemy, that so indefatigably seeks your ruin, and that so artfully disguises himself to deceive you. Keep close to God. Forsake [him] not. Be continually with him, near to him in the duty of prayer, that he would be your guard and your counsellor; that he would defend you from the wiles of the devil; that he would instruct you, and undertake to be your counsellor by the conduct of his own Holy Spirit.

SERMONS AND DISCOURSES, 1734-1738

OUR SCHEDULES REVEAL *what* and *whom* we love. What takes up the majority of our time? With whom do we spend our time during the course of the week? To what do we give time amid the rush of our lives? More than we might know (or care to admit), we discover our true commitments in our calendars.

Studies estimate that the average American Christian spends about an hour a week in devotions. Though few would suggest that believers should use a stopwatch in their studies, the point of Jonathan Edwards's counsel strikes home for many of us. We *need* to "keep close to God." We *need* to dwell "continually with him," to study his Word, and pray to him regularly. The basic priorities of our faith should not be strange to our ears and seldom on our lips.

The good news for weary travelers like us is that we are not responsible for operating our own spiritual power plant. The indwelling Holy Spirit makes us more than conquerors in all circumstances (Romans 8:37). The horsepower needed for a vibrant faith already resides within us. Our responsibility is to resist the world, the flesh, and the devil. Let us remember how good our God is, and how near he is to us. He is not far off; he is not hard to reach. Like the best father imaginable, he loves to draw near to his beloved.

The Helper, the Holy Spirit, whom the Father will send in my name, he will teach you all things and bring to your remembrance all that I have said to you. JOHN 14:26

January 27

JUST WEEKS BEFORE Jonathan Edwards died in 1758, his father, Timothy, passed away as well. Timothy Edwards came from a difficult background. His father worked hard as a merchant and lifted the family out of poverty. But Timothy's mother, Elizabeth (Tuthill) Edwards, cut a jagged path through life—repeatedly indulging in affairs and displaying a ferocious temper. Mental illness ran in the family. One of Elizabeth's sisters, for example, murdered her own child, and one of her brothers killed his sister with an axe.

Growing up, Timothy Edwards experienced significant instability. Little wonder that he, and the son he trained, held a dim view of human nature. Timothy responded to his childhood woes by intensifying his efforts to learn and advance. From start to finish, he pursued his desired ends with diligence. Timothy passed on this outlook to his son, Jonathan. Historian George Marsden sums up Timothy's fatherly approach as follows:

> Everything we know about Timothy Edwards suggests an intensely disciplined perfectionist, a worrier about details, a firm authoritarian who was nonetheless capable of good humor and warm affections toward his family. Jonathan Edwards never entirely escaped the hold this demanding yet affectionate father had over him. He followed closely in his father's footsteps and, except for greater reserve, closely resembled his father in standards and attitudes.[3]

No family is able to escape the effects of the Fall. No father will perfectly rear his children. Timothy Edwards had his own failings as a father, as did his son. But as Marsden shows, Timothy loved his son and demonstrated his love by seeking to launch Jonathan as a thinker and spiritual leader.

Undoubtedly, Timothy Edwards felt tremendous thankfulness to God as he watched his son from afar. Indeed, he saw that God's grace, and a ferocious work ethic, had overcome the darkness and turmoil of his own childhood home and set his offspring on a far different path. Whatever our background, and whatever our struggles, God's grace is greater still.

January 28

ON THIS DATE, Jonathan Edwards recorded his only diary entry from his early years at Northampton. In it, he says, "I think Christ has recommended rising early in the morning, by his rising from the grave very early." We see here the seriousness with which Edwards took the spiritual disciplines. He rose at four or five every morning so as to spend thirteen or more hours in study. He began the day with private prayer followed by family prayers. Before each meal, Jonathan led the family in devotions. At the end of the day, Sarah joined him in the study for prayer.

During his workday, Edwards dove into the life of the mind. At any given time, he was at work on numerous sermons, longer treatises, and a steady stream of outgoing mail. Yet he regularly stopped his labors to engage with his children and find "opportunities to converse with them singly and closely about the concerns of their souls," always being "careful and thorough in the government of his children." In response, his children "reverenced, esteemed and loved him."[4]

One writer sums up Edwards's serious focus, and intimidating demeanor as follows:

> No one reacted blandly to Edwards. He gave people a disturbing hunch that they were in the presence of a strangely different person. Sarah had sensed this and found it frightening when he first courted her. Clergymen who had settled for the routine, the safely popular options, resented a man like Edwards. His concentration repelled them. His moral force was a threat.[5]

But Edwards was also a kind and good man. The same author tells a memorable story:

> Long after Edwards' death it was learned that he had once heard of a "pure obscure man he never saw" who was in unusual need. Edwards, "unasked, gave a considerable sum to a friend, to be delivered to the distressed person," requesting that no one be told the donor's name.[6]

In his zealous focus, his care for his loved ones, and his heart for God, Edwards urges us on. He was a sinner just like us, but he labored to know the Lord and to lead others to do the same. We may not have his gifts or circumstances, but no one can stop us from emulating his zeal.

January 29

Holiness in the eyes of one that is spiritually enlightened is the chief beauty of all divine things: God and Christ [are] ravishingly beautiful upon the account of their infinite holiness. Holiness is the chief beauty of the way of salvation: holiness is the beauty of the Bible: holiness is the beauty of God's commandment: holiness is the beauty of heaven that makes it seem a pleasant and happy place in the eyes of one that sees by a spiritual light.
SERMONS AND DISCOURSES, 1734-1738

TYPICALLY WHEN WE THINK of heaven, we think of a happy place where nothing bad intrudes. Our popular cultural vision of the afterlife pushes us this way; we're told that heaven is a place where we'll be reunited with our favorite dog and play the best game of Frisbee golf imaginable. This seems to be what a common vision of heaven amounts to: reunion, playtime, and loved ones.

Nowhere is Jonathan Edwards more revolutionary for our day than in his vision of heaven. Edwards knew that eternity with God would mean all sorts of incredible blessings: perfect comfort, perfect peace, happiness at its height. But the chief point he made about heaven was this: Heaven is lovely not for sentimental reasons, but because of its nature. The redeemed will dwell with God in a place of perfect holiness, a fact that renders it "a pleasant and happy place."

The doctrine of the afterlife is no obstacle to delight. Rather, it is the gateway to joy. We must make sure, however, that our vision of heaven is first informed by Scripture. We have the ability to see blessed eternity in "a spiritual light." The natural man cannot see the true beauty of heaven. By divine grace, we can—and we will.

He will wipe away every tear from their eyes, and death shall be no more, neither shall there be mourning, nor crying, nor pain anymore, for the former things have passed away. REVELATION 21:4

January 30

A person is said to be justified when he is approved of God as free from the guilt of sin, and its deserved punishment, and as having that righteousness belonging to him that entitles to the reward of life. . . . A believer's justification implies not only remission of sins, or acquittance from the wrath due to it, but also an admittance to a title to that glory that is the reward of righteousness.

SERMONS AND DISCOURSES, 1734-1738

ONE OF A CHILD'S FIRST instincts when caught in wrongdoing is to explain. As the situation grows more serious, explanations multiply. Reasons abound. A detailed play-by-play is given. Sometimes, the sheer weight of information overwhelms the parents' senses. A dish lies broken on the ground, but we're deep in a back-story that stretches on like *Gone with the Wind*.

This instinct comes naturally to us. We all have a penchant for self-justification. We want to make ourselves look good. We want to show, even when caught in a misdeed, that there's a good reason for our behavior. The truth, however, is that we cannot ultimately clear ourselves. We are guilty before God because of our sin, and we have no true and lasting righteousness of our own.

In the moment we trust Christ, we are justified by faith (Romans 5:1). We are counted righteous in God's sight. Ten thousand spiritual gifts are ours—sin is canceled, wrath is overcome, and we have "admittance to . . . glory." Christ's own righteousness is ours (2 Corinthians 5:21). This is a tremendously freeing truth. The "reward of life" is ours. This and this alone is worth explaining in great detail.

> Since we have been justified by faith, we have peace with God through our Lord Jesus Christ. Through him we have also obtained access by faith into this grace in which we stand, and we rejoice in hope of the glory of God. ROMANS 5:1-2

January 31

Resolved, to live with all my might, while I do live.
LETTERS AND PERSONAL WRITINGS

I RECENTLY SAW A VIDEO of a pride of lions fighting with a honey badger. The honey badger is not a beautiful animal; it has little that would draw you to it, should you see one at the zoo. But the honey badger stands out nonetheless. It is one of the fiercest creatures on the planet. In this instance, the lions lash out at the little animal, which has clearly startled them. Despite the ridiculous odds, the badger somehow manages to get away from the pride. He lives to fight lions another day.

Witnessing such intensity in this determined little creature reminds me of the way Jonathan Edwards approached his earthly days. This most famous of his resolutions speaks to his strong, even fierce, will: He resolved before the Lord to give all his might to his tasks. Edwards trained under men who worked very hard. His grandfather was an eminent New England clergyman, and his father simultaneously pastored a church and taught school. From a very early age, Jonathan learned to put in long, hard hours to accomplish his goals.

We too want to marshal all our might for our duties before the Lord. We want to be the best husbands or wives we can be. We want to be the best children we can be. We want to be the best employees we can be. We want to serve our churches and strengthen them by our humble efforts. We want to help our neighbors and be witnesses of the gospel to them. God's saving grace is not weak; it does not create a dull spiritual state, but an energized one. I do not recommend fighting animals in the wild; I do recommend living with all your might, while you still may.

You shall love the LORD your God with all your heart and with all your soul and with all your might. DEUTERONOMY 6:5

February

✝

February 1

February 1757: A Dissertation Concerning the Nature of True Virtue *completed*

JONATHAN EDWARDS BELIEVED that if God created the world for his own glory, it means we cannot just live any which way we please. Edwards wrote two complementary books on this theme during his Stockbridge days. *The End for Which God Created the World* unfolds a rigorously God-centered philosophy of all things, while his *Dissertation Concerning the Nature of True Virtue* illumines what such a perspective looks like in ethics. *End of Creation* (the shorthand title) tells us why we should live for God; *True Virtue* shows us what shape a theocentric ethic would take. Neither book is for the faint of heart; both are dense, but both are also worth reading for serious students of theology and philosophy.

Edwards wrote at a time of growing interest in what we now call the Scottish Enlightenment. In the period between the American Revolution and the Civil War, there were some who argued that humanity is essentially good and benevolent, and that laws of morality could be proven in rational terms. In other words, one need not be religious to be good.

Edwards could not have disagreed more strongly. Though he does not quote Scripture in *True Virtue*, that treatise is a comprehensive defense of the uniquely Christian nature of goodness. He argues that "nothing is of the nature of true virtue in which God is not the *first* and the *last*."[7] True virtue "most essentially consists in . . . benevolence to *Being in general*."[8] This "Being" is clearly God. Edwards sought to cultivate a frame of mind he called "disinterested benevolence," by which he meant that the truly virtuous individual "does above all things seek the *glory of God*, and makes *this* his supreme, governing, and ultimate end."[9]

Edwards did not deny that unbelievers could do virtuous deeds. But none except the redeemed could perform *true* virtue, producing the righteousness that God intended. Edwards's argument merits serious attention as a counterpoint to modern ethical theories that base goodness in a secular understanding of reason. For Edwards, and indeed for many who track his arguments biblically, if there is virtue in the world, it must owe to a figure who is truly virtuous. Any other conclusion struggles to stand up, for it has no foundation for goodness.

Whether we surf the high tides of academic philosophy or not, these words apply to us. Day by day, we follow the Lord. We practice deeds in keeping with God's design and honor our great God, prompting the world to ask why we choose others-centeredness over selfishness. Living for God unburdens us, and releases us from the prison of our own selfish motives and desires. That's true virtue, goodness no one can deny.

February 2

Two things come to pass, relating to the saints' reward for their inherent righteousness, by virtue of their relation to Christ. First, the guilt of their persons is all done away, and the pollution and hatefulness that attends and is in their good works, is hid. Second, their relation to Christ adds a positive value and dignity to their good works, in God's sight. That little holiness, and those faint and feeble acts of love, and other grace, receive an exceeding value in the sight of God, by virtue of God's beholding them as in Christ, and as it were members of one so infinitely worthy in his eyes; and that because God looks upon the persons as persons of greater dignity on this account.

SERMONS AND DISCOURSES, 1734-1738

WE ALL MUST RECONCILE ourselves to the anonymous grind that is much of our lives. Our day-to-day existence sometimes seems less than what was promised. Didn't that high school graduation speech assure us we would change the world? Right now, we're doing well to change diapers. We're far, it seems, from the lofty dreams we once dreamed.

The Christian faith redeems the smallness of our existence. It charges our anonymous labors with spiritual electricity. Jonathan Edwards helps us to see that our lives have value not because people see us, but because God sees us. There is no such thing as an anonymous believer in the Kingdom of Heaven. Every born-again saint is known by God and loved by God. Our good works are not hidden from his sight.

Even our "faint and feeble acts of love" travel to God and are beheld by him. Though he is the only truly great being, he sees us as "infinitely worthy." In this, and in nothing else, we find our security. We are known and loved by God. No magazine may choose to profile us; no dinner may be given in our honor this month. It matters not. We are the Lord's, and our good works—however small, however quiet—are for him and no other.

For our sake he made him to be sin who knew no sin, so that in him we might become the righteousness of God.   2 CORINTHIANS 5:21

February 3

Time is very short, which is another thing that renders it very precious: the scarcity of any commodity occasions men to set an higher value upon it. . . . When bread is very scarce, they that have bread have but a little of it. They will be more choice of it, and will set an higher value upon it, because bread is what they must have or perish. . . . Time is so short, and the work is so great that we have to do in it, that we have none of it to spare. The work that we have to do to prepare for eternity must be done in time, or it never can be done.
SERMONS AND DISCOURSES, 1734-1738

ONE RARELY FEELS the passage of time more keenly than in summer. One minute, we're counting the months ahead, gleeful to have weeks and weeks to enjoy the season; the next minute, we're a little grumpy around our friends, lamenting where the time has gone.

We all exaggerate about time, though it ticks away rather predictably. Yet our sense that the days pass quickly is not off the mark. As Jonathan Edwards notes, "Time is very short . . . very precious." We have one life to live. We want our days on earth to be without number—at least some of the time—but they are not. They are indeed counted out. If we are to live for eternity, there is no time like the present.

This realization should not drive us into fear or frenzy. Instead, it should make us purposeful people. We have the ability to see every day as a vessel for God's glory. We may not all have the same financial resources, but we all have the same opportunity: a fresh twenty-four hours each day. God is so great, and the work of his Kingdom so enlivening, that there is simply no time like the present.

Teach us to number our days that we may get a heart of wisdom.
PSALM 90:12

February 4

Christ knew that hereby he should save sinners. He knew that God would accept of his sufferings, instead of the eternal damnation of sinners; and that poor sinners hereby would escape that dreadful misery, and would be saved. He knew that by his sufferings, as an act of obedience, he shall purchase glory for sinners; and therefore he took great delight in the thoughts of [it], and his heart was much upon it. It was exceeding pleasant to him to think how the justice of God would be satisfied, and perishing souls would have safety and deliverance through his blood. He thought of their being brought up from their depths of woe, and being advanced to glory by his pain and disgrace with great satisfaction. The thought of it was most sweet to him.

SERMONS, SERIES II, 1731-1732

BACK IN THE "GLORY DAYS" of high school basketball, I remember cold morning practices. The gym in Maine was so cold, in fact, that we did our prepractice stretching right next to the one heater in the facility. Every movement was painful. We wanted to be on the team; we didn't always want to do the work. The human heart is fickle.

Fickle is not a word that would apply to Jesus Christ. As Jonathan Edwards shows, Jesus lived a doxological life—that is, he always had the glory of his Father on his mind. According to Edwards, Jesus *yearned* to make atonement for the wretched. He *hungered* to satisfy the justice of God by giving his life as a ransom. He *lived* to obey the one who had sent him; in fact, he called it his *food* (John 4:34).

Jesus shows us what it means to live doxologically. This potent word captures the zeal of Christians who desire to give God maximum glory in every sphere and second of life. In such a framework, there are no unimportant moments. There is no meaningless Christianity. Whatever our role in the Kingdom, we have work to do. We have glory to gain for God. The human heart may be fickle, but our Savior and Redeemer is calling us back to the task at hand.

Since, therefore, we have now been justified by his blood, much more shall we be saved by him from the wrath of God. ROMANS 5:9

February 5

There are many ways that persons quench the Spirit. . . . Some {quench the Spirit} by entering into some contention and quarrel. {There is} nothing more contrary to the nature of the Holy Spirit than a spirit of hatred. . . . The Spirit of God is a spirit of love. The Apostles make the Spirit dwelling in us, and love dwelling in us, the same thing (1 John 4:12–13).
SERMONS AND DISCOURSES, 1734-1738

IF EVERYONE TALKS ABOUT LOVE, why do we sometimes struggle to put it into practice? The songwriters of our modern age, after all, have told us that "all we need is love." With certain folks, though, we honestly feel almost anything but love. Perhaps it is more difficult to genuinely care for and highly esteem others than we think.

This is why the Holy Spirit is so important to Christians. Though we may not find it easy to love certain people in our lives, Jonathan Edwards argues that the Holy Spirit is "love dwelling in us." To have the Spirit, in other words, is to have the capacity to love even our enemies. How grateful we can be to God for giving us the Spirit, and for giving us an unending ability to treat others as God-made beings.

This connection between love and the Holy Spirit helps us understand what "quenching the Spirit" means. We quench the Spirit when we quash love. We quench the Spirit when we choose bitterness over unity. We quench the Spirit when we enter a quarrel rather than swallowing hard and moving on. We all falter in these ways, but we have great hope despite our weakness. The Spirit lives in us. The Spirit is maturing us. The Spirit is love—not a shapeless or ambiguous emotion, but a divine commitment, a gift that no one can take away.

Do not quench the Spirit.   1 THESSALONIANS 5:19

February 6

There is a sufficient mediator. And though we are without strength, yet Christ has died for us, as 'tis said in the verse wherein is the text. He is sufficient in his purchase, and he is sufficient in his power. The Captain of our salvation is able to overcome that potent adversary of our souls. He came into the world to destroy the works of the devil, as 'tis said, 1 John 3:8, "For this purpose the Son of God was manifested, that he might destroy the works of the devil." He is ready to pity, and to help the helpless.

SERMONS AND DISCOURSES, 1734-1738

IT IS A BEAUTIFUL BIBLICAL TRUTH that Christ meets us in our lowness. We need not come to him in our finest clothes, our nicest apparel. Like the lowly folk observed in the Gospels who saw Jesus as their hope, we come to him in our wretchedness, and he does not refuse us. He is "ready to pity" us and help us.

We cannot forget that the same Savior who bends low is the Savior who destroys death. Jesus went to the Cross not merely to express oneness with us, to show us that he cares about the needy, but also to "overcome that potent adversary of our souls," as Jonathan Edwards points out. To those onlookers at Calvary, and even to the disciples, Christ's crucifixion looked like defeat. But it was anything but a defeat. For at the Cross, the devil's work was undone (Colossians 2:13-15).

At times, we feel as if we are "without strength." We grow weary; life is long; the days are a grind. How heartening, then, that we have a mediator who strengthens his people. So, whatever challenges lie before us today, we can know that our sin is washed away and our adversary has been defeated. Our salvation is finished, and our strong Savior stands close by, eager to help the helpless.

> But now He has obtained a more excellent ministry, by as much as He is also the mediator of a better covenant, which has been enacted on better promises. HEBREWS 8:6, NASB

February 7

Resolved, never to do anything, which I should be afraid to do, if it were the last hour of my life.

LETTERS AND PERSONAL WRITINGS

ANY HOUR COULD BE "the last hour" of our lives, as Jonathan Edwards suggests. When asked the common question, "What would you do if you had twenty-four hours to live?" like anyone, we might choose to spend time with loved ones, visit a beautiful scenic area, or complete as many bucket list items as time would allow.

As Christians, we might use our final twenty-four hours on earth in much the same way we would spend any other day. We would take time for prayer. We would read Scripture. We would give thanks to God for his good work in us. We all have individual interests, but as Christians we know that, while time is precious, true happiness stems not from "living it up" in a worldly way, but from "living upward," for God's glory and our good.

It's not a bad thing to enjoy the gifts of God's common grace, but as believers in eternal life, we have a bucket list the world cannot imagine. It involves, ultimately, living forever with God. Worshiping Christ with all the saints from all the ages. Shedding our sin and woes. If we found out we had twenty-four hours to live, I don't think most Christians would panic, or go into a traveling frenzy. Most, I believe, would do what the Spirit has trained us to do—and that is to put our hope and our delight in our loving Savior. So, regardless of how much time we have left, we should always be prepared to go to Jesus, to see him as he is, and to rest in his presence.

All the days of the afflicted are evil, but the cheerful of heart has a continual feast. PROVERBS 15:15

February 8

The directest course that you can possibly take to be thoroughly convinced of sin, is to set yourself with all your might to strive against it; not to allow any sin in any degree, no sinful act, or word, or thought; {to strive} against all sin, against profaneness, against self-righteousness, {against} wanderings of mind, {against} slothfulness in duty. Strive with all your might against all evil dispositions towards your neighbors, all manifestations of it, all evil-speaking, {all manifestations of} worldliness.

SERMONS AND DISCOURSES, 1734-1738

LET'S BE HONEST: We'd all like a little wiggle room. Those who minister to high school and college students know that young adults are curious about adulthood. They feel drawn to relationships, many of them, and they wish to clarify boundaries. "I know what stuff is out of the question," they ask in that halting teenage manner, "but how much physical contact is okay?"

The question comes from noble intentions, and premarried couples do need guidance. But in this line of inquiry we spot the tendency of our sin-tempted hearts. For all of us, whatever our age or station in life, "How much is okay?" is usually not the best question. A better question—whether we're 14 or 114—might be this one: "How holy can I be today?" In other words, to use Jonathan Edwards's vigorous language, how can I use all my energy to strive against every "manifestation" of worldliness?

This question is not legalistic; rather, it shows that we are thinking *theocentrically*, orienting our lives around the will of God. We cannot approach sin passively, after all. Sin is not passive. We have to plan against sin, scheme against it, and strive to overcome it. Thankfully, God is gracious to forgive us when our efforts fall short. But a biblical vision of godliness calls us back into the fray, and back to the question that grace itself creates: "How holy can I be today?"

> Put to death therefore what is earthly in you: sexual immorality, impurity, passion, evil desire, and covetousness, which is idolatry.
> COLOSSIANS 3:5

February 9

There is none like him, who is infinite in glory and excellency: he is the most high God, glorious in holiness, fearful in praises, doing wonders: his name is excellent in all the earth, and his glory is above the earth and the heavens: among the gods there is none like unto him; there is none in heaven to be compared to him, nor are there any among the sons of the mighty, that can be likened unto him. Their God is the fountain of all good, and an inexhaustible fountain; he is an all-sufficient God; a God that is able to protect and defend them, and do all things for them: he is the King of Glory, the Lord strong and mighty, the Lord mighty in battle: a strong rock, and an high tower.

SERMONS AND DISCOURSES, 1734-1738

THERE IS NO GOD like the true God. We scarcely dare to dream of such a being. We are accustomed, after all, to a hard and hardening world. We all face our own sorrows and woes. Our expectations soar to the clouds; we dare to believe that good can happen for us, but then those hopes crash and burn. Little wonder that we have a tough time believing in an ideal figure who loves us purely and unceasingly.

But such a God exists. This is the impossibly good news of Christianity. Jonathan Edwards loved little more than to meditate on God's greatness. God, as Edwards saw him in Scripture, is "infinite in glory and excellency," a constellation of perfection. He is so great, in fact, that try as we might, we cannot compare anyone to him. God is in his own category. We have no analogy, no metaphor, that can capture his essence, his goodness. He is sui generis: one of a kind.

Yet, God's goodness is not an abstraction. It is both personal and active. God *is* good, and he *does* good for us. He is strong and mighty, a high tower, the rock of our salvation. There is nothing we face that his grace cannot overcome. Even if our earthly lives are filled with challenges—even serious challenges—we must not forget: *There is none like him.* This impossibly Great Being loves us, and cares for us.

Remember the former things of old; for I am God, and there is no other; I am God, and there is none like me. ISAIAH 46:9

February 10

The people of God are the most excellent and happy society in the world. That God whom they have chosen their God, is their father; he has pardoned all their sins, and they are at peace with him; and he has admitted them to all the privileges of his children. As they have devoted themselves to God, so he has given himself to them: he is become their salvation, and their portion: his power and mercy, and all his attributes are theirs. They are in a safe state, free from all possibility of perishing: Satan has no power to destroy them. God carries them on eagles' wings, far above Satan's reach, and above the reach of all the enemies of their souls.

SERMONS AND DISCOURSES, 1734-1738

THE LOCAL CHURCH is a unique place. It is constituted for the purpose of worshiping God and making him known to the world. The church is not a social club, a political rallying point, or a community organization like any other. The church is unique among all the institutions of the earth. It is the gathering of Christ's blood-bought people.

For this reason, the church's very identity, in the words of Jonathan Edwards, is this: "the most excellent and happy society in the world." Edwards, who loved the church, sought to help his congregants see who they were intended to be, according to the grace of God. The church's "privileges" are greater than anything the world can afford us. Sin is pardoned; orphans are adopted; God's children are protected. Whatever our weekly worship looks like, it centers on these precious truths.

We must approach our congregational activity from this theological perspective. We enjoy one another, but we are not a social club. We promote God's truth in our community, but we are not a partisan group. We celebrate unity, but not in a New Age, anything-goes way. We are the people of Christ. God is our Father. We are not living for this world, but for the world to come. How can we not be joyful with a God like this as our possession?

Trust in him at all times, O people; pour out your heart before him; God is a refuge for us. PSALM 62:8

February 11

February 11, 1729: Solomon Stoddard dies; Jonathan Edwards becomes senior pastor of the church at Northampton

THE DEATH of Jonathan Edwards's maternal grandfather, Solomon Stoddard, left a vacant pulpit at the First Church of Northampton. A staunch Congregationalist pastor, Stoddard was called the Pope of the Connecticut River Valley—the most influential pastor in the New England colonies, commanding authority in both spiritual and political matters. Edwards referred to his grandfather as one of the greatest minds he had ever encountered, and he was well acquainted with the five seasons of revival seen under Stoddard's ministry.

Stoddard is not well known today, but his writings show a force and appeal not unlike his grandson's. In *The Safety of Appearing at the Day of Judgment in the Righteousness of Christ*, he exhorts readers to taste the encouragement of trusting Christ:

> When a saint is under greatest discouragements, if God does but open his eyes to see indeed this way of salvation by Christ, he will no longer stand insisting upon his fears, but, with comfort and joy, cast himself on Christ: the inward discoveries of the gospel make his temptations vanish; yea, he does not only rejoice in Christ, but can sometimes discern that sincerity which he was so doubtful of before.[10]

Edwards and all of Northampton were stunned when Stoddard died in 1729. He had served the town for sixty years and had pioneered theological solutions for a faltering church. Stoddard was one of the architects of the Halfway Covenant, which made provision for non-Christians to come under the church's care. Though widely critiqued now for this measure, Stoddard drew many followers in his day.

Many thought that Stoddard's right-hand man, William Williams, was the heir apparent to the Northampton pulpit, because Williams championed most of the same doctrines and spiritual causes. However, it seems that Williams encouraged his nephew, Edwards, to follow in his grandfather's footsteps in Northampton.

Upon Stoddard's death, the congregation asked Edwards—who had already assisted his grandfather's work—to assume all pastoral duties. Edwards pastored the Northampton congregation for more than twenty years, extending his family's spiritual reign in western Massachusetts to eighty years. At twenty-five, he was the sole pastor of a six-hundred-member church, the most influential New England church outside of Boston. Though we never know what God will call us to do, we do know that he will always give us the grace we need to do it.

February 12

We need the favor of God, but we can't purchase it. We have no price to offer for it, and we can't get a price. If we go to work never so diligently, and lay out our utmost strength, we can never get anything that will do to offer to God. We can't commend ourselves to the favor of God: we can do nothing to recommend ourselves. We need something to stand us in stead. . . . We have brought guilt on ourselves, and we can't deliver ourselves from it. We can't make any atonement for it. If we should offer thousands of rams, and ten thousands of rivers of oil, and our first born for our transgressions, and the fruit of our bodies for the sin [of] our souls, it would be of no avail (Micah 6:7).
SERMONS AND DISCOURSES, 1734-1738

WE HEAR A GOOD BIT today about the secularizing of our society. Everywhere we turn, the headlines tell us, the Western world is turning away from religion. But in truth, many people live deeply religious lives. They perform elaborate rituals. They offer sacrifices of various kinds. Billions of people continue to believe that they can cover their guilt by some kind of spiritual performance.

But there is absolutely no way for humanity to earn salvation. As Jonathan Edwards makes plain, we cannot "make any atonement" that will save ourselves. There is no ritual, no psychological coaching, no therapeutic plan, no religious service that can cleanse us of our guilt. Every last person on earth has a simple but desperate problem: We need someone to help us. We need a deliverer.

This sobering reality leads some people to despair, others to madness, still others to laziness. But born-again followers of Jesus have a different reaction. Our spiritual insufficiency leads us to delight in the God-sent Redeemer (John 17:18). We have stopped our self-salvation attempts. We trust the one who made the ultimate sacrifice, Jesus Christ. He stood in our stead. He took our place. The work is done; now, all of life is a gift.

By grace you have been saved through faith. And this is not your own doing; it is the gift of God, not a result of works, so that no one may boast. EPHESIANS 2:8-9

February 13

JONATHAN AND SARAH EDWARDS's third child, Esther, was a live wire. She wrote a journal from a young age that shows a mischievous spirit and counters certain stereotypes of colonial Christian women:

> Northampton, February 13, 1741. This is my ninth birthday and Mrs. Edwards, my mother, has made me stitch these sundry sheets of paper into a book to make me a journal. Methinks, almost all this family keep journals: though they seldom show them. But Mrs. Edwards is to see mine, because she needs to know whether I improve in composing; also whether I am learning to keep my heart with all diligence, [in] which we are all constrained to be engaged.[11]

Through Esther, we get a glimpse into the inner workings of the ever-busy Edwards household:

> Northampton, June, 1743. My mother has just come into the house with a bunch of sweet peas, and put them on the stand where my honored father is shaving, though his beard is very slight. We have abundance of flowers and a vegetable garden, which is early and thrifty. Our sweet corn is the first in town, and so are our green peas. My honored father of course has not time to give attention to the garden, and so Mrs. Edwards looks after everything there.[12]

Esther went on to marry a godly pastor and college president named Aaron Burr. The couple had two children, and Aaron Jr. grew up to be vice president of the United States. He later killed Alexander Hamilton in a duel, and ended up far from his evangelical roots. Esther's only remarks about her son foreshadow future trouble:

> Aaron is a little, dirty, noisy boy, very different from Sally almost in everything. He begins to talk a little, is very sly, mischievous and has more sprightliness than Sally. I must say he is handsomer, though not so good tempered. He is very resolute and requires a good governor to bring him to terms.[13]

Tragically, Esther Edwards Burr died young. Not long before her death, her two children fell ill. She expressed her total trust of God in one of her final letters:

God showed me that the children were not my own but his, and that he had a right to recall what he had lent, whenever he thought fit; and that I had no reason to complain, or say that God was hard with me. This silenced me. But O how good is God.[14]

This lively and godly woman died in 1758, leaving a remarkable testimony of faith and spirit.

February 14

February 14, 1748: Daughter Jerusha Edwards dies

JERUSHA EDWARDS was the flower of her father's eye. By all accounts, she had a sweet disposition and a deeply spiritual temperament. When David Brainerd came to the Edwards home in spring 1747, both Jonathan and Jerusha found much in common with the young missionary. Brainerd had spent himself in preaching the gospel to Native American tribes and now needed deep care for tuberculosis.

The ever-hospitable Sarah Edwards took Brainerd in and nursed him back to health. But Jerusha, too, tended to the courageous missionary and formed a bond with him. The two spent much time together, and both battled illness. Brainerd died on October 9, 1747, while still in residence with the Edwardses.

Jerusha seems to have inherited her father's strong spiritual temper but weak physical disposition. In early February 1748, she grew very ill, and within a week she passed away. Seven months later, her father spoke of his grief in a letter to Scottish minister John Erskine:

> It has pleased God, since I wrote my last to you, sorely to afflict this family by taking away by death, the last February, my second daughter in the eighteenth year of her age, a very pleasant and useful member of this family, and that was esteemed the flower of the family. Herein we have a great loss; but the remembrance of the remarkable appearances of piety in her, from her childhood, in life, and also at her death, are very comfortable to us, and give us great reason to mingle thanksgiving with our mourning. I desire your prayers, dear Sir, that God would make up our great loss to us in himself.[15]

Edwards was clearly crushed by the death of his beloved daughter. In a striking decision, he had Jerusha buried next to David Brainerd, her dear friend. Though no record of any romance between the two survives, it seems likely that David and Jerusha had so deep a connection that the two would have married, had their lives lasted longer, and had the "flower of the family" not been cut down so young. In his sorrow, Jonathan Edwards kept going, pressing on in faith in Christ—as every believer must.

February 15

How difficult a thing is it to convince men of the insufficiency of their own reason and abilities, to help them out of a natural state. These poor, feeble creatures look very big upon themselves. They little think how it is God that every day keeps 'em from falling into the most heinous wickedness imaginable, by the restraints that he lays on their corruptions; and how it is God that every moment keeps them from being destroyed by the devil, who, if God should give permission, would immediately fall upon them as a roaring lion. This arises from the grand conceit we naturally have of ourselves, and our ignorance of our own weakness.

SERMONS AND DISCOURSES, 1734-1738

WE ARE NOT OFTEN AWARE of the realities that enable us to live. Think of the ordinary working of our lungs, for example. On average, we take about 960 breaths an hour, 23,040 breaths a day, and 8,409,600 breaths a year. How many of these exhalations and inhalations do we notice? Maybe twenty per day? The other 23,020 we overlook. That's a lot.

Our true debt, however, is not to our bodies, but to God—in whom "we live and move and have our being."[16] In Jonathan Edwards's doctrine and biblical faith, God is the very foundation of reality. All creation exists because God upholds it. God is sovereign over all, ruling the cosmos, directing it according to his wisdom, preserving his creation. We live because he allows it; we breathe because he enables it; we are kept from destruction because he decrees it.

We could take a fearful view of this dependence. But the believing heart is offered something far better. We can worship the one who preserves us. We can thank Jesus that he absorbed on our behalf the righteous wrath of God. We can breathe deeply, and find many joys in our days, knowing that God has given us breath. And not just one; we give thanks for all 23,040, each one a blessing.

> Have you not known? Have you not heard? The LORD is the everlasting God, the Creator of the ends of the earth. He does not faint or grow weary; his understanding is unsearchable. He gives power to the faint, and to him who has no might he increases strength.   ISAIAH 40:28-29

February 16

February 16, 1758: Jonathan Edwards assumes office as president of the College of New Jersey

IN SEPTEMBER 1757, the trustees of the College of New Jersey (now Princeton University) wrote to Jonathan Edwards to offer him the presidency of the college. Edwards sought to shake off the call. He had books to write and a mission to lead, and his family had gone through a great deal in the previous ten years. He had no restlessness; he had settled down, and did not wish to start a new work.

When the trustees of the college persisted in their call, Edwards asked for a council of local ministers to help guide his thinking. The council met on January 4, 1758.

> When they published their judgment and advice to Mr. Edwards and his people, he appeared uncommonly moved and affected with it, and fell into tears on the occasion, which was very unusual for him in the presence of others: And soon after said to the gentlemen, who had given their advice, that it was matter of wonder to him, that they could so easily, as they appeared to do, get over the objections he had made against his removal, to be the head of a college, which appeared great and weighty to him. But as he thought it his duty to be directed by their advice, he should now endeavor cheerfully to undertake it, believing he was in the way of his duty.[17]

We do not know precisely why Edwards lost his composure in front of his peers, but it seems he felt the weight of the call. Leading a college in this era was tremendously difficult; Edwards would have more duties than he could count, and he was no longer a young man. He may also have wept at the thought that his cherished projects would now languish. He would not complete his history of God's work in the world; he would not complete his synthesis of the Old and New Testaments. He would expend himself as a teacher and a public figure. By any estimation, this was a weighty moment.

Nevertheless, Edwards ventured to Princeton, leaving Stockbridge in January 1758. His wife and several children stayed behind, and one of his daughters later said he left them in such a manner that indicated he might not see them again. He left the house, and then turned and said, "I commit you to God."[18]

Edwards lived in the president's home and was glad to see daughters Lucy and Esther, who lived in Princeton. He set about getting things in order, and the students were excited to have him as their president. He preached in chapel a few times and was installed at the school on February 16, 1758. However, not long after he arrived Edwards received an inoculation for smallpox, fell ill, and died. To the end, he sought to be faithful to the call of God.

February 17

Have your eye continually to God for his help in the whole affair, and in all that you do in that great work of seeking salvation. Take heed that you don't depend on your own strength. When praying and reading, or whatever duty you engage in, let it be with a sense of your own impotency. Don't go forth in your own strength. Go to God with all your difficulties. When you meet with temptation that you can't well get rid of, go to God to help you. When you find cause to complain of a hard heart and a blind mind, go to the fountain of life and light. When you are under temptation to discouragement or despair, go to God for help, in a sense of your own helplessness.
SERMONS AND DISCOURSES, 1734-1738

I WONDER IF we sometimes fail to pray because we feel . . . well, embarrassed. *I don't need to trouble God with that*, we think. *That's way too small a matter for him to worry about.* The Holy Spirit, in his kindness, generally convicts us of such wrong thinking. Yet we are tempted to return to such behavior often in our lives.

It can take a lifetime for the blessed truth of God's divine help to sink in. The instinct to pray for matters great and small forms over years. We feel as if we should have a handle on our business by now. But Jonathan Edwards is right: "Don't go forth in your own strength." Instead, "go to God for help." His power, and our own helplessness, are two sides of the same coin.

This doesn't mean we lie in bed all day, earning passive piety points. It does mean that we commit everything in our lives, as much as we can, to God's direction, God's leading. We are responsible for living wisely, yes, but the Lord never asks us to act alone. As the old hymn says of God: *I need thee every hour.* Yes, God, we need you. You will never let us go, and you will never turn us, your children, away.

Trust in the LORD with all your heart, and do not lean on your own understanding. PROVERBS 3:5

February 18

God is able to help you. He can do all things. He can enlighten you, and guide you in the right way: though it be a great and terrible wilderness that you travel in, yet your God can lead you in the right way to Canaan. God can restrain your corruptions; and not only so, but he can mortify and subdue them. He has all things in his hands, your reason and all your faculties: he has Satan in his power: he is stronger than he. . . . Satan can go no further than God shall permit him. God holds that roaring lion as it were on a string. And let him be never so fierce, and in so great a rage, he can't go beyond his tedder.
SERMONS AND DISCOURSES, 1734-1738

TRYING TO EXPLAIN some past wrong, I've heard some say, "The devil made me do it!" It's an easy pattern of thought to slip into. If we're not careful, we can lose sight of our moral responsibility. We can think to ourselves, *I would love to not sin, but sin is just too powerful.*

This is why we need to read the story of God's people throughout the Bible. Jonathan Edwards cites God's leadership of his covenant people, Israel, in Canaan. It wasn't easy for Joshua to bring the nation into the Promised Land (Joshua 1–5). But God was stronger than any ungodly tribe. He could overcome even the toughest, cleverest foe. As we see throughout the Old Testament, the Lord frequently intervened to aid his beloved in sticky situations (Exodus 14).

God is not limited by anyone or anything. He doesn't tremble at challenging circumstances. In fact, he often seems to stack the deck against himself, only to win a great victory, as in the conquest of the Promised Land. We may feel as if Satan has defeated us, and that we are out of God's divine reach. But this is not true. Through our repentance and faith, the Lord will draw near to us. He will guide us. The wilderness is great and terrible, but God is greater still.

Little children, you are from God and have overcome them, for he who is in you is greater than he who is in the world.   1 JOHN 4:4

February 19

God is very jealous of his own honor: he has often told us that he is a jealous God, and that his glory he will not give unto another. We ought therefore greatly to humble ourselves, and be sure [to] let us see to it that humility prevails and flourishes amongst us with other religion. . . . Let each one of us search and try our ways, and labor to become more as little children, to be low before God, and to walk humbly amongst men.
SERMONS AND DISCOURSES, 1734-1738

THIS IS THE AGE of the foodie. Now more than ever, excellent restaurant options abound. You want an Indian feast for lunch, oven-fired and tasting like the best of Mumbai? You got it. You want a sizzling hamburger made from cows raised within a twenty-mile radius? It's yours.

In a food-rich environment like ours, we have to steer clear of obvious failings (like gluttony). Beyond this, we need to redirect our appetites. You could say it like this: We need to be gluttons for God and the fruit of the Spirit (Galatians 5:22-23). As Jonathan Edwards urges, we should seek humility at all times. We want to fight "to be low before God."

How unusual this sounds. Not many people want to experience even a little bit of humiliation. As Christians, we have no greater example of humility than Jesus, who "emptied himself" and "humbled himself" on our behalf (Philippians 2:3-8). When opportunities for humility present themselves, as they inevitably will, we need not fear them. We can, by the grace of the Holy Spirit, embrace them. We are, after all, gluttons for God.

The reward for humility and fear of the LORD is riches and honor and life. PROVERBS 22:4

February 20

When God pours out his Spirit on a people, there are many blessed tokens of his presence and mercy amongst them. God is present everywhere, for he fills heaven and earth; but the way in which he is especially present with his people, is by his Spirit. When he pours out his Spirit on a people, he does as it were leave the heavens, and come down and dwells. And then there are many glorious tokens of his favor and mercy to be seen amongst them: it makes a most happy and blessed alteration amongst a people. When God is thus amongst a people, he brings salvation with him.

SERMONS AND DISCOURSES, 1734-1738

IT IS NOT UNCOMMON these days to hear people talk of feeling close to God. Our age may be less religious than some, but it is enduringly spiritual. People still hunger after a wondrous connection with ultimate reality. They want to be blessed by God, or whoever it is that upholds the cosmos.

In an experience-driven age, when everyone claims their own spiritual connection, we need to remember what the Holy Spirit actually does. In John 3, for example, Jesus links the Spirit with being *born again*. This is what we take as the most mystical of all realities: sinners confessing their unrighteousness to God and trusting Jesus to save them. When God sends the third person of the Trinity, the Spirit "brings salvation with him," a true salvation.

The initial ministry of the Spirit is conversion through divine mercy. The ongoing ministry of the Spirit involves conforming us to Christ through divine mercy. The Spirit blesses us in untold ways, but he is not a wild, careening presence in our lives. When God pours out his Spirit among us, the result is that we love the Father more, we love our Redeemer more, and we love our sin less. The Spirit-filled life is truly the best life we can imagine.

By this we know that we abide in him and he in us, because he has given us of his Spirit.   I JOHN 4:13

February 21

Resolved, to think much on all occasions of my own dying, and of the common circumstances which attend death.

LETTERS AND PERSONAL WRITINGS

To THINK MUCH ABOUT DEATH today can lead quickly to our peers labeling us as "morbid." In the age of elite living, of health food and juice cleansing, of technological solutions and wellness and mindfulness, thinking about the Grim Reaper seems ghastly. Unlike previous generations, we are a generation that wants to *beat* death and somehow overcome our mortality.

Death is not a good thing. But this mind-set of denial prepares us poorly for the brute realities of our existence. Death has a 100 percent success rate. We can try to pretend this is not so, or we can square with our circumstances. When Jonathan Edwards was just a young man—prior to marriage and prior to beginning his career—he made a promise to himself that he would think often of his own dying, and even, to narrow the point, "the common circumstances which attend death."

Edwards could think often about death because he didn't fear it. He had a living hope, a vibrant faith, and thus was freed from a trap that ensnares many others. One pastor has said that death is a trumpet blast of the apocalypse—that anytime a loved one passes away, we hear the distant sound of the coming day of days, when all accounts will be settled. Those who know Christ need not fear that trumpet. Let us prepare for death, prepare others for it, and know that one day we *will* beat death when we go into God's presence for eternity.

February 22

Without God's Holy Spirit, and his gracious presence, all other mercies will be in vain to them. They will do them no good. If God gives 'em aplenty of worldly good things—if they have health, if they have peace, if they have wealth, and flourish now so much in outward respects—it will avail them nothing. It will do them no good without this: yea, without this, all other blessings will prove curses, and will only work together for their ruin and destruction. Psalm 92:7, "When the wicked do grow as the grass, and all the [workers of iniquity do flourish; it is that they shall be destroyed for ever]."
SERMONS AND DISCOURSES, 1734-1738

CHRISTIANITY IS NOT a bottled-up little faith. It is a life-changing reality. Following the Lord in repentance and trust brings a spiritual tidal wave that washes over us. In trusting Christ, we may find ourselves in far healthier life patterns. We may take better care of our bodies, seeing them as vessels of holiness. We may live more wisely, wishing to make the most of each day (Ephesians 5:16). We may become better employees, taking our work more seriously as we seek to honor God with the fruit of our labor.

Yet we must take care. Faith is not a "life betterment pill" that we swallow. The benefits, in other words, are not the same as the cause. After all, if only our earthly life improves after we profess faith, what good is that? We are grateful for many blessings, but we are ones who treasure the Spirit of God. God's presence with us is sweeter than any earthly gift.

Walking with Jesus does not mean detachment from the world. It may well mean we have a fairly normal existence. It does mean, however, keeping all things in proper perspective. Seen through the eyes of faith, our jobs, possessions, and even our friends are great, but God is our delight. In a world entranced by momentary pleasures, we know this: If we have the Holy Spirit, we have everything.

It is the Spirit who gives life; the flesh is no help at all. The words that I have spoken to you are spirit and life. JOHN 6:63

February 23

If we profess that we have a spirit of love to everybody, we should show it in what we do. We should not love only in word and in tongue, but in deed and in truth. Religion towards God and duty to man, ought to run parallel: six of the Ten Commandments respect our duty to man. There should be a proportion kept up: when things are proportionable, then they are beautiful, and most acceptable to God.

SERMONS AND DISCOURSES, 1734-1738

IT'S FUNNY TO THINK ABOUT how little we have to do to have an impact on someone else. I can recall a summer day when my grandfather decided he was going to play soccer with me. He was a tender, loving man, but we did not usually play soccer. For reasons unknown, he launched into a game with me, and we had a truly memorable morning. Thirty years later, that day is still fresh in my mind.

It is easy to speak of love—even to teach about it. But it is harder to put love into practice. Scripture joins the two—word and deed—in an iron bond. It's not that we keep our mouths shut and only do good deeds; without words, there is no gospel to preach. But if there are no actions to back up our words, it obscures the living nature of divine truth.

We are all grateful for the influencers in our lives who pointed us to Christ and showed us the way to live by their actions. Their faith had a beautiful proportionality, to borrow from Jonathan Edwards's description of living "in word . . . in deed and in truth." That kind of mind-and-heart combination packs a powerful punch. Who knows who we can touch today? Our outreach, our effort to engage, might be as simple as a little time in the garden, a listening conversation, or some fancy footwork on a grassy field.

You shall not take vengeance or bear a grudge against the sons of your own people, but you shall love your neighbor as yourself: I am the LORD.
LEVITICUS 19:18

February 24

All is owing to Christ. . . . We did not deserve that Christ should thus deal with us, and should enter into such a sweet, and excellent, and happy union with us; for we are his enemies. How wonderful was it that the grace of Christ should so triumph over our enmity, especially considering after what manner this is brought about. Christ was not only first in seeking of it, but to make way for it. Though he was in the form of God, [he] became man, and laid down his life. Why should Christ make so much of us, who cannot be profitable to him, who can add nothing to his happiness and glory? What does Christ get by us poor, vile worms, that he should thus lay out himself for an union with us?

SERMONS AND DISCOURSES, 1734-1738

FOR SOME FOLKS, the deep things of life are a mental exercise. They have been given a quick and agile mind, and they feel as if they need to process everything like a human worker bee. Any statement, however harmless, leads to an intense philosophical discussion. They think they can single-handedly figure out the universe and its mysteries.

Thinking is great. God gave us minds by which to know him. But the truths of God are not laboratory samples. They regularly leave us speechless by their beauty. *Why would the Lord choose me?* we wonder in amazement. Part of being a Christian is thinking critically and carefully; another part is gazing in wonder at the kindness of God.

As much as we must use our minds to know the Lord, let us remember this as well: We cannot master the mind or heart of God. He has made us for himself. We do not deserve what Jonathan Edwards calls a "sweet, and excellent, and happy" union with our Savior. But we have it nonetheless. It all owes to the love of our Creator. The most theologically savvy Christian cannot improve on this simple, yet profound, statement: God loves us. All is owing to Christ.

You have died, and your life is hidden with Christ in God.
COLOSSIANS 3:3

February 25

God's love to his saints has had being from all eternity. God often in his Word is setting [forth] how great his love is to his saints, how dear they are to him. But this love of his to them, he had before ever they had any being. There it was in the heart of God of old. In former ages, thousands of years ago, in the ages before the flood, and when God created the world, there was that love; yea, and before the foundation of the world. And if we look back never so far, there is no beginning of it.

SERMONS AND DISCOURSES, 1734-1738

HAVE YOU EVER THOUGHT about the first ancestor of yours who thought about you? It's quite a matter to ponder. Perhaps it was your great-great grandmother; perhaps she prayed for future generations as she went about her daily work. Somewhere back in time, someone thought of us and wondered who we would be.

This exercise goes far deeper when we open it up to God. As Jonathan Edwards notes, God has loved "his saints . . . from all eternity." In fact, God's love for his people goes so far back that "there is no beginning of it." What a stunning truth. There was never a time when God had to turn his attention away from, say, the management of dark matter to begin contemplating whose names should be written in the Lamb's book of life. To make a people for himself was *always* the point.

This biblical teaching can seem so far beyond us that we're unable to dwell on it. But that's not the case. Every day we live, we should meditate on the "heart of God of old." He made all things for his glory, but his people are his precious possession. If we were to go all the way back, there we would find his love stored up for us. And if we were to travel all the way to our eternal future, there we would find his love waiting for us. More than we can ever hope to comprehend, God loves us.

Blessed be the God and Father of our Lord Jesus Christ, who has blessed us in Christ with every spiritual blessing in the heavenly places, even as he chose us in him before the foundation of the world, that we should be holy and blameless before him. EPHESIANS 1:3-4

February 26

There are many things that men possess which, if they part with, they can obtain 'em again. . . . But it is not so with respect to time. When once that is gone, it is gone forever. No pains, no cost will fetch it back. If we repent never so much that we have let it go, and did not improve it while we had it, it will signify nothing. Therefore we should be the more choice of it, while we have it; for that which is well improved is not lost; though the time itself be gone, yet the benefit of it abides with us.

SERMONS AND DISCOURSES, 1734-1738

WE'VE ALL HAD AT LEAST ONE long bus trip or flight that tested our patience. Cramped and confined, we end up silently haggling over the armrest with an aggressive seatmate; in terms of temperature, we're steaming, then freezing, then steaming again. When we get back to home and hearth, it's one of the more happy feelings we can have.

The challenges of travel remind us how good it is to have time and space on our own terms. To live in our own houses and be able to go wherever we'd like. And even though we have some obligations on our time, we also have much discretion. These are simple joys, but they're no less profound for their simplicity. Experiencing our freedom to choose motivates us to seize the hour and make good use of our days. Though we cannot regain the moments that have passed us by, we can make the most of the time we now have.

Daily, we must make a decision: Will we waste our time, or do we want to squeeze out every drop of goodness for the glory of God? As we consider the opportunities that lie before us, the wise words of Jonathan Edwards ring in our ears: "That which is well improved is not lost." Whether at home, at the office, or even while navigating armrest issues on the plane, we can redeem the time we've been given and please the God who holds the world in his hands.

> What is your life? For you are a mist that appears for a little time and then vanishes. Instead you ought to say, "If the Lord wills, we will live and do this or that." JAMES 4:14-15

February 27

When God is thus in the midst of a people, 'tis just cause of {joy and shouts}, that so great {and holy an one is amongst them}. 'Tis the greatest cause that a people can have to rejoice and to praise. Though they may be low in the world, they have greater cause of joy and thankfulness than if they abounded never so much in the wealth and good things of the world; more than if the earth should bring forth by handfuls [Genesis 41:47], or the abundance and wealth of the seas should be gathered together . . . and the heavens should shower down silver and gold and pearls on them, and the rock should pour out rivers of oil to them [Job 29:6]. They have greater cause to rejoice and praise than they that find great spoils.
SERMONS AND DISCOURSES, 1734-1738

THE NUMBER OF FINANCIAL INVESTMENTS we can make—and might need to make—shocks the senses. We have a 401(k), a college fund (or three), a rainy-day account, real estate, and maybe a cash-value insurance policy or two. And let's not forget *braces*, the prospect of which have kept many a young parent up at night.

In such a world as ours, it is not hard to find our joy and security in money. If things are going well, we're up; if the market drops, so do our spirits. How reassuring, then, to realize that our mood—and certainly our identity—need not be tied to any financial peak or valley. The one saved by God "may be low in the world," as Jonathan Edwards suggests, but has greater "abundance and wealth" than any tycoon can imagine.

It isn't hard to envy the rich, to say nothing of the super-rich. But we should not despise our fellow man, and we cannot underplay the wealth we have. It is true wealth, after all. Even as we live wisely and generously, we should recognize that we can do something far more important than buying braces or setting up a trust fund for future generations. We can seek to pass on the inheritance of faith to our family and loved ones. This may seem small in the eyes of an unbeliever, but its value is *priceless*.

Rejoice in the Lord always; again I will say, rejoice.
PHILIPPIANS 4:4

February 28

February 1755: A Dissertation Concerning the End for Which God Created the World *completed*

THE PURPOSE OF HUMAN EXISTENCE is not to live for oneself. It is to live for the glory of God. So Jonathan Edwards argues in his masterwork, *A Dissertation Concerning the End for Which God Created the World*. Edwards wrote this book while serving as a missionary in Stockbridge. We can scarcely fathom how he accomplished it amid his regular duties of weekly preaching, instruction of villagers, and familial care.

End of Creation (the shorthand title) lays out a rigorous case for *doxology* (glory to God) as the point of all things. Though not published until 1765, nine years after its completion, it represents Edwards's attempt to make good on his God-centered convictions. If God really is the focus of existence, then the purpose of our lives must center on him. In this text, Edwards connects our purpose to God's lovely being. His God is a God of absolute holiness, and thus intoxicating beauty.

According to Edwards's theology, Christians have the opportunity to delight in the beauty of God's character, and consciously return praise to God through a holy life.

> In the creature's knowing, esteeming, loving, rejoicing in, and praising God, the glory of God is both exhibited and acknowledged; his fullness is received and returned. Here is both an *emanation* and *remanation*. The refulgence shines upon and into the creature, and is reflected back to the luminary. The beams of glory come from God, and are something of God, and are refunded back again to their original. So that the whole is *of God*, and *in* God, and *to* God; and God is the beginning, middle and end in this affair.[19]

The purpose of life is not our own glory, but God's. The "whole is *of God* . . . and *to* God." Christians are not merely saved; Christians are not merely devoted to God; rather, Christians enter into the experience for which God made the cosmos—namely, the conscious enjoyment and glorification of God in all our existence.

Edwards's *End of Creation* deserves to be read alongside the great philosophical texts of the ages. It is a complex book, but offers a central insight that any Christian can understand and apply: My life is not my own. Everything is God's; God is the beginning, middle, and end of my life.

March

†

March 1

March 1729: Jonathan Edwards suffers physical collapse

SHORTLY AFTER ASSUMING the pastorate of Northampton's First Church in February 1729, Jonathan Edwards suffered a physical collapse that prevented him from preaching for a month. This illness left him frail and with a weakened voice. Edwards had thrown himself into his work, as was his custom, and no doubt felt considerable pressure to carry the load after his grandfather's death.

Part of the reason for his intense work ethic was his concern for the townspeople. Throughout his career, Edwards wrestled with the scourge of "nominal" Christianity among his parishioners. Many people had joined the church, or expressed faith over the years, as a result of Solomon Stoddard's preaching. But not all who confessed Christianity practiced it. More than any other burden he bore, Edwards opposed Christianity-in-name-only. For all his days, he sought to increase the spread of true Christianity and call out the false kind.

Aside from this theological effort, Edwards had also become a father not long before, and had the duty of preaching three times a week—Sunday morning, Sunday afternoon, and a lecture on Thursday. He spent huge blocks of time on his homilies, painstakingly crafting them for theological and spiritual effect. In addition to this already considerable workload, Edwards had ambitions of writing numerous theological texts.

The illness soon receded, but occasionally returned throughout his ministry. Edwards was not the healthiest of men, and suffered many physical breakdowns during his life, beginning when he was in college. Those closest to him feared for his life on several occasions. In retrospect, we can conclude that Edwards battled anxiety, stress, and overwork brought on by his grand aims. Though an unusually gifted man, he had to contend with the effects of the Fall in his daily life. He believed the Lord used a "low tide of spirits" to correct Edwards's natural tendency to self-sufficiency. His sufferings, some of which were self-inflicted, led him to prayer and greater dependence on God. We are not unlike him. Throughout our lives, we need the Lord to correct us, discipline us, and lift our heads once more.

March 2

A people that have such an one [the Lord] dwelling in the midst of them have the best comforter. He is the "God that comforts those that are cast down" [2 Corinthians 7:6]; yea, he is the God of all consolation [Romans 15:5]. He is a fountain of peace and comfort to such a people. He affords the best relief to poor, sad, and burdened souls. In him they may find rest [Matthew 11:29]. Those that have wandered, and have been tossed to and fro, and have found no rest, in him they have rest. They that have been afraid and terrified, in him they may have quietness and assurance forever.

SERMONS AND DISCOURSES, 1734-1738

WE CAN HAVE EVERYTHING and yet have nothing. The Bible unveils this sobering principle in its use of the word *poor*. Jesus, in his Sermon on the Mount, uses this word for financial poverty to illustrate a spiritual reality. If we recognize that we are poor in spirit and realize our need for God, we will inherit the Kingdom of Heaven (Matthew 5:3). On the other hand, if we don't recognize our need for God, then according to biblical wisdom we are impoverished beggars.

Some people mistakenly believe that the Bible forbids being wealthy, but Scripture paints a balanced portrait of earthly means. It isn't the wealthy who are faulted; it's those who are arrogant and stingy with their wealth (1 Timothy 6:17-19). That's a crucial distinction. The real point of Christian teaching, though, is not to lay out a money-management plan; it's to call the spiritually poor to find rest and relief and comfort in Christ.

In the modern era, rest (often thought of as leisure) is associated with money. But, in Scripture, rest is inextricably linked to Jesus. We can work like a whirlwind to achieve "security," and yet have none. We can plan for ease and comfort, but so wrap ourselves around worldly concerns that we find neither. It is imperative to know that true rest comes only through God. He is worth it all. We can have everything and yet have nothing. Conversely, in Christ, we have nothing and yet everything—what Jonathan Edwards refers to as "quietness and assurance forever."

Blessed be the God and Father of our Lord Jesus Christ, the Father of mercies and God of all comfort, who comforts us in all our affliction.

2 CORINTHIANS 1:3-4

March 3

When so great and holy a God dwells among a people, he [is] not only able to supply them with all good, but he himself is the sum of all good. God is theirs, and therefore they are happy, if they have nothing else. If all other things fail, the enjoyment of God is sufficient to make them completely happy. They that have God for their portion, they have a sufficient portion.
SERMONS AND DISCOURSES, 1734-1738

THE BILLIONAIRE John D. Rockefeller Sr. was once asked by a reporter, "How much is enough?" According to tradition, Rockefeller replied, "A little bit more." This mind-set is common not only among the rich, but also among people of all backgrounds. You need not have a billion dollars in the bank to live a restless, acquisitive life. The desire for more is universal.

This instinct—this capacity—for more, wasn't given us by God for the pursuit of money, however. He gave us appetites so we would pursue our ultimate fulfillment in him. But with our fallen nature, our hunger for more easily and inevitably goes astray. Our appetites give us a clue about the way things should be, not just the way things are. We want more, and more, and more because we were made for more.

In the words of Jonathan Edwards, our "great and holy" God is the "sum of all good." He not only meets the standard of goodness; he *defines* goodness. He is all we truly want. Prior to conversion, we indulge our desire for *more* only in lesser things. But when Christ gets hold of us, he sets us free to taste the delightful sufficiency of God the Father. What an encouragement! Few people on earth will ever become billionaires. But every person on earth can attain, by faith, *everything* that is in Christ Jesus. Our sufficiency is found in the all-sufficient one. And that, we can safely say, is all we need.

> The LORD is my chosen portion and my cup; you hold my lot. The lines have fallen for me in pleasant places; indeed, I have a beautiful inheritance. PSALM 16:5-6

March 4

Christ took great delight [in] the thoughts of his sufferings for sinners upon this account: he had his heart very much upon this way of glorifying [God]: he greatly rejoiced to think how God would be glorified in his sufferings; how this would be an occasion of showing forth his perfections to the views of men and angels. It rejoiced him to think how this would be an occasion of God's being praised by the angels; and of his having praise out of the mouth of babes and sucklings; and how he would be praised by all the host of heaven, the church of saints and angels forevermore. And therefore it was exceeding offensive to him that any should object against his suffering. It was an unpleasing thought to him, that God should miss of all this glory that he had so set his heart upon and settled upon for ages and generations.
SERMONS AND DISCOURSES, 1734-1738

OUR HEARTS ARE PRESET to steer clear of suffering. This makes sense. We depend on the avoidance of suffering to thrive and even to exist.

Understanding our instincts helps us see the wondrous strangeness of the life of Christ. Jesus embraced suffering in the Incarnation—in his gruesome death, of course, but also during his life on earth. He did so "for the joy that was set before him" (Hebrews 12:2), the reward of his Father's glory and good pleasure. Jesus didn't go to the Cross as a flameout. No, Jesus went to the Cross like an athlete at the peak of his performance, and he died victorious, in a blaze of holy glory. In making atonement for sin, he displayed "his perfections" to men and angels, to principalities and powers.

On this account, Jonathan Edwards is powerfully correct. Christ redeemed us, even as he redeemed suffering. He embraced the agony of life and death because he did not want his Father to "miss of all this glory." How instructive this is for us. The same one who transforms us has also transformed suffering. The ancient world saw no glory in the crucifixion of a king. But Jesus was a king like no other. As the bride of Christ, we are a people like no other. Whatever cross we must bear, we can bear it in the strength of our Redeemer.

Whether you eat or drink, or whatever you do, do all to the glory of God. I CORINTHIANS 10:31

March 5

The saints may be assured that God's love to them will be everlasting, because it hath already been from eternity. That love that is but of late beginning, may soon come to an end; but that which has been from eternity, will and must be to eternity. The love of men one towards another oftentimes grows up suddenly; and when men are soon hot, they are commonly soon cold. But the love of God to his saints is no sudden, upstart thing; but it has been in the heart unchanged from all eternity. This shows the constancy and immutability of it, and may put it out of doubt with those that are the objects of it, that it never will fail.
SERMONS AND DISCOURSES, 1734-1738

THINGS FAIL—frequently and unexpectedly (though you would think we would know better). The expensive new tires deflate on our way out of the shop. The new Internet+TV+Calling plan we just purchased results in one dropped connection after another. Even those flowers we picked up on the way home are dead a few days later.

If we're not careful, we can feel like a losing football team. Our minds become consumed by loss and failure. We're in a hard-as-nails world, after all. But there is one thing that doesn't fail in this world: the kindness of God. We may have to fight to continue grasping this truth, but we can *know* the love that has no temporal beginning or no temporal end.

We mustn't take this love lightly. We cannot soft-pedal it or use it as an excuse for unholiness. But neither can we fail to saturate ourselves with it. We need it. Even the best relationships, the deepest ones, begin at a point and end at a point. Death and separation are part of the cruelty of the Fall. But the difficulties of this world serve only to highlight God's warmth toward us. The God we worship and serve is not untrustworthy. He is a pillar of stability. The gadgets and plans we purchase? They will fail. God, on the other hand, will not.

Neither death nor life, nor angels nor rulers, nor things present nor things to come, nor powers, nor height nor depth, nor anything else in all creation, will be able to separate us from the love of God in Christ Jesus our Lord. ROMANS 8:38-39

March 6

There do meet in Jesus Christ, infinite highness, and infinite condescension. Christ, as he is God, is infinitely great and high above all. He is higher than the kings of the earth; for he is King of Kings, and Lord of Lords. He is higher than the heavens, and higher than the highest angels of heaven. So great is he, that all men, all kings and princes, are as worms of the dust before him, all nations are as the drop of the bucket, and the light dust of the balance; yea, and angels themselves are as nothing before him. He is so high, that he is infinitely above any need of us; above our reach, that we cannot be profitable to him, and above our conceptions, that we cannot comprehend him.

SERMONS AND DISCOURSES, 1734-1738

IT'S REALLY QUITE REMARKABLE what you can learn about celebrities today. There's the ever-present update about shopping: "Tom Cruise went to the *grocery store* yesterday!" Or you can indulge your interest in their vacations: "Reese Witherspoon is in the Bahamas and walked on the beach—it's true!"

Our culture encourages us to marvel at the daily rituals of mere mortals. This is not as God would have it. The figure we should be dazzled by is not a movie star, politician, or athlete. During his time on earth, Jesus walked among the ordinary people, and most ignored him. But he was altogether unique—dressed like a peasant, yet "higher than the heavens"; a crown jewel hidden in plain sight and overlooked by the celebrities of his day.

Biblical Christology—the theology of the person and work of Jesus Christ—is two-sided, bridging both the human and the divine. But before we try to understand his human nature, we would do well to linger for a moment on his divine nature. Jesus created the earth. He rules everything that is. By comparison, men and angels are as nothing before him. And yet this is the one who came to redeem us. This is *Immanuel*, God with us, the highest stooping to lift up the lowest, unrecognized by many, but treasured by all who know his true nature.

He is the radiance of the glory of God and the exact imprint of his
nature, and he upholds the universe by the word of his power.

HEBREWS 1:3

March 7

Resolved, never to do anything out of revenge.
LETTERS AND PERSONAL WRITINGS

BE VERY, VERY CAREFUL whose laptop you steal. In a true story you couldn't make up, a thief in Massachusetts grabbed a computer from a tech whiz's room. Using various programs, the techie found a way to hack back into his stolen computer. The first thing he found? A video of the thief dancing. He quickly posted it to YouTube, identified the criminal, and watched as two million people viewed the video. The laptop was eventually returned, and the thief brought to justice.

We must distinguish between justice and revenge. Christians seek justice to the fullest extent. But vengeance is a different matter. Vengeance is not ours to take. The one who has united us to himself through his work on the cross claims this duty for himself. We think here of Romans 12:19, where the apostle Paul tells a church that will suffer wrongs, "Beloved, never avenge yourselves, but leave it to the wrath of God, for it is written, 'Vengeance is mine, I will repay, says the Lord.'" Because of Christ's divine right, Jonathan Edwards charged himself not to do "anything out of revenge."

Edwards battled his temper throughout his life. He did not excuse his failings in this area. He took stock of his weaknesses and sought to reform them. He reminds us of the need to do the same. Knowing that God will by no means let the guilty off the hook frees us from feeling the need to avenge ourselves. We have a great opportunity when wronged: We do not merely stifle our hunger for revenge; we love our enemies—and by doing so heap coals on their heads.

If your enemy is hungry, give him bread to eat, and if he is thirsty, give him water to drink, for you will heap burning coals on his head, and the LORD will reward you. PROVERBS 25:21-22

March 8

There meet in Jesus Christ, infinite justice, and infinite grace. As Christ is a divine person he is infinitely holy and just, infinitely hating sin, and disposed to execute condign punishment for sin. He is the Judge of the world, and the infinitely just judge of it, and will not at all acquit the wicked, or by any means clear the guilty. And yet he is one that is infinitely gracious and merciful. Though his justice be so strict with respect to all sin, and every breach of the law, yet he has grace sufficient for every sinner, and even the chief of sinners.
SERMONS AND DISCOURSES, 1734-1738

I ONCE HEARD A TRUE STORY about a young man who got in trouble with the law. He'd done some foolish things and had to go to court for his misdeeds. This young gun was different, however. He was a Christian, and his father was the judge. On the dreaded day, the judge handed down his son's sentence, imposing a fine. He then called the young man to the front of the court, and handed him a twenty-dollar bill, paying the fine in full.

What a beautiful picture of what Christ has done. He is the "Judge of the world." We are fully accountable to him and have no claim on his grace. We are just like the young man awaiting his fate. We know we are guilty, and we know the judge is not lax when it comes to the law. He is "infinitely just" and will not fail to deal out justice in his court.

But this judge, too, motions us forward. He calls us to the front of the room. We can almost feel the heavy weight of divine justice landing on our shoulders. But the judge is not only the one who deals out justice, he is the payment for our sin. He gives us not a coin, a bill, or a check. He gives us himself; he yields his body and blood. He leaves us marveling at him every day we walk this earth. The judge has become the justifier, and the guilty have become the righteous.

It was to show his righteousness at the present time, so that he might be just and the justifier of the one who has faith in Jesus. ROMANS 3:26

March 9

There are conjoined in the person of Christ, infinite worthiness of good, and the greatest patience under sufferings of evil. He was perfectly innocent, and deserved no suffering. He deserved nothing from God, by any guilt of his own; and he deserved no ill from men. Yea, he was not only harmless, and undeserving of suffering, but he was infinitely worthy, worthy of the infinite love of the Father, worthy of infinite and eternal happiness, and infinitely worthy of all possible esteem, love, and service from all men. And yet he was perfectly patient under the greatest sufferings that ever were endured in this world.
SERMONS AND DISCOURSES, 1734-1738

NOT LONG AGO, I heard of a father and son who had an unusual bond. The boy was confined to a wheelchair and had no hope of walking. One day, the father decided to do something unusual. He entered his son in a race—a race in which the two of them would compete together. When race day arrived, the father pushed his son's wheelchair the full length of the course, while the son cheered him on and encouraged him. With that success behind them, the father and son began to enter one race after another, eventually attracting global attention.

How easy it is when trials come to opt out of hope. All around us, people are battling problems; and we have our own to face as well. Most folks just muddle through. But occasionally we get a spark; we hear of someone who is pressing on amid the hardship they face. We gain strength from such examples. We find ourselves with increased interest in going ahead, returning to the task at hand, pressing on.

Such acts of courage point to the greatest intervention of all time, when Jesus Christ took on the "greatest sufferings that ever were endured," shouldering the full weight of our sin and shame. He gives us both the power and the vision we need to overcome our own difficulties. True success, biblically defined, is not beating everyone else at their game. It is rising above sin and shame, shaking off discouragement, and following Christ to the end of the race. It does not all come in a rush; it comes one day at a time, one choice at a time.

Looking to Jesus, the founder and perfecter of our faith, who for the joy that was set before him endured the cross, despising the shame, and is seated at the right hand of the throne of God.   HEBREWS 12:2

March 10

His infinite condescension marvelously appeared in the manner of his birth. He was brought forth in a stable, because there was no room for them in the inn. The inn was taken up by others, that were looked upon as persons of greater account. The blessed Virgin being poor and despised, was turned or shut out; though she was in such necessitous circumstances, yet those that counted themselves her betters, would not give place to her; and therefore in the time of her travail she was forced to betake herself to a stable; and when the child was born, it was wrapped in swaddling clothes, and laid in a manger; and there Christ lay a little infant; and there he eminently appeared as a lamb. But yet this feeble infant that was born thus in a stable, and laid in a manger, was born to conquer and triumph over Satan, that roaring lion.

SERMONS AND DISCOURSES, 1734-1738

SOMETIMES WE TRICK OURSELVES. We think we want a travel adventure. We draft our schedule; we call ahead; we purchase the tickets. But then the actual adventure begins, and sometimes things spiral out of control. We think to ourselves, "I didn't sign up for this."

Nothing worth doing will come friction-free in this life. We have no greater example than Jesus, the God-man who embraced "infinite condescension" in coming to earth. At the greatest cost, he left his heavenly throne. The sovereign Lord became a "feeble infant" born to a humble young woman. Everything about Christ's earthly ministry was wearying and difficult. Yet he took it all on to destroy death and to ransom his people from Satan's tyranny.

Living a life that is dedicated to God is not easy, but it is worth it. It is an adventure, the kind that will stretch us and test us on a regular basis. Praise God, our faithfulness does not rest on our own shoulders. We follow a Savior who walked where we walk, and who triumphed where we would fail. His Kingdom, which advances this very day through the works of his people, continues its march. Soon, like Mary, we will see that we receive so much more than we signed up for—more than we ever could have imagined.

> She gave birth to her firstborn son and wrapped him in swaddling cloths and laid him in a manger, because there was no place for them in the inn. LUKE 2:7

March 11

Christ's holiness never so illustriously shone forth, as it did in his last sufferings; and yet he never was to such a degree, treated as guilty. Christ's holiness never had such a trial, as it had then; and therefore never had so great a manifestation. When it was tried in this furnace, it came forth as gold, or as silver purified seven times. His holiness then above all appeared in his steadfast pursuit of the honor of God; and in his obedience to him: for his yielding himself unto death was transcendently the greatest act of obedience, that ever was paid to God, by anyone since the foundation of the world.

SERMONS AND DISCOURSES, 1734-1738

IT WAS A STRANGE MOMENT between a baseball player and the umpire. After disagreeing on a called strike, the player stepped out of the batter's box. When the umpire told him to step back in, the batter refused. The ump gestured again, and again the hitter ignored him. Eventually, the umpire ejected the player from the game, the player went nuts, and the video went viral.

In a time when expressing ourselves is everything, following authority seems negotiable. We claim we are just "being authentic" when we do what we want, but not when we submit to those who lead us. Compared to countless earthly examples of "authentic" disobedience, the work of Jesus was unearthly. He came to earth not on his own, but to carry out the will of his Father. He embodied submission to God. He loved authority. He obeyed it perfectly.

What a challenge this is to our proud hearts. The Cross shows us that Jesus was truly the Son of God. His death, which Jonathan Edwards calls "the greatest act of obedience," reveals the character of a son who finds maximum pleasure in obeying the Father. Though very God himself, Jesus yielded himself to the Father's will, showing us the nature of our own sonship as adopted children (Romans 8:12-17). Disobedience might go viral, but obedience pleases the Lord.

When they came to the place that is called The Skull, there they crucified him, and the criminals, one on his right and one on his left.

LUKE 23:33

March 12

What are you afraid of, that you dare not venture your soul upon Christ? Are you afraid that he can't save you, that he is not strong enough to conquer the enemies of your soul? But how can you desire one stronger than "the mighty God"? as Christ is called (Isaiah 9:6). Is there need of greater than infinite strength? Are you afraid that he won't be willing to stoop so low, as to take any gracious notice of you? . . . Or, are you afraid that if he does accept of you, that God the Father won't accept of him for you? But consider, will God reject his own Son, in whom his infinite delight is, and has been, from all eternity, and that is so united to him, that if he should reject him he would reject himself?
SERMONS AND DISCOURSES, 1734-1738

IN HIS SONG "UNDERNEATH THE DOOR," musician Michael Card tells a story of trying to engage with his father, a busy doctor. His father performed life-saving surgeries during the day, and sought privacy when he came home at night. This was hard for a young boy to understand, so even when his exhausted father retreated to his study for hours, little Michael would slide pictures under the door to him, trying any way he could to connect with him.

Our family dynamics shape who we are, both for good and for ill. Therefore, it's not uncommon for us to carry our past experience into our walk with Christ. Sometimes we fear that we don't deserve the Father's attention. We worry that we will do something to cancel his grace. We know our own heart, and we calculate the odds of divine rejection. Instead of living in the joy of grace, we live in the sadness of alienation.

Our status as *justified* doesn't cancel our need to repent of our sin. Yet the wondrous news of the gospel is that God has "infinite delight" in his Son, who is "united" to us by the Cross and our conversion. The Son's death gave us life, and now the Father counts us as his own. He will not abandon us. He will not leave us to our own devices. The Father is near to us, and when we turn to him, he does not hold back. It is not merely that he is willing to receive us; it is that he is calling to us and urging us home.

Let us then with confidence draw near to the throne of grace, that we may receive mercy and find grace to help in time of need.
HEBREWS 4:16

March 13

THE PREACHING CAREER of Jonathan Edwards, like that of most pastors, consisted of a regular diet of biblical exposition. Most weeks went according to form. But certain points in Edwards's career bucked the norm. On an otherwise unspectacular Sunday in March 1737, Edwards had just reached the doctrine portion of his message. He was preaching on the following text: "Behold, ye despisers, and wonder, and perish: for I work a work in your days, a work which ye shall in no wise believe, though a man declare it unto you" (Acts 13:41, KJV).

Suddenly, as he recounted a few days later, things fell apart—specifically, the church's gallery.

> We in this town were, the last Lord's day (March 13th), the spectators, and
> many of us the subjects, of one of the most amazing instances of divine
> preservation, that perhaps was ever known in the land. Our meeting house
> is old and decayed, so that we have been for some time building a new
> one, which is yet unfinished. . . . In the midst of the public exercise in the
> forenoon, soon after the beginning of sermon, the whole gallery—full of
> people, with all the seats and timbers, suddenly and without any warning—
> sunk, and fell down, with the most amazing noise, upon the heads of those
> that sat under, to the astonishment of the congregation. The house was
> filled with dolorous shrieking and crying; and nothing else was expected
> than to find many people dead, or dashed to pieces.[20]

And yet, not a single person died in this horrific event:

> None can give an account, or conceive, by what means people's lives
> and limbs should be thus preserved, when so great a multitude were
> thus eminently exposed. It looked as though it was impossible but that
> great numbers must instantly be crushed to death or dashed in pieces.
> It seems unreasonable to ascribe it to any thing else but the care of
> providence, in disposing the motions of every piece of timber, and the
> precise place of safety where every one should sit and fall, when none
> were in any capacity to care for their own preservation.[21]

Most of our churchgoing experiences will likely be normal and without adverse incident. If you ever hear someone yearn for excitement in church, remind them of what Edwards and his congregation might say: Be careful what you wish for. You just might get it.

March 14

What is there that you can desire should be in a Savior, that is not in Christ? Or, where in should you desire a Savior should be otherwise than Christ is? What excellency is there wanting? What is there that is great or good? What is there that is venerable or winning? What is there that is adorable or endearing? Or, what can you think of that would be encouraging, that is not to be found in the person of Christ? . . . What is there wanting, or what would you add if you could, to make him more fit to be your Savior?

SERMONS AND DISCOURSES, 1734-1738

WE REGULARLY HEAR of congressional dealings in which bills have clauses added to them that benefit a limited group. The critics call it *pork*. A congressman wishes to draw federal funds for a new shipbuilding factory in his district, for example. In order to get the deal done, he agrees to allow a fellow legislator to add a provision for funding, say, a cheesemaker's museum. If, as they say, politics is the art of compromise, then bargaining is its currency.

The natural human heart tends to want to bargain. Even after the Spirit convicts us of our sin and draws us to Christ, we still find the "excellency" of our salvation "wanting," as Jonathan Edwards suggests. "Jesus is great," we say to ourselves, "but we'd love it if we could throw in something extra." Though we are free to bring all our requests to God, we know that our hearts can wander from the Lord and desire the wrong things. If we're not careful, our faith can morph into wish fulfillment. The cost of the Cross diminishes in our eyes as our lust for the things of the world grows.

Edwards's words hit hard. There is nothing lacking in Christ. In fact, all that is great, good, venerable, and encouraging may be found in him. If we pursue Christ, we gain *everything* of value, for all the treasures of God are found in him. There is nothing to add to Jesus—no clause, no exception. There is no bargaining with our Savior. He is fully sufficient. He has given us all we need, today and every day.

He is the head of the body, the church. He is the beginning, the
firstborn from the dead, that in everything he might be preeminent.
COLOSSIANS 1:18

March 15

Indeed I am fearful whether you will not be disappointed in New England, and will have less success here than in other places: we who have dwelt in a land that has been distinguished with light, and have long enjoyed the gospel, and have been glutted with it, and have despised it, are I fear more hardened than most of those places where you have preached hitherto. But yet I hope in that power and mercy of God that has appeared so triumphant in the success of your labors in other places, that he will send a blessing with you even to us, though we are unworthy of it. I hope, if God preserves my life, to see something of that salvation of God in New England which he has now begun, in a benighted, wicked, and miserable world and age and in the most guilty of all nations.

LETTERS AND PERSONAL WRITINGS

IF YOU'VE HEARD of New England, you're aware that it's known for its natural beauty, its solitude, and its seafood. In years past, New England was also known for its solid spiritual character. Founded on a vision to be "a city on a hill," its communities were established to achieve this spiritual goal.

Today, New England is known for its secularism. About 2 percent of the population professes to be evangelical, Bible-believing, gospel-confessing Christians. Reading the words that Jonathan Edwards wrote nearly three hundred years ago to the evangelist George Whitefield, one cannot miss the prophetic note he strikes. He shares his fear that the region, so uniquely blessed with sound preaching during the colonial period, was now "more hardened than most" other places. What was true in the 1740s has only become truer in our day.

But Edwards's sober reflection also includes evidence of hope, a little comet streaking across a dreary backdrop. He yearns to "see something of that salvation of God" in his homeland. Edwards never lost confidence in the sovereign mercy of God. Along with so many parts of our world, New England finds itself in a time of "gospel famine." There is little witness unto God, and many churches need help. Yet, as believers in the sovereignty of God, we cannot give in to despair. All around us, people need Christ. Today, let us pray for needy places and needy people. Let us ask God to visit a hardened people, and pray that we will see something of God's salvation in our time.

So neither he who plants nor he who waters is anything, but only God who gives the growth. I CORINTHIANS 3:7

March 16

By your being united to Christ, you will have a more glorious union with and enjoyment of, God the Father, than otherwise could be. For hereby the saints' relation to God becomes much nearer; they are the children of God in an higher manner, than otherwise could be. For being members of God's own natural Son, they are in a sort partakers of his relation to the Father: they are not only sons of God by regeneration, but by a kind of communion in the sonship of the eternal Son. . . . The church is the daughter of God, not only as he hath begotten her by his word and spirit, but as she is the spouse of his eternal Son.

SERMONS AND DISCOURSES, 1734-1738

FATHERS AND SONS have difficult relationships in Scripture. We think of David and Absalom, the heir to the throne who rejected his father's oversight and even went to war against him. The two never reconciled, and when David learned of his son's death in battle, he uttered one of the most piercing cries in all the Bible: "O my son Absalom, O Absalom, my son, my son!" (2 Samuel 19:4).

Thankfully, Scripture gives us a different example in God himself. The love of God the Father for God the Son reflects a special kind of bond. The two have the strongest possible affection for and interest in one another. To a degree that boggles our minds, the Father and Son share eternal love. The Son is the Father's gift to the world, and when the Son comes down to our lowly confines, the Father tells his disciples: "This is my beloved Son, with whom I am well pleased" (Matthew 3:17).

Whatever our past, whatever our history with our own fathers, we have hope. The Son of God unites our souls with his through his substitutionary death and life-giving resurrection. His saving work clears the guilty. We become children of God. We share fellowship with the Father through the Son. Today, all the privileges of sonship are ours. We are accepted, forgiven, and warmly welcomed. Even the fiercest pain and the darkest past are swallowed up by the Father's love.

In that day you will know that I am in my Father, and you in me, and I in you. JOHN 14:20

March 17

This was the design of Christ, to bring it to pass, that he, and his Father, and his people, might all be united in one. John 17:21–23, "That they all may be one; as thou Father art in me, and I in thee; that they also may be one in us; that the world may believe that thou hast sent me. And the glory which thou hast given me, I have given them, that they may be one, even as we are one; I in them, and thou in me; that they may be made perfect in one." Christ has brought it to pass, that those that the Father has given him, should be brought into the household of God; that he, and his Father, and his people, should be as it were one society, one family; that the church should be as it were admitted into the society of the blessed Trinity.

SERMONS AND DISCOURSES, 1734-1738

MANY PEOPLE RECALL forming a club as a child—hammering out rules, swearing some oaths, and going on adventures. As time wore on, however, the group began to drift apart. Soon, the club was no more, only a distant memory of days gone by.

Every earthly association, in truth, will end. All, that is, except one. The fellowship we have with God in this realm is not truly of this earth. The church does not create its own spiritual club; it partakes of the "society of the blessed Trinity," as Jonathan Edwards says. Our love is not our own; it does not originate with us. It spills over from heaven, giving us a taste of God's own happiness.

We have fellowship with one another because the members of the Godhead have fellowship with one another. Unity is not our achievement. It is a divine reality. We are "one family" in Christ. Soon, we will go to be with the whole family of God forever. The unity and love and care that our churches have fought to preserve will no longer require effort. Our lives are not static. They are headed somewhere. With all the people of God, we are part of the "society" of God—and always will be.

That they may all be one, just as you, Father, are in me, and I in you, that they also may be in us, so that the world may believe that you have sent me. JOHN 17:21

March 18

The thoughts of the perfect humility with which the saints in heaven worship God, and fall down before his throne, have often overcome the body, and set it into a great agitation. A great delight in singing praises to God and Jesus Christ, and longing that this present life may be, as it were, one continued song of praise to God; longing, as the person expressed it, to sit and sing this life away; and an overcoming pleasure in the thoughts of spending an eternity in that exercise: a living by faith to a great degree; a constant and extraordinary distrust of own strength and wisdom; a great dependence on God for his help, in order to the performance of anything to God's acceptance.

THE GREAT AWAKENING, 1758

IN 1734 AND 1735, a revival broke out in Northampton, Massachusetts, where Jonathan Edwards pastored the First Church. Some critics decried these events, arguing that what the pastor claimed was a work of God was nothing more than emotional excitement. Edwards defended the revival—the first major instance of what is called the First Great Awakening—in print.

He pointed out that he had witnessed in the life of his own family the effects of what had taken place in town. Though he does not directly identify his wife, Sarah, he speaks of a person who felt "a great delight in singing praises to God, and exhibited "a great dependence" on the strength of God. The preaching of God's Word drew church members such as Sarah away from themselves and toward God.

We have a hard time pinpointing the mystical works of the Lord. We are finite creatures. But when we draw near to God and find increased joy in him, we can safely say that he is moving in us. When we lessen our grip on our own self-sufficiency and confess that God alone is our help, we may be certain that the Spirit is working in us. These are what we could call *everyday miracles*. It is not that our trials are over; it is that God is growing us spiritually in the midst of them. This is the extraordinary work of God, and we pray for it daily.

You are the LORD, you alone. You have made heaven, the heaven of heavens, with all their host, the earth and all that is on it, the seas and all that is in them; and you preserve all of them; and the host of heaven worships you. NEHEMIAH 9:6

March 19

[An example of evangelical piety:] . . . A vehement and constant desire for the setting up of Christ's kingdom through the earth, as a kingdom of holiness, purity, love, peace and happiness to mankind: the soul often entertained with unspeakable delight, and bodily strength overborne at the thoughts of heaven as a world of love, where love shall be the saints' eternal food, and they shall dwell in the light of love, and swim in an ocean of love, and where the very air and breath will be nothing but love.

THE GREAT AWAKENING, 1758

NEARLY THREE HUNDRED YEARS after revival first broke out in western Massachusetts, we still hear about unusual movements of God today. Sometimes we get reports of drastic effects, or garbled sayings. Jonathan Edwards's report of revival in Northampton reminds us that the chief fruit of a sudden spiritual harvest is loving God.

It is surprisingly rare to find believers who will speak openly of the things of God. We find it easier to discuss work circumstances, or football scores, or PTA concerns than to talk about our sovereign, loving Lord. Whether our churches experience a remarkable number of conversions or not, we can know that God is at work when people are drawn into "thoughts of heaven," thoughts of God, and thoughts of his love.

Let no one stop us from discussing these things. These are the greatest subjects our minds can contemplate and our tongues can express. Through prayer and study of the Bible, let us seek "eternal food." Let us "swim in an ocean of love," giving ourselves over to God. Let us talk about God, no matter what others think of us. This is "evangelical piety" that the world and the church need to see.

Seek first the kingdom of God and his righteousness, and all these things will be added to you.   MATTHEW 6:33

March 20

[An example of evangelical piety:] . . . A wonderful access to God by prayer, as it were seeing him, and sensibly immediately conversing with him, as much oftentimes (to use the person's own expressions) as if Christ were here on earth, sitting on a visible throne, to be approached to and conversed with; frequent, plain, sensible and immediate answers of prayer; all tears wiped away; all former troubles and sorrows of life forgotten, and all sorrow and sighing fled away.
THE GREAT AWAKENING, 1758

How OFTEN DO WE CARRY our burdens on our own backs? Too often. But God is ready to hear us. As Jonathan Edwards tells us, we need not learn some super-doctrinal language in order to talk with the Father. We have "a wonderful access to God," and we should seize it. We may approach our ruler and talk with him. We can pray the same way as we talk: "plain" and "sensible" words work very well. Our Father hears them all.

What happy news this is. There is no delay of access for the child of God to the person of Christ. Now, and at any time, we may draw on him for strength, worship him, rejoice in his perfections. Nothing is stopping us; nothing is holding us back. Christ is here, and near to us. He gives us full entry to the Father's mansion, and encourages us to talk with him, lifting up our petitions, requests, confessions, and thanksgiving.

Prayer is not an escape from the world. It will not *physically* launch us into the heavens (that would make for an interesting church prayer meeting), but it can bring the peace of God to our hearts, causing them to soar. Prayer is the active exercise of trust. In prayer, we hand our cares and hopes to God, and commit them to him. Soon, Christ will wipe away every tear from our eyes, once and for all. Even before that great day, however, prayer relieves our heavy load. Peace is ours; sorrow and sighing flee away. Such is the privilege of those who pray.

Do not be anxious about anything, but in everything by prayer and
supplication with thanksgiving let your requests be made known
to God. PHILIPPIANS 4:6

March 21

I am bold to say, that the work of God in the conversion of one soul, considered together with the source, foundation and purchase of it, and also the benefit, end and eternal issue of it, is a more glorious work of God than the creation of the whole material universe: it is the most glorious of God's works, as it above all others manifests the glory of God.

THE GREAT AWAKENING, 1758

DURING THE TWENTIETH CENTURY, the world witnessed the rise of several political movements that supposedly promoted the interests of "the people." For decades, communist governments promised to lift their people up. In truth, the reverse happened. Millions of ordinary, peaceable citizens died at the hands of dictators in China, the Soviet Union, and Cambodia. Those who said they were for the people proved decidedly against them.

There is no such treachery in the Kingdom of Heaven. Souls matter to God, and every individual counts. Jonathan Edwards writes that heaven rejoices over the "conversion of one soul" more than the making of the "whole material universe." His point harkens back to Genesis 1:26-27, which tells us that on the sixth day of creation, God poured forth all his artistry, making the man and the woman in his own image and likeness. Humanity, we could say, is an enchanted race.

Following the Fall, however, we lost our holy status and wandered far from the Lord (Genesis 3). But this was not the end of the story. Jesus, the true shepherd, plunged into the darkness, seeking out his lost sheep (John 10:11-18). He died to rescue and redeem sinners. Many people will tell us that they are on our side, but we must never forget: Only God is truly on our side. He loves us not in theory, but in truth—sin-overcoming, body-sacrificing, life-giving truth.

Even when we were dead in our trespasses, [God] made us alive together with Christ—by grace you have been saved. EPHESIANS 2:5

March 22

March 22, 1758: Jonathan Edwards dies of complications from a smallpox vaccination

IN FEBRUARY 1758, Jonathan Edwards was inoculated for smallpox. He was treated by William Shippen, a widely respected Philadelphia physician. Edwards had no qualms about the vaccination; in fact, as a respected community leader, he received it in part to provide an example to show other colonists that they need not fear medical advances.

While at first everything seemed to be going well, Edwards eventually contracted smallpox on his mouth and throat. This prevented him from swallowing liquids, which were essential to preventing fever. He had just begun his presidency at the College of New Jersey. In great pain, his fever raging, and unable to eat or drink, Edwards lasted for several weeks. The close of his life was not pleasant; he was far from his wife, from his beloved children, and from the comfort of home.

> In late March, knowing that his time was now short, he called his daughter Lucy to his bedside and said: Dear Lucy, it seems to me to be the will of God, that I must shortly leave you; therefore give my kindest love to my dear wife, and tell her that the uncommon union that has so long subsisted between us, has been of such a nature, as I trust is spiritual, and therefore will continue for ever. And I hope she will be supported under so great a trial and submit cheerfully to the will of God. And as to my children, you are now like to be left fatherless, which I hope will be an inducement to you all to seek a Father who will never fail you.[22]

Just before he died on the afternoon of March 22, he reportedly cried out, "Now, where is Jesus of Nazareth, my true and never-failing friend?" A preacher right to the end, he rallied himself for one final word: "Trust in God, and you need not fear." Edwards's God-centered death speaks volumes to us. We need to be ready to die; we need to remember that the Father will never fail us.

March 23

When a people oppose Christ in the work of his Holy Spirit, it is because it touches 'em in something that is dear to their carnal minds; and because they see the tendency of it is to cross their pride, and deprive them of the objects of their lusts. We should take heed that at this day we be not like the Gadarenes, who when Christ came into their country in the exercise of his glorious power and grace, triumphing over a legion of devils and delivering a miserable creature, that had long been their captive, were all alarmed because they lost their swine by it, and the whole multitude of the country came, and besought him to depart out of their coasts: they loved their filthy swine better than Jesus Christ; and had rather have a legion of devils in their country, with their herd of swine, than Jesus Christ without them.
THE GREAT AWAKENING, 1758

JESUS RUINS EVERYTHING. That's what it looks like to unholy eyes, anyway. Nowhere does he more clearly upset the earthly order than in his engagement with finances. Jesus rarely got people more angry than when he applied his teaching to personal wealth and the making of money.

So it was in the case of the Gadarene swine. Jonathan Edwards doesn't mince words in his description of the situation: "They loved their filthy swine better than Jesus Christ," and preferred "devils" to the divine (Matthew 8:28-34). This pattern continues in the book of Acts, where the preaching of the gospel upset local tradesmen. The preaching of Christ produced an actual riot in Ephesus, for example (Acts 19). So much for making friends and influencing customers!

Clearly, these people got the equation wrong. They were offered the saving presence and power of Jesus, and yet were annoyed by the disruption of their material interests. It's not hard to see the parallels to our day and age. Following Jesus may place us in difficult situations, possibly at work. What if we are asked to affirm unbiblical sexual ethics, for example? How will we respond? We cannot forget that Jesus is not only Savior—he is Lord. Jesus loves to ruin our ungodly truces with the world; this he did in days past, and this he will do in our lives today.

> Do not lay up for yourselves treasures on earth, where moth and rust destroy and where thieves break in and steal, but lay up for yourselves treasures in heaven, where neither moth nor rust destroys and where thieves do not break in and steal. For where your treasure is, there your heart will be also. MATTHEW 6:19-21

March 24

We ought not to be, in any measure, like the unbelieving Jews in Christ's time, who were disgusted both with crying out with distress and with joy. When the poor blind man cried out before all the multitude, "Jesus, thou Son of David, have mercy on me!" and continued instantly thus doing, the multitude rebuked him, and charged him that he should hold his tongue, Mark 10:46–48 and Luke 18:38–39. They looked upon it to be a very indecent noise that he made; a thing very ill becoming him to cause his voice to be heard, so much and so loud, among the multitude.
THE GREAT AWAKENING, 1758

NOT LONG AGO, I read a story about a basketball coach. This coach, according to the article, had made his workplace into a hostile environment. What had he done, we wonder—had he made the players run extra laps? Scheduled practice for 7:00 a.m.? Dyed the uniforms a weird color?

No, the coach had spoken openly about being a Christian. In other words, he brought his faith into the workplace. He hadn't harassed anyone, or dismissed non-Christian players from the squad. As best one could tell, the coach had lived out his faith at work and had represented himself as a born-again believer. For this, he drew fire.

This is not a new phenomenon. Celebrating the redemption we receive from God and calling upon him openly have always caused Christians to be rebuked, and even persecuted. Satan spins the lie that reality is secular, God is a delusion, and faith is offensive. But no matter how little the Christian faith may be esteemed by the world, it should never be silenced. We should not hush those who are "crying out" to God. In fact, we ourselves should regularly cry out, showing more regard to God than to anyone else. With humility and grace, we want God's Word to be heard "so much and so loud" in our world.

He answered, "I tell you, if these were silent, the very stones would cry out." LUKE 19:40

March 25

Another thing that some have found fault with, is abounding so much in singing in religious meetings. Objecting against such a thing as this seems to arise from a suspicion already established of this work: they doubt of the pretended extraordinary love and joys that attend this work, and so find fault with the manifestations of them. If they thought persons were truly the subjects of an extraordinary degree of divine love, and heavenly rejoicing in God, I suppose they would not wonder at their having a disposition to be much in praise. They won't object against the saints and angels in heaven singing praises and hallelujahs to God, without ceasing day or night; and therefore doubtless will allow that the more the saints on earth are like 'em in their dispositions, the more they will be disposed to do like 'em.
THE GREAT AWAKENING, 1758

IT WAS SAID THAT British prime minister Winston Churchill hated almost nothing more than whistling. Churchill once silenced a boy who dared to whistle a tune while walking down the street. No doubt Churchill was sorting out some global issue as he walked, but the image is a humorous one nonetheless. Who tells someone to stop whistling on a city street?

In his day, Jonathan Edwards faced similar objections. As the church revived and love of Christ spread, singing abounded. But churchgoers with little joy in their hearts for God did not like this trend. They rejected this new practice, the vocal praising of God. Edwards, to his credit, defended those who enjoyed "singing praises and hallelujahs" to God. He found it the very business of heavenly saints and angels, and the heartbeat of earthly believers.

We might think, *That's great, but I haven't been blessed with an operatic voice. Besides, the worship team does the work for me.* We can't forget that we are called to raise our voices *together* (Ephesians 5:18-20). Singing is not about performance, really. Singing, and all corporate worship, is remembering, treasuring Christ, and making war on the devil by defying our doubts and declaring God's praise. On whistling, we may claim a policy of neutrality; on singing, the church cannot help but raise its voice. Sing with joy, Christian.

Make a joyful noise to the LORD, all the earth! Serve the LORD with gladness! Come into his presence with singing! PSALM 100:1-2

March 26

There is no way that Christians in a private capacity can do so much to promote the work of God, and advance the kingdom of Christ, as by prayer.
THE GREAT AWAKENING, 1758

WHEN SHOCKING NEWS HITS, what is your first reaction? We've all heard at least one story about a husband who panicked when his pregnant wife announced she was in labor. We can try to prepare ourselves for such moments, but in truth there is no way to know how we will respond. The father-to-be may spin like a top at this exciting news, uncertain of what exactly he should do.

Whether we are facing something big or small, our first instinct as Christians should be to pray in any and all circumstances. We're told to "pray without ceasing" (1 Thessalonians 5:17), but nowhere does it say this must be in some type of formal service drawn out over several hours. More likely, the apostle Paul's injunction means that we will pray "in a private capacity," which as Jonathan Edwards suggests is a powerful action that "can do so much to promote the work of God, and advance the kingdom of Christ."

We mustn't downplay the importance of prayer. It is even more important than action. God has staked so much on our petitions and requests and offerings of gratitude. In his wise providence, the Lord oversees the world, and carries out his will, by involving and using our humble, meager prayers. If we knew how powerful our prayers were, we would pray more often and with greater fervor. Here, then, is just such an opportunity: Prayer matters. So, let us pray continually.

If you abide in me, and my words abide in you, ask whatever you wish, and it will be done for you. JOHN 15:7

March 27

If some Christians in the land, that have been complaining of their ministers and struggling in vain to deliver themselves from the difficulties they have complained of under their ministry, had said and acted less before men, and had applied themselves with all their might to cry to God for their ministers, had as it were risen and stormed heaven with their humble, fervent and incessant prayers for them, they would have been much more in the way of success.
THE GREAT AWAKENING, 1758

WHEN DIFFICULTIES ARISE between friends, there is no guarantee of a restored friendship. There is, however, a surefire way to make the disagreement go nuclear: Vent. Tell others. Choose undisciplined speech over discretion and patience.

In such instances, we trick ourselves into thinking it is better to speak than to be patient. It is remarkable how venting—which feels so right in the moment—creates further trouble. "The tongue is a small member, yet . . . how great a forest is set ablaze by such a small fire!" (James 3:5). This is true in all of life, and it is true in the life of the church. As a longtime pastor, Jonathan Edwards knew of what he spoke.

Edwards knew the ideal, as do we. In his day, if people had "said and acted less before men" when the Great Awakening broke out, unity in God's Word might have held fast. Instead, opinions abounded, and people were quick to speak and slow to listen. This sad episode chastens us today. We must use great care in our speech with one another. Before we "reply all" on the e-mail chain, we should pray. Before we go public with our disagreement, we should seek dialogue. Before we are quick to break fellowship, we should consider "the way of success," which in the church means the preservation of unity in the truth.

He told them a parable to the effect that they ought always to pray and not lose heart. LUKE 18:1

March 28

Resolved, that I will live so as I shall wish I had done when I come to die.
LETTERS AND PERSONAL WRITINGS

I'VE SEEN COMMERCIALS that say, in effect, "Life is short, so why not do what you want?" It's a clever question. It urges us to pack in as much as we can for our own fulfillment. Jonathan Edwards understood this common human instinct. Yet his simple resolution speaks to something far greater than selfish pursuits.

We will all come to a point when we'll look back on our lives. But Christians will revisit the past through an entirely different set of lenses than unbelievers. We cannot help but look at all our doings, all our goings-on, from a distinctly God-centered perspective. We want a life that leaves no regrets, that is full of God. Full of his mercy. Full of his goodness. Full to overflowing with his heavenly strength and overcoming grace.

One thing I know: On my deathbed, I will not look back and wish I had loved God less. I will not wish I had gratified the desires of the flesh more. I will not think of the churches I belonged to and sigh over the Sunday-morning brunches I missed by attending services. When you and I look back and see a long line of faithfulness in our lives, we will not wince. We will rejoice. We have not yet come to our final hour; the days stretch out before us. So let us now live as we shall wish we had done when we come to die.

In this the love of God was made manifest among us, that God sent his only Son into the world, so that we might live through him.
I JOHN 4:9

March 29

He waded through the sea of blood and wrath. His love failed not when he began to enter it, nor when he was in the midst of it. He willingly and freely gave himself up a victim for divine wrath for his enemies.

SERMONS AND DISCOURSES, 1734-1738

IT IS NOT HARD TO AFFIRM that "Jesus loves me." Many would agree that "Jesus died on the cross in our place." But fewer people believe that Jesus substituted himself in order to become "a victim for divine wrath," in Jonathan Edwards's arresting phrase. Jesus paid for our sin, yes, but some believe that God's fury against sin is unjust.

We must beware of those who would "correct" Scripture and instruct God in his doctrine. The Bible teaches us what theologians call "penal substitutionary atonement." Jesus went to the cross to pay the penalty for sin, namely death, and by his bloody sacrifice washed our unrighteousness away. His perfect offering, the fulfillment of the ancient sacrifice of bulls and goats (Leviticus 16), satisfies divine justice and absorbs all the holy wrath of God against sin.

God did not kill Jesus, as some say. But the Father did send the Son to die for our salvation. "It was the will of the [Father] to crush him" (Isaiah 53:10). There is no true parallel to this gift. Without it, without Christ entering the "sea of blood and wrath," we have no hope, for we otherwise must satisfy God's holy anger ourselves to clear our guilty hearts. This we cannot do. But Jesus could, and did. Biblical love is not cheap; grace wasn't purchased at a discount. Our rescue came at infinite cost, for Christ did not fail. Neither, by his power, will our faith.

> Whoever believes in the Son has eternal life; whoever does not obey the Son shall not see life, but the wrath of God remains on him.
>
> JOHN 3:36

March 30

From a letter to Rev. Benjamin Colman:

None can give an account, or conceive, by what means people's lives and limbs should be thus preserved, when so great a multitude were thus eminently exposed. It looked as though it was impossible but that great numbers must instantly be crushed to death or dashed in pieces. . . . Such an event, may be a sufficient argument of a divine providence over the lives of men. We thought ourselves called on to set apart a day to be spent in the solemn worship of God, to humble ourselves under such a rebuke of God upon us, in the time of public service in his house, by so dangerous and surprising an accident; and to praise his name for so wonderful, and as it were miraculous, a preservation. The last Wednesday was kept by us to that end; and a mercy, in which the hand of God is so remarkably evident, may be well worthy to affect the hearts of all who hear it.

LETTERS AND PERSONAL WRITINGS

FOR MOST PEOPLE, tragedy drives us one of two ways: either we get angry, or we feel gratitude. Believing in a big God, Jonathan Edwards called his congregation to give thanks to God for preserving every life when the gallery of the church building in Northampton collapsed during a midweek service in 1737 (see March 13). Despite this terrible event, Edwards wanted the people to "praise [God's] name for so wonderful" a deliverance.

This terrible event in Northampton reminds us of our own daily choices. We may see the events of physical trials or other challenges as unjust, and grow angry at the Lord. Or, as Edwards urges, we may consider anew our undeserving nature, and praise God that he has worked out his sovereign will. This is one of the strongest evidences that Christianity is real and genuinely life-changing: We respond to trials with faith and trust.

All around us, people act as if they are entitled to health and ease of life. But no one can stake such a claim in our fallen world. Still, we worship a God who does all things well, and who uses even the worst things on earth for his glory and our good. The Christian church, after all, does not follow a genie from a bottle, but a God who became a man and descended to a cross. His atoning death is not the end—he rose, and he carried us with him, out of the depths, out of the pain, out of the collapsing world in which we live.

Every word of God proves true; he is a shield to those who take refuge in him. PROVERBS 30:5

March 31

THE HAPPY SEASON of 1740 and 1741 gave way to a time of discouragement for Jonathan Edwards. He had an open war of the printed word with Charles Chauncy, pastor of First Church, Boston, which took a great deal of time and energy. Chauncy opposed what he saw as emotionalism in response to the preaching of the "revivalists" of the day, but Edwards was determined to vindicate the awakenings in the judgment of history. Then, in March 1744, a local event threatened to capsize Edwards and his ministry.

What came to be known as the "bad book" incident arose from the lewd curiosity of a number of young men who got hold of a book on midwifery that included some illustrations of the female anatomy.[23] According to later reports, they used the information to joke inappropriately with some young women in town. Most of the young men involved were affiliated with First Church, Northampton, where Edwards pastored.

This behavior was common to young men, but not honorable. When Edwards learned of this failure of character, he did not hold back from the pulpit. He informed the church of the young men's conduct, and read off a list of names of people who were ordered to give testimony before a committee assembled to judge the affair. In reading his list, however, he failed to distinguish between perpetrators and witnesses. A number of prominent families bristled at what they perceived as Edwards accusing the innocent.

Pastoral matters of this kind are notoriously tricky. Some historians have criticized Edwards for going public with the disciplinary process, but the affair was *already* public. Further, while Edwards looks like a prude to some in retrospect, a cleric getting heated up over minor mischief, the young men had not treated the young women with respect. In the pastor's response—which is definitely quite strong in retrospect—we see his desire to protect the young women under his care and his zeal for holiness.

Eventually, the main perpetrators confessed to minor offenses, but major damage had been done to Edwards's ministry. His pastoral authority seemed to have lessened, and his rosy portrait of post-revival Northampton—possibly, in his hopes, the seedbed for the millennial Kingdom—appeared less accurate. The "bad book" incident portended further trouble for Edwards, who soon lost his pulpit in Northampton. This event speaks of the need today for churches that do not allow unregenerate individuals into membership, and for teams of elders who will shepherd and protect the flock under their care.

April

✝

April 1

IN APRIL 1734, a young man in Northampton fell ill and died suddenly, causing great grief among his peers in the community. Edwards took this opportunity to charge the young men and women to count the sands of time. They had lived for worldly pleasures, many of them, and the death of their friend signaled the fate that awaited every child of Adam.

Further tragedy happened soon after, as Edwards recounted in a letter:

> This was followed with another death of a young married woman, who
> had been considerably exercised in mind, about the salvation of her soul,
> before she was ill, and was in great distress in the beginning of her illness;
> but seemed to have satisfying evidences of God's mercy to her, before her
> death; so that she died very full of comfort, in a most earnest and moving
> manner warning and counselling others. This seemed to contribute
> to render solemn the spirits of many young persons; and there began
> evidently to appear more of a religious concern on people's minds.[24]

Edwards preached a series on justification by faith alone. His strong theological response cemented his authority in Northampton, and led to a revival. Faith in Christ, he said, is the instrument which "justifies, or gives an interest in Christ's satisfaction and merits, and a right to the benefits procured thereby, as it thus makes Christ and the believer one in the acceptance of the Supreme Judge. 'Tis by faith that we have a title to eternal life, because 'tis by faith that we have the Son of God, by whom life is."[25]

These doctrinal messages awakened Northampton like a thunderclap: "The work of conversion was carried on in a most astonishing manner," Edwards noted, "and increased more and more; souls did as it were come by flocks to Jesus Christ."[26] Edwards had long heard the stories about his grandfather's revival work, and his father had experienced these revitalizing showers in his own ministry, as well. Now Jonathan saw an outbreak of gospel grace, all through strong biblical preaching on the means by which every sinner may be made right in the sight of God.

Historians cite this revival in Northampton, which spread to other towns, as one of the keys to the First Great Awakening—a movement that involved numerous other preachers, resulted in the conversions of thousands of people, and helped to usher in a new season in the history of the Protestant church. It also crystallized an identity—*evangelical*—grounded in the new birth that millions around the world still take for their own. The beginning of the First Great Awakening reminds us to pray for conversions, and for the strengthening of the church in our own day.

April 2

From a letter to Rev. George Whitefield:

I hope, if God preserves my life, to see something of that salvation of God in New England which he has now begun, in a benighted, wicked, and miserable world and age and in the most guilty of all nations. It has been with refreshment of soul that I have heard of one raised up in the Church of England to revive the mysterious, spiritual, despised, and exploded doctrines of the gospel, and full of a spirit of zeal for the promotion of real vital piety, whose labors have been attended with such success. Blessed be God that hath done it! who is with you, and helps you, and makes the weapons of your warfare mighty. . . . May you go on, reverend Sir! and may God be with you more and more abundantly, that the work of God may be carried on by a blessing on your labors still, with that swift progress that it has been hitherto, and rise to a greater height, and extend further and further, with an irresistible power bearing down all opposition! and may the gates of hell never be able to prevail against you! and may God send forth more laborers into his harvest of a like spirit, until the kingdom of Satan shall shake, and his proud empire fall throughout the earth and the kingdom of Christ, that glorious kingdom of light, holiness, peace and love, shall be established from one end of the earth unto the other!

LETTERS AND PERSONAL WRITINGS

ON FEBRUARY 12, 1740, Jonathan Edwards wrote a letter to evangelist George Whitefield, who had raised a ruckus in England through his "out of doors" preaching of the gospel. Too lively for formal (and sometimes spiritually listless) Anglican pulpits, Whitefield simply moved outdoors to open fields and preached to the common man. Edwards loved a faithful preacher, and so invited Whitefield to fill the pulpit at Northampton, which he did in October 1740.

It is clear in Edwards's letter that he is thrilled at what the Lord was accomplishing through Whitefield. He shows no jealousy, and savors the unusual nature of the English evangelist's ministry. The focus is plain for both men: the "mysterious, spiritual, despised, and exploded" message of Christ, which so many, both in England and the American colonies, had forgotten or forsaken.

The Lord enacted a remarkable spiritual resurgence through a band of preachers in this period, Edwards and Whitefield included. Whatever our role in God's church, we can promote the greatness of God and the sweetness of Christ in our day. We may not be global evangelists, but we can point our friends, neighbors, coworkers, and family to Jesus. The gospel message is still mysterious to many, and still despised by most. But it is powerful to save, and where recovered and unleashed, it will explode.

The harvest is plentiful, but the laborers are few. MATTHEW 9:37

April 3

From a letter to Rev. George Whitefield:

I have joyful tidings to send you concerning the state of religion in this place. It has been gradually reviving and prevailing more and more, ever since you was here. Religion is become abundantly more the subject of conversation; other things that seemed to impede it, are for the present laid aside. I have reason to think that a considerable number of our young people, some of them children, have already been savingly brought home to Christ. I hope salvation has come to this house since you was in it, with respect to one, if not more, of my children. The Spirit of God seems to be at work with others of the family. That blessed work seems now to be going on in this place, especially amongst those that are young. And as God seems to have succeeded your labors amongst us, and prayers for us, I desire your fervent prayers for us may yet be continued, that God would not be to us as a wayfaring man, that turns aside to tarry but for a night, but that he would more and more pour out his Spirit upon us, and no more depart from us; and for me in particular, that I may be filled with his Spirit, and may become fervent, as a flame of fire in my work, and may be abundantly succeeded, and that it would please God, however unworthy I am, to improve me as an instrument of his glory, and advancing the kingdom of Christ.

LETTERS AND PERSONAL WRITINGS

FOLLOWING GEORGE WHITEFIELD'S visit in October 1740, Jonathan Edwards sent him an update on how the work was advancing. Before the evangelist came, Edwards shared his desire that the work of awakening would "rise to a greater height" as many trusted Christ and God vindicated his cause. In his December report to Whitefield, Edwards shared that the evangelist's visit had a major effect in Northampton. The evangelist lit a fire that had not gone out.

This is a notable moment of humility. Edwards was already a famous preacher in his own right, but he had invited the oratorical genius of his day into his pulpit. Edwards had already led a revival in the mid-1730s, but he sought another through Whitefield's ministry. Edwards could have simply thanked the evangelist for his labors and closed the note. Instead, he told Whitefield of the Spirit moving, even in his own home, after the 1740 visit.

The two men did not agree on everything. They each had their flaws. But they shared a strong, unquenchable thirst for God and his gospel. They longed to play some part in "advancing the kingdom of Christ." This led them to recognize and act on the truth that there was room for more than one figure in God's great undertaking. This example speaks to us, nearly three hundred years later, and urges us to lay aside envy and embrace the good that God is doing in others. We dwell together in a Kingdom where all must decrease, so that Christ can increase.

I thank my God in all my remembrance of you, always in every prayer of mine for you all making my prayer with joy, because of your partnership in the gospel from the first day until now.   PHILIPPIANS 1:3-5

April 4

From a letter to a young convert, Deborah Hatheway:

I would advise you to keep up as great a strife and earnestness in religion in all parts of it, as you would do if you knew yourself to be in a state of nature and was seeking conversion. We advise persons under convictions to be earnest and violent for the kingdom of heaven, but when they have attained to conversion they ought not to be the less watchful, laborious and earnest in the whole work of religion, but the more; for they are under infinitely greater obligations. . . . Don't leave off seeking, striving and praying for the very same things that we exhort unconverted persons to strive for, and a degree of which you have had in conversion. Thus pray that your eyes may be opened, that you may receive your sight, that you may know your self, and be brought to God's foot, and that you may see the glory of God and Christ and may be raised from the dead, and have the love of Christ shed abroad in your heart.

LETTERS AND PERSONAL WRITINGS

JONATHAN EDWARDS WROTE this letter to Deborah Hatheway when she was eighteen years old and a recent convert to Christ. She had little background with the faith and no pastor at the time that Edwards contacted her. She had come to faith in nearby Suffield and asked Edwards to write her with advice about living for the Lord. Edwards had duties at every turn, but he found time to write this young woman and offer her counsel.

The key point in his letter is the idea that one should seek God in as "earnest and violent" a manner after conversion as before it. When we come to faith, we may feel much urgency and zeal to know God. But after the joyful shock of conversion ebbs, our passion for the Lord may cool. Edwards warned young Deborah of this tendency of the heart, and called her not to "leave off seeking, striving and praying" for God to saturate her with his presence and blessing.

This is strong language, yet there is a key to godliness in it. We need to be "earnest and violent" in striving after God. God will never refuse our coming to him. He delights in such zeal, such holiness. He loves to bless those who pass on such counsel; this letter, just an ordinary missive from a pastor to a needy believer, was printed, reprinted, and reprinted again in the century after Edwards wrote it. By 1875, nearly 350,000 copies were in circulation. God honored Deborah's humble request, it seems, even as he will honor ours.

I do not consider that I have made it my own. But one thing I do:
forgetting what lies behind and straining forward to what lies ahead, I press
on toward the goal for the prize of the upward call of God in Christ Jesus.

PHILIPPIANS 3:13-14

April 5

From a letter to Deborah Hatheway:

Be always greatly abased for your remaining sin, and never think that you lie low enough for it, but yet don't be at all discouraged or disheartened by it; for though we are exceeding sinful, yet we have an advocate with the Father, Jesus Christ the righteous, the preciousness of whose blood, and the merit of whose righteousness and the greatness of whose love and faithfulness does infinitely overtop the highest mountains of our sins.

LETTERS AND PERSONAL WRITINGS

THE BUSINESS OF DIPLOMACY involves dealing on a regular basis with one's competitors, allies, and enemies. Nations host glittering galas for visiting dignitaries to make deals and seek peaceful solutions to problems, but all are aware that each government will seek to protect its own interests. A practical realism must guide the formulation of diplomacy.

As Christians, we must be similarly realistic about our situation. We cannot pretend that our spiritual condition is thriving when it is not. We must deal with our enemy—sin—in direct and honest terms. As Jonathan Edwards charges young Deborah Hatheway, we should feel "abased" over unrighteousness, for "we are exceeding sinful." At the same time, we must not "be at all discouraged" by our iniquities, for Christ's merit and fidelity to us "infinitely" overcomes our sin.

This balance is not always easy to maintain. We must beware of tilting in one direction or the other—too severe or too lenient. We must know our own hearts and seek counsel from wise believers in our local communities. Two rhythms must regularly operate in our lives: an honest awareness of our sin, and an even greater awareness of the forgiving blood of "Jesus Christ the righteous." Coming to terms with our lowness leads us to rejoice anew in God's greatness.

A woman of the city, who was a sinner, when she learned that he was reclining at table in the Pharisee's house, brought an alabaster flask of ointment, and standing behind him at his feet, weeping, she began to wet his feet with her tears and wiped them with the hair of her head and kissed his feet and anointed them with the ointment.

LUKE 7:37-38

April 6

From a letter to Rev. James Robe:

I am persuaded we shall generally be sensible, before long, that we run too fast, when we endeavor by our positive determinations to banish all fears of damnation from the minds of men, though they may be true saints, if they are not such as are eminently humble and mortified, and (what the Apostle calls) "rooted and grounded in love" [Ephesians 3:17]. . . . When love is low in the true saints, they need the fear of hell to deter them from sin, and engage them to exactness in their walk, and stir them up to seek heaven; but when love is high, and the soul full of it, we don't need fear. And therefore, a wise God has so ordered it that love and fear should rise and fall like the scales of a balance.

LETTERS AND PERSONAL WRITINGS

IT ISN'T POPULAR NOWADAYS to talk about hell. Churches that claim to be Christian advertise their distance from the old testimonies and the previous generations. Hell, it seems, is a downer of a doctrine. It doesn't please the ear or tickle the fancy. Better to leave it to the past and effectively pretend it doesn't exist.

But this will not do for true believers, Jonathan Edwards argues. When Christians wander from the truth, "they need the fear of hell" to return them to spiritual consistency. Edwards did not mean that born-again believers could lose their salvation. He meant that drifting Christians should think once more about the justice of God and God's wrath. We will not take God lightly if we take damnation seriously. We think of the effects of an earthly fire. There is little frivolity near a burned-out house, still smoldering with glowing embers.

Remembrance of hell won't paralyze true Christians. Edwards believed it would "stir them up to seek heaven," a glorious result. The love of God that the sinning heart ignored would now return to view. The soul would drink of God and be full. How we need these words today. There is never a time to take God lightly; it is always right to remember the wages of sin, and to praise God for the payment Christ made to deliver us from death.

> For this reason I bow my knees before the Father, . . . that Christ
> may dwell in your hearts through faith—that you, being rooted and
> grounded in love . . . may be filled with all the fullness of God.
> EPHESIANS 3:14, 17, 19

April 7

If we ought ever to exercise our affections at all, and if the Creator has not unwisely constituted the human nature in making these principles a part of it, when they are vain and useless; then they ought to be exercised about those objects which are most worthy of them. . . . All the virtues of the Lamb of God, his humility, patience, meekness, submission, obedience, love and compassion, are exhibited to our view, in a manner the most tending to move our affections, of any that can be imagined . . . So has God disposed things, in the affair of our redemption, and in his glorious dispensations, revealed to us in the gospel, as though everything were purposely contrived in such a manner, as to have the greatest possible tendency to reach our hearts in the most tender part, and move our affections most sensibly and strongly.
RELIGIOUS AFFECTIONS, 1746

OUR MINDS AND HEARTS weren't made for secular, godless things. Every ability we have, every appetite and emotion, was made ultimately to know and relish the things of God. There was no reason for the human race to come into existence but to display and glory in the perfections of its Maker.

This helps us understand the very function of our hearts and minds. We do not do God a favor by thinking about him a little; we do not honor Christ by giving him a few minutes every day. God has "disposed things," Jonathan Edwards avows, to "move our affections most sensibly and strongly" toward him. When we worship our great God and Redeemer with heart and mind alive to his kindness, we fulfill our original purpose.

So many around us will not join us. They will use their emotions and words and gestures and conversations to do anything but glorify God. They will be enthusiastic, emotional, affected, and moved about all sorts of things in life without ever dwelling on that which is most important. What an opportunity this sad reality gives us as believers. That which is "vain and useless" we leave behind. The object that is "most worthy" we adore. God is too interesting, and too kind, for us to be consumed by anything else.

You make known to me the path of life; in your presence there is
fullness of joy; at your right hand are pleasures forevermore.
PSALM 16:11

April 8

MOST OF THE EDWARDS CHILDREN kept their father's faith, but not all. No one stands out more in this regard than Pierpont, the youngest of the eleven siblings. Born just as Edwards's pastoral career in Northampton came to a fiery close, Pierpont spent his childhood in Stockbridge. He had a quick mind and was said to be able to "think in Indian," demonstrating his facility for social engagement (and later business and politics).

Pierpont graduated from Princeton in 1768 and became a lawyer. After serving in the Continental Army during the Revolutionary War, he became a political figure in Connecticut, successfully pressing for the passing of the US Constitution in 1788. After Benedict Arnold committed his act of treason, Pierpont oversaw Arnold's estate. He later served in the Connecticut House of Representatives, filled the role of United States attorney for his state, and was appointed as a judge by President Thomas Jefferson in 1806.

The 1910 edition of *Encyclopedia Britannica* described Pierpont Edwards as "a brilliant but erratic member of the Connecticut bar, tolerant in religious matters and bitterly hated by stern Calvinists, a man whose personal morality resembled greatly that of Aaron Burr." Burr was no pillar of the faith. Pierpont Edwards helped to create the Masonic Grand Lodge and was head of all Connecticut Masons, showing that the capacity for organization and leadership so evident in the father resided also in the son.

The legacy of Jonathan Edwards extended into the nineteenth century in public affairs in considerable part because of Pierpont. He was an uncle of famous citizens such as Aaron Burr Jr., Theodore Dwight, and Timothy Dwight IV. His daughter Henrietta married Eli Whitney, who invented the cotton gin. This missionary child, raised on the frontier under the watchful care of Jonathan and Sarah, excelled in his lifelong pursuits but traveled a good way from his Christian roots. We note that Christian parents cannot save their children; we pray for God to work, we love our children as best we can, and we trust his wisdom in all that comes to pass, however unexpected.

April 9

From a letter to Mary Edwards:

My greatest concern is for your soul's good. Though you are at so great a distance from us, yet God is everywhere. You are much out of the reach of our care, but you are every moment in his hands. We have not the comfort of seeing you, but he sees you. His eye is always upon you. And if you may but be sensibly nigh to him, and have his gracious presence, 'tis no matter though you are far distant from us.

LETTERS AND PERSONAL WRITINGS

ONE OF THE CENTRAL TASKS of parenthood is to help our children find comfort. There are good reasons to direct our children toward sound thinking during their moments of fear. "No, there are no monsters in the closet. No, the thunder is not going to make the house fall down. Yes, Daddy and Mommy are here in the house, keeping you safe."

But the truth is that we fathers and mothers cannot in the end keep our children from all harm. We are not omnipotent. We can, however, train our little ones to see that they must place their faith in someone much bigger than we are. This is where true comfort and security originate. As Jonathan Edwards wrote to his fifteen-year-old daughter Mary, "You are every moment in his hands," whether near or far from home.

It is essential for every parent, every child, and indeed every Christian to keep this wise saying close to our hearts. In any stage of life, no person can guarantee our health and flourishing. Only God watches over all. His Spirit lives in every believer, giving us intimate closeness with our sovereign Lord by his Spirit (1 Corinthians 6:19). There is nowhere we can go that he does not watch over us; there is nothing we can walk through, not even the valley of the shadow of death, that he does not walk with us.

As a father shows compassion to his children, so the LORD shows compassion to those who fear him. PSALM 103:13

April 10

From a letter to Rev. William McCulloch:

I am now separated from the people, between whom and me there was once the greatest union. Remarkable is the providence of God in this matter. In this event, we have a great instance of the instability and uncertainty of all things here below. The dispensation is indeed awful in many respects, calling for serious reflection, and deep humiliation, in me and my people. The enemy far and near will now triumph; but God can overrule all for his own glory. I have now nothing visible to depend upon for my future usefulness, or the subsistence of my numerous family. But I hope we have an all-sufficient, faithful, covenant God to depend upon. I desire that I may ever submit to him, walk humbly before him, and put my trust wholly in him.

LETTERS AND PERSONAL WRITINGS

WE ARE FREED BY THE CROSS of Christ to be honest about our pain. So it was for Jonathan Edwards when he wrote to fellow pastor William McCulloch. The First Church of Northampton had recently dismissed Edwards from his pastorate, and the cost was great. In terms we can all understand, Edwards was embarrassed—it was "indeed awful"—and uncertain about the future—"I have now nothing visible to depend upon for . . . the subsistence of my numerous family." Nearly a dozen mouths to feed, and no job by which to support them.

That Jonathan Edwards, the peerless preacher of his day and the greatest theologian and philosopher in American history, would be fired—from the church he had pastored for more than twenty years, and his grandfather for sixty years before him—ranks as one of the stranger moments in evangelical Christian history. Edwards's life was not without its troubles. He lost his job. He was unemployed for a time. He scraped around for work. He battled depression.

What makes him a figure to emulate is his tenacity in the face of adversity. He looked to the "all-sufficient, faithful" God, who made "covenant" with his people and kept it. We may discern in Edwards's words that he is struggling for faith. "I desire," he says plainly, "that I may . . . put my trust wholly in him." This was a challenge, but by faith he clung to Christ, and so must we.

The LORD is a stronghold for the oppressed, a stronghold in times of trouble. PSALM 9:9

April 11

Resolved, to live so at all times, as I think is best in my devout frames, and when I have clearest notions of things of the gospel, and another world.
LETTERS AND PERSONAL WRITINGS

A FEW YEARS AGO, I read a story about the writer Elisabeth Elliot, whose earthly life was coming to a close. For two hours during the writer's visit, Elliot did not say a word and seemed lost in her thoughts. Her husband spoke for her, and closed the interview by summing up how his wife handled dementia: "It was something she would rather not have experienced, but she received it." At this point, Elliot looked up, nodded, and spoke for the first and only time that day: "Yes."[27]

Old age comes at great cost for many, including the loss of memory. But every believer, young and old, must fight through the fog of our culture to hold fast to what is true. We want to walk, as Jonathan Edwards says, in our "devout frames," propelled by our "clearest notions . . . of the gospel." We do not want to drift, in other words, through the hours and days allotted to us. We don't want to lose our spiritual clarity and theological sharpness. We want to stay close to the Word, and close to God.

Every day we must return to the great truths of our salvation and let them have first place. Every day, we must return to "another world," the realm of glory. We all face the possibility of drifting; our sights can wander, and our thoughts will sometimes grow cloudy. But if we will resolve to live for what is best, the fog will lift and we will see the Lord. He will ask us to follow him even into eternity itself, and we will say, "Yes."

They shall come and sing aloud on the height of Zion, and they shall be radiant over the goodness of the LORD, over the grain, the wine, and the oil, and over the young of the flock and the herd; their life shall be like a watered garden, and they shall languish no more. JEREMIAH 31:12

April 12

From a letter to Lady Mary Pepperrell:

Let us think, dear Madam, a little of the loveliness of our blessed Redeemer and his worthiness, that our whole soul should be swallowed up with love to him and delight in him, and that we should salve our hearts in him, rest in him, have sweet complacence and satisfaction of soul in his excellency and beauty whatever else we are deprived of. The Scripture assures us abundantly of his proper divinity, so that we consider him that came into the world in our nature and died for us, as truly possessed of all the fullness of that infinite glory of the Godhead, his infinite greatness and majesty, his infinite wisdom, his infinitely perfect holiness and purity, righteousness and goodness.

LETTERS AND PERSONAL WRITINGS

JONATHAN EDWARDS was a theologian of action. He worked roughly thirteen hours a day, closely guarded his spiritual life, and urged his congregation ever onward into holiness. Yet the Northampton pastor knew that the Christian faith called for rest as well as action. When William Pepperrell, Mary Pepperrell's husband, passed away, it was as if a great tree had fallen in a New England forest. Before his death, Pepperrell, a successful merchant, had made his fortune from a shipping business, had become a war hero, and had retired to a grand home in Kittery, Maine.

Though Edwards had polite relationships with the New England aristocracy, he did not merely extend his sympathies to Lady Pepperrell. Instead, he lifted her eyes to Christ and urged her to "rest in him." Even the wealthiest among us cannot help but be "deprived" of that which we love in the world, but there is "infinite glory" in Christ.

The theological nature of this letter stands out. Edwards did not feel he was burdening Lady Pepperrell with his words about Jesus. He believed that the best and most lasting things in life are found in God. Death was not an escape from truth; death brought the preciousness of biblical truth home to the heart. We remember this counsel in our difficulties. Whatever we are deprived of, no one can rip Christ away from us. His "infinite greatness and majesty" spill into every season, run through every moment, and bear us through every burden. We have rest in him, now and always.

I was beside him, like a master workman, and I was daily his delight, rejoicing before him always. PROVERBS 8:30

April 13

From a letter to Lady Mary Pepperrell:

Having found him who is as the apple tree among the trees of the wood, we may sit under his shadow with great delight and his fruit may be sweet to our taste. Christ told his disciples that in the world [they] should have trouble, but says he, "In me ye shall have peace." If we are united to him, our souls will be like a tree planted by a river that never dieth. He will be their light in darkness and their morning star that is a bright harbinger of day. And in a little [while], he will arise on our souls as the sun in full glory. And our sun shall no more go down, and there shall be no interposing cloud, no veil on his face or on our hearts, but the Lord shall be our everlasting light and our Redeemer, our glory.

LETTERS AND PERSONAL WRITINGS

JONATHAN EDWARDS was a tall man who loved tall trees. He often walked among them, meditating as he slipped past huge oaks and massive firs. A great tree is a symbol of strength, thick and sturdy, its roots going down into the ground almost as far as its branches stretch into the sky. In Scripture, the image of a tree points us to God (Psalm 1:1-3).

Trees are symbolic of a great truth—namely, God's loving provision. As Edwards notes in his letter, the "apple tree" yields fruit that is "sweet to our taste." In another of his writings, he speaks of the flavor of the apple as synonymous with the delicious "taste" of Christianity. In the eighteenth century, apples were a delicacy, one of the sweetest foods to be found. To lay claim to the apple tree "among the trees of the wood" was to gain the treasure that many seek but only some find.

This, Edwards told the grieving widow Mary Pepperrell, is how we understand Christ. Death and trials seem to drain our days of beauty. But the excellency of Christ is such that we may taste it at any time. The antidote to despair is Christ-centered beauty. We savor the sweetness and beauty of Christ, thankful that we have found the apple tree—the choicest one—among all the trees of the wood.

I have said these things to you, that in me you may have peace. In the world you will have tribulation. But take heart; I have overcome the world. JOHN 16:33

April 14

From a letter to Timothy Edwards:

It is indeed comfortable, when one is in great pain, languishing under sore sickness, to have the presence and kind care of near and dear earthly friends; but this is a very small thing, in comparison of what it is, to have the presence of an heavenly Father and a compassionate and almighty Redeemer. In God's favor is life, and his lovingkindness is better than life. Whether you are in sickness or health, you infinitely need this. . . . For he is a God of infinite mercy and he delights to show mercy for his Son's sake; who is worthy, though you are unworthy; who came to save the sinful and the miserable some of the chief of sinners.

LETTERS AND PERSONAL WRITINGS

IF YOU OFFERED PEOPLE PERFECT health for the rest of their lives or a relationship with God, which would they choose? This is not a silly question. It's a decision that people make today, particularly in our age of rising life expectancy and better health care. Many would not miss a session at the gym for any reason, but they make a practice of neglecting the local church. In our sin, we would rather live well *without* God than live forever *with* him.

We don't need to choose between Christianity and flossing our teeth (alas). We do, however, need to know that whether we face "sickness or health," we have a finite need of bodily health, but an infinite need for an "almighty Redeemer." As Jonathan Edward's son Timothy battled an illness while a student at the College of New Jersey (later Princeton University), Edwards drew his son's attention to God. His direction may sound pointed, but the Puritan approach to life that Edwards embraced placed great weight on preparing for eternity.

This God-centered perspective will lift us out of self-pity and depression when we suffer. We need not blink away our pains and illnesses; we should pray for relief. But even when "languishing," we should never cease to remember that we have God's "favor" and "lovingkindness," which are "better than life" itself. Even as we ask God for bodily help (James 5:13-18), we praise him for giving us a better gift than strength and fitness. Our greatest need is met; the challenge we face is only for a little while.

I will have mercy on whom I have mercy, and I will have compassion on whom I have compassion. ROMANS 9:15

April 15

From a letter to Esther Edwards Burr:

I would not have you think that any strange thing has happened to you in this affliction: 'tis according to the course of things in this world, that after the world's smiles, some great affliction soon comes. . . . You are like to spend the rest of your life (if you should get over this illness) at a great distance from your parents; but care not much for that. If you lived near us, yet our breath and yours would soon go forth, and we should return to our dust, whither we are all hastening. . . . And above all the rest, use riding in pleasant weather; and when you can bear it, riding on horseback; but never so as to fatigue you. And be very careful to avoid taking cold.

P. S. Your mother has also an inclination that you should sometimes try a tea made of the leaves of Robin's plantain, if it be known at Newark by that name; she says she has found it very strengthening and comfortable to her in her weakness.

LETTERS AND PERSONAL WRITINGS

IT IS A CLASSICALLY HUMAN RESPONSE: When we encounter a trial, we wonder, How could this happen to me? If we double down on our self-pity, we chime in, I've been living such a consistent life lately—God owes me better than this! It is natural to think that God owes us blessings—when truthfully we have no such claim on his grace.

In writing to his sickly daughter, Esther Edwards Burr, Jonathan Edwards offered wise counsel. He urged her, as a loving father would, to "avoid taking cold," for instance. But he also reminded her of the tough nature of life in a fallen world. Sickness hits, and does not quickly leave. Families are separated by distance. Even if we share life, we draw near to the end of our lives hour by hour, and will soon "return to our dust."

Edwards loved his daughter. He loved her enough to remind her of certain hard truths. This fallen world is not a kind, nice, easy place. He wrote these truths to Esther not to discourage her, but to strengthen her for the road ahead. So we must do with one another, whether as a parent, a friend, or a fellow church member. We need to ready one another for the bumps and bruises of life in this broken place. Such honesty of counsel may mark us as strange in a climate of "positive thinking" and self-help therapy. But the gospel equips us to be honest, and still more than this, to be hopeful. We have hope—great hope—not because we know every trial will be resolved in this life, but because God is our God and he will not abandon his chosen.

For those who love God all things work together for good, for those who are called according to his purpose. ROMANS 8:28

April 16

From a letter to his son Timothy:

Therefore, there is your only hope; and in him must be your refuge, who invites you to come to him, and says, "He that cometh to me, I will in no wise cast out" [John 6:37]. Whatever your circumstances are, it is your duty not to despair, but to hope in infinite mercy through a Redeemer. For God makes it your duty to pray to him for mercy which would not be your duty, if it was allowable for you to despair. We are expressly commanded to call upon God in the day of trouble; and when we are afflicted, then to pray.

LETTERS AND PERSONAL WRITINGS

OURS IS AN ERA that seeks an explanation, or perhaps an excuse, for most any behavior. I realized the popularity of the "backstory" while viewing a children's movie. Instead of merely presenting us with a villain, like many cartoon films, the filmmaker used multiple scenes to show why a mean teddy bear had achieved its peak level of meanness. The message seemed plain enough: We're not actually bad people; we've just had bad things happen to us.

Our contemporary culture tempts us to believe we are prisoners of our environment. It is true that we are shaped by forces beyond our control. But we have no excuse for our spiritual condition. To flip this: We must act responsibly in our own lives. "Whatever your circumstances are," Edwards wrote to his ailing son, "it is your duty not to despair, but to hope" in Christ. This is a throwback mind-set, so ancient it might just be progressive. *Don't get lost in yourself,* the elder Edwards says. *You are responsible for avoiding despair. Instead, give yourself over to hope in God.*

We need such strong-voiced exhortations in our day, when everyone wants to give an excuse but no one wants to clean up the mess. Our duty is to pray. Our duty is to steer away from anxiety. "Do not be anxious about anything," the apostle Paul advises in Philippians 4:6. This is not a recommendation. It is a command. We have meaningful encouragement for believers swimming the deep waters of this world. But we cannot settle for only reminding them of their great worth and God's great love for them. For the weak—and we will all come face-to-face with our weakness at some point—we also must encourage them to place their hope in God and to not despair. Pray, for this is your duty. God will in no way cast out your prayers, just as he will not cast you out.

All that the Father gives me will come to me, and whoever comes to me
I will never cast out. JOHN 6:37

April 17

From a letter to his daughter Esther Edwards Burr after the death of her husband:

I thank you for your most comfortable letter; but more especially would I thank God that has granted you such things to write. How good and kind is your heavenly Father! How do the bowels of his tender love and compassion appear, while he is correcting you by so great a shake of his head! Indeed, he is a faithful God; he will remember his covenant forever; and never will fail them that trust in him. But don't be surprised, or think some strange thing has happened to you, if after this light, clouds of darkness should return. Perpetual sunshine is not usual in this world, even to God's true saints. But I hope, if God should hide his face in some respect, even this will be in faithfulness to you, to purify you, and fit you for yet further and better light.

LETTERS AND PERSONAL WRITINGS

WE DON'T OFTEN HEAR much about biblical covenants. But *covenant* is a great biblical word. In Genesis 12, the Lord forms a people for himself by making a covenant with Abraham. He extends this promise through Moses, and David, and fulfills his plans and purposes in Jesus Christ. Christ is the head of the new covenant, and all who are washed by his blood are members of his covenant people (2 Corinthians 3, 5; Hebrews 9-13).

This is what Jonathan Edwards means when he tells his bereaved daughter Esther that God "will remember his covenant forever." Now a widow, Esther must know and trust that God loves her and will keep her. Apparently, she has found some peace after her husband's death. But "clouds of darkness" frequently roll in on us like a springtime thunderstorm. "Perpetual sunshine" we cannot expect.

For this reason, we must not forget this important truth: God will remember his covenant forever. He has made a people for himself (1 Peter 2:9). He has bound himself to his chosen race, made of every tribe, tongue, and nation on earth. He will not abandon us, even if it feels like he has. Yet he may, for a little while, choose to "hide his face in some respect." Like Esther Burr, we are called to walk by faith, to trust God by faith, and not to trust our sight, clouded as it may sometimes be.

The steadfast love of the LORD never ceases; his mercies never come to an end; they are new every morning; great is your faithfulness.

LAMENTATIONS 3:22-23

April 18

Resolved, to maintain the strictest temperance in eating and drinking.
LETTERS AND PERSONAL WRITINGS

CHRISTIANITY EXALTS THE SOUL, but in doing so, it does not devalue the body. In the earliest days of the church, pastors and theologians wrote a good deal about the threat of Gnosticism, a religion that taught that the soul is good, but the body is not. Such a system promotes a lack of respect for our physical being. Though some would charge that the Bible holds such a view, it does not.

Instead, we should care for our bodies. We don't want to starve them, but neither do we wish to bloat them. The body is not a tomb, a prison for the soul. It is the unique creation of Almighty God. He made man and woman; he gave each a distinctive form, and he did so for his own glory (Genesis 2). We should not worship the body. But neither should we dishonor our bodies.

We are responsible for being good stewards of everything God has given us, including our bodies. Jonathan Edwards sought to do this in a characteristically intense way—by challenging himself to the "strictest temperance" in dietary matters. He sought to master his flesh and not be ruled by it. He knew biblically that the human body is the "temple of the Holy Spirit" (1 Corinthians 6:19). These words remind us of the origin of our bodies: We have them "from God," as Paul says. We are not our own. Whatever specific dietary choices we make, we want to eat and drink and exercise in a uniquely Christian way. We want to use prudence and temperance; we want to master our appetites; we want to joyfully care for the body God has given us. We are not Gnostics; we are Christians.

No one ever hated his own flesh, but nourishes and cherishes it, just as Christ does the church. EPHESIANS 5:29

April 19

But to see God is this: it is to have an immediate and certain understanding of God's glorious excellency and love. There must be a direct and immediate sense of God's glory and excellency. I say direct and immediate to distinguish from a mere acknowledging that God is glorious and excellent by ratiocination, which is a more indirect and mediate way of apprehending things than intuitive knowledge. A true sense of the glory of [God] is that which never can be got by ratiocination. If men argue that God is holy, that never will give a sense of his amiable and glorious holiness. If they argue that he is very merciful, that won't give a sense of his glorious grace and mercy. It must be a more immediate discovery, that must give the mind a real sense of the excellency and beauty of God. He that sees God, he has an immediate view of God's great and awful majesty, of his pure and beauteous holiness, of his wonderful and enduring grace and mercy.
SERMONS AND DISCOURSES, 1730-1733

GOD DOES NOT EXIST TO BE STUDIED. He exists to be worshiped.

It is possible, as Jonathan Edwards makes plain, to see that God is awesome by "ratiocination" an archaic term that means "the process of reason." But we cannot gain a "true sense" of God from an intellectual dissection of his being, a purely analytical study of his character and works. We must pursue the "real sense" of God.

This is not special pleading on Edwards's part; he is not introducing a different standard for Christianity than for science, or math, or art, or any part of life. Picking up some travelogues about the Caribbean pales in comparison to setting foot on its white sands. Eating authentic spaghetti in Rome beats reading about it in an online review any day. Seeing a wide receiver leap into the air to catch a game-winning touchdown transcends later reporting about it.

So it is with Christianity. Scripture is not a dry and dusty book from which we must detach ourselves to truly know God. Rather, "the word of God is living and active" (Hebrews 4:12). It grabs us by the collar and reveals to us the holy mind of God. It gives us the "true sense" and allows us to see "God's great and awful majesty." Christians who love and devote themselves to the Word, and who doggedly seek the "real sense" in the Bible, are not rationalistic. We are not studying to know God for purposes of pride and gain. We study to know God because we love him. In all our contemplation of the divine, we seek pleasure in him, emerging wide-eyed over the beauty and excellencies of God.

God, who said, "Let light shine out of darkness," has shone in our hearts to give the light of the knowledge of the glory of God in the face of Jesus Christ. 2 CORINTHIANS 4:6

April 20

The more perfect views that the saints have of God's glory and love in another world is what is especially called seeing of God. Then they shall see him as he is. Their light, which now is but a glimmering, will be brought to clear sunshine; that which is here but the dawning, will become perfect day. Those intellectual views which will be granted in another world are called seeing God: because the view will be as immediate as when we see things with our bodily eyes. God will as immediately discover himself to their minds, so that the understanding shall as immediately behold the glory of God and his love as a man can behold the countenance of his friend that he looks in the face.

SERMONS AND DISCOURSES, 1730-1733

NONE OF THE FIVE SENSES is more important to one's being a person than sight. This does not discount the other senses, nor does it suggest we are less than human if we're blind. But far more than we know, we depend on sight for second-by-second functioning. On average, the human brain takes in 400 billion bits of information per second, and about 60 percent of the brain is used for sight. This means that our eyes act as the gateway to just about everything we do.

This is why, Jonathan Edwards suggests, it is so significant that we will one day see God "as he is." For now, we see only the "glimmering"; we behold the "dawning." Soon, however, the same eyes created to behold the God-made world will gaze upon the Maker himself. Our sight then will be "immediate." Seeing God will be as natural as reading this book, figuring out how much coffee is left in your cup, and basking in the smile of a dear friend.

It will be as natural, but it will be far, far better. In fact, it will be so satisfying to see God that we can scarcely scratch the surface of the experience. We know that the moment will not pass; the sunny skies will not grow murky and convoluted; the friend will not depart. God will be our all, and will shine on all without interruption, without damage. After a lifetime of night, it will be "perfect day." And once it has dawned, it will never leave.

Now we see in a mirror dimly, but then face to face. Now I know in part; then I shall know fully, even as I have been fully known.

I CORINTHIANS 13:12

April 21

The pleasure of seeing God is so great and strong that it takes the full possession of the heart; it fills it brimful, so that there shall be no room for any sorrow, no room in any corner for anything of an adverse nature from joy. There is no darkness can bear such powerful light. It is impossible that they that see God face to face, that behold his glory and love so immediately as they do in heaven, should have any such thing as grief or pain in their hearts. When once the saints are thus come into God's presence, tears shall be wiped from their eyes and sorrow and sighing shall flee away [Revelation 21:4]. The pleasure will be so great as fully and perfectly to employ every faculty. The sight of God's glory and love will be so wonderful, so engaging to the mind, and shall keep all the powers of it in such strong attention, that the soul will be wholly possessed and taken up.

SERMONS AND DISCOURSES, 1730-1733

OUR WORLD TELLS US that it is human nature to doubt. Skepticism seems more sensible to many than trust. We can understand why—to a point. We break promises, and promises to us are broken; we make friends, and lose them; we trust our leaders, and they defy our trust.

As Christians, however, we start from a different place in our thinking. The fundamental fact of the cosmos is that God rules over it and does all things well (Mark 7:37). Yes, the earth suffers from a vindictive curse occasioned by Adam's sin (Genesis 3:1-13). But evil is not stronger than God, and doubt is not more *real* than truth. Skepticism may be appealing as a posture, but it will not sustain us in the wilds of our earthly existence. We need something more, something substantial, something that will hold us steady when everything else is shaken.

The power of the Christian faith is such that it clears the heart of anything "of an adverse nature from joy." Doubt does not bring joy; it corrupts joy. It picks apart true happiness like ants slowly eating a cob of corn. Doubt is not the resting state of the believer. Already the light of Christ floods our hearts in conversion, and leaves no place for darkness. Already the gloomy, gray skepticism of this world has fled us. Soon, it will not be even an afterthought, for we will be "wholly possessed" by God, unveiled and unhidden.

He will wipe away every tear from their eyes, and death shall be no more, neither shall there be mourning, nor crying, nor pain anymore, for the former things have passed away.   REVELATION 21:4

April 22

We must not think to excuse ourselves by saying that it is God's work, that we cannot purify our own hearts; for though it be God's work in one sense, yet it is equally our work in another; James 4:8, "Cleanse your hands, ye sinners; and purify your hearts, ye double-minded." If you do not engage in this work yourselves, and purify your own hearts, they will never be pure. If you do not get a pure heart, the blame of it will be laid to your own backwardness. The unclean soul hates to be purified. It is opposite to its nature; there is a great deal of self-denial in it. But be content to contradict the nature and bent of your own heart, that it may be purified; however grating it may be to you at first, yet consider how blessed the issue will be.

SERMONS AND DISCOURSES, 1730-1733

"TRUST THYSELF: every heart vibrates to that iron string." In one form or another, we have all heard this kind of advice. This quotation is from Ralph Waldo Emerson's famous 1841 essay on self-reliance. Such an exhortation appeals to our fallen hearts; we want to hear that we should look inside, not outside ourselves, for wisdom.

However, Emerson's advice runs counter to biblical thought. According to the prophet Jeremiah, the human heart is "desperately wicked" (Jeremiah 17:9, NLT). Even after conversion, we must be careful about listening to ourselves. We must fight our own hearts at times. We must *not* trust ourselves. We need to trust God. The Bible is clear here: Even as Christians, we may lie to ourselves, deceive ourselves, and find ways to enter into sin in secret. James 1:13-15 warns us, for example, about tempting ourselves to sin, picturing us as laying a trap for our own heart.

Jonathan Edwards proves a far wiser counselor than Ralph Waldo Emerson. We must all be ready and willing to "contradict" our "own hearts." We must search our motives, try the spirits, and examine our desires. This work is not easy; it will be "grating" at first, Edwards assures us. But he is right in saying that we cannot wash our hands of washing our hands. We must take ownership of our spiritual lives. An unclean soul hates to be purified, but the pure in heart love the work of purification. Don't trust yourself; trust God.

Draw near to God, and he will draw near to you. Cleanse your hands, you sinners, and purify your hearts, you double-minded. JAMES 4:8

April 23

Let us earnestly cry to God, that he would pour out his Spirit upon us to revive our first love and excite us to the doing of our first works: and particularly that God would pour out his Spirit on this part of the land, and in this town. Though we are so dead, God is able to revive us; he is able soon to make a great alteration amongst us. . . . If God gives his people a heart to cry mightily to him, and pours out his spirit upon us, it will be a happy omen that God is not as yet about to forsake us, and that he will not remove our candlestick out of its place.
SERMONS AND DISCOURSES, 1730-1733

ONE REMARKABLE THING about Christianity is that God never grows tired of hearing our repentant pleas. You might think it would be different; it is clear that Christ's disciples, for example, assumed there must be limits to the number of times they would be expected to forgive the guilty. Drawing from the Hebrew number for perfection, they thought that *seven* might suffice to meet the expectations of God's Kingdom. But Jesus shattered the low expectations of his followers. He set the bar for forgiveness at "seventy times seven," an exaggerated number meant to reframe their previous notions of mercy (Matthew 18:21-22, NLT).

Jonathan Edwards drives us to this truth by encouraging the church to ask God again and again to "revive our first love." He preached these words to a congregation that had witnessed revivals in the past under his grandfather, Solomon Stoddard. But even aside from a return to those glory days—a phrase meant quite literally—the people of God must regularly experience revival. We are prone, after all, to leave our first love, and to forget the first things of the faith.

The good news is this: Wherever we are in our faith, God will jump-start us. He may send us fresh trials as we call upon him, but even such occurrences are meant to vivify our faith. Through the eyes of Adam, we see such happenings as purely bad. Through the eyes of Jesus, we recognize that even pain comes as a gift, an opportunity to draw closer to God. Wherever we are today, whether at a high point or a low ebb, we can cry out to God for refreshing from the Holy Spirit. Nothing is stopping us—truly nothing—from repenting, from adoring God, and from drawing close to him. He will not forsake us.

What father among you, if his son asks for a fish, will instead of a fish give him a serpent; or if he asks for an egg, will give him a scorpion? If you then, who are evil, know how to give good gifts to your children, how much more will the heavenly Father give the Holy Spirit to those who ask him! LUKE 11:11-13

April 24

It is a shame for persons that have a hell of eternal misery to avoid and a heaven of eternal happiness, that are in a few days to be called before God to be judged for eternity, to grieve because their fellow worm gets more of this earth than they, and to be so engaged in their plotting and contriving how to pull down their neighbor, as if they had nothing else more worthy to be minded by 'em. It is of infinitely greater concern to you that your soul may be saved, than who shall be in this or that profitable post. If men see the vanity of the world, they would envy not [a] man because he has more of it than he.
SERMONS AND DISCOURSES, 1730-1733

AT ANY GIVEN MOMENT, our perspective may be off. It isn't hard for us to make mistakes—it comes easily. Our view gets cloudy, as if we're looking through smudged binoculars. We don't see life with the depth and wisdom that God intends for us to have. The world doesn't look pleasing and pleasant, full of the grace of God. Without a proper perspective, things look dreary and gray.

As a pastor, Jonathan Edwards dealt with congregants who lost sight of what was most important. Like many of us, they felt concerned about material concerns. So they fought over a "profitable post" in town. They lost perspective in doing so. Instead of reaching out to their neighbors, they sought to step over them. In the meantime, they lost their grip on the greatest gift in their possession: "eternal happiness."

It isn't difficult to fall into this trap. Earthly concerns grow so great; eternal concerns diminish to almost nothing. Before long, we're staring at the wrong realm, lost in our own petty issues. Today we must lift our gaze. Our lives here matter, but we must devote ourselves to the things of God. We should seek heavenly treasure at all times. We have something far greater than a growing financial portfolio or a trophy job. We have the sure hope of eternal life. With such a future as this, why would we envy anyone else?

> Do not lay up for yourselves treasures on earth, where moth and rust destroy and where thieves break in and steal, but lay up for yourselves treasures in heaven, where neither moth nor rust destroys and where thieves do not break in and steal. MATTHEW 6:19-20

April 25

Which do you think is the happiest man? He that minds his own concerns, seeking his own salvation and eternal happiness, and is not uneasy at others' prosperity, has not his own calm at all disturbed, let who will be advanced; he [that] is willing to leave it with providence to promote whom God will to earthly honor and wealth? Or he that frets himself about such a man's getting money easily, and about his growing great, and for fear he will think himself bigger than he; he frets himself, it may [be], about the honor that is put upon him, his being advanced to some post, or having a higher seat in the meeting house, or some such thing? "A sound heart is life of the flesh: but envy rottenness to the bones" (Proverbs 14:30).

SERMONS AND DISCOURSES, 1730-1733

WE HAVE ALL HEARD the phrase, "Nice guys finish last." It speaks to a certain approach to life—we drive fast, break the rules, and look out for ourselves. If we don't—or so goes the thinking—we'll get left behind. How interesting that we naturally consider it bad to be nice, and nice to be bad.

The human heart is always looking for excuses to grow in selfishness. "Nice guys finish last" gives us the kind of open door we want. But if we were to actually follow this desire, we would be like the unwise person that Jonathan Edwards identifies. We'd envy others; we'd "fret"; we'd find ourselves overtaken by those who have a "higher seat," a nicer house, or healthier children. Selfishness, even to the point of hating our neighbors, is not simply a modern concept. It is as old as humanity.

There is a better way to live: as believers who are zeroed in on "eternal happiness." As believers who have reconciled with God and inherited all things in Christ. As believers who are happy when others prosper. As believers whose identity isn't tied up in "earthly honor and wealth," who work hard and are grateful for what they get, but are not a tangle of twisted motives that must produce impressive results for onlookers. As believers who are living for God, and thus are freed from envy, the fear of finishing last, and the misery that such sins cultivate.

A tranquil heart gives life to the flesh, but envy makes the bones rot.

PROVERBS 14:30

April 26

April 26, 1730: Daughter Jerusha Edwards born

JERUSHA WAS THE SECOND CHILD of Jonathan and Sarah Edwards, preceded by Sarah (1728), and followed by Esther (1732), Mary (1734), Lucy (1736), Timothy (1738), Susannah (1740), Eunice (1743), Jonathan, Jr. (1745), Elizabeth (1747), and Pierpont (1750).

It appears Jerusha came to faith when the great evangelist George Whitefield visited Northampton and preached the gospel in October 1740. She remained close to her father and mother throughout her young life. Her father later said of her that she greatly respected her godly parents, and sought to honor them:

> Exceeding contrary to these was the disposition of that person I am
> speaking of, being a remarkable instance of honor, respect and duty
> to [her] parents; not only maintaining a most strict and conscientious
> regard to their counsels, but disposed to ask their counsels in all
> important affairs, studiously, and with great care and concern, to please
> them, and to avoid anything that might be grievous to them; seeming
> ever deeply concerned for their comfort and ready to her utmost to
> exert [herself] to that end.[28]

According to her father's description, Jerusha seems a model Christian. She displayed a godly spirit and cared only for the glory of God, two classically Edwardsean traits:

> [She was] very indifferent about all things whatsoever of a worldly
> nature, setting her heart [on another world], manifesting a relish
> [and] appetite [for divine things] as her supreme good.
>   [She] declared in words, showed in deeds, [that she was] ever more
> ready to deny herself, earnestly inquiring in every affair which way
> she could most glorify God, and do most service, and be under best
> advantages for her soul's good.[29]

We do not know a great deal more about Jerusha, but we do have clear evidence that Edwards enjoyed a special closeness with his second daughter. He nurtured her understanding of spiritual things, rejoiced when she came to faith as a child, and later spoke of her in the highest terms. This father-daughter relationship, anchored in God, reminds us how strong familial bonds may be, and how much joy they bring us when functioning as the Lord intends.

April 27

Be often reflecting and considering what a miserable, lost condition you was in when God found you, when he came by his grace and called you to himself. Consider what a helpless condition you was in and how you must inevitably have perished if God had not here pitied you, if Christ so had not here sought you, and in his love and his pity redeemed you. Remember how unable you were to do anything with your own heart to make yourself better and to work conversion in yourself. Remember how you wandered about seeking rest and finding none, and how God came to you in the midst of your distress and darkness. Remember how barren and desolate the wilderness appeared to you. Did you imagine then those barren rocks would ever yield you anything for your food and refreshment?
SERMONS AND DISCOURSES, 1730-1733

THE FIRST SIGN that someone is not getting enough rest is that they talk about not getting enough rest. Many people get seven or eight hours of sleep and are satisfied. Those who burn the candle at both ends, however, struggle through life. Some nights they get only three hours; other nights six. Sleep becomes like a holy grail, a far-off goal that no one can attain. It is painful to know this sort of person, for he or she never seems able to taste the simple goodness of sleep.

Yet, as much as we need sleep, we need spiritual rest far more. Outside of faith and repentance in Christ, however, such rest is elusive. Not wishing to fully commit our lives to Christ in the flesh, we seek any number of practices and helps. We use breathing exercises to calm ourselves. We do yoga to master our bodies. We meditate and try to clear our minds. Emptiness is the desired result.

God is not a far-out guru. He doesn't want us to empty ourselves; he wants to fill us. He stands ready to give us more of Jesus—more grace, more love, more power over sin, more hope, more comfort, and more rest. Before we met Jesus, we could find none of these things. We sampled earthly pleasures, to be sure. But we found the world "desolate." But in Christ, the barren land has turned into a garden for us. God has rescued us from our "distress and darkness." What more do we need that we don't already have? Let us rest, and sleep, and labor, in Christ.

[God] saved us and called us to a holy calling, not because of our works but because of his own purpose and grace, which he gave us in Christ Jesus before the ages began. 2 TIMOTHY 1:9

April 28

Rejoice and praise God the more; the consideration of these things should have this effect upon you. A man that is perishing, and seems far from help, and it seems very unlikely he should have any, when he is delivered, it will affect him the more to consider how forlorn his case was. The greater the misery and the more helpless the condition, the greater the deliverance, and the greater will the joy be, if you are aright sensible both of the misery of your former and the happiness of your present state. . . . You will the more praise his grace, that he was pleased to make so great a difference and to cause such light to spring out of such darkness, that he should seek and save you when you was lost, that he should take you out of the miry clay and set your feet upon a rock, that he should take you when you was a beggar from the dunghill and set you {upon a rock}.

SERMONS AND DISCOURSES, 1730-1733

WE SOMETIMES SEE a friend or coworker and think, *Wow, that person is a real hard case. She will never come to Christ.* It's not a thought we often give voice to, but we're tempted to *think* it. At a human level, it seems to make sense to see certain folks as "far from help" or beyond reach. After all, we too, in our unrepentant state, tried to get as far from God as we could.

The miracle of Christianity is that *no one* is beyond the reach of God. Such a location on earth, whether physical or spiritual, simply does not exist. No one can escape God when he pursues them. No one is too far from him to find salvation. We know this from our own experience. To varying degrees, we all remember "how forlorn" we once were, as Jonathan Edwards describes it. We did not want the Lord; we wanted anything, and anyone, but him.

God loves to win the toughest customers, the ones bristling in their anger at the divine. God loves to save the proudest achievers, the ones whose lives are intricately arranged to avoid admitting weakness in any area. God loves the hard cases. When he saves us, he helps us continually by showing us our former misery and present happiness. This is what he does, in reality, for all of us. We made ourselves poor; God has made us glad. No one is beyond the reach of God. Know this about others, and know this about yourself.

Count it all joy, my brothers, when you meet trials of various kinds, for you know that the testing of your faith produces steadfastness. And let steadfastness have its full effect, that you may be perfect and complete, lacking in nothing. JAMES 1:2-4

April 29

The saints receive by Christ the most quiet and sure rest and peace. By his redemption they obtain or will obtain the most perfect rest and sweet repose of mind. They may lay themselves down and sleep and awake, the Lord sustaining of them. They may dwell quietly and without fear of evil. They may set their hearts at rest, and may enjoy undisturbed quietness without having anything to fear. And that with good reason, for by Jesus Christ they enjoy the most perfect safety. They are thoroughly secured from all evil. He that is in Christ, he has the almighty God to be his defense. He is secured from all those evils and that misery he was exposed to while in a natural condition. . . . From the top of the highest mountain of God he may behold the dreadful work that storms make amongst miserable mankind below and himself be out of their reach, enjoying the most undisturbed tranquillity in Jesus Christ, his strong rock.
SERMONS AND DISCOURSES, 1730-1733

INSECURE IS A WORD that fascinates me. It is often used today to describe people who are unsettled, who cannot find confidence in who they are. People who derive their identity from the opinions of others. If they are not affirmed—and even celebrated—their spirits plummet. The common wisdom today is that such individuals need a good deal of attention and encouragement, so we should shower them with praise.

Insecure people are what Christians once would have called "man-centered." Their condition, in other words, is not fundamentally psychological, but spiritual. They worship the wrong God—namely, themselves. Under the guise of humility, they think that life is about *them*, when it truly is—and should be—about God. We know that Jesus saves us from sin, Satan, death, and hell. And that is quite a bill of deliverance. But we must add one other enemy to the list: *ourselves*.

By looking to Christ, we find our lasting identity and everlasting security. We are no longer insecure, for we enjoy "perfect safety in Christ." Christ is our life (Colossians 3:4). The "evils" and "misery" we so long faced have met their match in our Savior. He has disarmed unrighteousness and made a mockery of pride. These theological truths mean everything to us. We cannot be happy by looking to ourselves. We must look to Christ. We may struggle to feel settled and confident at times, but God is our Father and Christ our "strong rock," the giver of "undisturbed tranquillity" in a place where nothing is stable.

The effect of righteousness will be peace, and the result of
righteousness, quietness and trust forever. ISAIAH 32:17

April 30

He is a perfect, a complete savior. His righteousness is perfect, both active and passive. He completely answers all our needs. This should move us to trust in him. Hereby is also signified his strength, his ability to save and defend. He is a strong rock and high tower; let us therefore fly to him. They that are in Christ, their "place of defense is the munitions of rocks" [Isaiah 33:16]. Hereby is signified his everlastingness and unchangeableness. This should move us to trust in him, for he is an everlasting redeemer, and will be the everlasting portion of all that are his. His being, his glory, and his love will never fail. . . . The rock shall sooner be removed out of its place, than Christ shall depart from anything that he has engaged.

SERMONS AND DISCOURSES, 1730-1733

MYTHOLOGIST JOSEPH CAMPBELL famously identified the longing in the human heart for a true hero. In his book *The Hero with a Thousand Faces*, Campbell describes how we crave stories about people who go on difficult journeys, overcome great odds, and return home victorious.[30]

Campbell was correct in at least one respect: We do hunger for a hero. We know that we cannot save ourselves. Our desire is not primarily psychological, but theological. The witness of the human conscience shows us right from wrong. Though we try to deny it, deep down we all know we have gone astray (Romans 2:14-16). Whether we know the full revelation of God or not, we will all perish without someone to save us.

This is why Jesus Christ stirs us so. Our hearts are made for him. He is perfect in every way. He "completely answers" every need we have, as Jonathan Edwards observes. He is as strong as the mighty rushing ocean in all its potency. He is an immovable rock, a high tower that no one can assault or throw down. Our God doesn't put the spotlight on us, our strength, or our capacity to save. He meets the longing of our hearts in Christ, and draws us to marvel at the Messiah, the true hero, the one whom no foe can overcome. The rock will not move.

He is like a tree planted by water, that sends out its roots by the stream, and does not fear when heat comes, for its leaves remain green, and is not anxious in the year of drought, for it does not cease to bear fruit.

JEREMIAH 17:8

May

†

May 1

THE ORIGINAL PROBLEM OF HUMANITY? Original sin.

Countering those who argued for an optimistic view of mankind, Jonathan Edwards wrote the book *Original Sin*, which was published in 1758, after his death. After completing *The Freedom of the Will* in 1754, Edwards had a larger vision for writing about the major "doctrines of grace." While ministering in Stockbridge, Edwards observed the growing influence of a pastor named John Taylor, whose teaching downplayed human depravity and argued that sin and guilt were entirely personal. Taylor contended that Adam's fall represented no one but Adam himself, and thus denied the doctrine of original sin.

Throughout his life, Edwards had seen firsthand the effects of the Fall. He grew up with a grandmother who committed foul deeds. He witnessed much death and suffering as a pastor in Northampton. He lost his ministerial post in the town due to a group that despised his growing insistence on restricting church membership and access to Communion to those whose conversion could be verified. No person whose eyes are open in this world can fail to gain proof that it is fallen. Still, then as today, various theological leaders argued against the doctrine of mankind's fall in Adam and pushed for a rosier view of the human condition.

In *Original Sin*, Edwards charges that Adam's sin not only corrupted all of human nature, but the guilt from his sin was also passed to all humanity. For this reason, Edwards claims, God deals with humanity collectively through federal heads, representative leaders, not individually as John Taylor had argued. Responding to Taylor, Edwards couches his argument in typically God-centered terms.

> A propensity to that sin which brings God's eternal wrath and curse
> (which has been proved to belong to the nature of man) is evil, not only
> as it is *calamitous* and *sorrowful*, ending in great *natural evil*, but as it is
> *odious* and *detestable*: for by the supposition, it tends to that *moral evil*,
> by which the subject becomes odious in the sight of God, and liable,
> as such, to be condemned, and utterly rejected and cursed by him.[31]

Edwards's point is a powerful one: If human nature is inherently good, why do all people display evil tendencies? What accounts for such inclinations? Only the Christian worldview adequately explains the evil and suffering in the world. But such reasoning doesn't satisfy the sinful human heart, which quests for nothing less than exoneration, acquittal, getting off the hook. Edwards knew himself to be a sinner, and he taught that everyone is a sinner, and that our only hope is in Christ—not in any way in ourselves. The pastor still speaks.

May 2

Resolved, whenever I do any conspicuously evil action, to trace it back, till I come to the original cause; and then both carefully endeavor to do so no more, and to fight and pray with all my might against the original of it.
LETTERS AND PERSONAL WRITINGS

WE HAVE WITHIN US a battle of motives. Usually, when caught out in sin, we respond by citing good intentions but poor actions. The problem, so to speak, is in the follow-through, not the desire. But though our motives are generally good, we also have evil ones. Frankly, it's hard to admit this; it is the prickly part of our personality that we continually wish to hide. Years after coming to faith, we still have a tough time owning up to our wrongdoing.

A halfway approach to fighting sin is no approach at all. Acknowledging that damage has been done, but not fully searching out the immoral reason behind our words or actions, is like plucking off the top of a weed. It appears to the eye that the weed has met its match, but nothing of the sort has happened. Before long, and perhaps simply to spite us, the weed grows back doubly strong. So it is with our unwillingness to take responsibility for the evils we commit. If we fail to truly confess and repent, we may succeed in snapping off the outward part of our wrongdoing while leaving the bitter root intact.

There is a better way: When we do what Edwards labels a "conspicuously evil action," we must "trace it back," discovering the evil motive in our hearts that fueled our actions. Then we must "carefully endeavor" to fight against it, and devote ourselves to prayer to this end. This is sound guidance on a tough matter. We should resolve to take no half-measures with our unrighteousness. Starting right now, we need to reckon with our wrongdoing. We must "fight and pray" against it. Though we cannot totally erase our sin—only Jesus can do that—we can make major progress in our quest for holiness by admitting we are wrong and taking action with God and man to make things right.

> Let your ear be attentive and your eyes open, to hear the prayer of your servant that I now pray before you day and night for the people of Israel your servants, confessing the sins of the people of Israel, which we have sinned against you. Even I and my father's house have sinned.
> NEHEMIAH 1:6

May 3

If you are under convictions, you have a precious opportunity, which if you knew the worth of it, you would esteem it as better than any temporal advantages. You have a price in your hands to get wisdom that is more valuable than gold or silver. It is [a] great privilege to live under the means of grace, to enjoy the word and ordinances of God, and to know the way of salvation. It is a greater advantage still to live under a powerful dispensation of the means of grace under a very instructive, convincing ministry. But 'tis a much greater privilege still to be the subject of the convincing influences of the Spirit of God. If you have those, you have a precious advantage in your hands, and if you should lose it, 'tis questionable whether ever you will have the like advantage again.
SERMONS AND DISCOURSES, 1730-1733

THE OPPORTUNITY WE GAIN through Christian preaching is this: the chance to die to ourselves and live to God. The message of the gospel is thus different from any other religious, spiritual, or self-help promise. In other systems of belief, we may trust the message and gain a great deal. In the modern positive-thinking world, for example, buying into the model (often literally) improves us, enhances our lives, makes us better. But it can't save us. In Christianity, the initial message is to come and die to ourselves. Only then can we "live under the means of grace."

It's no wonder why Jesus tells his followers to "count the cost" (Luke 14:27-29). The message of conversion is indeed a costly one. We surrender everything we love in the world, everything to which we have devoted ourselves, everything on which we have based our identity. Yet this truth is "more valuable than gold or silver." If we come under the influence of the gospel, we have the opportunity to leave the world behind, and live in Christ. We can die to ourselves and become alive in him.

We have a "precious opportunity" to gain wisdom, as Jonathan Edwards describes it. And we have need of this wisdom, for we must regularly battle the flesh. We cannot forget the costly nature of the faith. The Spirit works his "convincing influences" in us, giving us power over the flesh. God has not promised to prosper us financially; but he has promised to prune us spiritually. The Word of God, bringing the conviction of God upon us, is no hindrance to happiness. Today, we have a "great privilege" to die to ourselves, as we first did upon our conversion. This may not yield the kind of material gain that other people have, but it honors God, and it secures for us the blessings of eternity. In other words, we have a great deal to gain—much more than we can even comprehend.

Seek the LORD while he may be found; call upon him while he is near.
ISAIAH 55:6

May 4

To exhort those that are under convictions, to seek earnestly that their convictions may be thorough: that is, that you be brought to see your helplessness and that you deserve God's eternal wrath. Men are not thoroughly sensible of their misery till they see they are helpless, nor of their guilt. The way to obtain the end of your convictions, that is, to have God appearing and manifesting himself to you in his redeeming love in Christ, is to have your convictions become thorough. When your convictions are thorough, then are you prepared for a sight of Christ as your redeemer. Don't rest, therefore, till you have obtained thorough convictions or till you are sensible of your helplessness and your deserving of eternal misery, and that it would be just with God to inflict it upon you.
SERMONS AND DISCOURSES, 1730-1733

WHEN GOD SAVES US, he shows us that we are not okay apart from him. We are "deserving of eternal misery," as Jonathan Edwards told his flock long ago. Edwards sought to awaken those who took their faith for granted. But even if we do not, even if we seek to obey the Lord, it is still useful for us to think afresh of God's great rescue of us and of all his chosen ones.

The fact that God has given us Christ means, simultaneously, that the best possible thing *has already happened*, and the worst possible things *cannot* happen. Jesus has saved us through his atoning death. This is the best possible outcome we can imagine. Because Christ's shed blood covers the wrath of God on our behalf, we cannot fall into judgment. We will not suffer the torment of hell. The worst possible outcome cannot occur. Christ has made it so.

Remembering these two truths frees us from two besetting problems. First, we could search the world for something better than Jesus. We know, however, that this is an empty pursuit. There is nothing better than Jesus. Second, we could live our lives in fear of some unnamed terrible event. But whatever we could imagine, it cannot be worse than experiencing God's everlasting punishment for sin. Nothing compares, however awful. We see, then, that Jesus is a remarkable Savior. He undertook the worst so we could experience the best. If we have never trusted in his name, now is the hour to do so. If we have long trusted him, we can rest assured that God's redeeming love shall sustain us forever.

He has delivered us from the domain of darkness and transferred us
to the kingdom of his beloved Son, in whom we have redemption,
the forgiveness of sins. COLOSSIANS 1:13-14

May 5

Labor to see your own wickedness. And to that end, be very much in self-reflections and confessions. As you have power in measure over your own thought, turn your thoughts often upon your own sins. And be very particular in setting your own sins in order before your own eyes. And be very particular and frequent in confessing them to God. Keep a catalogue of your sins in your mind and be often reading of it and often spreading of it before God, for 'tis the greatness of your guilt that you want to be sensible of. And in order to [do] this, 'tis of necessity that you have your sins in your view.

SERMONS AND DISCOURSES, 1730-1733

JONATHAN EDWARDS GAVE some stern counsel to his Northampton congregation as he sought to awaken in them a deeper faith. Some of his congregants had heard hundreds, even thousands, of sermons, and yet seemed to have gleaned nothing from them. So, week after week, the eminent pastor rehearsed the basic duties of the Christian life, striving to help his people understand that simply going to church did not equate with serious-minded faith.

As Christians, we should not become lost in contemplation of our sin. Instead, we look to Jesus. But we should heed Edwards's counsel as followers of Christ. It is possible, after all, to deceive ourselves when it comes to our spiritual practice. Some are prone to regular discouragement, but others are tempted to do enough just to get by. We act as if everything is great while failing to face down our real problems. Perhaps our marriages look strong, but need some serious repair in places. Perhaps our children look fine on the surface, but need cultivation we are not giving them. Maybe we don't sin in gross, embarrassing, public ways, but are we trapped in quieter patterns that dishonor the Lord?

Let us not live in denial. Let us reckon with our failings. Let us open our eyes to our sin. Perhaps most important, let us pray that God would uncover what we are hiding, and reveal what we are whitewashing. The Lord loves such prayers. We think, for example, of Hosea 14:4, where God responds to the prayer of a wayward people: "I will heal their apostasy; I will love them freely, for my anger has turned from them." It is time to be honest about our need for spiritual growth. Let us pray for our sin to come to light—and once it has, let us come once more before the Cross.

Nothing is covered up that will not be revealed, or hidden that will not be known. LUKE 12:2

May 6

When Christ made his solemn and triumphant entry into Jerusalem . . . the whole multitude of the disciples, of all sorts, especially young people, began to rejoice and praise God, with a loud voice, for all the mighty works that they had seen, saying, "Blessed be the king that cometh in the name of the Lord! Peace in heaven, and glory in the highest!" The Pharisees said to Christ, "Master, rebuke thy disciples." They did not understand such great transports of joy; it seemed to them a very unsuitable and indecent noise and clamor that they made, a confused uproar, many crying out together, as though they were out of their wits; they wondered that Christ would tolerate it. But what says Christ? "I tell you, that if these should hold their peace, the stones would immediately cry out" [Luke 19:37–40].

THE GREAT AWAKENING, 1758

CROSSFIT, if you're not already aware, is an intensive workout program that combines cardio and weightlifting exercises. I've learned that you don't have to ask someone whether they do CrossFit. If they do, they'll tell you. It may be something about the program's difficult nature that triggers the need to announce personal participation. But this isn't unique to workout routines. We don't have a problem telling people about the stuff we value highly—whether it's a new truck, a refinished kitchen, or a band we love.

How strange, then, that we often feel the need to stifle our praise of God. We have our reasons, of course; we've all experienced a time when someone overheard one of our prayers, or a spiritual conversation, and reacted negatively. Within seconds, they've vacated their table at the coffee shop. Though the sinful human heart despises the things of God, we know that God's mercy and grace are worth sharing. Like the Pharisees mentioned by Jonathan Edwards in today's reading, the world wants to rebuke our praise. We cannot help but offer it anyway.

We should not muzzle ourselves. We should not quiet our lips. We should praise our king with assurance. The whole earth is filled with the glory of God. The heavens declare his praise. The skies proclaim his handiwork. Scripture tells of his works and his ways. We need not be obnoxious in celebrating our Savior, but neither should we be oblivious to God's greatness. We have received all the riches of heaven itself. With boldness and grace, let us proclaim the Good News. We shouldn't have to be asked whether we follow Christ. The people around us should know.

All the earth worships you and sings praises to you; they sing praises to your name. PSALM 66:4

May 7

In 1731, Jonathan Edwards traveled to Newport, Rhode Island, to purchase a young slave girl, named Venus. The Edwards family often had a single slave in the home to help Sarah with her tasks. Throughout his career, Edwards wrestled with the institution of slavery. On the one hand, he believed that he and his slaves were equal before God: "We are made of the same human race. . . . Both have one Maker, and . . . their Maker made 'em alike with the same nature."[32] On the other hand, Venus was not indentured and she was not free to go. She was a slave.

The Northampton church received slaves into membership, and did not have separate classes of members. And Edwards's views continued to evolve when he moved to Stockbridge. Unlike many of his fellow colonists, he advocated for the welfare of Native Americans under his care, and went so far as to oppose members of his own extended family for their failure to treat all members of the community well. In terms of how he treated slaves, Edwards seems to have been a benevolent overseer, such that his slaves were more like indentured servants than chattel property.

Without question, this is a great blight on the legacy of Jonathan Edwards. It is worth noting that Edwards's own son, Jonathan Jr., later repudiated his father's practice, as did one of the pastor's key students, Samuel Hopkins. Though Puritan New England accepted slavery to its shame, there were some brave dissidents who raised strong objections to it. Samuel Sewall, a Puritan judge, thundered against slavery in a tract titled *The Selling of Joseph: A Memorial*, published in 1700. "Man Stealing," he wrote, "is ranked amongst the most atrocious of Capital Crimes."[33]

Today, we grieve over Edwards's firsthand involvement with slavery. It raises tough questions for us, as do the significant sins of other past leaders. Martin Luther sometimes expressed anti-Semitic views. John Calvin did not prevent the killing of Michael Servetus, an anti-Trinitarian theologian in Geneva. Ulrich Zwingli oversaw the martyr's deaths of several Anabaptists. George Whitefield was an indifferent husband and father. The list could go on—and does.

We should not excuse or whitewash the failings of the historical figures we respect. We should be honest about them, even as we should approach them with the same fair-mindedness we ourselves would want. No person is spotless; no one will get everything right. Tragically, we all err, sometimes in grievous ways. We should not seek to deny or revise the Christian past; we should instead practice properly biblical theology, and fight sin wherever we can. There is only one truly righteous man. He is the redeemer of all his children, all of whom fall short of his holy standard.

May 8

Examine whether or no you are new born.

1. *Whether or no you are, "as little children," humble (Matthew 18:3–4).*
2. *Whether or no "as new born babes, you desire the sincere milk of the word," whether [you are] governed by spiritual appetites (1 Peter 2:2).*
3. *Whether you are a "follower of God, as a dear child" (Ephesians 5:1), and "walk as a child of the light" and of the day Ephesians 5:8], [and] follow God: [a] child with a filial disposition, [with] love, reverence, [and] dependence as a little child on a father, imitating, obeying in everything.*

SERMONS AND DISCOURSES, 1730-1733

THE SERIOUSNESS OF CHRISTIANITY is unlike anything else we've experienced. It's true, Christians can sometimes earn the reputation of being overly uptight. We want to guard against that, especially because overflowing joy is a major gift of God to his blood-bought people. But we also stand apart from the world in fundamental ways. Life is not a joke. It is not a game. We are sinners. Eternal matters are at stake.

So it is that true religion marks us as different. Our faith is not a mere interest in heaven, but rather a matter of heaven and hell. Above all else, we are called to examine whether we are in Christ (2 Corinthians 13:5). "Test yourself," the apostle Paul tells us. So it was that Jonathan Edwards summoned his hearers in Massachusetts to examine their hearts. Were they humble? Did they desire to know God's Word? Were they "governed by spiritual appetites"? Did they seek, at even a basic level, to follow their holy Father?

These were not trick questions. Edwards did not wish to bring his people down, but to lift them up. When we revisit such matters as these, we who are born again will remind ourselves of our first priorities. Our present walk with Christ is not about having a position, or being listened to by others, or making ourselves great. It is about the simple things: humility, spiritual hunger for God, obeying the Father. In a world prone to silliness, the Christian faith is serious, and it yields serious change, and serious joy.

Do not marvel that I said to you, "You must be born again." JOHN 3:7

May 9

The redeemed have all their good of God. God is the great author of it; he is the first cause of it, and not only so, but he is the only proper cause. 'Tis of God that we have our Redeemer. 'Tis God that has provided a Savior for us. Jesus Christ is not only of God in his person, as he is the only begotten Son of God; but he is from God as we are concerned in him, and in his office of mediator; he is the gift of God to us: God chose and anointed him, appointed him his work, and sent him into the world. And as it is God that gives, so 'tis God that accepts the Savior. As it is God that provides and gives the Redeemer to buy salvation for us, so it is of God that that salvation is bought: he gives the purchaser, and he affords the thing purchased.
SERMONS AND DISCOURSES, 1730-1733

WHEN I WAS GROWING UP, if someone invited you over for dinner, they made the entire meal. Nowadays, it seems that things have changed. An invitation to dinner may also be an invitation to cook. For reasons that are hard to pin down, as a society we seem to have embraced a more communal way of food preparation.

On a culinary level, it may feel weird to be served a great meal and have nothing to contribute except our appetite. It may go against our grain to receive kindness in such a lavish way. Yet, that is Christianity in a nutshell. We gain all our good from God, and we gain all of God in the process. There is nothing we have done to earn the gift, except blaspheming and belittling our Maker. But, with grace that never ceases to amaze us, he pardons the guilty. "He gives the purchaser" of our salvation, and he gives himself without measure or limitation. All the good we have, we have "of God." He is the "great author" of every blessing we receive.

With grace so great as this, it may take us a lifetime to stop fidgeting at the table. "It is finished," Jesus said as he breathed his last. Atonement was made. We struggle to comprehend this impossibly good news, but it never changes. There is no dish for us to prepare. There is nothing we can add to God's kindness. We are fully responsible for obeying the Lord, but we contribute nothing to our salvation. The mediator has done what we could not do. Our call now is to revere him, walk after him, and taste all his delights.

By grace you have been saved through faith. And this is not your own doing; it is the gift of God. EPHESIANS 2:8

May 10

We are more apparently dependent on God for happiness, being first miserable, and afterwards happy. 'Tis more apparently free and without merit in us, because we are actually without any kind of excellency to merit, if there could be any such thing as merit in creature excellency. And we are not only without any true excellency, but are full of, and wholly defiled with, that which is infinitely odious. All our good is more apparently from God, because we are first naked and wholly without any good, and afterwards are enriched with all good.

SERMONS AND DISCOURSES, 1730-1733

MERIT, the term Jonathan Edwards uses here, is a very important one in theology. What role does merit—acceptable obedience that clears the guilty—play in the Christian life? Where do we get it? Does it come from within us, or from someone outside of us?

Protestants and Catholics disagree about numerous issues, but none more profound than this one. According to Catholic tradition, the grace of God is imparted to us, and becomes a kind of engine in us. According to the Protestant reformers, however, God's righteousness is imputed to us, such that we are *counted* righteous. Our good works give *evidence* that we are accepted in the beloved, but they are not the basis of our acceptance.

Our unredeemed selves are "without merit." We do not have "any true excellency." What's more, we are "full of . . . that which is infinitely odious." We have no hope of producing internal righteousness that will acquit us in God's courtroom. Our only hope is in the merit of Jesus, our Savior. It is not "creature excellency" that we need, but what we might call "Christological excellency." We need the perfect merit of Jesus, with his unblinking obedience, for salvation. This is what God supplies to us through faith, and this is what blesses us "afterwards . . . with all good." The pressure is off, and the answer is plain: Christ alone gives us the merit we need.

God, being rich in mercy, because of the great love with which he loved us, even when we were dead in our trespasses, made us alive together with Christ—by grace you have been saved—and raised us up with him and seated us with him in the heavenly places in Christ Jesus.

EPHESIANS 2:4-6

May 11

We are dependent on God's power through every step of our redemption. We are dependent on the power of God to convert us, and give faith in Jesus Christ, and the new nature. 'Tis a work of creation: "If any man be in Christ, he is a new creature" (2 Corinthians 5:17); "We are created in Christ Jesus" (Ephesians 2:10). The fallen creature can't attain to true holiness, but by being created again; Ephesians 4:24, . . . Yea, 'tis a more glorious work of power than mere creation, or raising a dead body to life, in that the effect attained is greater and more excellent. That holy and happy being, and spiritual life which is reached in the work of conversion, is a far greater, and more glorious, effect than mere being and life. And the state from whence the change is made, of such a death in sin, and total corruption of nature, and depth of misery, is far more remote from the state attained than mere death or nonentity.

SERMONS AND DISCOURSES, 1730-1733

"GOD IS DEAD." We have heard this slogan, perhaps from the "New Atheists," perhaps from its originator, philosopher Friedrich Nietzsche. The claim is not a neutral one, to say the least. The human heart does not, at its core, wish to know God or give him glory. We are hungry to be masters of our own domain, however we express it.

Wherever we settle, we do not want to give God the glory. We know he exists, but we do not honor him as God (Romans 1:21). This is partly why, even after coming to faith in Christ, we still feel a hitch in our spirit about God being totally, comprehensively sovereign. We feel as if we must have *some* part in the affair for it to really take root in us. Surely we need to add our part, chime in, lend a hand, and pull ourselves up. This is just how things work, right?

Jonathan Edwards cuts to the quick. In salvation, and in all things, he writes, we are dependent on God's power, with no asterisks or qualifications. We do all the sinning; God does all the saving. The one who carries out this work deserves all the glory, and that is precisely what God should receive. He does not share his glory with any other. It is his alone. Though foolish speculation may speak to the contrary, God is alive, and he is redeeming sinners from their sin. No slogan, no book, and no lecture can overturn this truth. This is our conviction and our confidence.

You have been filled in him, who is the head of all rule and authority
. . . having been buried with him in baptism, in which you were also
raised with him through faith in the powerful working of God, who
raised him from the dead. COLOSSIANS 2:10, 12

May 12

God knows wherein the happiness of his own creatures does consist; and the blessedness of that state which his infinite wisdom has contrived for the perfection of happiness consists very much in serving of God. And doubtless, that which is a part of the happiness of heaven is pleasant and delightful here in this world. A life of fervent serving of God is a pleasant life. Wisdom's "ways are ways of pleasantness, and all her paths are peace" [Proverbs 3:17]. He, therefore, that desireth "life, and would see good days, let him eschew evil, and speak no guile" [1 Peter 3:10]. This doctrine should encourage those that have chosen God's service, to serve him with the greater cheerfulness. It should endear the service of God to you, to consider that your future and eternal blessedness so much consists in it.

SERMONS AND DISCOURSES, 1730-1733

WHAT A GIFT IT IS to learn to work at a young age. We aren't given glamorous jobs, most of us, when we're bright-eyed and energetic. I recall mowing a cemetery, busing tables at a local restaurant, and raking blueberries. I had my moments when I would have rather been playing basketball, but I look back with gratitude at those early learning experiences.

We understand at a basic level that we need something purposeful to do. Most parents know this. Christian parents, however, have far more incentive to see their children develop skills and take on bigger projects. We follow a Savior who worked hard at his earthly job for years, and then worked tirelessly to advance his Father's Kingdom (John 4:34). Those who watched Jesus may well have concluded, as Jonathan Edwards does, that a life of fervently serving God is a pleasant life.

Whatever our age, we must take care that we are pursuing such a pleasant existence. We joke about laziness, but it is a sin against God, and it robs us of the joy that he intends for us to have. Work did not begin with the Fall; work predates the Fall, and work of some kind will be part of our heavenly future. We all need rest, and we should not idolize our work. When we know this biblical balance, we are freed to reject our culture's vision of labor that sees it as a curse, and instead serve the Lord—whatever our vocation—with "greater cheerfulness." Few around us may do so, but it is no matter. We are not working for men, but unto the Lord.

Her ways are ways of pleasantness, and all her paths are peace.

PROVERBS 3:17

May 13

Faith is a sensibleness of what is real in the work of redemption; and as we do wholly depend on God, so the soul that believes doth entirely depend on God for all salvation, in its own sense, and act. Faith abases men, and exalts God, it gives all the glory of redemption to God alone. It is necessary in order to saving faith, that man should be emptied of himself, that he should be sensible that he is "wretched, and miserable, and poor, and blind, and naked" [Revelation 3:17]. Humility is a great ingredient in true faith: he that truly receives redemption receives it "as a little child"; Mark 10:15, "Whosoever shall not receive the kingdom of heaven as a little child, he shall not enter therein."

SERMONS AND DISCOURSES, 1730-1733

SOMETIMES, people's logic is a strange thing. We hear, for example, about the need to steward the earth. This is a good message; in fact, if you study Scripture, you'll see that it is grounded in God's will. But it always surprises me when I hear about public figures who fly on private planes to attend gatherings that promote global stewardship. Is there something missing, logically, in this equation?

We all crave a mode of righteousness that leaves us in the right, but free to do whatever we want. We're excited to preach the message, but we'll continue to do as we please. Some people have a similar view of what it means to become a Christian. They think they can check a box, raise their hand, or respond to an altar call, and that closes the deal. No transformation necessary; no assembly (of the saints) required. But this is not true faith. It's merely a gesture, a surge of emotion, or a perfunctory religious activity.

True faith does not rest lightly upon us; true faith overtakes us. When God gives us eyes to see the beauty of Christ, we are humbled to the dust. We can no longer exalt ourselves, nor persist in our twisted practices. We are worms, and Christ is King. This is why evangelical faith and humility go hand in hand. Whatever stage of the journey we've reached, we crave and pursue self-forgetfulness. Our beliefs and our practice do not clash; they sing the same song. We practice what we preach, and no longer live as hypocrites. We enter the Kingdom as little children, subject to the King, and are always welcome in his court.

> Truly, I say to you, whoever does not receive the kingdom of God like a child shall not enter it. MARK 10:15

May 14

In short, it is the very soul of piety to apprehend and own, that all our springs are in him, the springs of our present grace and comfort, and of our future glory and blessedness, and that they all entirely flow through Christ by the efficacious influence of the Holy Spirit. . . . Such doctrines as these, which by humbling the minds of men, prepare them for the exaltations of God. He has finally owned and prospered in the reformed world, and in our land especially in the days of our forefathers; and we hope they will never grow unfashionable among us. For, we are well assured, if these which we call the doctrines of grace ever come to be contemned or disrelished, vital piety will proportionably languish and wear away, as these doctrines always sink in the esteem of men, upon the decay of serious religion.

SERMONS AND DISCOURSES, 1730-1733

THERE WILL BE NO HINDRANCE on our worship of God in heaven. We will never pause to marvel at human instruments; we will not have to suffer the ear-slicing shriek or the tooth-rattling thunder of a wayward sound system; we will not be distracted by that pinstriped suit worn by a member of the worship team. We will worship God without disturbance or interruption. Our souls will be full, and yet we will want still more of God; and we will be satisfied.

The life of the church is a foretaste of this greater delight. Though we don't yet reside in the new heavens and new earth, the happiness of that future realm has already dawned in our hearts. We have been given the "doctrines of grace," truths from the Word of God on divine salvation and rulership, that cast down the pride of men and exalt God's wisdom. The more we savor God's providence, his shepherding of all things for the flourishing of his people and the fulfillment of his perfect will, the more we will enjoy "vital piety," as Jonathan Edwards terms it. The truth leads to hope; doctrine leads to joy.

We do not always honor the doctrines of grace by how we live. Sometimes we quarrel, grow haughty, or break fellowship over minor matters. When this occurs, it is no fault of God's or his gracious, sovereign will. Where the sovereignty of the Lord is celebrated, and humility is cultivated, piety will flourish. This is true in our congregations; it is true in our hearts. By contrast, where we oppose God and his holy prerogatives, we will see our love grow cold. May the Lord give us great confidence in him, and a thriving, living, active faith grounded in his grace. The worship of God in eternity has begun, whether the sound system works or not.

In him we live and move and have our being.   ACTS 17:28

May 15

It is therefore most meet and suitable that certain times should be set apart wherein men should be required to throw by all other concerns, that their minds may the more freely and entirely be engaged in spiritual exercises, and duties of religion, and God's more immediate worship, so that religion may not be mixed and the mind may be disengaged; and that those times should be fixed and settled, that the church may agree therein, that they should be the same for all, that men mayn't interrupt one another but may rather assist one another by each other's example. For example has a great influence in such cases. If there be a time set apart for public rejoicings and there be generally manifestations of joy given, the general example seems to inspire men with a spirit of joy and mirth; one kindles another.
SERMONS AND DISCOURSES, 1730-1733

CHRISTIAN CHURCHES DO NOT all agree on everything about the Sabbath. Some who believe we must keep the Ten Commandments, forbid work on Sunday; others emphasize the first day of the week, the day of Christ's resurrection, as the day for rest and worship (Acts 20:7). Most believers would agree, however, about the importance of weekly worship.

It is strange to live in a cultural transition period. Sundays have become a prime day for youth sports; in some cities, Sunday brunch seems to be the new worship service, complete with avocado toast and mimosas, a kind of secular Communion. In such a culture, Christians seem a bit strange to outsiders. But our willingness to set aside time for God matters. Few things show genuine spirituality more than arranging our weekly calendars around the worship of God. How we spend our time, after all, tells us where our priorities lie, and what our hearts love most.

We all need times for "spiritual exercises," when we indulge "a spirit of joy and mirth" together. There is so much to be troubled by in this world; there is so little opportunity for deep joy. The fellowship of the body of Christ opens for us a door into another world, a world where God is not crowded out or downplayed, but treasured. The focus of our services is not us, though we may participate. The focus is on Christ, and thus we are relieved from our thrones and deliciously rebuked for our pride. We need "holy," set-aside times more than ever in this age of perpetual connection and smartphone saturation. For more than duty, but not less than delight, let us assemble together.

For everything there is a season, and a time for every matter under heaven. ECCLESIASTES 3:1

May 16

If God held sinners in a state of condemnation, and as the objects of his hatred and wrath, it would be utterly incongruous that they should have his Spirit. It is utterly unbeautiful and inharmonious that a person have anything of those holy, sweet, humble dispositions and motions of heart, which are a participation of the divine nature, given him while he is held as the object of God's utter displeasure and loathing. Therefore, when a person feels the Spirit of God in those divine dispositions and exercises, it assures him that God does not hold him as an enemy, but that he is in a state of favor with God.

THE "MISCELLANIES"

MANY PEOPLE SAY they have been given signs from God. They tell us they have heard from God and he has told them what to do. They say they have impressions from God that he has used to guide them. They recount instances when a chance occurrence has triggered a life change. We listen to these accounts with interest and empathy; we yearn for everyone to come home to God. But we also know that outside of conversion, none of us has access to the Lord.

We hear it said that people today are secularist in their outlook. Surely, many are. But many are not, as well. I sometimes wonder whether our age has grown more spiritualistic, not less. Many turn to their own intuition, their own foundationless spirituality, for assurance, comfort, and guidance. Our hearts go out to them. But though they seek our affirmation, we cannot offer it to them. We do not rest when people around us are spiritual; we rest when people around us have the Holy Spirit.

But how do we know whether we have the Spirit? We know because the Word tells us that the Spirit indwells every believer (1 Corinthians 3:16). This is how, to use Jonathan Edwards's vibrant language, we have any "holy, sweet, humble dispositions" toward God. If we have faith in Christ and produce spiritual fruit in keeping with repentance (Matthew 3:8), we may know that the Spirit resides in us. Having the Spirit does not depend on our following an experiential barometer, the equivalent of running like a madman around a rural parking lot in search of cell phone coverage. Having the Spirit depends on our believing the truth. We must remember what a precious treasure we have—life in the Spirit, not in the flesh.

In him you also, when you heard the word of truth, the gospel of your salvation, and believed in him, were sealed with the promised Holy Spirit.

EPHESIANS 1:13

May 17

The happiness of the reasonable creature don't consist in idleness but rather in action. The perfection and excellency of man consists in his faculties and principles. God hath endowed man with noble and excellent faculties and powers far above the beasts, wherein consists the natural image of God. . . . But 'tis more excellent in the creature to be in action than in a state of inactivity. While men's powers of action lie dormant and inactive, they are useless; they are as if men had them not. . . . God created man for action, as is evident by his giving of him those powers of action which he hath. By his giving of him such noble and excellent powers of action as he hath done, it is evident that he made him for action.

SERMONS AND DISCOURSES, 1730-1733

US SENATOR BEN SASSE of Nebraska tells a humorous story from his days as a college president. Some students who were helping to put up a Christmas tree wound the lights around the bottom half. When a staff member walked by after a while, she was thankful for the effort, but surprised that the lights went only halfway up. The staff member asked the students what had happened. Did they run out of lights? No, they answered. There was no ladder. The staff member dispatched them to get a ladder, and thus complete the task. Christmas was saved.

There is in our bones a desire for inaction. Whatever our training (or lack thereof), we want an excuse—and a way out—of responsibility. In Scripture, however, we cannot miss the fact that the first man and woman were not created for lounging around. They were created for *action*, to use Jonathan Edwards's catalytic word. The first couple was called to "have dominion" over creation, to work it, steward it, and treat it well (Genesis 1:26-27). Even after the Fall (Genesis 3), Adam and Eve still had vocations to pursue, and glory to give to God. Humanity didn't fall into some kind of cryonic sleep after the events in Genesis 3; the man and woman continued their lives of action, working the ground and bearing children.

In our day, we may receive the message that work stinks and vacation is awesome. As the children of God, we have a duty to reject this message. "God created man for action," Edwards points out, and so it is. We will find happiness through diligent undertaking. Let us not fall prey to the lie that the lazy are fulfilled. They are not. What is fulfilling is this: putting the Christmas tree up right. Enjoying a job well done. Working as God worked, with eagerness, creativity, and purpose.

We are his workmanship, created in Christ Jesus for good works,
which God prepared beforehand, that we should walk in them.

EPHESIANS 2:10

May 18

The serving of God is the most excellent kind of action that man is capable of. If man's happiness consists in action, doubtless it consists chiefly in that kind of action which is most excellent. 'Tis the most excellent kind of action that man is capable of, because 'tis not only the action that man by his noble powers was most fitted for, but as 'tis the exercise of the most excellent principles of the heart. That principle of heart that is the greatest beauty of man is holiness, a principle of love to God. This principle was that wherein man's primitive excellency consisted, which he lost by the fall. And this principle is that wherein consists the beauty of the angels in heaven.

SERMONS AND DISCOURSES, 1730-1733

SERVING GOD OFTEN seems so humble compared to the bigger enterprises of the world. Folks out there are starting global businesses, and we're pouring juice for the youth group? Politicians are pursuing world peace and cutting deals, and we're editing a spreadsheet? The author we follow is on an international tour, and we're trying to get a toddler to eat peas?

It is striking how often Jesus cites quiet, lowly people as examples of vibrant Christianity. The tax collector who abased himself. The woman who gave just a tiny amount, but for whom the sacrifice was everything. Mary serving Jesus and his disciples without complaint. These people all served the Lord. They did not call attention to themselves, but rather offered their service to God.

Jonathan Edwards is right: Our "happiness consists in action." We were not made to wilt; we were made to work. Yet we must remember that God assigns our lot in his Kingdom. We should not obsess, in other words, over the roles we are given; we should serve to the fullest wherever we are placed. It may be a very public position; it may be an unnoticed one. It matters not. Whether on speaking tours or slicing turkey, when we serve God, we are doing what we were made for, and we are putting holiness into action.

Those whom he foreknew he also predestined to be conformed to the image of his Son, in order that he might be the firstborn among many brothers. ROMANS 8:29

May 19

The service of God is an imitation of God, as it is the exercise of holiness; but 'tis an imitation of Jesus Christ, as it is a subjecting to God's authority. Christ, when he was in this world, he obeyed God perfectly; he was obedient even unto death. He delighted to do God's will, as it was written; Psalms 40:8, "I delight to do thy will, O my God: yea, thy law is within my heart." And in heaven, Christ will be subject to the Father; 1 Corinthians 15:28, "And when all things shall be subdued unto him, then shall the Son himself be subject unto him that put all things under him, that God may be all in all." It will be a great pleasure to 'em to be conformed to, and to imitate, the Lord Jesus Christ.

SERMONS AND DISCOURSES, 1730-1733

IN RECENT YEARS, officials in many Western countries have tried to change the language of gender on official documents. In some places, birth certificates no longer list "Father" or "Mother," but "Progenitor A" and "Progenitor B." These terms sound like they belong to a strange science-fiction novel, but they don't.

As Christians, we sometimes wonder how to describe the Trinity, one of the mysteries of our faith. Without much awareness of what the Bible teaches, we might think of the members of the Trinity as Divine Person A, Divine Person B, and Divine Person C. But they are not so bland as this. The New Testament unveils the Godhead, the holy three-in-one, as Father, Son, and Holy Spirit. The three persons of the Trinity always relate in such a way that displays their unity, their oneness, but also reveals their distinct personhood—their *threeness*, if you will.

The uniqueness of the Son shines in his willingness to obey his Father. Christ is the true Son, who followed the call of his Father into the world (Hebrews 1:1-2). He is the sent one (John 13:20) who "obeyed God perfectly." Jesus came to earth to do the Father's will and accomplish the Father's mission. His Sonship speaks to our own adoption as children of God: We are not members of the Kingdom to achieve fame. We exist to imitate the Son to the praise of the Father. It may sound like a story too good to be true, but it's not. This isn't science fiction; we're living in the story of God.

When all things are subjected to him, then the Son himself will also be subjected to him who put all things in subjection under him, that God may be all in all. I CORINTHIANS 15:28

May 20

Hence we may learn something of the nature of the heavenly state. They are not idle but active.
'Tis true the heavenly state is a state of rest: they that enter into heaven, they enter into Christ's
rest. And 'tis also a state of reward for what they have done: when those that are in the Lord
die, "they shall rest from their labors; and their works do follow them" [Revelation 14:13].
But this don't hinder but that their state will be a state of action and employment. We need
not suppose that they spend their time in doing nothing: no, the saints never are so active as in
heaven. As it is said of the angels, that they are as a flame to signify their activity in serving
of God, so may it be said of the glorified saints (Luke 20:36).
SERMONS AND DISCOURSES, 1730-1733

THE TRUE DIVISIONS in this world aren't political or geographical. They are over
how to properly spend a vacation. There are basically two camps: those who
view time off as an opportunity to stretch themselves, sample new cultures, and
travel ceaselessly; and those who favor rest over recreation, and prefer sitting by
the pool, drinking something cool, and taking a nice nap. The first group wants
to rev it up; the second group wants to quiet down.

Jonathan Edwards rarely took a day off. He worked hard. When he gazed
past this world into eternity, he saw our eternal state as a blend of rest and action.
When we die, we "enter into Christ's rest." In other words, we have no more work
to do to get across the finish line. We are home. Christ is everything to us. But
that doesn't mean we'll sit around playing harps for eternity. We will be active in
serving God in eternity, living in "a state of action and employment." Rest and
activity in perfect balance.

No one knows for certain what exactly our moment-by-moment experience
of eternity will be like. It is clear that Adam and Eve worked *coram deo*—in the
presence of God—in the Garden of Eden before they fell away from him. Even
in a sinless paradise, they served God. They were created for such labor, and so
are we. We may not know all that heaven will be, but we know this: It will be
beyond our wildest dreaming and better than any vacation by a factor of infinity.

I heard a voice from heaven saying, "Write this: Blessed are the dead
who die in the Lord from now on." "Blessed indeed," says the Spirit,
"that they may rest from their labors, for their deeds follow them!"
REVELATION 14:13

May 21

IN MAY 1724, Jonathan Edwards was offered a position at Yale College as a tutor. He and the church at Bolton had an understanding that his pastorate was temporary, and two weeks later Edwards returned to New Haven.

The educational regimen did not lack for rigor. Six days a week, the community went to chapel at 6:00 a.m. Following this, the tutors listened to the students recite their readings—repeating sentences from certain theology textbooks—for the rest of the day, with an hour and a half break for lunch. The community gathered for prayer from 4:00–5:00 p.m., then supper, free time, and studying until lights-out at 11:00 p.m.

What the student body possessed in duty, they lacked in devotion. After Yale's rector, Thomas Cotton, defected to Anglicanism, the school did not fill the position until 1726. Edwards was left holding the bag, and found himself sinking due to the weight on his shoulders. His diary entries from that period are heavy, even morose:

> Wednesday, Sept. 30. It has been a prevailing thought with me, to
> which I have given place in practice, that it is best, sometimes, to eat
> or drink, when it will do me no good, because the hurt, that it will
> do me, will not be equal, to the trouble of denying myself. But I have
> determined, to suffer that thought to prevail no longer. The hurries of
> commencement, and diversion of the vacancy, has been the occasion
> of my sinking so exceedingly, as in the three last weeks.[34]

The gloom of this season did not last forever. But Edwards's time as a tutor reminds us that he—as with every believer—went through tough seasons, seasons of discouragement, stress, and overwork. He did not stop working; he did not depart the church. He kept reading the Word and praying, he was faithful to his local congregation, and eventually things improved. No Christian can avoid rough patches in a fallen world; we can, however, press on toward the upward call that is ours in Christ (Philippians 3:14).

May 22

The redeemed have all their inherent good in God. Inherent good is twofold: 'tis either excellency or pleasure. These the redeemed not only derive from God, as caused by him, but have them in him. They have spiritual excellency and joy by a kind of participation of God. They are made excellent by a communication of God's excellency: God puts his own beauty, i.e. his beautiful likeness, upon their souls. They are made "partakers of the divine nature," or moral image of God (2 Peter 1:4). They are holy by being made "partakers of God's holiness" (Hebrews 12:10). The saints are beautiful and blessed by a communication of God's holiness and joy as the moon and planets are bright by the sun's light. The saint hath spiritual joy and pleasure by a kind of effusion of God on the soul. In these things the redeemed have communion with God; that is, they partake with him and of him.

SERMONS AND DISCOURSES, 1730-1733

SOME PEOPLE HAVE THE GIFT of tending plants. They can nurture even a tiny would-be flower to full bloom, winning prizes along the way. I am not such a person; I keep such people in business. My wife once gave me a plant for my office. It was my best intention to help it reach its full plant-based potential; alas, I failed that little green shrub. Miserably.

Part of the problem was the lack of light in my office. When a plant-saving office visitor intervened, she immediately moved the plant to a spot in the sunlight. It was noteworthy to see how quickly the plant responded to the light. This reaction speaks to the effect that God has on the souls of the redeemed. Like beams of sunlight streaming through a floor-to-ceiling window, the Lord communicates his holiness to his people. We "partake of" and participate in the very goodness of God himself.

This does not mean that we *become* God. Such a view obscures the distinction between the creature and the Creator. But we do receive God's grace, just as the plant receives sunlight. Through the Holy Spirit, we gain all the blessings of God, and enjoy God's pleasure. The fruit of the Spirit comes to life in us. We do not become part of God, but we do become like God, as we have union and fellowship with him. Thankfully, with the Lord, the blinds are never closed, and water is not withheld—two other factors in the death of my plant. We drink God's grace to the full, and are never turned away or forgotten.

He has granted to us his precious and very great promises, so that through them you may become partakers of the divine nature, having escaped from the corruption that is in the world because of sinful desire.

2 PETER 1:4

May 23

[The] Use of this doctrine [is] to warn all persons carefully to examine themselves before they come to the Lord's Supper, that they don't seal their own damnation. . . . If upon self-examination, you find yourself unfit in these respects, it won't excuse you from coming. One wickedness don't excuse [you], though, 'tis true, if [you] will continue, you had much better stay away than come. But the end of examination is that you may amend before you come. If there be any now about to approach that are in any of these mentioned ways {of wickedness}, I forewarn them in the name of Jesus Christ not to presume to touch till they have taken up a resolution. If you live in any known way of wickedness, don't come here to eat and drink damnation to yourselves.

SERMONS AND DISCOURSES, 1730-1733

THE LORD HAS SO CONSTRUCTED the Christian life that it is hard for us to thoughtlessly entrap ourselves in sin. He has given us the Holy Spirit, who convicts us of sin (John 16:8). He has ordained that we would hear the Word every Sunday. He has called us to observe Communion, and to examine ourselves before partaking (1 Corinthians 11:28). The takeaway is clear: Even as the redeemed of God, we still must regularly assess our sin, and regularly repent.

This spiritual seriousness goes against our grain. The old nature doesn't rule us, but it does pull at us and try to entice us to slip into sleepy spirituality. *I'm fine*, we think. *Things are humming along. Nothing big to repent of.* Yet the Lord's Supper will not let us slumber. We know at an instinctive level that we should not take it lightly. This ordinance calls us to "examine" ourselves, and to do so with judgment on our minds, as Paul tells the Corinthians.

The Lord's Supper warns us. It also comforts us. The ritual action of consuming the bread and wine speaks to what we must do daily—feed on Christ. There is no hypertheological approach to this needed exercise. There is not an enhanced Lord's Supper for the super-Christian. We all take the same elements, and God honors us and ministers to us as we do. If we are in Christ, the judgment we must consider is canceled. Praise God. The Lord's Supper is thus not only a remembrance of what has been done. It is a victory meal, for soon we will be with the High Priest, the one who not only made atonement for sin, but made it by his body and blood.

Let a person examine himself, then, and so eat of the bread and drink of the cup. I CORINTHIANS 11:28

May 24

Nothing foreseen, foreseen excellency or endeavors of the elected, is the motive that influences God to choose them; but election is only from his good pleasure. God's election being the first thing that causes any distinction, it can be no distinction that is already the foresight of which is to [be] considered as prior, that it influences God to choose them. It is not the seeing of any amiableness in these above the rest that causes God to choose them rather than the rest. God don't choose men because they are excellent, but he makes them excellent because he has chosen them. 'Tis not because God considers them as holy that he chooses them; he chooses them that they might be holy; Ephesians 1:4–5, "According as he hath chosen us in him before the foundation of the world, that we should be holy and without blame before him in love: having predestinated us unto the adoption of children by Jesus Christ to himself, according to the good pleasure of his will."
SERMONS AND DISCOURSES, 1730-1733

THE CHRISTIAN CHURCH features plenty of debates over theological matters. In fact, many Christians think—or have been subtly trained to think—that doctrine creates division. Better to keep things plain and basic, for we can agree on the ABCs of the faith. Such a mind-set, though perhaps well-intentioned, means that we sidestep many biblical truths the Lord wants us to confront—and embrace.

It is no secret that some Christians take issue with "election"—that is, God, by his sovereign will, choosing some to be saved. But even if we hesitate over God's sovereignty in salvation, we cannot help but affirm that we are not in the driver's seat in much of our lives. We did not choose our eye color. We did not preselect who our ancestors would be one hundred, five hundred, or a thousand years ago. We did not carefully screen possible parents and choose the man and woman we thought ideal for our personal vitality. All this was *done*. It was fixed by God's sovereign will.

God did not choose us because he saw something good in us. He loved Jacob, and hated Esau, because of his decree, not their individualized character (Romans 9). We were not saved because we were lovely and God was drawn to our innate beauty. We were saved because we were unlovely and God chose to reconcile us to himself in Christ. The wisdom of God, as seen in doctrines like "election," hits the wisdom of man hard. But we know which is better. We know, as well, who is sovereign, and who is not—and thus we know whom to worship.

He chose us in him before the foundation of the world, that we should be holy and blameless before him. In love he predestined us for adoption to himself as sons through Jesus Christ, according to the purpose of his will.
EPHESIANS 1:4-5

May 25

Let Christians take heed so to walk that they mayn't dishonor their pedigree. You are of a very honorable race, more honorable by far than if you were of the offspring of kings and had royal blood in your veins. You are a heavenly offspring, the seed of Jesus Christ, the children of God. They that are of noble race are wont to insist greatly upon the honor of their families. They value the ensigns of the honor of their families, the coat of arms, and the like. How much more careful should you be of the honor of your descent, to see to it that you in nothing behave yourself unworthy of the great God, the eternal and omnipotent king of heaven and earth whose offspring you are.

SERMONS AND DISCOURSES, 1730-1733

IT IS A WONDROUS THING to discover facts about your ancestors. When we learn about our heritage, we may discover stories of perseverance under distress. We may marvel at the lineage of faith we uncover, or lament at how little godliness runs through our ancestry. When we study history, it seems almost miraculous that we are *who* we are and *where* we are, given the odds faced by past generations.

This is true not only of our blood relatives, but also of the family of God. We are a unique and even quirky people. We have a spiritual family tree that stretches back thousands of years and transcends every division known to mankind. We are a holy race and a chosen people, crossing over every ethnicity, tribe, tongue, and geographic location. We give thanks for our immediate roots and the unique backstory of our bloodlines. But we who know God belong to a much greater family, one that spans the globe and human history.

This holy family has a head: Jesus Christ. Some, as Hebrews 11 instructs us, had to look ahead to the greater David, the Messiah; others, like us, look back to Jesus, the author and perfecter of our faith. Yet we all may give praise to God for this spiritual "pedigree." We are the offspring of God, knitted together with every God-fearing person from the beginning of time. Soon, we will meet this bustling, diverse, beautiful family, and together we will extol the one who has made us, who were not a people, into the family of God.

All these, though commended through their faith, did not receive what was promised, since God had provided something better for us, that apart from us they should not be made perfect. HEBREWS 11:39-40

May 26

JONATHAN EDWARDS, JR. WAS the Edwards child who most closely approached his father in intellectual ability. Raised in Stockbridge for the majority of his early years, Jonathan Jr. learned Mahican, a Native American tongue, and was also fluent in languages spoken by the Algonquin and Iroquois tribes.

Jonathan Jr. studied at Princeton, graduating in 1765. In a course that resembles his father's vocational path, he became a tutor at Princeton (1767-1769) and then a pastor in New Haven, Connecticut (1769-1795) and Colebrook, Connecticut (1796-1799). The younger Jonathan Edwards concluded his life's work in Schenectady, New York, where he took the presidency of Union College in 1799, and served until his death on August 1, 1801. Like his father, he died while serving an academic institution as president.

Jonathan Jr. largely upheld his father's theological legacy, defending the biblical doctrine of exclusive salvation through Christ, while modifying his father's concept of the will. He is best known for his abolitionist stance, declared with fervor and logic in a 1791 homily, titled, "The Injustice and Impolicy of the Slave Trade." Without naming his famous father (who held slaves), Jonathan indicted him for his sin:

> Let such inquire how it is possible, that our fathers and men now alive, universally reputed pious, should hold negro slaves, and yet be the subjects of real piety? . . . But to steal a man or to rob him of his liberty is a greater sin, than to steal his property, or to take it by violence.[35]

Jonathan Jr. concluded his homily—which had very little exposition of the biblical text—with a flourish that evoked the theme of light, one of his father's favorite word pictures:

> It hath appeared with great clearness in France, and produced remarkable effects in the National Assembly. It hath also shone in bright beams in Great Britain. It flashes with splendor in the writings of Clarkson and in the proceedings of several societies formed to abolish the slave trade. Nor hath it been possible to shut it out of the British parliament. This light is still increasing, and in time will effect a total revolution.[36]

On this count, the younger Edwards—carefully breaking with his father, in print—proved right. Today, centuries after Jonathan Jr.'s death, we give thanks that the light of Christ "is still increasing," and that none can stamp it out.

May 27

Every Christian is allowed as near an access to God and as free a use of sacred things as the priests were of old. God under the law dwelt in the tabernacle and temple; they were the symbols of his presence, and these places were holy. They might go into the holy place to minister before the Lord, but if any other that was not of the seed of Abraham came nigh, they were to be put to death; Numbers 3:10, "And thou shalt appoint Aaron and his sons, and they shall wait upon their priest's office: and the stranger that cometh nigh shall be put to death." But now all are allowed to come nigh. We are all allowed a free access to God to come with boldness and confidence.

SERMONS AND DISCOURSES, 1730-1733

I WAS ONCE IN WASHINGTON, DC, for a quick trip. As I was headed down some stairs in a hotel, on my way to a meeting, all of a sudden a thickset man in a jet-black suit stopped me in my tracks. Just then, a member of the presidential cabinet swept past, with multiple Secret Service agents in tow. My access to the stairs was interrupted. I was definitely not moving from my post, seeing those agents all around.

There are so many places in the world we cannot go. We have passwords and stop signs and blaring alarms. We do not have access to a great many things in life. The same ought to be true in the spiritual realm. We have no *right* to know God. We have no claim on his divine favor. We cannot sue God in cosmic court and have him give us what we want. There is no key card that will swipe open the gates of heaven for the unrepentant.

How incredible that every believer has unreserved "access to God." It was not always so; the nation of Israel had strict rules that regulated their coming near to God. Only the high priest could enter the Holy of Holies, and then only once a year. But now, through Christ, we may all enter the presence of God. We are a kingdom of priests (1 Peter 2:9), and we have "free access" to our God. These spiritual privileges matter more than we know. We may not go everywhere we'd like to on earth. So be it. But we may enter the presence of God at any time, and we will live with him forever in a world made right, dwelling with the Lamb as he is, where he is.

In Christ Jesus you who once were far off have been brought near by the blood of Christ. EPHESIANS 2:13

May 28

They will forever be employed in heavenly works, and shall be diligent in it. They shall not cease day nor night. They shall rest from their labors, for although they will still be employed in the service, yet it will be no labor to them. It won't then be as 'tis now. . . . There will be no difficulty or no need of labor and striving, no weariness. They will be active in holiness easily, freely, and naturally as the sun shines. They will have no need of ceasing, to take their rest; it will be all rest. It will be refreshment to them, and not labor, to do the will of God.
SERMONS AND DISCOURSES, 1730-1733

THE ENERGY OF CHILDREN never ceases to amaze me. All day long, the family has bustled about, playing together, cleaning up a room together, taking a nice outdoor walk. When evening hits, it is often the case that the parents (and grandparents) find a quiet place on the couch, thinking the day's doings are done. But then—like slices of toast—up pop the youngsters. After more than twelve hours of energetic output, they still have enough gas in the tank for a few more sprints around the house.

We love to see the cheerful energy of children. In fact, in our little ones, we see a picture of how humanity was made to live. We were made to be "active in holiness," as Jonathan Edwards argues; but this is a challenge for us. In a spiritual sense, it's tempting to pursue the couch over the Cross. But God has a better way for his people. He wants us not merely to work, but to "be employed in heavenly works" for all our days.

The pursuit of holiness is not a minor matter for evangelical Christians. Through the work of Jesus Christ, heaven has broken into our world (Matthew 4:17), and we may now engage in the same activity that will captivate us in eternity. Our lives here on earth and our lives in heaven should not be dissonant, or even that different from one another. Though it is not yet completed, the age to come has dawned. In this very hour, God gives us the chance to be active in holiness. There are many tasks to carry out, and much that calls for our attention here. But we are more than worker bees, scurrying about without a greater cause. We are, and we shall be, workers unto God, not wilting in the task, but gaining refreshment from it.

Give glory to the LORD your God before he brings darkness, before your feet stumble on the twilight mountains, and while you look for light he turns it into gloom and makes it deep darkness. JEREMIAH 13:16

May 29

Let your walk be such as will bear to be examined in the light, such as will bear to be examined by the power of God's word. Frequently try them by the light yourself; [this is] the character that Christ gives of those that do; John 3:21, "But he that doeth truth cometh to the light." Do such things only as if they were known and published in the light, [and] would appear honorable and worthy. Never allow of things that you would have cause to be ashamed of, if they should be declared in the light. Practice such as would be honorable in the light. This seems to be what the Apostle means by "walking as children of light" (Ephesians 5:8); for it follows in the next verse, "For the fruit of the Spirit is in all goodness and righteousness and truth." Do that which appears honorable when things come to be brought to light at the day of judgment. Christ tells us, "Whatsoever [ye have] spoken in darkness shall be heard in the light" [Luke 12:3].

SERMONS AND DISCOURSES, 1730-1733

THE IMAGE HAS STAYED with me for a long time. After a lengthy flight, I grabbed my carry-on from the overhead bin and walked off the plane. As I proceeded through the concourse, I noticed a flight crew walking ahead of me. Just then, one of the pilots paused and knelt down. Had he dropped his car keys? No. He was bending over to pick up a candy wrapper from the ground. When he straightened up, he walked over to a trash can, threw away the wrapper, and went on his way.

It was a simple lesson, but it lodged in my memory. Here was a pilot—at the top of his profession. He did not have to pick up someone else's trash. He could have easily pretended he didn't see it and left it for the janitor to retrieve. But he didn't. He saw a need and took action to correct it. And he wasn't concerned whether anyone even noticed. I've often thought about that pilot as an example of how to act when we think no one is watching. We face situations like that every day. When no one is looking, who are we? Are we the same person "in the light," as Jonathan Edwards puts it, as we are in the dark?

Scripture condemns what James calls a "double-minded" approach (James 1:8). One moment we're all in, our hands raised in public worship. In the next moment, we're gratifying our lusts, confident that no one can see us. But someone always can. The Lord sees everything we do, and he will examine "in the light" every seemingly inconsequential decision we make. This is one way to know whether we are mature in the faith and growing in godliness: Are we the same person in public that we are in private? Are we living in the dark as we would live in the light?

Whatever you have said in the dark shall be heard in the light, and what you have whispered in private rooms shall be proclaimed on the housetops. LUKE 12:3

156

May 30

Resolved, to study the Scriptures so steadily, constantly and frequently, as that I may find, and plainly perceive myself to grow in the knowledge of the same.
LETTERS AND PERSONAL WRITINGS

CHRISTIANS SHOULD NOT COME to the Bible like wandering tourists, popping in to this place or that for a while before lazily venturing on to the next destination. Instead, we should consider ourselves *theologians*. This may sound strange to evangelical ears, particularly in our day. Many people have learned to be intimidated by theology. They think only a tiny percentage of the church has a right to think deeply and study widely.

But every Christian, in a way, is a theologian. We have all received the gift of God's special revelation in the Bible. For all of us, the law of the Lord is a lamp to our feet and a light to our path (Psalm 119:105). We should all search the Scriptures "steadily, constantly and frequently," as Jonathan Edwards suggests. Whether we have a degree in theology or not, we may all be students of the Word, and of the God it reveals. Every Christian has this privilege.

This was Jonathan Edwards's constant desire—to study the Scriptures and grow steadfastly in knowledge. We need not all become pastors or missionaries as he did. But we can all come to the Bible for enrichment and advancement in our faith. No one is keeping us from continual study; no one is forbidding us from gaining knowledge. So, starting today, think of yourself not as an aimless visitor to God's revelatory book, but as a theologian—an explorer in search of great treasure. Equip yourself. Grow in the knowledge of God—steadily, constantly, and frequently.

They read from the book, from the Law of God, clearly, and they gave the sense, so that the people understood the reading. NEHEMIAH 8:8

May 31

We have the tidings of willingness to restore us to our first state of happiness that we were wrath-driven from when we fell, of being restored to a like innocency and holiness and the image of God, to have our naked, deformed, loathsome souls covered and made to shine with the communication of God's glory (2 Corinthians 3:18). After we have despoiled ourselves of all our primitive excellency and loveliness and become odious and in the image of Satan, we may have God's beauty put on us again; yea, we may be brought to perfect holiness as spotless as that which we lost. God is willing to restore our whole man, to exalt our faculties to a like strength and vigor with that which we had before, and our bodies to the like beauty and life. This corruptible may put on incorruption and this mortal immortality.

SERMONS AND DISCOURSES, 1730-1733

A FEW YEARS AGO, I read a story of a young man in Detroit. He saw the decline of his beloved city, and though he had no money and little experience, he decided to buy and rehabilitate a property. The work, in sum, was scary, slow going, and little-supported. Some nights he felt lonely; often he wanted to give up. But he persevered, and like many others in this city, he restored a ruined home. He purchased the house at auction for only $500, but the experience was priceless.

Reclamation projects like this inspire us. Yet we Christians get to witness something so much greater than a domestic rebuild. We ourselves become a new creation (2 Corinthians 5:17). Once, we were "despoiled" and primitive, living in the desert, doomed to die. Now, the Spirit has made his home with us, and we display "God's beauty." We have no guarantee of getting a supermodel contract, of course, but the inner renovation peeks through. We gain strength we never had; we brim with vitality we never knew.

This is not a short-term project. There's no camera crew that is going to swoop in and—*bang!*—in thirty days, the deal is done. Sanctification, growing in godliness, takes a lifetime. The gospel is not cosmetic surgery of the soul. The gospel remakes from the inside out, and as we walk with Christ by faith, he makes us more and more godly over time. Our filthy mouth improves. Our envious comments recede. Our lazy habits change. Our poor marital communication turns a corner. We do not lose all our sin until we go to glory, but God does work in us. He reclaims us, hour by hour, day by day, and he never leaves the site.

We all, with unveiled face, beholding the glory of the Lord, are being transformed into the same image from one degree of glory to another. For this comes from the Lord who is the Spirit. 2 CORINTHIANS 3:18

June

✝

June 1

THE 1734 NORTHAMPTON REVIVAL soon expanded throughout New England and the Northeast. What began as a local pastoral response to two tragic deaths spread to churches in Massachusetts, Connecticut, New York, and New Jersey. The revival even drew the attention of some British preachers and theologians, who came to witness it firsthand before going back to their own parishes.

But the showers of refreshing in this life often give way to seasons of regression. In the summer of 1735, Satan struck back in Northampton. He landed a notable target in Joseph Hawley II, a wealthy merchant in the town. Hawley excelled at numerous ventures: He had a sawmill, a boat, a large farm, and a store that sold household goods and even silk handkerchiefs. Hawley was a civic leader, having been elected townsman and town clerk more times than one could count. But there was a wildness in the Hawley family, a streak of melancholy and perhaps mental illness that afflicted numerous members. Jonathan Edwards later commented on this:

> In the latter part of May, it began to be very sensible that the Spirit
> of God was gradually withdrawing from us, and after this time Satan
> seemed to be more let loose, and raged in a dreadful manner. The first
> instance wherein it appeared, was a person putting an end to his own
> life by cutting his throat. He was a gentleman of more than common
> understanding, of strict morals, religious in his behavior, and a useful and
> honorable person in the town; but was of a family that are exceedingly
> prone to the disease of melancholy, and his mother was killed with it.[37]

The death of Joseph Hawley II effectively brought the firstfruits of revival to an end in Northampton. Deaths by suicide were reported in other locations as well, events which Edwards and others described as Satan's attacks on the extraordinary work of God. The Hawley tragedy took a heavy toll on Edwards, though he reasoned through it theologically. By the summer of 1735, his own health had deteriorated, and he left town for an extended trip to New York and New Jersey.

Hawley's son—Joseph Hawley III—later clashed with Edwards, and emerged as one of the principal leaders of the opposition in Northampton. The younger Hawley became a major political figure in Massachusetts, more eminent for a time than even John Adams, but he came to regret his role in Edwards's dismissal in 1750. Like his father and grandmother, Hawley struggled with depression and had a turbulent relationship with the church.

Moments like these in Edwards's life remind us that pain is never far off in this world, but the grace of God can strike suddenly and turn things upside down.

June 2

The wrath of God drove us out of paradise, but the grace of God invites us to return. The Son of God in the name of his Father comes and calls to us to return from our banishment; he ceases not to call us. He beseeches us to return again. He is come forth on purpose to make known those joyful tidings to us. Christ calls us away from this cursed ground, that brings forth briars and thorns, to a better country. Our first parents were driven away very loath and unwilling to go, but we are invited back again.

SERMONS AND DISCOURSES, 1730-1733

GROWING UP, many of us heard what C. S. Lewis and J. R. R. Tolkien used to call *fairy stories*. For Lewis and Tolkien, a fairy story was not a silly tale of make-believe, but a mythical exploration of the pain and beauty of the real world. Their stories, leading us into the worlds of Narnia and Middle-earth, made us long for a warrior king, an enchanted homeland, and a thrilling adventure. When we were young, the imaginative seemed within reach, mythical as it was.

The shocking news is that the fairy stories of our youth—and beyond—pale in comparison to the truth. The Christian faith is not drab and dreary. We are on a grand adventure with God. The stakes are impossibly high. The human race was driven "out of paradise," Jonathan Edwards tells us, but the Son of God has come as a deliverer, and to invite us back again. He destroyed the works of the devil by his death (1 John 3:8) and now leads us "to a better country" by the message of his Word.

Today, we need to remember who we are following. We are not following a passionless bureaucrat, but a warrior king. We are not bound for a listless loca-tion, but the new heavens and new earth. Our lives are not drained of purpose, but are brimming with holy potential. There is no greater adventure than this; there is no better story than the one we are living.

In Christ God was reconciling the world to himself, not counting their trespasses against them. 2 CORINTHIANS 5:19

June 3

Christ undertook to lead us to the tree of life, and he went before us. Christ himself was slain by that flaming [sword]; and this sword, having slain the Son of God appearing in our name, who was a person of infinite worthiness, that sword did full execution in that. And when it had shed the blood of Christ, it had done all its work, and so after that was removed. And Christ arising from the dead, being a divine person himself, went before us; and now the sword is removed, having done its execution, already having nothing more to do there, having slain Christ. There is no sword now, and the way is open and clear to eternal life for those that are in Christ.

SERMONS AND DISCOURSES, 1730-1733

LONG BEFORE THE BIBLE unveils the name and person of the Messiah, we hear God promise a Savior. After the Fall, the Lord speaks to the deceptive serpent, saying, "I will put enmity between you and the woman, and between your off-spring and her offspring; he shall bruise your head, and you shall bruise his heel" (Genesis 3:15). Scholars call this promise the *protoevangelium*, or "first gospel."

We note the vengeful nature of the woman's "offspring." He will not come in a spirit of peace. He comes to destroy the serpent. He comes to make war. Further, his victory is assured. The Lord does not give odds to the devil in the Garden. He perfectly foretells the serpent's future: doom and destruction. The devil will, however, strike his own blow in this apocalyptic death match, engineering Christ's crucifixion through wicked rulers and a hostile people.

None of this caught God off-balance. It was foretold that Jesus would come as a holy warrior to face down his foe. Genesis 3:15 charts what the New Testament Gospels show us. Christ, Jonathan Edwards says, "went before us." He suffered "execution," dying to honor the justice of God, represented so vividly as a "sword," a great and terrible weapon. But the way of Christ is not a way of defeat. In dying, the Son of God crushed the serpent's head. He rose from the dead. For believers, "there is no sword now," and eternal life awaits. The conquering hero will one day welcome us home, a liberated nation and a set-apart people.

For our sake he made him to be sin who knew no sin, so that in him we might become the righteousness of God.   2 CORINTHIANS 5:21

June 4

A selfish spirit is very unsuitable to the nature and state of mankind. He that is all for himself and none for his neighbors deserves to be cut off from the benefit of human society, and to be turned out among wild beasts, to subsist as well as he can. A private, niggardly spirit is more suitable for wolves and beasts of prey than for human beings. Loving our neighbor as ourselves is the sum of the moral law respecting our fellow creatures, and helping of them and contributing to their relief is the most natural expression of this love.

SERMONS AND DISCOURSES, 1730-1733

WE HAVE ALL EXPERIENCED times when we needed help but received none, or someone needed our help and we failed to give it. We met with a friend who could use serious encouragement, but we turned the conversation back to us. We heard a church member share a prayer request, but quickly allowed it to slip from our minds. We listened to someone tell us of hardship, only to laugh it off with a joke. We've all acted selfishly and let other people down.

Christianity declares war on selfishness. The Lord targets our inclination to look out for number one. He summons us to two—and only two—great commandments: to love him, and to love our neighbor (Matthew 22:34-39). That's it. All his teaching, he says, points to these two immutable principles. They are intertwined. We cannot bask in the overflowing kindness of our Sovereign and at the same time ignore our neighbor.

This is why Jonathan Edwards does not hold back in his sermon about a selfish spirit. He denounces the vice of selfishness in the strongest terms; the person who is "all for himself" deserves being "turned out among wild beasts." This pastoral word shows us the priority of charity in Christianity. This is true of our finances; it is also true of our time and attention. In the moment, helping others is often costly. But rest assured: The eternal reward will make the cost worth it.

You shall love your neighbor as yourself. MARK 12:31

June 5

You yourselves are not your own; 1 Corinthians 6:19–20, "Ye are not your own, for ye are bought with a price; your body and your spirit are his." And if you yourself are not your own, so then neither are your possessions your own. You have by covenant given up yourself and all you have to God; you have disclaimed and renounced any right in yourself, as in anything that you have, and given God all the absolute right. And if you are a true Christian, you have done it from your heart. Your money and your goods are not your own. They are only committed to you as stewards, to be improved for him who committed 'em to you; 1 Peter 4:9–10, "Use hospitality one to another without grudging. As every man hath received the gift, even so minister the same one to another, as good stewards of the manifold grace."

SERMONS AND DISCOURSES, 1730-1733

BELIEVING IN GOD makes all the difference when it comes to our possessions. In theological terms, if we know that everything we have is a gift from God, we are freed from anxiety regarding what we own. We may love our homes, our cars, and our clothes, but if we know that God has given them to us and that we cannot keep them eternally, we are freed to be generous.

In his pastoral ministry, Jonathan Edwards worked hard to help his people understand this reality. We need not fall prey to covetousness—of wanting more and more and more. Strangely, this is what often happens to the human heart. Gaining more wealth and possessions does not necessarily free us from the love of money. As we acquire more, we guard our possessions more jealously. It's a bitter and ironic development.

Selfishness with our money is not only a failing of the will; it is a misunderstanding of our identity. Here's the good news: The Lord loves to free fearful and stingy people from their shackles. We have the freedom to release our stranglehold on our possessions. Instead of being treasure hoarders, we can live as wise stewards of our money and our goods. Why should we live under the unpleasant fiction that we are lords of our own domain? We are not. Our bodies, our houses, and our bank accounts are the Lord's. Let us be who are we are freed to be, a wise and generous people.

Show hospitality to one another without grumbling. As each has received a gift, use it to serve one another, as good stewards of God's varied grace. I PETER 4:9-10

June 6

Resolved, never to count that a prayer, nor to let that pass as a prayer, nor that as a petition of a prayer, which is so made, that I cannot hope that God will answer it; nor that as a confession, which I cannot hope God will accept.

LETTERS AND PERSONAL WRITINGS

WE HAVE TREMENDOUS freedom in prayer. We have the model prayer taught to the disciples by Jesus (Matthew 6:9-13). We read numerous other prayers in Scripture. But we are not confined to a fixed outline of words. We are exhorted to "pray without ceasing" (1 Thessalonians 5:17). Yet as much as we have freedom, we also have direction in what we should pray about. Our prayer priorities should match the priorities of the New Testament.

This means that we should ask God to build his church, and to send the gospel to the ends of the earth (Matthew 28:16-20). We should pray that in our lives and in the ministry of the local church, Christ would be magnified. We want him to increase, and ourselves to decrease (John 3:30). We want our children to know the Lord, and we want to live holy lives before their watching eyes (Colossians 3:20-21). We pray for persecuted brothers and sisters and ask the Lord to give them faith, hope, and courage in their times of trial (Matthew 5:11-12). We want the glory of God to fill this realm; for it to cover the globe as the waters do (Habakkuk 2:14).

We could list more such matters for prayer. These are key areas of the faith and practice of God's people. We do not want to pray idly and glancingly; we do not want to center our prayers on ourselves, though we'll surely lift up many things we need to the Lord. Like Jonathan Edwards, our goal in our intercession is to offer that which we surely "hope that God will answer." God wants us to go to him about matters great and small; but it is sadly easy for us to pray about many things, and forget to ask God to grant that which he has promised he will give. We have great freedom in prayer. Let us pray without ceasing, and ask God to bring to pass what he has promised.

When they had prayed, the place in which they were gathered together was shaken, and they were all filled with the Holy Spirit and continued to speak the word of God with boldness.   ACTS 4:31

June 7

Consider that God tells us that he shall look upon what is done in charity to our neighbor that is in want as done unto Him, and what is denied unto them as denied unto Him; Proverbs 19:17, "He that hath pity upon the poor lendeth to the Lord." God has been pleased to make our needy neighbors his receivers. . . . In Matthew 25:40, there Christ says to the righteous on his right hand, who had supplied the wants of the needy, "in that ye have done it to one of the least of these my brethren, ye have done it unto me." In like manner, he says to the wicked, who had not shown mercy to the poor, "inasmuch as ye did it not to one of the least of these, ye did it not to me" (Matthew 25:45). . . . If Christ himself was here upon earth and dwelt amongst us in a frail body, as he once did, and was in calamitous and needy circumstances, should not we be willing to supply him? Should we be apt to excuse ourselves from helping him?

SERMONS AND DISCOURSES, 1730-1733

You MAY HAVE SEEN the TV show where CEOs go undercover in their own organizations to see how the company functions at ground level. The setup often involves an elaborate physical disguise, feigned ignorance of daily workplace tasks, and a surprise reveal at the end. "That bumbling worker you trained," the CEO informs the startled employee, "was me."

It turns out that Christianity has a surprise of its own. When we give to the poor, as Jonathan Edwards observes, we give to God. One of the major marks of true Christian faith is generosity to those in need. Giving out of the overflow of our resources to help a struggling neighbor is a sure sign that God has claimed not only our heart, but our wallet or purse as well.

It stuns us that Christ identifies not with the high and mighty, but with the poor and lowly. His teaching on charity is the ultimate "reveal." It upends our expectations and calls us to relax our grip on our money. As Edwards notes, it is the "righteous" who have "supplied the wants of the needy" and thereby ministered to God. This is not simply an opportunity for believers; it's a calling. With wisdom and discretion, let us find ways to give to the poor, to be stingy with the devil, and to be rich in good works (1 Timothy 6:17-19).

Whoever is generous to the poor lends to the LORD, and he will repay him for his deed. PROVERBS 19:17

June 8

Christ denied himself to help us, though we are not able to recompense him; so we should be willing to lay out ourselves to help our neighbor freely, expecting nothing again. Christ loved us, and was kind to us, and was willing to relieve us, though we were very hateful persons, of an evil disposition, not deserving any good, but deserving only to be hated, and treated with indignation; so we should be willing to be kind to those that are an ill sort of person, of a hateful disposition, and that are very undeserving. Christ loved us, and laid himself out to relieve us, though we were his enemies, hated him, had an ill spirit towards him, had treated him ill; so, as we would love Christ as he hath loved us, should {we love those who are our enemies, hate us, have an ill spirit toward us, and have treated us ill}.

SERMONS AND DISCOURSES, 1730-1733

IT ISN'T HARD to say that we're Christians. If we keep the definition vague, the shoe seems to fit. We go to church, do what we're supposed to do at work, and write a check once in a while to a worthy cause. With this low threshold, the faith doesn't seem all that challenging; it fits comfortably into a typical American lifestyle, and we experience little discomfort.

But when we dig into the priorities of true Christianity, that laxness seems woefully deficient. The standard of Christ is not simply to love people who love us back, or to love humanity in a general sense. The standard of Christ is to love our enemies, and pray for those who persecute us (Matthew 5:44). Such teachings present us with a major challenge. It's no easy thing to love someone who acts hatefully toward us. Our every instinct runs away from love in such situations.

Christianity brings about a quiet revolution in the human heart. One of its chief effects is to awaken a full range of compassion and kindness to the people we encounter. Faith grabs hold of the truly repentant, and upends us, making friends of those who once were enemies. "Christ loved us" when we "hated him." Now, God gives us the strength, the otherworldly ability, to emulate our Savior and love those who despise us. Few practices are more challenging—or more revealing of the authenticity of our faith.

If while we were enemies we were reconciled to God by the death of his Son, much more, now that we are reconciled, shall we be saved by his life. ROMANS 5:10

June 9

A true sense of the divine and superlative excellency of the things of religion; a real sense of the excellency of God, and Jesus Christ, and of the work of redemption, and the ways and works of God revealed in the gospel. There is a divine and superlative glory in these things; an excellency that is of a vastly higher kind, and more sublime nature, than in other things; a glory greatly distinguishing them from all that is earthly and temporal. He that is spiritually enlightened truly apprehends and sees it, or has a sense of it. He don't merely rationally believe that God is glorious, but he has a sense of the gloriousness of God in his heart. There is not only a rational belief that God is holy, and that holiness is a good thing; but there is a sense of the loveliness of God's holiness. There is not only a speculatively judging that God is gracious, but a sense how amiable God is upon that account; or a sense of the beauty of this divine attribute.
SERMONS AND DISCOURSES, 1730-1733

THERE IS NO SUCH THING as an indifferent angel. Throughout Scripture, we catch glimpses of the worship angels offer to God. They are not checking their watches as they worship the high and holy one. They fall on their faces; they cry out in praise; they thrill to be in God's presence. It's safe to say the angels *live* to worship God.

If there are no indifferent angels, there should be no such thing as an indifferent Christian. God has claimed us for his own; he has opened our eyes to his surpassing glory and greatness. Christ is our King. We know these truths rationally, but our knowledge goes deeper still. God gives us what Jonathan Edwards calls a "true sense" of his excellency and glory. This is what distinguishes nominal faith, faith in name only, from true and saving faith. Everyone can see that God is an exalted being. Only believers, however, can lay hold of the "true sense" of God, and thus delight in him.

The loveliness of God's character overpowers the indifference of our hearts. We value the world God has made, but we see in the Lord "a glory greatly distinguishing" him from everything else. Between God and his creation there is a massive gap. He is qualitatively greater than anything else, so great in fact that we can fairly say that nothing compares to him. No one can separate the Christian from God; no foe can take away the "true sense" of his beauty and worth. We have an access to God that the angels long to have, for we are given all the privileges of sonship in Christ (Galatians 4:1-6). We might fool ourselves at times, but with truths like these in mind, we cannot forget: There is no such thing as an indifferent Christian.

God, who said, "Let light shine out of darkness," has shone in our hearts to give the light of the knowledge of the glory of God in the face of Jesus Christ. 2 CORINTHIANS 4:6

June 10

The mind of man is naturally full of prejudices against the truth of divine things: it is full of enmity against the doctrines of the gospel; which is a disadvantage to those arguments that prove their truth, and causes them to lose their force upon the mind. But when a person has discovered to him the divine excellency of Christian doctrines, this destroys the enmity, removes those prejudices, and sanctifies the reason, and causes it to lie open to the force of arguments for their truth. Hence was the different effect that Christ's miracles had to convince the disciples, from what they had to convince the scribes and Pharisees. Not that they had a stronger reason, or had their reason more improved; but their reason was sanctified, and those blinding prejudices, that the scribes and Pharisees were under, were removed by the sense they had of the excellency of Christ, and his doctrine.

SERMONS AND DISCOURSES, 1730-1733

JESUS CHRIST IS THE STRANGEST figure of them all. When he came to earth, he proved that he was the Son of God. He did things no mere man could do. But to a surprising degree, people did not receive him. They did not welcome him. They did not even want him in their midst. The greatest man came to town, and no one seemed to realize it.

It's almost comical to read the Gospels and observe the responses to Jesus. Even though he heals the sick, raises the dead, and feeds the crowds, his deeds do not quiet objections, but fan them into a flame. We know why. The natural mind, as Jonathan Edwards points out, is "full of prejudices." In our unredeemed state, we are a seething collection of biases, just waiting to react. We hate God (Romans 8:7). We despise nothing more than "the truth of divine things." When confronted with this truth, whether in word or deed, we lash out. We refuse to believe.

Praise God that he doesn't leave us in the swamp of our suspicions. Through the Word, he opens our eyes to the "divine excellency of Christian doctrines." As we study Scripture, the scales fall off our eyes. Once captive to "blinding prejudices," we are now captivated by the blinding light of Christ. The Lord uses our minds in this spiritual revolution, but he also seizes our hearts for his own. As believers, we savor the truth taught by Jesus. But he is more than the sum of his teachings. He *embodies* truth in his very being, and so we follow him without question. He transcends our categories. He possesses spiritual power that we cannot deny, that grips us even now, and that the world glimpses but cannot comprehend.

This, the first of his signs, Jesus did at Cana in Galilee, and manifested his glory. And his disciples believed in him.   JOHN 2:11

June 11

When it is said that this light is given immediately by God, and not obtained by natural means, hereby is intended, that 'tis given by God without making use of any means that operate by their own power, or a natural force. God makes use of means; but 'tis not as mediate causes to produce this effect. There are not truly any second causes of it; but it is produced by God immediately. The Word of God is no proper cause of this effect: it don't operate by any natural force in it. . . . It conveys to our minds these and those doctrines; it is the cause of the notion of them in our heads, but not of the sense of the divine excellency of them in our hearts. . . . that notion that there is a Christ, and that Christ is holy and gracious, is conveyed to the mind by the Word of God: but the sense of the excellency of Christ by reason of that holiness and grace, is nevertheless immediately the work of the Holy Spirit.

SERMONS AND DISCOURSES, 1730-1733

THERE IS NO WORLD WITHOUT GOD. There is no salvation without Christ. And there is no faith without the Holy Spirit. The first two statements make good sense to us—but the third might sound odd. After all, we're told to "have faith" from many corners of our world today. I recall reading the counsel given to a struggling man by a former pastor: "Somehow it will all be okay," he said. This works out to a generic exhortation: "Have faith." Not faith in God—just faith in general.

How tragic such counsel is. As the church, we do not cling to "somehow" theology. We believe in "someone" theology. In other words, we have faith in God—immovable, unshakable faith—because of the Holy Spirit. The Spirit enables us to see the "excellency of Christ" and to trust God and his Word. Without the Spirit, we cannot know God, and we cannot taste true comfort. With the Spirit, we gain what Jonathan Edwards calls "the sense of the divine excellency." Said more simply: The Spirit opens our hearts to love God.

There is no rational way to gain this love. To know and love God, and to live a life of overcoming faith, we need the Holy Spirit. The good news is that we don't need to perform rituals to access the Spirit. He indwells all believers (1 Corinthians 3:16). Following our moment of first repentance, the Spirit resides in us, renews us, and gives us faith to trust God. We have hope because the Spirit gives us hope in God, and enables us to see that God is with us and for us, in the lean times and the harvest seasons, and no one can take God away from us.

God, who said, "Let light shine out of darkness," has shone in our hearts to give the light of the knowledge of the glory of God in the face of Jesus Christ. 2 CORINTHIANS 4:6

June 12

This doctrine may lead us to reflect on the goodness of God, that has so ordered it, that a saving evidence of the truth of the gospel is such, as is attainable by persons of mean capacities, and advantages, as well as those that are of the greatest parts and learning. If the evidence of the gospel depended only on history, and such reasonings as learned men only are capable of, it would be above the reach of far the greatest part of mankind. But persons, with but an ordinary degree of knowledge, are capable, without a long and subtile train of reasoning, to see the divine excellency of the things of religion: they are capable of being taught by the Spirit of God, as well as learned men. . . . And babes are as capable of knowing these things, as the wise and prudent; and they are often hid from these, when they are revealed to those; 1 Corinthians 1:26–27, "For ye see your calling, brethren, how that not many wise men, after the flesh, not many mighty, not many noble, are called. But God hath chosen the foolish things of the world."

SERMONS AND DISCOURSES, 1730-1733

IN OUR WORLD, wealth is concentrated in the hands of a few. Power belongs to a select group of political leaders. Fame skews to celebrities. Let's be honest: Most of us are not destined for great riches, great authority, or great popularity. The forecast for most people on this planet speaks of anonymity, hard work, and far less influence than we might desire.

But in the Kingdom of God, we are rich beyond reckoning. The spiritual resources available to us are not limited in any way. We do not need great ability, erudition, or intelligence to enjoy God; thriving Christians do not depend on a noble heritage, a vast financial portfolio, or a job in elite sectors of society. There need not even be a connection to godliness in our past. We may, without any religious background at all, "see the divine excellency" of God. All who place their faith in Christ, and repent of all their sin, learn wisdom from "the Spirit of God."

One cannot help but marvel at the dynamics of this spiritual kingdom. God has ordered it to stand out and stand apart from the worldly kingdom. There is much to slog through here on earth. We frequently face frustration from our lack of agency. It's hard enough to renew a driver's license, let alone clear away the more substantial hardships we encounter on a regular basis. But for the church, there is no impediment to knowing Christ, to treasuring God, to learning spiritual truths. Nothing is held back from us; nothing good is denied to the children of God; God withholds no part of himself from his church. Today, whatever difficulties you face, savor this truth: Your access to God is infinite, and the goodness of God is your portion and your strength.

Consider your calling, brothers: not many of you were wise according to worldly standards, not many were powerful, not many were of noble birth. But God chose what is foolish in the world to shame the wise; God chose what is weak in the world to shame the strong.

1 CORINTHIANS 1:26-27

June 13

Resolved, to strive to my utmost every week to be brought higher in religion, and to a higher exercise of grace, than I was the week before.
LETTERS AND PERSONAL WRITINGS

YOU ARE NEVER TOO OLD to keep working on your craft. I read a story some time ago about a 102-year-old woman who decided, late in her nineties, to finally complete a PhD she had started in the mid-1930s. As a Jew, this woman had been forced to flee Germany when the Nazis came to power. After working in the medical field for many years, she decided—decades later—that she would defend her thesis. So she did. At 102, she received a PhD from the University of Hamburg.

The story made international headlines, but it stands out to me as not just a curiosity, but as a metaphor for the Christian life. We never get to a place in our walk with Jesus where we cease to doggedly pursue him. As long as there is light in our eyes and breath in our lungs, we seek to know the Lord better and better. We think of the apostle Paul, who communed with his Savior while imprisoned in Rome, and was led by the Holy Spirit to write letter after letter to nascent churches throughout the Greco-Roman world. He could have given up the game; he could have sat back after an exhausting ministry career and waited for heaven. But he kept working, kept growing, and kept after that which mattered most.

So it is for every Christian. Not one of us gets to a point where, walking along a forest trail, we stop suddenly and exclaim, "That's it. I've got all the God I can ever gain. I'm full." No one ever *masters* God. We pursue him and pursue him, and learn more and more, and fight to obey, every hour we have.

Grow in the grace and knowledge of our Lord and Savior Jesus Christ. To him be the glory both now and to the day of eternity. Amen.
2 PETER 3:18

June 14

This is the most excellent and divine wisdom, that any creature is capable of. 'Tis more excellent than any human learning; 'tis far more excellent, than all the knowledge of the greatest philosophers, or statesmen. Yea, the least glimpse of the glory of God in the face of Christ doth more exalt and ennoble the soul, than all the knowledge of those that have the greatest speculative understanding in divinity, without grace. This knowledge has the most noble object that is, or can be, viz. the divine glory, and excellency of God, and Christ. The knowledge of these objects is that wherein consists the most excellent knowledge of the angels, yea, of God himself.

SERMONS AND DISCOURSES, 1730-1733

THE HUMAN MIND IS conditioned to crave wisdom. We are informational creatures, hungering after enlightenment. We read annotated entries on the meaning of song lyrics; we debate the intention of our favorite film director in a given scene; we hunt for nutritional facts that will unlock lasting health for our bodies; we parse the latest announcement from our hometown sports team. We constantly seek and take in information.

Our goal is often to acquire wisdom in our fields of interest. Yet for all our efforts, God has already given us the most important material we can imagine. The Bible is a feast of knowledge. It yields true enlightenment, for it educates us as it shapes our deeds. Even a quick encounter with divine wisdom can spark an overhaul of the way we think, talk, and act. Scripture, after all, targets the very depths of our being. God is not after a part of us; he wants our entire person.

The Christian mind vacuums up wisdom wherever it can be found. Coming to faith increases our curiosity, and in no way dampens it. This matters for our education, our engagement of the arts, our cooking, and yes, even our fandom. But our curiosity cannot terminate in these areas. Once given a taste for "divine wisdom," we crave more. Once we gain "the least glimpse" of divine glory, we yearn for more. This encounter with the wonders of wisdom is no one-time miracle. Every day affords us new opportunities to learn more about God, to watch as he transforms our thinking, and to practice holy wisdom.

If any of you lacks wisdom, let him ask God, who gives generously to all without reproach, and it will be given him.

JAMES 1:5

June 15

We ought not to be content with this world, or so to set our hearts on any enjoyments we have here as to rest in them. No, we ought to seek a better happiness. If we are surrounded with many outward enjoyments and things are comfortable to us; if we are settled in families and have those friends and relatives that are very desirable; if we have companions whose society is delightful to us; if we have children that are pleasant and likely, and in whom we see many promising qualifications, and live by good neighbors, and have much of the respect of others, have a good name and are generally beloved where we are known, and have comfortable and pleasant accommodations: yet we ought not to take up our rest in these things. We should not be willing to have these things for our portion, but should seek happiness in another world.
SERMONS AND DISCOURSES, 1730-1733

THE HUMAN HEART INCLINES toward stability. We want things nailed down. We want to be able to achieve equilibrium. Sure, we've had some past struggles. But now, in the present, they have ended. Now we can breathe deeply, rest up, and finally enjoy our surroundings. As one example of this mind-set, the vision of retirement that beckons to many of us promises us this lasting peace, and motivates many people during the long, hard hours of the week.

The problem is this: Nothing is bolted down in this life. We cannot finally lay hold of security and comfort on this earth. There is no once-for-all way to opt out of trials, challenges, and frustrations. Once our suffering ebbs, there is no guarantee it won't return. We want to believe that we're finally in the clear; we desperately want it to be true. We want our homes, families, careers, bodies, and communities to thrive. But as Jonathan Edwards reminds us, there is no ultimate "rest in these things."

Our happiness does not reside here. We "seek a better happiness," the happiness of another world. In our eternal home, no sudden jolt will destroy our peace. No market spasm will wipe out our inheritance. No illness will grip us or a loved one. In this better world, God is the "portion" of his people. He will not merely provide our happiness; he will *be* our happiness. He offers us rest, eternal rest, and he ensures by his own sovereign guardianship that we enjoy it.

There remains a Sabbath rest for the people of God, for whoever has entered God's rest has also rested from his works as God did from his.
HEBREWS 4:9-10

June 16

We ought to seek heaven by traveling in the way that leads thither. The way that leads to heaven is a way of holiness; we should choose and desire to travel thither in this way, and in no other. We should part with all those sins, those carnal appetites, that are as weights that will tend to hinder us in our traveling towards heaven, Hebrews 12:1, "let us lay aside every weight, and the sin that doth so easily beset us, and let us run with patience the race that is set before us." However pleasant any practice or the gratification of any appetite may be, we must lay it aside, cast it away, if it be any hindrance, any stumbling block, in the way to heaven.
SERMONS AND DISCOURSES, 1730-1733

PRIOR TO OUR CONVERSION, sin sometimes seemed like fun, at least from a distance. It enticed us. It promised us a garden of delights, and we believed it. Most people, of course, don't fully act on their appetites. Thankfully, due to the restraining influences of God's common grace, most sinners act on only a fraction of their base desires. But this does not stop the fallen heart from esteeming sin, worshiping ungodliness, and yearning to act on it.

For Christians, the spell that sin casts upon the human heart is broken. When Christ saves us, he unmasks sin. He shows us that sin is not what uplifts us; instead, every sin functions as a *weight* that eventually will send us crashing to the ground. As Jonathan Edwards observes, sin still may disguise itself as "pleasant" to us. But the Spirit's voice is stronger than the devil's whisper. We know the facts. We know that our "carnal appetites" do not satisfy us, but leave us doubled over in pain. We know that holiness, by contrast, is pure pleasure, and obedience to God is pure delight.

We need this mentality as we travel "the way that leads thither" to glory. When temptations arise, as they inevitably will, we need to remember their true nature. We want a greater pleasure, and a greater happiness, than sin can afford. Sin is not too big for us, too scary and awful; sin is too small for believers. The true pleasure-seeker craves holiness, knowing that God rewards those who seek him (Hebrews 11:6; 1 Peter 1:15-16). There is no greater gift or outcome than this. So, as temptations pop up today, we laugh at Satan's schemes. We give sin a wide berth. We keep on traveling the way to God, our faces scanning the horizon. We are on our way to something better, something lasting, something certain.

Since we are surrounded by so great a cloud of witnesses, let us also lay aside every weight, and sin which clings so closely, and let us run with endurance the race that is set before us. HEBREWS 12:1

June 17

How worthy is heaven, that your life should be wholly spent as a journey towards it. To what better purpose can you spend your life, whether you respect your duty or your interest? What better end can you propose to your journey than heaven? Here you are placed in this world, in this wilderness, and have you your choice given you, that you travel which way you please; and there is one way that leads to heaven. Now where can you direct your course better, than this way? What can you choose better for your journey's end? All men have some aim or other in living. Some mainly seek worldly things; they spend their days in the pursuit of those things. But is not heaven, where is fullness of joy, forever and ever, much more worthy to be sought by you?

SERMONS AND DISCOURSES, 1730-1733

"YOU ONLY LIVE ONCE." In recent years, this slogan—sometimes abbreviated YOLO—has become the cry of a generation. It signifies the desire of many to live without moral or social constraints. If your earthly existence is all you have, you should do whatever you want with the time you have left. If we extended the phrase, it might go something like this: "You only live once, so live for this earth."

We could propose a different version, couldn't we?

"You only live once—so live for heaven."

That's what Jonathan Edwards argues. There simply is no better way to live than to journey toward God. The narrow way, in other words, is not narrow in pleasures. It is not deprived of joy. The narrow way is the way that leads to "fullness of joy, forever and ever." If we live for God now, by the power of God, we gain everything. We become the richest and happiest people on earth.

Heaven, after all, not only lies in the future. It has broken into our day and age. We are presently saved, even as God will soon complete our salvation. We have rest from our labors, even as God will soon give us total and unceasing rest. We have come into the eternal city, even as God will soon remake the whole earth into the new Jerusalem. All this is already our possession, though the journey is not yet completed (Hebrews 4:1-11). We have nothing greater to live for than the Kingdom of Heaven. There is no better cause, no grander purpose. You only live once. Let us therefore live for heaven, not earth.

Everyone who has left houses or brothers or sisters or father or mother or children or lands, for my name's sake, will receive a hundredfold and will inherit eternal life. MATTHEW 19:29

June 18

How can you better apply your strength, and use your means, and spend your days, than in traveling in the road that leads to the everlasting enjoyment of God, to his glorious presence, to the city of the new Jerusalem, to the heavenly Mount Zion, where all your desires will be filled and [there is] no danger of ever losing your happiness? No man is at home in this world. Whether he chooses heaven or no, yet here he is but a transient person. Where can you choose your home better than in heaven? The rest and glory of heaven is so great that 'tis worthy that we should desire it above riches, above our fathers' houses or our own, above husbands, or wives, or children, or all earthly friends. It is worthy that we should subordinate these things to it, and that we should be ready cheerfully to part with them for heaven whenever God calls.

SERMONS AND DISCOURSES, 1730-1733

EVERYONE LEAVES THE EARTH with unfinished business. We strive, by God's grace, to do the best we can while we're here. We want to love our families; we want to serve our church; we want to work well in our vocations. Yet the fact is plain: We cannot bring all the disparate threads of our endeavors to perfect resolution. We cannot guarantee in our own strength and by our own name that our families, our church, our businesses will hold together after we depart the earth. In one way or another, we leave matters undone when we die.

This reality can easily unsettle us. We want our legacy, our lineage, our efforts, to be certain, fixed, so we might strain our bodies and hearts to that end, thinking we can bring things to resolution. But we can't. What freedom—tremendous freedom—there is in commending our feeble works to God, and leaving them in his hands. Christians, after all, do not operate under the delusion that we control our days. We strive to labor well here, but we are uniquely ready to depart this world to go to God.

What a difference this makes. The Holy Spirit is in the process of preparing us all to "cheerfully" slip the surly bonds of earth. We will not thrash against the will of God. We have *Christ-centered confidence*, knowing that God has ordered our days. In Christ, all things resolve. So we commend even our most cherished ones to him, knowing that our spouses, our children, our dearest friends are in his care. We leave unfinished business here—we all do. But we follow the one who will bring every molecule of the universe to its proper resolution. We do all things insufficiently; God does all things well.

They were astonished beyond measure, saying, "He has done all things well. He even makes the deaf hear and the mute speak." MARK 7:37

June 19

June 19, 1748: John Stoddard dies

MANY OF US HAVE lost loved ones. Some have lost several people they loved within months. The 1740s were such a season for Jonathan Edwards. After his daughter Jerusha died in February 1748, his uncle John Stoddard passed away in June. Stoddard was the son of Solomon Stoddard and for many years the chief justice of the court of common pleas for the county of Hampshire. He served as a military leader in Boston and was an intimate of Massachusetts governor Jonathan Belcher.

John Stoddard had long been a stalwart supporter of Jonathan Edwards. Historian George Marsden writes, "Probably no eighteenth-century clergyman in America sustained a closer relationship to so powerful a regional magistrate."[38] At some level, Edwards drew strength from the kind of righteous public leadership that Stoddard provided the colony. He was close to his uncle, and saw in him a picture of godly stability that made Massachusetts a unique place, one that could possibly be a light for all people.

Stoddard and Edwards saw eye to eye on theological issues, and during the controversy over the awakenings in the early 1740s, Stoddard defended his nephew's views in print. He also provided valuable counsel in pastoral situations that Edwards faced. Stoddard was one of the last links to the stable and supportive infrastructure that Edwards grew up in. He was a valuable help to Edwards as various elements threatened the stability of the Northampton church.

But every man or woman has a time limit on their usefulness. The Lord called Stoddard home, and Edwards was left with one less ally. Not long afterward, Edwards decided to challenge the longstanding practice of "open Communion" in his Northampton congregation. He believed that only those giving visible evidence of godliness should take the Lord's Supper. This development, along with the loss of Stoddard and several other events, put Edwards in a weak position. His bumpy situation reminds us that we have no easy protection against conflict and suffering in this life. Even the colony's most famous pastor could not forever forestall the conflict heading his way, one that led to his ouster from Northampton.

June 20

We should travel on as a way of obedience to all God's commands, even the difficult, as well as the easy, commands. We should travel on in a way of self-denial, denying all our sinful inclinations and interests. The way to heaven is ascending; we must be content to travel up hill, though it be hard, and tiresome, and contrary to the natural tendency and bias of our flesh, that tends downward to the earth. We should follow Christ in the path that he has gone; the way that he traveled in was the right way to heaven. We should take up our cross and follow him. We should travel along in the same way of meekness and lowliness of heart, in the same way of obedience, and charity, and diligence to do good, and patience under afflictions.
SERMONS AND DISCOURSES, 1730-1733

TWENTY YEARS AFTER MY FINAL cross-country practice, it is the hill runs I remember most. Many aspiring athletes face this toughest of endurance tests. A hill run is rather simple: You stand at the base of a small hill and think about almost anywhere you would rather be. You run up the hill and back down again. Then you do it again, and again, and again, until you collapse on the ground, ruing the day you signed up for the glory of youth sports.

But the silver lining of hill running is this: There is no undertaking that strengthens the body and mind more than charging up a mound of dirt. The exercise is as much mental as it is physical. If you can execute the task, and do it over and over, you will gain mastery over your weakness. You will silence your excuses. Even if you're sore afterward, you will marvel at the effect of your persistence. You fought the mountain and won.

Such discipline applies to the Christian walk as well. The narrow way is not generally a downhill trot. Often, as Jonathan Edwards suggests, "we must be content to travel up hill." We must persevere. We must fight for character. We must pray for discipline. We must "take up our cross and follow" Christ. There is nothing easy about this. It is not always fun. But spiritual hill running is always worth it. Killing sin, returning daily to the Word and prayer, curbing our temper, speaking up courageously—we do not practice these virtues by accident. As we climb, we remember that we are not alone. The one who traveled this road before is with us now, having won the prize and finished the race. Our strength is not in ourselves; it is in him.

Since we are surrounded by so great a cloud of witnesses, let us also lay aside every weight, and sin which clings so closely, and let us run with endurance the race that is set before us. HEBREWS 12:1

June 21

It profits us not to have any knowledge of the law of God, unless it be either to fit us for the glad tidings of the gospel, or to be a means of our sanctification in Christ Jesus, and to influence us to serve God through Christ by an evangelical obedience. And therefore we stand in the greatest necessity of a divine revelation. And it was most fit and proper that, when God did give us a revelation—Christ—that it should not only contain those peculiar truths which purely and in every respect depend on revelation, as the doctrines of Christ's mediation and justification through him, but that this revelation should contain everything that belongs to divinity, either to be known or practiced. For it all depends on revelation, in the way in which it is necessary for us to know it.
THE "MISCELLANIES"

CHRISTIANS POSSESS A GIFT that is almost unfathomable in its greatness. We know the mind of God. Through the agency of the Holy Spirit, we have come to trust Scripture. We see it as a lamp to our feet and a light to our path. As Jonathan Edwards says, we are able to know "everything that belongs to divinity, either to be known or practiced." There is nothing, in other words, that we lack as we pursue the knowledge of God. All that our Maker wants us to have, we have.

We may not have heard a great deal about the doctrine of biblical sufficiency. We actually sometimes hear more about the insufficiency, or perhaps the inadequacy, of the Word of God. *The Bible addresses some topics*, some would contend, *but it doesn't touch on the ones we need for it to handle.* In some instances, we turn to a mystical approach to the faith, and expect God to speak from the sky in direct response to our questions. In others, we grow angry at the Lord for leaving us in this unfair predicament.

Neither approach breeds healthy Christianity. Both intellectually and spiritually, we need to believe in the doctrine of biblical sufficiency. Like the New Testament, the Old Testament was written for our instruction in the faith (Romans 15:4). The details of our personal situations will take time to iron out, but we have what we most need. The Scripture reveals Christ, and Christ is not a part-time Savior, or an absentee Lord. He is our sovereign, our ruler, and in him we have all the riches of God, and all we need for godly living today. Let us go to him, and go to his Word, and drink deeply of everything that belongs to him.

In him all the fullness of God was pleased to dwell, and through him to reconcile to himself all things, whether on earth or in heaven, making peace by the blood of his cross. COLOSSIANS 1:19-20

June 22

IN JUNE 1750, America's most famous pastor—then and now—was fired by his church. It is a matter that even today, nearly 270 years later, still shocks the eye.

There were several factors in play. Jonathan Edwards had fought a long battle over his salary with the leaders of the First Church. The "bad book" incident had not been well resolved. Most significantly, Edwards had attempted to tweak the membership and Communion practices of the church, unsettling many who preferred Solomon Stoddard's more open practices. Under Stoddard one did not necessarily have to be converted to join the church and take Communion. Edwards wanted to change this, having grown more and more uneasy over the years with a congregation that seemed to include both saints and the religiously interested (though not converted). In truth, the mixed nature of the Northampton congregation caused Edwards terrific headaches.

Jonathan Edwards, it should be noted, was a superlative theologian, but not the best administrator. He sometimes went heavy where a gentler touch might have helped; he sometimes took controversies public that might have been better resolved in quiet. But even if Edwards had handled all matters before him with perfect grace, his congregation did not agree with his vision of the church as an assembly of saints only. Stoddard had taught them differently, and even twenty years after his death, he cast a long shadow.

The innovation that so entangled Stoddard in debate, the Halfway Covenant, ended up ending the pastoral career of his grandson in Northampton. After Edwards tried to change the church's membership policies in late 1748, the church committee broke with him. Edwards, they decided, could not present his views to the people. His changes were rejected. On June 22, Edwards was dismissed from the church, with only 10 percent of the congregation voting to keep him. He preached his last sermon as pastor of Northampton on July 1. America's most eminent pastor was out of a job.

This sorry affair shows us two things. First, the doctrine of the church matters greatly. The way the church is set up, though sometimes downplayed in evangelical circles, has tremendous import. Second, no one is immune to embarrassment in this world. Less than a decade prior, Edwards had hailed Northampton in print as evidence of a global outbreak of Christianity. Now he was jobless. His example commends humility to us even as it reminds us to cling to God, who truly is our one stable possession in this life.

June 23

The obedience of Christ excels all others, because . . . the works or acts [that] was required of him by the law that he was under, and that he performed, were superlatively excellent, for it was a work of the highest love to God and love to creatures, and he in this work exercised a love to both immensely excelling all others, which gave an exceeding value to the work in the eyes of the Father.

THE "MISCELLANIES"

GOD WANTS US TO OBEY HIM. Obedience is not optional for believers (John 14:15). This means we should always choose to honor God rather than pleasing men. We will not always hear the clamor of applause when we obey the Lord. Obedience, in fact, could come at a terrible cost to us, and even to our loved ones. In many countries in the world, Christians face tough and even deadly consequences for sharing their faith in accordance with the great commission (Matthew 28:16-20).

Yet God does not desire weary, trudging obedience. He wants us to emulate his Son, who laid down his life for the joy set before him (Hebrews 12:1-2). The death of Jesus on the cross was not only a righteous step on his part. His crucifixion was "a work of the highest love," in the words of Jonathan Edwards. In obeying the will of God, Christ loved his Father. In making atonement for the sins of a fallen race, Christ loved sinners like us. There is no other love like this; it is the greatest act of love imaginable.

We are not called to make atonement for our sins—praise God—for we cannot do so. We are, however, summoned to the same way of love as our Savior (John 13:34-35). We are united to Christ, and because of him, we can call God *Father* and not foe (Romans 8:15). It is not a slavish, fearful commitment that drives our efforts to obey our heavenly Father. It is love and joy that propel us onward. We seek the good of our neighbor, just as Christ instructed us, as we strive to honor our Father. God is eager to reward his faithful servants. Knowing this, and recalling the example of Jesus, enables us to count every momentary problem as nothing in comparison to the reward of obeying God.

I have come down from heaven, not to do my own will but the will of him who sent me.   JOHN 6:38

June 24

Flesh, i.e. corruption, is by the first birth, but the Spirit or grace and holiness is by the second birth; and as all corruption is by the first birth, so the mortifying of that corruption, and all the restoration of holiness or the Spirit, is by the new birth. The new birth in Scripture is represented as a new creation, but the whole work of sanctification, in the whole progress, is a work of creation. In every step and degree of that restoration, something is brought out of nothing, and there is the very same almighty, creating power needed and exerted, as there is in the first beginning of this work on the soul.

THE "MISCELLANIES"

THE CHURCH CELEBRATES the conversion of sinners. What a joyous occasion it is when unbelievers repent of their evil ways and turn to follow Christ. We have a name for these stories of coming to faith: We call them *testimonies*. For those who love God, the narrative of redemption never grows old. It is always uplifting to hear how the Spirit has regenerated a lost soul.

In truth, the Spirit's work doesn't stop with the moment of conversion. Testimonies don't stop at salvation. Scripture doesn't teach that we hit our spiritual pinnacle when we are freshly born again. Instead, the Bible presents our Christian walk in terms of a lifelong call to holiness (Colossians 3:1-11). We become "a new creation" when God saves us, but his work in us will continue for the rest of our days—decades for many of us. We are given holy status by our conversion, but we are made progressively holy as God carries out our sanctification.

This reality reframes our truncated understanding of the Christian life. We need God to move in us for redemption, but also for every aspect of our growth in godliness. It is grace that saves us and grace that grows us. God's active love drives "every step and degree" of our ongoing "restoration," as Jonathan Edwards sums it up. Something living and vital is wrought from what formerly suffered decay. Habits are overcome. Speech patterns are overhauled. Poor thinking is renewed. We are given spiritual life by God's lavish kindness, and that same favor prunes us like thriving plants to bring us to full spiritual health. It is right to share our testimonies of our new birth; it is equally right to tell the marvelous story of our ongoing sanctification in Jesus.

If then you have been raised with Christ, seek the things that are above, where Christ is, seated at the right hand of God. Set your minds on things that are above, not on things that are on earth. For you have died, and your life is hidden with Christ in God. COLOSSIANS 3:1-3

June 25

When we speak of God's happiness, the account that we are wont to give of it is that God is infinitely happy in the enjoyment of himself, in perfectly beholding and infinitely loving, and rejoicing in, his own essence and perfections. And accordingly it must be supposed that God perpetually and eternally has a most perfect idea of himself, as it were an exact image and representation of himself ever before him and in actual view. And from hence arises a most pure and perfect energy in the Godhead, which is the divine love, complacence and joy.

WRITINGS ON THE TRINITY, GRACE, AND FAITH

It's NOT UNCOMMON TO HEAR people encourage one another by saying things like, "You're perfect just the way you are." We understand the statement, and we're grateful for a little encouragement where we can find it. But though we may not realize it in the moment, this statement is incorrect. There is only one being who is perfect. Despite the flattering look of those new shoes, we are not flawless.

God is the only one who is perfect. There is no flaw in him, no sin, and thus he deserves our total adoration. It would be a bit weird if we said of ourselves to others, "I'm extremely happy in my enjoyment of myself." We are not like God; we do not have his "essence and perfections," as Edwards instructs us. But God is God. As such, he would err if he failed to find infinite satisfaction in his own perfection. Instead, he lives and always has lived in pure celebration of all his greatness.

Knowing the character of God reframes our spiritual life. God is whole and pure; we are not. He is divine, and infinite, and holy. He deserves worship, not us or any other fallen person. Nothing in this world, however much we may appreciate it, qualifies as God; we dare not worship the creation, the human body, the mind, the scientific accomplishments of humanity, athletes, celebrities, or anything other than God. It is the perfect character of God that causes us to find total and unceasing happiness in him. We are never more like God than when we love, and rejoice in his essence and perfections.

Behold, I am the LORD, the God of all flesh. Is anything too hard for me? JEREMIAH 32:27

June 26

The things of divinity are things of superlative excellency, and are worthy that all should make a business of endeavoring to grow in the knowledge of them. There are no things so worthy to be known as these things. They are as much above those things which are treated of in other sciences, as heaven is above the earth. God himself, the eternal Three in One, is the chief object of this science; in the next place, Jesus Christ, as God-man and Mediator, and the glorious work of redemption, the most glorious work that ever was wrought; then the great things of the heavenly world, the glorious and eternal inheritance purchased by Christ, and promised in the gospel; the work of the Holy Spirit of God on the hearts of men; our duty to God, and the way in which we ourselves may become like angels, and like God himself in our measure: all these are objects of this science.
SERMONS AND DISCOURSES, 1739-1742

AT MANY COLLEGES and universities today, it isn't easy to find a course on Christianity. It was not always so. Many schools were founded for the purpose of promoting the Christian faith and training preachers of the gospel. In most cases, "the things of divinity" were not the only subjects of the school; the sciences, mathematics, literature, philosophy, and other disciplines received significant attention. But during the nineteenth century, the curriculum flipped. By the twentieth century, the study of God at many schools was an afterthought.

Jonathan Edwards valued many fields of inquiry. He read voraciously in a wide range of subjects. Yet he knew that not all knowledge deserved equal billing. The things of divinity called not only for awareness, but also for adoration and application. What a unique approach to learning this seems in our day of spiritual inattention. The Trinity, Christ, redemption, heaven—these are not dry and dusty matters. Doctrine is captivating. The study of God and his works is the most compelling field there is.

No believer is barred from learning what Edwards referred to as "this science." Secular universities may have moved on from the great questions of faith, but we need not. No one is holding us back from learning about God. We have every chance to study the Word and to drink deeply of its delicious truth. Devoting ourselves to the things of divinity, the study of God, will not weaken or intellectualize our walk with Jesus. Knowing God always brings personal transformation, and always foments living worship. The school of Christ is never closed, and it accepts all repentant students.

Though by this time you ought to be teachers, you need someone
to teach you again the basic principles of the oracles of God.
HEBREWS 5:12

June 27

Resolved, to be strictly and firmly faithful to my trust, that . . . Proverbs 20:6, "A faithful man who can find?" may not be partly fulfilled in me.
LETTERS AND PERSONAL WRITINGS

SEVERAL YEARS AGO, Evites were all the rage. Perhaps what stood out most about Evites was the "Maybe" option in response to an invitation. This was revolutionary. You didn't have to commit either way. You sent back neither a hard no nor an unnuanced yes. You were in the middle, and that was a comfortable place to be.

We're currently in a "maybe" age. We struggle to commit to things, whether huge or inconsequential. All communication seems open-ended; there is little need to leave on time, for example, when you can simply text your friend, "On my way!" as you begin final preparations. Your "timely" message provides cover for the fact that you're now going to arrive twenty minutes after you said you would. But though we all act inconsiderately at times, as Christians we have a higher call. We want to be faithful men and women of God. We want to be faithful in loving God; we want to be faithful in showing respect to our friends.

A "maybe" age is a great time to grow into a "yes or no" individual. Long before Evites, Jonathan Edwards had this desire. He yearned to be "strictly and firmly faithful" in all that he promised. In an informal age, manners and basic courtesies seem unimportant. We tell ourselves that it's the general direction of the heart that matters. But here's the rub: basic courtesies speak to broader commitments. The way we treat people reveals what we really think about them. It is tough to find a faithful friend, and always has been. Through Christ, we can be that friend to others.

Let what you say be simply "Yes" or "No"; anything more than this comes from evil. MATTHEW 5:37

June 28

The things of divinity not only concern ministers, but are of infinite importance to all Christians. . . . They are about those things which relate to every man's eternal salvation and happiness. The common people cannot say, "Let us leave these matters to ministers and divines; let them dispute them out among themselves as they can; they concern not us," for they are of infinite importance to every man. Those doctrines which relate to the essence, attributes, and subsistencies of God, concern all; as it is of infinite importance to common people, as well as to ministers, to know what kind of being God is. For he is the Being who hath made us all, "in whom we live, and move, and have our being"; who is the Lord of all; the Being to whom we are all accountable; is the last end of our being, and the only fountain of our happiness.
SERMONS AND DISCOURSES, 1739-1742

THERE IS NOTHING MORE practical than the study of God. The study of God produces the worship of God. It is impossible for a true Christian to delve deeply into the works and mind of God and not be affected. There is a marvelous connection here. The great truths of Scripture fire our souls and foster love for the Almighty.

In order to worship God well, we must learn doctrine. This doesn't necessarily mean we must obtain a theological degree (though that is not a bad thing). Nor does it mean we must enroll ourselves in formal classes or training courses. It does mean, however, that every believer should at the very least ponder and treasure "the things of divinity," as Jonathan Edwards calls them. Theology is not to arm us for debate; theology is for the study of God and for worship.

Too many Christians have come to believe that theology only breeds controversy. That as we begin taking in biblical teaching, we must be careful lest we ignite disagreements within the church. For certain, we must all guard our hearts. But theology will not waylay godly people. The knowledge of God is of "infinite importance." It renews our minds. It focuses us on ultimate reality. It calls us to live differently in light of what we have investigated. Theology does not center on learning a storehouse of facts, after all, but in drawing near to the God who made us and redeemed us. Theology leads to worship, and worship pleases the Lord. Let us begin to learn Christian doctrine and never stop.

You are good and do good; teach me your statutes. PSALM 119:68

June 29

The same may be said of the doctrines which relate to the manner of a sinner's justification, or the way in which he becomes interested in the mediation of Christ. They equally concern all; for all stand in equal necessity of justification before God. That eternal condemnation, to which we are all naturally exposed, is equally dreadful. So with respect to those doctrines of divinity, which relate to the work of the Spirit of God on the heart, in the application of redemption in our effectual calling and sanctification, all are equally concerned in them. There is no doctrine of divinity whatever, which doth not some way or other concern the eternal interest of every Christian. None of the things which God hath taught us in his Word are needless speculations, or trivial matters; all of them are indeed important points.
SERMONS AND DISCOURSES, 1739-1742

IF YOU ENTER A CONVERSATION over a debated doctrinal point, you may hear folks say, "This area isn't really a major deal, is it? We can agree to disagree." We should all practice a spirit of humility when we discuss and debate; we have all witnessed the sad effects of an ungracious, unyielding temperament. Yet we should also take care that we do not rank the teaching of the Word of God. We should not downplay doctrine. All God's truth is precious; all God's truth is relevant.

The sentiment expressed above is not new in Christian circles. Jonathan Edwards heard it in his day just as we do in ours. He labored to help his church understand that disagreements over doctrine do not demand that we turn off our brains. Instead, we should eagerly and attentively search for understanding. Christians have debated the finer points of justification, effectual calling, and sanctification for centuries, even millennia. But this fact does not render such matters *trivial* or *needless*. Where the Word of God speaks, we hearken. We study. We learn. Where necessary—and this will prove applicable for us all—we correct our thinking per the Bible's guidance (and often a friend's influence).

Edwards says it well: "There is no doctrine of divinity whatever" that is a waste of time. Every attempt to study God is an attempt to draw nearer to him. The Lord does not desire indifferent Christians; Christ did not die to purchase a disinterested church. God wants us to worship him in spirit and in truth (John 4:24). Sadly, we will not always agree with one another in this life. But we must not cease to seek the Lord. Doctrine is for life.

Give me life according to your word! PSALM 119:25

June 30

However diligently we apply ourselves, there is room enough to increase our knowledge in divine truth, without coming to an end. None have this excuse to make for not diligently applying themselves to gain knowledge in divinity, that they know all already; nor can they make this excuse, that they have no need diligently to apply themselves, in order to know all that is to be known. None can excuse themselves for want of business in which to employ themselves. There is room enough to employ ourselves forever in this divine science, with the utmost application. Those who have applied themselves most closely, have studied the longest, and have made the greatest attainments in this knowledge, know but little of what is to be known. The subject is inexhaustible.

SERMONS AND DISCOURSES, 1739-1742

DURING OUR GROWING-UP YEARS, it may take a while for global geography to sink in. As children, we may have struggled to understand the concept of a round earth. Children sometimes worry about falling off the edge of the earth if they venture too far. We can't blame them; after all, the earth beneath their feet *seems* flat, and they've all seen a flat map, and it has edges.

But just as there is no point at which we arrive at the ends of the earth, neither is there an end to God and our study of God. We will never reach a point where there is nothing more to learn or understand about him. We will never be justified in thinking, *I have zeroed in on the Lord, and I can honestly say I don't need to think about him for a while.* No, his attributes are inexhaustible; we will never come to the end of our learning about his character and nature. We will always want more of him; we will always be right to "diligently apply" ourselves to the gaining of wisdom and the increase of knowledge.

Sometimes, we believers might act as if we have gained everything we need to know about God. After reading Scripture for years, we might think we have gotten what we need out of the Bible. But the Scripture is a limitless book. Those who engage it will find that there is always "room enough to increase our knowledge in divine truth." May we all pray for God to increase our hunger for deeper, richer Bible teaching. May we all recommit ourselves to the "divine science." This discipline, unlike any other, repays the diligent.

Great is the LORD, and greatly to be praised, and his greatness is unsearchable. PSALM 145:3

July

†

July 1

THE MOST SHOCKING EVENT in Jonathan Edwards's life was his firing from the church in Northampton in 1750. Equally as shocking, perhaps, was the fact that he filled the Northampton pulpit for another year after his dismissal. Though Edwards had no obligation to continue, he was asked by the church's committee to preach throughout 1750 and into 1751. It wasn't until a group of discontented church members voted not to invite him anymore that Edwards finally vacated the pulpit. Apparently, the people would rather have no preaching at all than listen any longer to their former pastor.

One can only imagine the humiliation, pain, and confusion that Edwards must have felt. He was forty-six years old, with a large family still to provide for, and he had lived in Northampton for more than two decades. He was easily the town's most prominent figure, yet now he was out of work. He eventually accepted a call to Stockbridge, Massachusetts, on the western frontier of the colony, but Stockbridge was not an easy place to minister.

In his formal "farewell" sermon on July 1, 1750 (before anyone knew that many more awkward months of supply-preaching would follow), Edwards left the congregation on a hair-raising note. Pastor and people, he argued, would meet again:

> Having briefly mentioned these important articles of advice, nothing
> remains; but that I now take my leave of you, and bid you all farewell;
> wishing and praying for your best prosperity. I would now commend
> your immortal souls to him, who formerly committed them to me;
> expecting the day, when I must meet you again before him, who is the
> Judge of quick and dead. I desire that I may never forget this people,
> who have been so long my special charge, and that I may never cease
> fervently to pray for your prosperity. May God bless you with a faithful
> pastor, one that is well acquainted with his mind and will, thoroughly
> warning sinners, wisely and skillfully searching professors, and
> conducting you in the way to eternal blessedness.[39]

Thus began a year of uncertainty in the life of Jonathan Edwards. Though his own weaknesses factored into his dismissal, Edwards tried to handle his humiliation in a God-honoring way. We will all find ourselves in challenging circumstances; how will we respond?

July 2

Be assiduous in reading the holy Scriptures. This is the fountain whence all knowledge in divinity must be derived. Therefore let not this treasure lie by you neglected. Every man of common understanding who can read, may, if he please, become well acquainted with the Scriptures. And what an excellent attainment would this be! . . . When you read, observe what you read. Observe how things come in. Take notice of the drift of the discourse, and compare one scripture with another. For the Scripture, by the harmony of the different parts of it, casts great light upon itself. We are expressly directed by Christ, to "search the scriptures," which evidently intends something more than a mere cursory reading.
SERMONS AND DISCOURSES, 1739-1742

WHEN MAPPING DIRECTIONS to a destination, an alternate route often presents itself. This new possibility triggers a range of questions: Is this path more scenic? What will traffic be like? Is this route worth the extra two minutes of travel time? Some of us might do better with just one option!

Thankfully, when it comes to our sanctification—our growth in godliness—we have only one route: the Bible. Nowhere else will we find the very wisdom of God laid out for us. Like a compass on a wilderness trail, Scripture points us continually to Christ. But while we may discover our Savior and Lord in the pages of the Bible, we should not misunderstand God's holy Word. Though the core message is easy enough to understand, the Scriptures are not simplistic. It takes work to comprehend the intelligence of God. We need to be "assiduous" in studying it.

Jonathan Edwards's love for the Bible encourages us. It is not always easy to find the horsepower necessary to dive into the Word on a daily basis. We might feel sluggish as we begin. But searching the Scriptures always rewards our efforts. As we grow in our understanding of the Word, we begin to see connections we never glimpsed before. The parts emerge as a musical "harmony," and our faith is stretched and strengthened as we read portions of Scripture we have not previously explored. God bids us to come to the waters of life not merely for a sip, but to drink, and drink deeply, from his wellspring of wisdom.

His delight is in the law of the LORD, and on his law he meditates day and night. PSALM 1:2

July 3

As to the acts in which this virtue exerts itself: in one word, it is in pursuing the glory of God. 'Tis not all holy fervency of spirit that is properly intended by zeal, but it is a holy fervor of mind as it relates to practice only, or the pursuit of the glory of God, as those things that are well-pleasing to him. And therefore 'tis a being "zealous of good works," as the expression is in the text. . . . But 'tis love with respect to that exercise of it that there is in pursuing his glory that is called zeal. . . . So the hatred of sin and the jealousy for God's honor that is properly comprehended in zeal is exercised in opposing sin and that which is opposite to God's glory. So the courage and fortitude that is in zeal relates to action, that action that is in pursuing God's glory.

SERMONS AND DISCOURSES, 1739-1742

WE HAVE ALL HEARD the term *religious extremists*. Though at times it is used rightly, we should ponder what it communicates about religion itself. It suggests there is grave danger in taking spiritual things too seriously. If we ramp up our interest in the things of God, we place ourselves on a highway to danger—and even damage to ourselves and others. Better then, in the thinking of our culture, to dampen our religious conviction. Lukewarm tolerance is thought wiser than intense devotion in our era.

The problem with many of the conflicts motivated by so-called religious extremists is not generally their zeal, but their wrongheaded thinking. It isn't wrong, in other words, to be zealous; it's wrong to be zealous toward the wrong ends. It is right to have what Jonathan Edwards calls a "holy fervency of spirit" for God and his glory. In fact, if we come away from a biblical encounter with God and do not feel passion for the divine, we should ask if something is wrong with us.

The Spirit produces in believers a panoply of virtues: love, joy, peace, patience, and more. The fruit of the Spirit thus creates balanced Christians. But all our pursuit of God depends on zeal. The magnificence of our Redeemer summons love, and love creates action. We should eagerly kill our sin. We should passionately speak of God to unbelievers. We should joyfully serve our local churches. We should display "courage and fortitude" as witnesses for Christ. The Spirit does not make us religious wackos. But the Spirit does create believers who cannot be restrained from loving God, telling of God, and living for God.

Our great God and Savior Jesus Christ . . . gave himself for us to
redeem us from all lawlessness and to purify for himself a people for
his own possession who are zealous for good works. TITUS 2:13-14

July 4

Everything that is lovely in God is in him, and everything that is or can be lovely in any man is in him: for he is man as well as God, and he is the holiest, meekest, most humble, and everyway the most excellent man that ever was. He is the delight of heaven. There is nothing in heaven, that glorious world, that is brighter and more amiable and lovely than Christ. And this darling of heaven, by becoming man, became as a plant or flower springing out of the earth; and he is the most lovely flower that ever was seen in this world. Canticles 2:1—there 'tis said of Christ, "I am the rose of Sharon, and lily of the valleys."
SERMONS AND DISCOURSES, 1739-1742

FEW THINGS IN LIFE are more refreshing than a leader who wears his or her title lightly. I read a story recently about the queen of England. Apparently, every once in a while, she goes for a stroll in the area near the royal palace in London. She dresses in ordinary clothes and calls no attention to herself. Occasionally, people have even asked her if she's ever seen the queen!

Unfortunately, such lack of pretense is in short supply today. Our sinful hearts struggle to embrace humility. Most people need no coaching on "Ways to Maximize Your Pride." Narcissism comes naturally to us. Yet we have a bracing antidote—the person and work of Jesus Christ. Jesus truly had reason to feel superior to his neighbors and associates. He's the Son of God, after all. Others around him thought they were great; yet it was Jesus who created the universe. Others thought they were impressive; yet Jesus communed directly with the Father. But for all his inherent awesomeness, Jesus exuded a lowly spirit. He was, as Jonathan Edwards identifies, "the holiest, meekest, most humble" person that ever lived.

What a rebuke this is to us. When our thoughts run to ourselves and our self-sufficiency, we need to dwell afresh on Christ. We want a lowly spirit like his. We should cry out to God to make us holy like him, meek like him, and humble like him. We remember the order of the Kingdom of Heaven: It is the lowly who inherit the earth. No one has ever ridden into the throne room of God on the wave of pride that surges in every human heart. Only the humble and the weak will see the Lord. Let us root out our pride with intensity. We may or may not see the queen of England, but we will soon see the King of all creation.

The sacrifices of God are a broken spirit; a broken and contrite heart, O God, you will not despise. PSALM 51:17

July 5

The wrath of God is like great waters that are dammed for the present; they increase more and more, and rise higher and higher, till an outlet is given, and the longer the stream is stopped, the more rapid and mighty is its course, when once it is let loose. . . . There is nothing but the mere pleasure of God that holds the waters back that are unwilling to be stopped, and press hard to go forward; if God should only withdraw his hand from the floodgate, it would immediately fly open, and the fiery floods of the fierceness and wrath of God would rush forth with inconceivable fury, and would come upon you with omnipotent power; and if your strength were ten thousand times greater than it is, yea, ten thousand times greater than the strength of the stoutest, sturdiest devil in hell, it would be nothing to withstand or endure it.

SERMONS AND DISCOURSES, 1739-1742

MOST PEOPLE WHO SEEK an uplifting start to their day do not immediately turn to passages of Scripture that threaten judgment. I recall preaching at a church years ago and meeting with the other leaders before the service to go over the liturgy. For the Old Testament reading, I had selected a text that spoke of judgment, and a staff member voiced concern. A passage on divine wrath, he said, was not comforting. It was a topic he clearly thought best to avoid.

The Bible, though, doesn't sidestep the issue of God's hatred of sin. Scripture presents God as burning with anger against sin. Wrath is not an attribute of God; it is the exercise of his divine justice in a sinful world. But God is glorified in the exercise of vengeance for sin. He is not a toothless deity somewhere up in the sky. The Lord is holy to the core. Sin cannot come into his presence. Evil cannot exist alongside him. He is a God of perfect love, and he is a God of perfect justice. We praise his name for both of these attributes.

We rightly feel fear and wrenching sorrow at the prospect of judgment on people we love. Like Jonathan Edwards, we should feel compelled by the prospect of God's "omnipotent power" destroying the wicked to tell unbelievers the truth. We may feel hesitant to talk about God's wrath. We may think that people will only respond to the comforting parts of biblical doctrine. But this is not true. God uses the reality of divine judgment to compel sinners to take their plight seriously. Our duty is not to edit the Bible; our duty is to tell the truth and show fellow sinners that Jesus has taken God's judgment on our behalf.

Vengeance is mine, and recompense, for the time when their foot shall slip; for the day of their calamity is at hand, and their doom comes swiftly. DEUTERONOMY 32:35

July 6

O sinner! Consider the fearful danger you are in: 'tis a great furnace of wrath, a wide and bottomless pit, full of the fire of wrath, that you are held over in the hand of that God, whose wrath is provoked and incensed as much against you as against many of the damned in hell; you hang by a slender thread, with the flames of divine wrath flashing about it, and ready every moment to singe it, and burn it asunder; and you have no interest in any mediator, and nothing to lay hold of to save yourself, nothing to keep off the flames of wrath, nothing of your own, nothing that you ever have done, nothing that you can do, to induce God to spare you one moment.
SERMONS AND DISCOURSES, 1739-1742

WE DO NOT INSTINCTIVELY savor judgment. We might even feel guilty as modern-day Christians for continuing to believe that God everlastingly punishes the wicked. Such a conviction sounds medieval; it doesn't seem to fit with our kinder and gentler sensibilities. We may feel pressure, therefore, to soften our doctrine and play down its rougher edges.

But here's the reality behind the wrath of God: No criminal escapes the deserved sentence. All get their due. This concept makes sense to the human heart. We groan when we hear of evil dictators successfully fleeing justice. We are left speechless when a politician jumps back into office after ruining his or her family. We ache when we learn of white-collar crimes that leave ordinary people without their hard-earned savings. In each of these instances, our conscience points us to the truth. It is wrong for the guilty to avoid justice. It is abominable when the wicked go free.

Praise God that he doesn't fail to uphold his divine standard. God is not lax. He is not asleep. The unrighteous may slip the bonds of earthly justice, but no one outruns God. Unrepentant sinners, despite what they may want to believe, are not going to be okay. They "hang by a slender thread" over the "bottomless pit." They have no salvific ability in themselves; they stand condemned before God. We do not pray for their destruction; we pray for their rescue. We know they are in "fearful danger," and only the Lord can save them. Though in this life we may see a glaring lack of moral balance, in the life to come, we will praise God for calling all people to account, and not allowing the guilty to go free.

The vision awaits its appointed time; it hastens to the end—it will not lie. If it seems slow, wait for it; it will surely come; it will not delay.
HABAKKUK 2:3

July 7

You have reason to wonder, that you are not already in hell. 'Tis doubtless the case of some that heretofore you have seen and known, that never deserved hell more than you, and that heretofore appeared as likely to have been now alive as you: their case is past all hope; they are crying in extreme misery and perfect despair; but here you are in the land of the living, and in the house of God, and have an opportunity to obtain salvation. What would not those poor damned, hopeless souls give for one day's such opportunity as you now enjoy!

SERMONS AND DISCOURSES, 1739-1742

WE WILL NEVER FIND ourselves in a place of justified ingratitude to God. If the Lord has saved us, we have cause to praise him. Every day that we live gives us recurring "reason to wonder" why God has made us his own, even as so many just like us, who deserve to go to hell just as we do, turn away from him. We will never fully plumb the depths of this truth. God leaves us in *wonder*, as Jonathan Edwards phrases it.

We have no claim on God's mercy. Yet in the wisdom of our Maker, we find ourselves as "new creation[s]. The old has passed away; behold, the new has come" (2 Corinthians 5:17). For the rest of our lives, following this grand remaking, we will shake our heads in awe at God's mercy. We are like those saved by a heroic lifeguard at the beach. One minute, we are drowning; the next minute, we're on dry ground. No one can snatch us away from safety.

Thinking about damnation is not an exercise in defeatism for Christians. If we forget what we are saved from, we will surely forget the miraculous nature of our salvation. Christianity does not begin with a life-improvement program; Christianity begins in smoldering ruins, as God lifts us out of the pit, the smell of smoke still clinging to our clothes. Today, we should meditate on our deliverance. We may face trials of many kinds, but we have infinite reasons for gratitude to God.

We . . . were by nature children of wrath, like the rest of mankind. But God, being rich in mercy, because of the great love with which he loved us, even when we were dead in our trespasses, made us alive together with Christ. EPHESIANS 2:3-5

July 8

July 8, 1741: Preaches sermon titled "Sinners in the Hands of an Angry God"

THE MOST FAMOUS SERMON in American history—and probably all of extrabiblical history—was not preached in an urban pulpit. It was not delivered in one of the Top 100 Fastest-Growing Churches. It was not heard by thousands of people. It was delivered by Jonathan Edwards to a small congregation in minuscule Enfield, Massachusetts (later Connecticut). One of the most-read messages ever was delivered by a pulpit-supply preacher in the New England countryside.

"Sinners in the Hands of an Angry God" fits in with one strand of Edwards's preaching: his attempt to awaken sinners by alerting them to the sure and certain dangers of hell. Though Edwards preached sermons on many other topics, his rhetoric rarely reached greater heights of eloquence than in "Sinners." Nearly three hundred years later, the prose still crackles:

> Your wickedness makes you as it were heavy as lead, and to tend downwards with great weight and pressure towards hell; and if God should let you go, you would immediately sink and swiftly descend and plunge into the bottomless gulf, and your healthy constitution, and your own care and prudence, and best contrivance, and all your righteousness, would have no more influence to uphold you and keep you out of hell, than a spider's web would have to stop a falling rock. Were it not that so is the sovereign pleasure of God, the earth would not bear you one moment; for you are a burden to it; the creation groans with you; the creature is made subject to the bondage of your corruption, not willingly; the sun don't willingly shine upon you to give you light to serve sin and Satan; the earth don't willingly yield her increase to satisfy your lusts; nor is it willingly a stage for your wickedness to be acted upon; the air don't willingly serve you for breath to maintain the flame of life in your vitals, while you spend your life in the service of God's enemies. God's creatures are good, and were made for men to serve God with, and don't willingly subserve to any other purpose, and groan when they are abused to purposes so directly contrary to their nature and end. And the world would spew you out, were it not for the sovereign hand of him who hath subjected it in hope.[40]

When the Enfield congregation heard this message, many cried out in terror, and implored Edwards to show them the way to Christ. He did, and when he repreached the sermon, more were converted. (This despite the fact that when Edwards had delivered the same sermon in Northampton in June 1741, it had no visible effect on his people.)

So it was that Enfield, and Edwards, made history. Much like the ministry of a much greater preacher, a man from Nazareth, one could scarcely imagine spiritual impact coming from a less likely place than Enfield. But the providence of God knows no restraint and observes no man-made laws. We do well to remember this truth in our time, and with regard to our lives.

July 9

Be sensible you are not out of danger of the devil and a corrupt and deceitful heart, even in your highest flights and best frames. It is a great mistake [to think] that there no danger of going astray because God is near you. Indeed, there is great encouragement in it that you shall be succeeded in a way of vigilance and circumspection. But to think that even then you han't need of the greatest watch and care, and are not in great danger without it, is presumption. 'Tis a presumption by which many herein have been woefully answered.

SERMONS AND DISCOURSES, 1739-1742

MANY AN ATHLETIC COACH could tell you that the most dangerous time in a game is when your team has a comfortable lead. Senses that were sharp grow dull; players take chances they normally wouldn't try; intensity wanes as the feeling of inevitable victory dawns. Often, the other team, bristling with embarrassment, mounts a comeback. In a fair number of games, the comeback falls short, but not before it leaves everyone feeling unsettled.

A similar principle applies to the Christian life. When it seems we have found equilibrium; when we have cleared the brush from our lives and finally reached a place of rest and health, we're prone to think, *Surely, now we will finally taste the lasting victory and peace we have sought for so long.* And it may even prove true—for a while. But as Jonathan Edwards cautions his people, we must take care in our "highest flights and best frames." We have a diligent foe who seeks our undoing. We cannot ever coast with regard to our familiar sins. We must always, in this life, practice "vigilance and circumspection."

This need not lead us to a defeatist, gloomy brand of faith. But it should balance us and keep us ever ready. In a much greater way than any athlete, the soldier at war knows never to grow soft while deployed. The battle may die down for a spell, even a lengthy season, bringing great refreshment. But we cannot lose our wartime mentality (2 Corinthians 10:3-6). We post guard against the flesh; we keep a watch out for the devil's temptations; we do not allow ourselves to grow spiritually lax.

As it is said, "Today, if you hear his voice, do not harden your hearts as in the rebellion." HEBREWS 3:15

July 10

Nothing is more hateful and abominable, nothing so contrary to the spirit of the gospel. [Pride is] the sin of the devils. Nothing is so pernicious in its consequences. The Spirit is very often quenched by it. 'Tis frequently the means of persons' losing the comfortable presence of God. In some that have been exalted high, the consequences have been most woeful. The devil commonly comes in at the door in all the delusions that zealous persons are led away with. . . . Therefore strive that you may be kept humble. Persons are never so safe as when kept truly humble and dependent, [as] little children. [And they are] never so much in danger as when spiritual pride rules.

SERMONS AND DISCOURSES, 1739-1742

THE IRONY OF THE Kingdom of God is rich: If we wish to be exalted, we must become humble. This is the pathway to true greatness. Exaltation does not lie in flattery, behind-the-scenes maneuvering, burnishing our image, elite public relations management, or any other form of human strategy. The way of the Lord is different from the way of the world. If we would emulate Jesus, we will not seek the right-hand seat among the power brokers. Instead, we take on the role of a servant.

Humility is also our greatest defense against the devil. Satan's primary strategy does not consist of poking us with a cartoon pitchfork, or making us think there are ghosts in the attic. Instead he looks for ways to entice us to forget the Lord. This is particularly true when we are "exalted high," as Jonathan Edwards points out; it is then that spiritual warfare grows very intense indeed. This internal battle need not have sound effects or creepy voiceovers, though; it centers in our moment-by-moment decisions. Will we glory in our excellent abilities? Will we celebrate our achievements as owing to our own efforts? Or will we acknowledge what God has done, thank him for his kindness, and give him all the praise?

The sharpest testing of our character comes in opposite experiences: the worst times and the best times. In calamity or in triumph, there are two ways to live. Will we live for ourselves, and allow pride to rule our hearts? Or will we live for God, and "strive" for humility, thinking of ourselves as "little children" before the Lord? Whatever our station, let us seek the humble role of the servant.

God opposes the proud but gives grace to the humble.   JAMES 4:6

July 11

Resolved, to ask myself at the end of every day, week, month and year, wherein I could possibly in any respect have done better.
LETTERS AND PERSONAL WRITINGS

No two believers are the same, of course, but I've noticed a difference between some younger Christians and some veteran Christians. The younger group is aware of their sin; they can still taste a little bit of the poison it emptied into their system. They hate sin and are restless to identify it and put it to death.

As we go along in our faith, we can slip into thinking that all is well. And yet our spirituality never goes much below surface level. We don't talk much about the things of God; we assume them. We don't work on our marriages to strengthen them; we simply float along. We don't strategize for spiritual growth and theological learning; we are content with what we have.

However long we've been Christians, we need to press on. We need to persevere in the faith. Like Jonathan Edwards, we should regularly take stock of how "in any respect" we can improve our character. We should ask fellow church members how we can grow in grace. We should inquire of friends and family members to discover our character flaws and address them. We should especially pray that God would expose our sin and help us to change by his Spirit's power. In all seasons, we want to avoid taking the Christian faith for granted, and see it as a precious, undeserved gift from Almighty God.

Let us test and examine our ways, and return to the Lord!
LAMENTATIONS 3:40

July 12

Without a revelation now extant, or once extant, having some remaining influence by tradition, men would undoubtedly forever be at a loss what God expects from us and what we may expect from him; what we are to depend upon as to our concern with God, and what ground we are to go upon in our conduct and proceedings that relate to him; what end we are to aim at, and what rule we are to be directed by, and what good and what harm is to be expected from a right or wrong conduct. Yea, without a revelation, men would be greatly at a loss concerning God, what he is, what manner of being, whether properly intelligent and willing, a being that has will and design, maintaining a proper, intelligent, voluntary dominion over the world.
THE "MISCELLANIES"

CHRISTIANS START THEIR WITNESS to unbelievers from this point: God is knowable. He has made the world. By his Word, his finished and perfect revelation, we may know who our heavenly Father is, and what he wants from us. What a gift it is to know the will of God. Even those who do not study Scripture have revelation from God, both in Creation and in their hearts (Romans 1–2). They can plainly see the power and wisdom of God displayed in the earth; they know God's moral standard through their conscience, the divine law written on their hearts.

All humanity lives some version of the God-designed life. We cannot help but do so. Even the most hardened atheist depends on the laws of gravity to walk to the grocery store. The college student who believes that the universe is chaotic relies on God-guaranteed order as he drives down the road. The scientist who teaches in her classroom that humanity is an evolutionary accident, and thus there is no greater moral code or reason to love others, feels love when she holds her newborn child. The wisdom and power and design of God are not hidden. The world points in one direction: to him.

What explosive joy this truth should prompt in the Christian heart. We do not take divine ownership and rulership for granted. We *love* the providence of God. We know that God works all things according to the counsel of his holy, perfect will. We have a heavenly Father. We are not lost in the cosmos. God is knowable. We know him, and he is bringing his perfect will to pass.

As I passed along and observed the objects of your worship, I found also an altar with this inscription: "To the unknown god." What therefore you worship as unknown, this I proclaim to you. The God who made the world and everything in it, being Lord of heaven and earth . . . gives to all mankind life and breath and everything. ACTS 17:23-25

July 13

Conversation between God and mankind in this world is maintained by God's word on his part, and prayer on ours. By the former he speaks to us and expresses his mind to us; by the latter we speak to him and express our minds to him. Sincere and a suitable high friendship towards God, in all that believe God to be properly an intelligent, willing being, does most apparently, directly and strongly incline to pray. And it no less disposes the heart strongly to desire to have our infinitely glorious and gracious friend expressing his mind to us by his word, that we may hear it.

THE "MISCELLANIES"

WE SOMETIMES HEAR prayer described as "talking with God." This definition begs for further explanation: How exactly do we talk with God? Does he communicate with us through audible words? Will he give us impressions in our hearts in response to our prayers? Will he cause our eyes to fall on just the right text at just the right moment?

Prayer need not be confusing for us. Jesus taught his disciples to pray, and we are instructed to pray likewise (Matthew 6:9-13). We need not feel pressure to invent some new way to petition God; we already have the Son of God's direction. But still we wonder: How does he communicate with us in prayer? Jonathan Edwards's answer is this: God drives us deeper and deeper into his Word. This is essentially what Jesus promised his band of disciples (John 16:12-15). They would not read the Bible like a dusty legal code; they would receive God's Word as true, living, and applicable.

Edwards's summation helps us remember the gift of the Word of God, and the privilege of prayer. The Word really is a lamp to our feet and a light to our paths (Psalm 119:105). As we give God our adoration, petitions, requests, and heart groanings, the Spirit opens our eyes to see wondrous things in the Scripture. It isn't that prayer will usually yield a direct response, like a voice from the clouds. It's that prayer draws us nearer to God. The Spirit illumines God's sufficient revelation. We gain wisdom, and thus humbly step forward in faith. In all this, we have "a suitable high friendship" with God. He ministers to us, and as we talk with him, our eyes are opened and our hearts are filled.

Open my eyes, that I may behold wondrous things out of your law.
PSALM 119:18

July 14

God saw it necessary that a Mediator should be provided in order to man's salvation, because it was not proper that a sinner should be united to God without a Mediator. It was necessary that the Mediator should die for sinners. And if the sinner was saved on his account, it was not possible that that cup should pass from him, because propriety required it. So God will not bestow the benefits of the Mediator on them that are not united to him, because there is no propriety in it. It is not proper that they should have communion with Christ who have no union with him.

THE "MISCELLANIES"

I RECENTLY HEARD a story about a Texas Ranger called in to stop a riot in a remote town. When he arrived in the town, he was greeted by the mayor. The mayor, having expected a whole group of lawmen, looked disappointed and said, "Just one Ranger?" The Ranger nodded and replied, "Just one riot."

This story reminds me of the human predicament. We have just one major problem: sin. For this terrible problem, God has provided just what we need: Jesus Christ. As Jonathan Edwards says, Christ is the Mediator appointed by the Father to "die for sinners." Outside of Jesus, we have no other rescue, no other hope. But Christ does not offer us an unfinished salvation. He did not come to earth, make atonement for sin, and leave the rest up to someone else. Jesus has united himself to us; we have "union with him."

How grateful we should be that Jesus gives us ongoing communion with him. If we did not have this vital connection with him by faith, we would wander alone in this world, waiting for heaven without help or assistance. Praise God that Christ promised us the Holy Spirit, who seals the bond we have with our Savior. We are not alone. Christ is ours, and he never withholds himself from us. We have a sin problem, but Jesus does not tire of our fighting it. He gives us daily strength to overcome our besetting unrighteousness. We have just one problem and just one solution—but Jesus is all we need.

There is one God, and there is one mediator between God and men,
the man Christ Jesus.

I TIMOTHY 2:5

July 15

If you trust in God, you shall be delivered from all evil, and you shall dwell in God's secret hiding place, and be safe under the shadow of his wings. And he will deliver you from the snare of the fowler. You need not be afraid of the terror by night, nor of the arrows that flieth by day. You shall, through Christ's strength, be able to quench the fiery darts of the devil. God will give his angels charge concerning you, to keep you from evil. And you shall have Satan subdued under your feet. You shall tread upon the lion and adder, and trample the young lion and the dragon under feet.

SERMONS AND DISCOURSES, 1734-1738

WE READ THE GRAND narratives of the Old Testament and feel inspired. What a mighty work the Lord did through Joseph! How wonderfully did he work through Esther to save the Jews! How gracious of him to call the dreaded Ninevites to repentance despite Jonah's reluctance to take the message to them.

But what about us? We don't have ancient kings to face down, but we have scary health issues. We have relational challenges that have not resolved. We bear scars from the past that we don't tell others about, but that plague us on a daily basis. Most people have battles like these, but we tend to downplay such matters, bearing them alone. In doing so, we can end up forgetting that God is Lord of the small as well as the big. He rules and rescues his people in dramatic ways; he helps and strengthens us in the quiet moments of life.

We must never forget that God is the hiding place of every Christian. This is as true of the tired carpenter or the weary mother as it is of the missionary facing persecution. The same God watches over all his people. No one is left exposed and unprotected. We are all safely hidden under God's wing. It is as true today as it was in ancient times.

Fear not, for I am with you; be not dismayed, for I am your God; I will strengthen you, I will help you, I will uphold you with my righteous right hand. ISAIAH 41:10

July 16

If the torments of hell are to last a very long time, ages of ages, the torments of the sinners of [the] old world till the end of the world and after that, so long that the time is often and almost constantly represented figuratively as everlasting, lasting forever and ever, then it must be because sinners in hell all this while are obstinate and, though they [are] free agents as to this matter, yet willfully and perversely refuse even under such great means to repent, forsake their sins and turn to God. . . . Though they feel the dreadful effects of it and know that they must be continued many ages under them if they refuse, yet they resolutely go on in their strong and desperate enmity and opposition.

THE "MISCELLANIES"

WE WILL NOT TASTE the eternal torments of hell. What a comfort this is; what a summons to daily thankfulness to God. We should not forget, however, that we are tempted to grow "obstinate" toward God. The hostility that unrepentant unbelievers harbor toward the Lord—an anger that continues in hell, as Jonathan Edwards argues—may flare up in our own hearts. Confronted with a pattern of sin, we may resist our friend's rebuke; made aware by the Holy Spirit of a need to apologize, we may forgo the opportunity.

For this reason, we need to remember how evil such stubbornness is. But for the grace of God, we would give full vent to this hard-heartedness. We would follow our angry instincts all the way to damnation. We have within us still the power to undo ourselves. We could blow up our marriages, lose our children, sow discord in our churches, compromise our testimony among unbelieving friends, and worse. We carry within us the seeds of our own earthly destruction.

How we should praise God for the strength of his grace. He is not a weak savior. He has gotten hold of willful, perverse creatures like us, and he has turned us around. We will not suffer in hell. The power of our "strong and desperate enmity" to our Creator is broken by Christ. We must still fight the hardness of our hearts as believers, but we need not fear the forcefulness of sin. Hell cannot claim us. Grace is stronger. God is greater.

You were dead in the trespasses and sins in which you once walked, following the course of this world, following the prince of the power of the air, the spirit that is now at work in the sons of disobedience.

EPHESIANS 2:1-2

July 17

The Levitical priesthood lasted long, but finally gave place to that of Christ. But Christ gives place to no other, is not to be succeeded by another sacrifice by which the damned that have rejected this shall at last be saved. For by the oath of God he is a priest forever. He hath an everlasting priesthood. 'Tis plainly implied in Hebrews 8 that God, finding fault with the ancient priesthood and sacrifices, removed 'em, as not making anything perfect, not completing the designs of God's holiness, wisdom and grace, to make way for the priesthood and sacrifice of Christ, which he finds no fault with, and by which perfection is arrived at, and which therefore God establishes with a design never to remove it or introduce any other, but that this should continue forever as an unchangeable priesthood.
THE "MISCELLANIES"

WHAT A MIRACLE THE incarnation of Jesus Christ is. Jesus took on human form. We could think about this truth for the rest of our lives and never exhaust its depths. Jesus, the very image of God and true Son, came to bring the promises of God to fulfillment. As the great High Priest, he brought to an end the sacrificial system that formerly guided the people of God. In this role, he offered the ultimate sacrifice for sin, bringing to an end the practice of slaughtering bulls and goats to signal the remission of iniquity.

Jesus will never leave this role. He is our eternal High Priest. God will never "remove" this priest, nor will he "introduce any other" in the age to come. The finality of Christ's work leads us to rest in him. We need to obey the Lord, but we have no responsibility for adding to the finished work of Christ. Nothing hangs in the balance; no accounts remain open. God sent the perfect sacrifice for sin, and in so doing completed the line of priests with Christ.

We are left to marvel at the "perfection" of this offering. We have freedom from guilt, from the need to justify ourselves, from the desire to look good in front of others. What more could we want? What more could anyone give us? Jesus' work is so final, so perfect and complete, that it suffices for all eternity. Jesus is the Temple (John 2:19). Jesus is the perfect sacrifice for the sins of the world (1 John 2:2). Jesus is our great High Priest (Hebrews 7:25). All that remains for us to do in the wake of his coming is to savor Jesus and walk as he walked.

When Christ had offered for all time a single sacrifice for sins,
he sat down at the right hand of God. HEBREWS 10:12

July 18

JONATHAN EDWARDS GREW UP under Congregationalist pastors who saw themselves fighting three major threats to sound doctrine: Roman Catholicism, Anglicanism, and Arminianism. The first controversy of Edwards's young life came when Yale rector Timothy Cutler defected to Anglicanism, taking several protégés with him. When an Anglican cleric named George Berkeley secured a large gift of books for Yale, Puritan concerns about the school increased.

Edwards himself did not hesitate to enter the roiling contest of doctrine. On July 8, 1731, he traveled to Boston to deliver a lecture entitled "God Glorified in Man's Dependence." In this lecture, he defended Calvinism against the Arminian system that he saw spreading across New England. Edwards did not mince words. Reading his lecture in a high-tenor voice, he left little doubt where he stood:

> Man was dependent on the power of God in his first estate, but he is more dependent on that power now; he needs God's power to do more things for him, and he depends on a more wonderful exercise of his power. It was an effect of the power of God to make men holy at the first; but more remarkably so now, because there is a great deal of opposition and difficulty in the way. 'Tis a more glorious effect of power to make that holy that was so depraved and under the dominion of sin than to confer holiness on that which before had nothing of the contrary. 'Tis a more glorious work of power to rescue a soul out of the hands of the devil, and from the powers of darkness, and to bring it into a state of salvation, than to confer holiness where there was no prepossession or opposition; *Luke 11:21–22*, "When a strong man armed keepeth his palace, his goods are in peace; but when a stronger man than he shall come upon him, and overcome him, he taketh from him all his armor wherein he trusted, and divideth his spoils."[41]

This lecture marked a turning point in Edwards's career. The Boston clergy quickly saw that Solomon Stoddard's grandson had the familial gifting and vigor. The blood of the fathers ran strong in the next generation.

Edwards's lecture was published in due course, helping to catapult the young preacher (then only twenty-seven) into colonial prominence. Though Edwards loved the daily work of the ministry, his trip to Boston shows that he did not dodge controversy by softening his stances. He held his doctrine firmly and preached it strongly. He leaves us a model to follow in loving and standing boldly for the truth.

July 19

Drawing men to Christ is the fruit of his being lifted up on the cross. Christ buys or redeems men that they may be his. He redeems 'em from their sins, from all iniquity, that he may purify them to himself, a peculiar people zealous of good works. They are redeemed from their vain conversation by the precious blood of Christ. And 'tis by conversion, by faith, that men become actually his, come to him, and are brought into his possession. God, in giving them faith, brings them to him and gives 'em to him, and they give themselves to him. He purchases his spouse that he may present her to himself.

THE "MISCELLANIES"

THE ATONEMENT DOES NOT make salvation possible. When Christ died on the cross, he did not merely give us his best shot. He didn't make a good faith gesture and hope things would turn out. He didn't leave an offering of love and pine for us to take it. We cannot view the Cross as Jesus' doing all he could to save us but without the actual power and ability to buy us back from the dead.

The Atonement does not make salvation *possible*; it makes salvation *actual*. As Jonathan Edwards notes, the "precious blood of Christ" has covered the sin of his "spouse," the collection of redeemed sinners known as the church. We are "redeemed" in full by his work on the cross. We were in the worst state, the most desperate of circumstances; we had no hope, and no agency to spring ourselves from our miserable state. We were on our way to execution when Jesus suddenly intervened. He bought us for himself. He made us his own. He didn't offer only the *possibility* of redemption; with a strong hand and a sure voice, he called us to himself, and we came.

When we think and sing of the Cross, we should know that our sin was canceled there, and our debts were removed (Colossians 2:13-15). There, the bride was washed (Ephesians 5:25-27). God effects and seals our salvation when he gives us faith to trust in the atonement of Christ—this is when we "become actually his," as Edwards makes clear. Ours is a sure and certain salvation.

Husbands, love your wives, as Christ loved the church and gave himself up for her, that he might sanctify her, having cleansed her by the washing of water with the word. EPHESIANS 5:25-26

July 20

God, in justifying a sinner by faith, looks on him as the sinner by that act of faith looks on himself, for doubtless there is an agreement between the act of God in justifying and the act of the person which God requires in order to his justification. But in the act of that faith which God requires in order to a sinner's justification, he looks on himself wholly as a sinner, or ungodly. He has no consideration of any goodness or holiness of his own in that affair, but merely and only the righteousness of Christ. And thus he seeks justification of himself, as in himself ungodly and unrighteous, by the righteousness of another.
THE "MISCELLANIES"

ONE OF THE STRONGEST DESIRES we feel is the urge to justify ourselves. When trouble breaks out, trouble we have caused, we declare our good intentions. We wound people with our words and then say that we "didn't mean" to hurt them. Perhaps we throw in an explanation about why our mood was sour.

We are finite creatures, it is true. But the doctrine of justification frees us from this kind of excuse making. We need not soften our shortcomings; we should not explain away our sins. We know at a theological level that God sees us accurately, after all. He has not saved us because we are virtuous—not even a little bit. He hasn't looked into our hearts and found a residue of righteousness. He has saved us on the basis of the pure, spotless "righteousness of Christ," and Christ alone. When conversion strikes in the human heart, we do nothing more than agree with God about our need for salvation. Christ is pure; we are not. We desperately need "the righteousness of another," as Jonathan Edwards puts it.

This high-level doctrine matters tremendously for everyday Christianity. Though redeemed and justified by Jesus, we still slip into our old habits. We know we shouldn't excuse our unrighteousness; God has shown us this in our personal miracle, our deliverance from death. But if we are not careful, we will edit our apologies and tweak our confessions. When we observe our hearts sliding in this way, we should return to the doctrine we love. The excuses have ended. True repentance can begin.

> I have suffered the loss of all things . . . in order that I may gain Christ
> and be found in him, not having a righteousness of my own that
> comes from the law, but that which comes through faith in Christ, the
> righteousness from God that depends on faith. PHILIPPIANS 3:8-9

July 21

The glory of God in our justification is greatly secured and advanced by these two things: 1. that our justifying righteousness is the righteousness of God, the righteousness not of an human but a divine person, so that a divine person is the author of it and the value of it arises from the dignity of the divine nature; and 2. as the very bond of union, by which we are united to this divine person so as to be interested in his righteousness, is that principle and act of the soul by which we know that the righteousness is thus the righteousness, and by which we cordially and with all our hearts ascribe it wholly to him and give him all the glory of it.
THE "MISCELLANIES"

GOD RELENTLESSLY PURSUES his glory. He does this throughout our lives. Conversion comes only from the Lord, and he gets all the glory. But his involvement with those he has redeemed never diminishes. All our righteousness and every good deed we perform is given to us by God. Whenever we obey the Lord as we should, we never take the credit for ourselves. Every virtuous act, every time of prayer, every act of service stems from God, and accrues to God. He is the righteous one, and he is the one who gives us his righteousness in Christ.

In this way, we see that the Christian life really and truly is about God, not about us. There is never a point in our walk with him that we start to deserve some credit. We cannot call God, make an appointment, and hash out with him the terms of glorification. "Yes, Lord, you saved me, and that was great—fantastic, really—but I'm wondering if now I could get some of the renown. Could we maybe think about a 70/30 split? 60/40? Please know I still want you to be the main stakeholder here."

When we find ourselves slipping into this mind-set, we need to go back to basics. We have not earned our righteousness; we have not generated it. God has reckoned us righteous in Christ; he has imputed all Christ's goodness to us. The Holy Spirit, who lives in the justified, produces fruit in us. This is why all the virtues of Christ are called the fruit of the Spirit. How kind of God to work in us all our days to make us glorious in his sight. Truly, this is not our own doing. It is all of God, and because it is all of God, it is all for God.

> Worthy is the Lamb who was slain, to receive power and wealth and wisdom and might and honor and glory and blessing!
> REVELATION 5:12

July 22

Christ, when he institutes the Lord's Supper, speaks of his blood as that which was shed for the remission of their sins (compare Luke 22:19–20 and Matthew 26:28). Christ tells his disciples that, if he washed them not, they had no part with him, and tells them that they were clean, excepting Judas (John 13:8, John 13:10–11). Christ declares himself their friend, and teaches 'em to call his Father their Father, and declares that the Father had received him already to favor, and was ready to answer their prayers because they had loved him and believed in him, and tells 'em that he gives 'em his peace, etc. Christ says, John 5:24, that he that believed on him should not come into condemnation, but had eternal life, and was passed from death to life; and, John 3:18, that he that believed on him was not condemned.
THE "MISCELLANIES"

MANY FOLKS AROUND us are more than happy to talk about love—even God's love. Few people oppose, at least initially, the concept of being welcomed by another. But we must take care in our discussions of love. The cultural form of love we hear about on TV shows and in pop music amounts to accepting people for who they are. Modern love doesn't really *do* anything. It's an emoji, an endless smile, that flashes on your screen all day, every day.

Love in the Bible looks very different. The Father giving his spotless Son as a willing sacrifice defines biblical love. This type of love necessitates transformation, as Jonathan Edwards points out. Christ warned his disciples of laziness, taught them to pray, and bestowed upon them "his peace." This love is anchored in an iron promise: The disciples had "passed from death to life" and would not suffer condemnation. Biblical love is costly, for both giver and recipient. Out of his love for us, Christ died; for love of God, we die to ourselves.

Secular love gives a hug, but cannot transform lives. Biblical love gives us Christ and all his benefits. There is an infinite gap between these two visions of deep affection. One gives and asks nothing, in the end. The other gives and asks everything. As we teach about and share the love of Christ with our family members, neighbors, and coworkers, we must explain what true love involves. At its height, love does not mean launching out into the world free of any obligations, subject to no one. Love at the summit is the Father giving the Son for us, and the Son bringing us to the Father. There is no greater love than this.

Greater love has no one than this, that someone lay down his life for his friends. JOHN 15:13

July 23

As the children of Israel were redeemed out of Egypt that they might serve God, so are we redeemed by Jesus Christ; not that we might be at liberty to sin, but that we might be at liberty from sin, that so we might serve God. They were delivered from serving their old masters, the Egyptians, that so they might serve God. So we are redeemed from the service of sin, that we might henceforth serve God; being "made free from sin," we are become "the servants of righteousness" [Romans 6:18], as Romans 6 throughout.

THE "BLANK BIBLE"

THERE MAY BE NO DOCTRINE more misunderstood than that of Christian liberty. For some, Christian liberty means you can basically do what you want as a believer, and God is fine with it. Sure, you shouldn't commit unbiblical acts. But Christ has freed us from the need to manage our spirituality. We're liberated.

There is much here to think through. Yes, the blood of Christ has ransomed us from Satan. How marvelous is this! We are no longer slaves to sin, it is true; the law, with its demands, is fulfilled in Christ (Matthew 5:17-20). But we are not saved to do whatever we please; we are saved for holiness. The blood of Christ frees us "from sin" in order to "serve God." We are saved by the holy King to live as holy subjects under his holy rule. It is true that we no longer live in darkness; but it is also true that we now live in the light, and are called to be light in a dark place (Matthew 5:13-16).

Let us glory in our freedom. Sin no longer entraps us and poisons us. Death has no sting. Hell does not own us; it does not bid us come, knowing we are unable to resist. We are liberated from the power of Satan and his evil influences. How strong and mighty is Christ! How free we truly are. We are free, and free to be holy, free to worship our crucified and resurrected King, free to sing and pray and treasure God. This is Christian liberty at its essence—and we possess it, all of it.

He has delivered us from the domain of darkness and transferred us
to the kingdom of his beloved Son, in whom we have redemption,
the forgiveness of sins. COLOSSIANS 1:13-14

July 24

[Leviticus 4:20. "And the priest shall make an atonement for them, and it shall be forgiven them."] It is not meant that the sacrifice, in itself considered, made a true atonement for any sin, or that any iniquity whatsoever should on account of these sacrifices simply considered, without true repentance and faith in the mercy of God, be forgiven. For the Old Testament does sufficiently teach that sacrifices are nothing without sincere prayer or faith, of which prayer is the expression. . . . It was not the sacrifice that was the true bread of God and a sweet savor to him, but the offerer became accepted and the object of God's delight through faith, of which prayer was the expression.
THE "BLANK BIBLE"

THE HUMAN HEART has a natural interest in religious ritual. We crave the order and simplicity of a liturgical service. Even when people avoid the church, they still seek out a version of it. To observe shoppers lost in the world of the mall, or sports fans performing their regular chants, or music fans singing along to their favorite band, is to witness the human appetite for greater reality and ordered ritual.

We cannot find what our hearts seek, however, without God. Even God-ordained religious endeavors mean nothing without faith. *Faith* does not mean a fuzzy belief in something bigger than ourselves; biblical faith means that small, deficient creatures trust in their Creator to offer a way back home. Biblical faith depends on a basic awareness that we need the Lord, and only he can cleanse us and bring us into his presence. The average God-fearing Israelite in the Old Testament did not know all the particulars of theology. They did know this: They needed "true atonement" that they could not provide.

We approach God in the same way today. It is right to join and attend a church, and to participate fully in its shared life. But it is not the liturgy we observe or the service we attend that grants us God's favor and the promise of heaven. Church matters because "sincere prayer" is offered there to God. Church matters because the body of Christ together expresses "delight through faith." God does not want man-directed, man-centered worship. He takes no pleasure in the mere observance of old rituals. He wants the heart. He wants *us*.

It is impossible for the blood of bulls and goats to take away sins.
HEBREWS 10:4

July 25

Resolved, to endeavor to my utmost to deny whatever is not most agreeable to a good, and universally sweet and benevolent, quiet, peaceable, contented, easy, compassionate, generous, humble, meek, modest, submissive, obliging, diligent and industrious, charitable, even, patient, moderate, forgiving, sincere temper; and to do at all times what such a temper would lead me to. Examine strictly every week, whether I have done so.
LETTERS AND PERSONAL WRITINGS

JONATHAN EDWARDS was what we might call a "great man of God." Even non-Christians would (and do) consider him a great man, even if they choose to ignore the faith component of his life. We find figures of this kind throughout history, and they have both outsized strengths and weaknesses. The same bulldog spirit that drives them to epic courage can render them difficult family members. The tenacity that compels them to vindicate their cause may not easily switch off, tiring them out, and leaving them with little energy for others.

Edwards was a rare great man who hungered to grow in his walk with God. He saw spiritual virtues, not worldly accolades, as the chief measure of a leader. Before his formal ministry career began, he called himself to account, identifying numerous godly traits that he needed to cultivate: meekness, modesty, submissiveness, and charity among them.

Like the rest of us, the young Edwards did not always meet his own standards. Throughout his career, Edwards sometimes mishandled pastoral matters. But a part of why we still read and seek to emulate this imperfect man is that he did not want to be a great man. He yearned to be a great man *of God*. He had his eyes locked on something greater than fame; he wanted to know the Lord, and taste an abundance of heavenly rewards. His example encourages us to practice biblical virtues through the Spirit's enabling, and to put aside the habits and behaviors the world esteems. We are not trying to become famous; we are trying to grow in grace.

Put on then, as God's chosen ones, holy and beloved, compassionate hearts, kindness, humility, meekness, and patience. COLOSSIANS 3:12

July 26

[Numbers 14:17. "Let the power of my Lord be great," etc.] Here God's pardoning great, and aggravated, and manifold sin, and showing mercy to the very unworthy, is mentioned as a manifestation of the high and glorious all-sufficiency of the divine nature. Therefore the declared design of the gospel, which is to magnify the infinite riches of free grace, is most worthy of God. Such exceeding goodness to enemies and vipers does greatly show the infinite height, fullness, and glory of the Divine Being, and may well be looked upon as the most exalted manifestation of the divine excellency that ever was. This therefore is a confirmation of the divinity of the gospel of Jesus Christ.
THE "BLANK BIBLE"

MANY FOLKS CAN UNDERSTAND a good portion of the Bible's teaching. Precepts such as "Do unto others as you would have them do unto you," for example, resonate with most people. The average man or woman wants to be treated with dignity and respect; they think it only fair, furthermore, that they treat others the same. The need for humility, caring for one's family, striving for personal growth—these things cause little offense for most.

But the core of the biblical message throws us off. The incarnated Christ throws in a doozy of a plot twist. We expect him to come and teach people, to move among the masses, and maybe even to perform some surprising feats. Free bread for thousands. Awesome! But what we don't expect, and perhaps do not want at some level, is for Jesus to die for his enemies and justify the ungodly. This makes little to no sense to the human heart. As he so often does, Jesus reorders things, upending our expectations, overturning our nice and neat plans for an easy existence.

Jesus wades into the muck and mire of earthly society and brings a new order, a new code, a new law. His law is a law of love (John 13:34). He in no way downplays the justice of God, but he shows us something impossibly glorious, the "infinite riches of free grace" found in the gospel, as Jonathan Edwards contends. Now, "enemies and vipers" may come into his Kingdom. Through repentance, we who are his foes gain entrance to heaven through the doorway of the Cross. What a scandal this is; what evil this news occasioned from Christ's enemies. But this plot twist holds true today. Truly, God does the impossible—and through his power, so may we.

By grace you have been saved through faith. And this is not your own doing; it is the gift of God, not a result of works, so that no one may boast. EPHESIANS 2:8-9

July 27

[Deuteronomy 4:21–22.] In this Moses was a type of Christ. God was angry with Moses for their sakes; so God was as it were angry with Christ for our sakes. He bore the wrath of God for our sakes. Our iniquities were laid upon Christ; our guilt lay upon him. And so he in some respect partook of our guilt. So Moses partook of the guilt of the children of Israel when, by their rebellion, they provoked his spirit so that he spoke unadvisedly with his lips. And Moses was as it were a sacrifice for them: he died in the wilderness; and they lived, and went in to possess the good land.

THE "BLANK BIBLE"

WHAT A MAN MOSES WAS. He walked into the courtroom of the most powerful man on earth and defied him. He led God's people out of Egypt. He received the Ten Commandments, the cornerstone declaration of the Lord in the old covenant era. Most amazing of all, Moses saw the glory of God personally. In a biblical scene that overloads our imaginations, Yahweh passed by Moses, giving his chief prophet a vision of his magnificence.

Yet Moses had his downs as well as his ups. When the people of God rebelled, Moses grew angry with them. Anger was a recurring theme in his life. Before God appointed him to lead the people, Moses killed a man in a conflict. The picture that emerges of Moses in different parts of his life not only impresses us, but sometimes scares us. Moses led the Israelites well, but he was not a perfect man. His very life would end in disappointment when he died without being allowed to enter the "good land," as Jonathan Edwards terms it.

But Moses was not an end unto himself. As "a type of Christ," he points us to Jesus, the greater Moses. Jesus, too, went into the wilderness; he too led an exodus from Egypt, the land of death and destruction. But unlike Moses, Jesus never failed. He represented us before God and brought the law of God with him, descending from heaven to teach us the "law of love," a better law than the law of Moses (John 13:34; Hebrews 7:19). Jesus not only walked before us, showing us the way to God; Jesus *is* the way to God. His arms held back the waters of judgment as he took on himself the punishment for sin we deserved. We read of Moses and marvel at his faith and courage. But Moses, our brother, points us to one who is greater and calls us to follow the greater one all the way to the promised land.

All we like sheep have gone astray; we have turned—every one—
to his own way; and the LORD has laid on him the iniquity of us all.
ISAIAH 53:6

July 28

In 1726, Jonathan Edwards became the pastoral assistant at the First Church of Northampton, Massachusetts. He served under his eminent grandfather, Solomon Stoddard. Finally, after numerous twists and turns, Edwards had found the pastoral job he long desired.

But there was more afoot. For some time, Edwards had courted young Sarah Pierpont, a minister's daughter. In the summer of 1727, he wed his tall, elegant bride in New Haven. Edwards did not record much about the courtship, though a receipt for some of the wedding expenses survived—a lute string, white gloves, and silver buckles. Despite the lack of comment about the marriage in his papers, Edwards's private thoughts on Sarah leave no doubt that he had fallen deeply in love with her some years prior.

By all accounts, Sarah was a marvelous match for Jonathan. She managed the household, which left Jonathan time in the study, which was often thirteen hours a day. Still, the pastor made time to read and teach the Bible to his family and to pray with Sarah. The couple had eleven children, and the achievements of their family through the centuries speaks to an uncommon partnership. One scholar estimated that by 1900 the Edwards family had produced

- thirteen college presidents
- sixty-five professors
- one hundred lawyers and a dean of a law school
- thirty judges
- sixty-six physicians and a dean of a medical school
- eighty holders of public office

As time has worn on, the Edwards tree has borne much fruit. It all began with a tall, socially reclusive young man marrying a tall, sweet-spirited young woman on a summer's day in New Haven. So it is that God has ordained marriage. So much blessing can come from such a common union: one man and one woman joined together before God, the two becoming one flesh (Genesis 2:24).

July 29

[Psalms 8:5–9. "For thou hast made him a little lower than the angels."] . . . *Now the advancement of the human nature, or crowning of it with glory and honor, is twofold. There was that that was done at God's first work, when God first created man, whereby God gave him dominion over this lower world and the other creatures in it, herein making man but a little lower than the angels, those thrones, dominions, principalities, and powers above [Colossians 1:16]. . . . And Secondly, the second exaltation, or crowning with glory and honor, of which this was but a shadow, is that which is performed in God's second work in actual uniting the human nature to the divine, whereby the human nature was exalted not only to an honor and dominion that was an image of God's, but actually to God's honor and dominion.*
THE "BLANK BIBLE"

HUMANITY WAS MADE FOR THIS EARTH. The Lord made mankind to have "dominion over this lower world" as an emblem of God's authority in heaven. Even before the Fall, God intended for Adam and Eve to be fully here. They were not to yearn to go somewhere else; they were laden with "glory and honor," given tasks of great dignity and worth, and made to display the glories of God.

Yet God had still greater hopes for humanity, as Jonathan Edwards notes. The Lord is specially glorified by humanity's interest in "God's honor and dominion." God is a sharing God. His generosity is dumbfounding to brutes like us. From the beginning, the Lord wished to elevate his creation, to give us his very own blessings, none of which we merit in our own strength. Even Adam before the Fall could not lay claim to this elevation of status. But God wanted him, and all his chosen race, to have it.

God is a giving God. He is stupendously generous. We can lose sight of this truth, for our hearts are fickle, and our lives can fill with trials. But nothing we experience reworks the character of the Lord. He never changes. He doesn't ebb and flow, wax or wane. He doesn't promise good to us only to forfeit on his assurances. God has always intended to lift his people up. This desire comes from nothing but pure kindness on his part. We have no claim on God; we have no right to demand gifts from his hand. But his hand, we find, is always full, and always reaching out to us, always giving us what we do not merit and could never earn.

What is man that you are mindful of him, and the son of man that you care for him? Yet you have made him a little lower than the heavenly beings and crowned him with glory and honor. PSALM 8:4-5

221

July 30

Summer 1721: Jonathan Edwards's summer conversion experience

IN THE SUMMER OF 1721, during his first year of master's studies, Jonathan Edwards experienced what he would later describe as a conversion experience. Having been reared in the Puritan tradition, he had a robust understanding of conversion. Edwards believed what his father and grandfather preached: He knew his soul would live forever, and he hated his depravity. In his final years at Yale, however, he still entertained doubts about God's sovereignty.

Edwards had long nurtured a quiet rebellion in his heart. Even as he learned staunch Puritan doctrine, he resisted the greatness of God's power. He longed to know the Lord, but could not reconcile himself totally to an all-ordaining God. His resistance finally crumbled in the spring of 1721 as he meditated on 1 Timothy 1:17: "Now unto the King eternal, immortal, invisible, the only wise God, be honor and glory for ever and ever. Amen" (KJV). He later spoke about that moment:

> As I read the words, there came into my soul, and as it were diffused through it, a sense of the glory of the divine being; a new sense, quite different from anything I ever experienced before. Never any words of Scripture seemed to me as these words did. I thought with myself, how excellent a Being that was; and how happy I should be, if I might enjoy that God, and be wrapt up to God in heaven, and be as it were swallowed up in him.[42]

Edwards laid down his intellectual weapons that day. The absolute sovereignty of God had long presented him with a seemingly impossible difficulty; he did not feel he could totally trust the Lord. But as the Spirit moved in his heart, he ceased to see the total lordship of Christ as a damaging doctrine, and embraced it as a life-giving grace.

Prior to this conversion experience, Edwards had excelled in the study of God's Word. But he had not met the object of his studies. On this day, through meditation on the Word, that all changed. The truth that had repelled him became the truth that compelled him. We never know how Scripture will grab us, free us, and bless us when we just make time to read it and ponder it.

July 31

[Matthew 16:26. "For what is a man profited if he gain the whole world, and lose his own soul? Or what shall a man give in exchange for his soul?"] The preciousness or value of anything above other things will appear by comparing it with other things, considering of it either as to be sold for them, or to be bought with them. If it be considered as to be sold for them, then the preciousness of it above them appears in the unprofitableness of the bargain. If it be considered as to be bought with other things, then its superior value appears by their insufficiency to buy it. The preciousness of the soul is set forth in this verse both these ways as being more precious than the whole world.

THE "BLANK BIBLE"

IN SPIRITUAL TERMS, the soul is the most "precious" part of our person, to use Jonathan Edwards's language. For many people, though, the soul receives the least care and attention. We know that we should mind our bodies; we do not fail to dedicate ourselves to the passions of our hearts. But we find the soul—our spiritual self—harder to engage, and easier to ignore. Many people, in fact, completely neglect to care for their souls.

But the soul needs care, doesn't it? The soul is eternal. Little though we examine and stoke such interest, the soul has a capacious desire for something greater than itself. We know that we are not the end of all things. We want something bigger, and we yearn for something lasting. Our hearts are made, after all, for God. We lost our connection to God in the Fall, but we did not lose our capacity for God. We did not lose our need for him. We lost him, and in so doing, lost everything.

As Christians, we have now regained it all. We have come to Christ, who restores our relationship with God. We have swallowed eternity whole. We may now care for our souls on a daily basis.

> What will it profit a man if he gains the whole world and forfeits his soul? Or what shall a man give in return for his soul?
> MATTHEW 16:26

August

✝

August 1

Resolved, whenever I hear anything spoken in commendation of any person, if I think it would be praiseworthy in me, resolved to endeavor to imitate it.
LETTERS AND PERSONAL WRITINGS

THE HEART THAT IS SECURE in God is able to do what few imagine: It can hear someone else complimented, and avoid growing either jealous or despairing. It is not so for the insecure among us. If we are not content with who we are, we will hear others commended and covet what they have—or else become morose due to the fact that we do not measure up.

If our roots go down deep in the Lord, we will not bridle when others around us receive plaudits. The Spirit's work in us will instead produce *joy* for the one being honored. We will not merely avoid jealousy; we will feel *love*. The times when others are complimented and we are not, perhaps even pointedly so, offer us a terrific test of our true character.

Jonathan Edwards received much praise in his life. This was true even at the time when he penned this resolution; he had already excelled in his studies and gained attention for his writings. Yet his heart, like ours, was not immune to bitterness. Knowing this, he set himself up to choose a better way when tempted to dive into envy. Rather than growing angry, he expressed his wish to "endeavor to imitate" the virtues spotted in others. How we all need such a perspective. The goal of our lives is not to be made great; the goal of our lives is to lift high the banner of God. We should praise God that he uses imperfect vessels like us; we should leave the scorekeeping to him alone.

Let us consider how to stir up one another to love and good works.
HEBREWS 10:24

August 2

Spiritual enjoyments are satisfying also in a respect that worldly enjoyments are not, in this, that they answer the expectation of the appetite. When the appetite is high to anything, the expectation necessarily is so. Appetite to a particular object implies expectation in its nature. It is an expectation without reflection. . . . The man expected to have a great occasion of happiness, but he don't find himself much, if anything, more happy than he was before. But it is not so with spiritual enjoyments. They fully answer and satisfy the expectation. They find themselves as much happier as they expected.

THE "BLANK BIBLE"

THERE IS NO TRUE HAPPINESS outside of God. I recall hearing a Super Bowl-winning quarterback say after the big win, "I thought to myself: *Is that all there is?*" He had climbed the mountain; he had what millions of people dream of, and yet he knew he had not found lasting happiness. In fact, he could not—not in this world.

We understand why we want more happiness than this world affords. As Jonathan Edwards argues, we have "appetites" that are too great for earth. Momentary accomplishments cannot satisfy us. Fleeting successes will not "answer the expectation of the appetite." Humanity will launch and relaunch this fruitless quest nonetheless; the futile search for joy outside of God goes on as it has for ages.

Christians can never say of God, "Is that all there is?" for God never fails to meet our expectations. He never breeds disappointment. God has given us the appetites we have. He made them so that we would drink our fill of him. The longing for eternity, and the quest for undying happiness, come to an end in God. The "spiritual enjoyments" he gives exceed any hopes we could have. The curse is broken. We know an exception to the rule. Jesus entered into our pain and our discouragement, and he has led a way out of captivity for us. Despair and fruitlessness die in the death of Jesus; hope and true happiness rise in his resurrection.

I am the bread of life; whoever comes to me shall not hunger, and whoever believes in me shall never thirst. JOHN 6:35

August 3

"I go to prepare a place for you." What must most naturally be understood by this speech of Christ is that he was going to prepare or make ready a place for them. . . . So if a person was fitting his house for the reception of a beloved bride, it would be by putting it in every respect under such circumstances as should be most for her delightful entertainment. Thus Christ, that loved the church and gave himself for her, after he had redeemed her, went to heaven to prepare the palace of his eternal abode for reception by beautifying and adorning it, and increasing its glory. Hence [we] may argue that at Christ's ascension the glory of heaven was greatly increased, and made a more happy and blessed seat.

THE "BLANK BIBLE"

WILL HEAVEN BE EVERYTHING we hope for? More than a few Christians have asked this question. As students of God's Word, we must admit that heaven is wrapped in some mystery. To those of us who gaze up at it, it seems enshrouded, a land above the clouds. It is possible for our wandering hearts to start questioning whether heaven will meet our expectations. After all, we're all accustomed to disappointment—the beach vacation gone awry; the new house with the leaky roof; the job search that doesn't pan out.

We must correct our tendency to lowball heaven. More than any other Christian thinker, Jonathan Edwards thought about what heaven would be like. He saw from Scripture that it is a place prepared for us by Christ as a man readies his home "for the reception of a beloved bride." Heaven yields "delightful entertainment." There is a special shine and sparkle to the blessed realm following "Christ's ascension," for heaven welcomed home its champion. Christ came to sit at the Father's right hand, but not only this (Hebrews 1:3). He went to prepare heaven for *us*.

Two things are certainly true for us today. First, the world in some way is going to let us down. We will face difficulties and challenges we would rather avoid, whether great or small. Second, the afterlife is coming, and it will blow our minds. We will go to a place that is beautiful, adorned with glory, and ready to receive the bride of Christ, the church. Perhaps we know so little about heaven because God knows we could not absorb the glory of what we will soon see.

In my Father's house are many rooms. If it were not so, would I have told you that I go to prepare a place for you? JOHN 14:2

August 4

[Romans 8:29: "For whom he did foreknow, he also did predestinate to be conformed to the image of his Son."] This is the sum of what the elect are predestinated to, viz. "to be conformed to the image of his Son," to be made like his Son, and to have communion with him in his holiness and in his happiness. They are predestinated to be conformed to his Son in his death, in dying to sin and the world, and in his resurrection, by being quickened from being dead in trespasses and sins, and also in their bodies being raised, Christ the first fruits, and afterwards those that are Christ's at his coming. . . . This glory, this excellency and happiness that consists in the saints' being conformed to Christ, is the sum of the good that they are predestinated to; and the whole of their conformity to Christ is what the Apostle has respect [to], and not only their being made like him in conversion and sanctification.

THE "BLANK BIBLE"

As MUCH AS WE MIGHT pretend otherwise, uncertainty in life is a daily reality for us. Will our bank account survive the next downturn in the market? Will our health hold up against sickness, misfortune, and accidents? Will family and friends remain true? One conversation can damage even a decades-long relationship. More than we sometimes care to admit, so much of life is unstable.

The love of God cuts through our uncertainty like a bullet train through the fog. Nothing about the love of God is weak or up for grabs. God's absolute sovereignty means that those whom he loves, he blesses. This is what we take away from the theological term *predestination*, which refers to God's setting of our course long ago. The Lord has personally seen to it that all his chosen people will "have communion with [Christ] in his holiness and in his happiness." The Lord has fixed our path; he saved us in the beloved. Because of this, we will be conformed to the image of Christ. We will grow in godliness. We will die "to sin and the world."

How strange that predestination should seem to some only a debating topic. God's sovereignty is not a matter of debate in the Bible. Predestination does not rob us of joy; predestination is the grounds for our eternal security. It is a theistic fireworks show bursting with beauty. We do not know what the economy holds or the government will do. But we do know that God will bring to completion what he has started. We will grow in godliness, in conformity to Christ. It is guaranteed by our Lord himself because he is a predestining God, a sovereign God. How can we not trust him amidst our daily uncertainty?

Those whom he foreknew he also predestined to be conformed to the image of his Son. ROMANS 8:29

August 5

Summer 1752: Misrepresentations Corrected, and Truth Vindicated *published*

CONFLICT IN OUR DAY may ignite in a matter of minutes. Controversies in the mid-eighteenth century often played out over several years. If the argument went to print, as Jonathan Edwards's dispute over Communion with Rev. Solomon Williams did, it might take half a decade for the two sides to exchange views.

This was the case with the Communion controversy. Solomon Williams, who was Edwards's cousin and a pastor in Connecticut, went to press in opposition to Edwards's policy of "closed Communion." He took the general line that their grandfather, Solomon Stoddard, had, but he overstated his case and misrepresented Edwards's position.

This did not bode well for Williams, who was left holding the bag after his brother, Elisha, abandoned the project. Elisha was the more gifted thinker and writer of the two, but he stepped away for a variety of reasons (perhaps to avoid conflict with his formidable cousin). Solomon Williams published *The True State of the Question* (abbreviated title) in 1751, arguing that Edwards had made it nearly impossible for anyone to take Communion, so high was the bar set for a "credible profession."

In *Misrepresentations Corrected, and Truth Vindicated*, Edwards did not hold back from scrutinizing Williams's position in great detail, pointing out numerous overstatements, and distancing Williams's position from their grandfather's. Also, Edwards further clarified his beliefs about conversion, the nature of the church, and eligibility for Communion.

We get a taste for the fierce nature of the argument in passages such as this:

> If an attendance on these public duties was in its own nature a
> profession of orthodoxy, or even piety; yet the reason of mankind
> teaches them the need of joining words and actions together in public
> manifestations of the mind, in cases of importance: speech being the
> great and peculiar talent, which God has given to mankind, as the
> special means and instrument of the manifestation of their minds one
> to another. Thus, treaties of peace among men are not concluded and
> finished, only with actions, without words. Feasting together was used
> of old, as a testimony of peace and covenant friendship; as between
> Isaac and Abimelech, Laban and Jacob, but not without a verbal
> profession. Giving the hand, delivering the ring, etc. are to express
> a marriage agreement and union; but still a profession in words is
> annexed.[43]

Edwards's response did not lead to an easy resolution of the matter. However, two years after Edwards's death Joseph Hawley III, the principal head of opposition in Northampton, repented—both privately and publicly—of his role in the whole sorry business. Though theologians and pastors continue to debate Edwards's views on Communion, many evangelicals today hold similar views.

August 6

[First Corinthians 1:30. All our good is contained in these four things mentioned, viz. "wisdom, righteousness, sanctification, and redemption."] . . . Here in this verse is shown our dependence on each person in the Trinity for all our good. We are dependent on Christ, as he is made to us wisdom, etc. We are dependent on the Father, in that 'tis of that he is made these things to us. 'Tis the Father that has given him, and sent him into the world. And 'tis the Father that accepts of him, that what he has done may procure these benefits for us. We are dependent on the Holy Spirit, as 'tis of him that we are in Christ. 'Tis he that brings us to close with Christ, and gives us faith in him, whereby we come to receive of him these benefits.
THE "BLANK BIBLE"

THE TRINITY IS A GRAND THEOLOGICAL REALITY. We know that we are beings made by God for his glory. We know that God saves us. We know that the church is supposed to be the body of Christ. But how do we *apply* the doctrine of the Godhead?

In truth, the Trinity matters immensely for our daily walk. First, the Godhead is the central fact of all existence. The Trinity is not a debatable matter for the church; we must affirm one God in three persons as the summary biblical teaching on God. These persons are Father, Son, and Spirit. We did nothing to create or identify the Trinity; they have revealed themselves to us. As Jonathan Edwards argues, we *need* each member of the Trinity. The Father has "given" and "sent" Christ on his errand of salvation. Christ is our wisdom, and the one who gives us the benefits of salvation. The Spirit unites us to Christ and "gives us faith in him."

Every believer has a Trinitarian faith. Take away the Holy Trinity and we are paupers; we are without God himself. Give us the holy Trinity and we are rich beyond belief. As the people loved by the Godhead, we have all the benefits the Father intends for us to possess. We have wisdom for all situations and seasons. We have the very righteousness of Christ credited to us. We are made holy by God, sanctified in the Spirit. We are redeemed now, and will be fully redeemed when the Son returns and gathers all his people to himself. When we unfurl all the work of the triune God in our lives, the question for us is not, "How does the Trinity matter?" but, "What could we do without the Trinity?"

And because of [God] you are in Christ Jesus, who became to us
wisdom from God, righteousness and sanctification and redemption.
I CORINTHIANS 1:30

August 7

[Second Corinthians 13:14. "The grace of the Lord Jesus Christ."] What is signified in each part of this benediction is the sum of all that good that the elect have by the redemption of Christ. This is called "the grace of the Lord Jesus Christ," having respect to the way that we have this good through him, viz. by partaking of the fullness of that our head. He is full of grace, and we partake of his fullness, and grace for grace. The gift is first bestowed on our head, given into his possession as our head; and we partake of the gift or grace in him. "The love of all." All is of the love of the Father as its first spring, as he is the first mover, and head, and fountain of all in the affair of our redemption.
THE "BLANK BIBLE"

NOT LONG AGO, I saw a documentary on some former soccer players who had clearly struggled to find their way after retiring from the game. They had fame and fortune, but comparatively little happiness. One player, however, stood out: He had two young children, one of whom had cerebral palsy, and he had resolved, along with his wife, to help his little girl learn to walk. She had succeeded, and now could even play sports with her family.

We are always deeply touched by such portraits of fatherhood. They move us because they remind us of our heavenly Father. The Father at his core is loving and strong. He rules and initiates as the Father to the holy Son, Jesus Christ. He gave his Son as a gift to us, sending him into the world and appointing him as our redeemer (John 3:17). As Jonathan Edwards notes, God is the "first spring" and the "head" and "fountain" of the symphonic masterwork of salvation.

Everything that is good can be found in our heavenly Father. Everything that is loving can be found in him, as well. You may not have a great relationship with your earthly father—maybe you've struggled to connect with him, understand him, or grow close to him. Whatever the case, whenever we see an example of an authoritative, virtuous, loving, strong father in the world, we know that we're seeing a reflection of our much greater heavenly Father. This Father did not spare his own Son, but gave him up for us. Earthly relationships will fade away. In Christ, you may gain nothing less than all "the love of the Father" for all eternity.

The grace of the Lord Jesus Christ and the love of God and the fellowship of the Holy Spirit be with you all. 2 CORINTHIANS 13:14

August 8

THE SUMMER OF 1751 was a tough time for Jonathan Edwards. After roughly a year of pulpit supply in Northampton, the venerable preacher accepted a call to the evangelical mission in Stockbridge, Massachusetts, a missionary village set up to evangelize the Native Americans. In the eyes of the political leaders at the time, this effort would help to secure the allegiance of the native tribes even as King George's War unfolded against the French.

Stockbridge was a beautiful town just off the Housatonic River. The outpost consisted mainly of Mahicans, but over time some Mohawks and members of other tribes began to settle there as well. The Mahicans became famous to succeeding generations of Americans through James Fenimore Cooper's novel *The Last of the Mohicans.* Cooper modeled his Native American characters on Mahican Indians from Stockbridge whom Edwards would have known.

Edwards spent the next seven years in Stockbridge. While there, he produced the bulk of his major theological works, even as he advocated for the welfare of the Native Americans under his care, wresting control of the town's school from members of his extended family, the Williamses. This family, well-known in Stockbridge, had not cared well for the Native American children, and Edwards saw to it that the school offered spiritual and intellectual instruction.

Edwards changed up his preaching in Stockbridge. A sermon on 2 Peter 1:19 shows that he drastically modified his speaking style from his Northampton days:

> You see how it is [in] the spring. When the sun shines on the earth and trees, it gives 'em new life, makes the earth look green. It causes flowers to appear and give a good smell. So it is in the heart of a man when the light of God's Word shines into it. . . . The light, when it shines into the heart, is sweeter than the honey, and the gospel will be a pleasant sound to you when you come to understand it.[44]

The familiar themes—light, the beauty of Creation, the power of the Word—were all there. Though Edwards and his family traveled a rough road to get to the mission, they had persevered, and they enjoyed several good years on the frontier. The colony's leading pastor became a missionary, giving posterity an example of endurance, grit, and gospel focus in very tough times. We need just such a perspective on whatever God brings into our lives.

August 9

Christians have their blessedness in heavenly places, for they are not of the world. That is not their country, not their home. Their inheritance, their house, their treasure, their food, their ornaments, their friends, society, and entertainments are "in heavenly places." Their enjoyments are not in an earthly paradise, for they are not of the first Adam, who was of the earth, earthy. They are taken out of that stock. They are the children of the second Adam, who was a quickening spirit and the Lord from heaven. . . . Because they belong to Christ or are in Christ, their blessings are spiritual and "in heavenly places," and not earthly, in Eden, or any other earthly country.
THE "BLANK BIBLE"

THIS WORLD IS NOT OUR HOME. No country will perfectly represent us and meet all our dreams and expectations. We know not to put our trust in any one government, for we are citizens of a better country. Still, we cannot stop our hearts from longing for lasting rest and peace and success in this world. If we're not careful, we can start placing our hope in earthly leaders and nations and forget what we know about the Kingdom of God.

As Christians, we should be good citizens wherever God plants us. But as a people, we are unlike any other. We are "not of the world," as Jonathan Edwards plainly states. Wherever we find ourselves, it is not our true home. This truth, again, is easy to affirm, but harder to put into practice. We naturally crave a lasting home and a righteous administration. These desires are not flawed; they are given to us by God. We are made to be the people of God—unified and happy—dwelling in the place of God under God's holy rule. Until Christ returns, we retain these rightful longings, and must regularly do battle with over-realized earthly hopes. But as long as we are here on earth, we are going to be disappointed by kings and governments, nations and organizations.

The flip side of this principle is stupendously encouraging. We are "the children of the second Adam," Jesus Christ. We have every spiritual blessing in him. We are not sitting by, left here by Jesus without anything useful to do until he comes back. Christ is leading a new exodus right now—leaving a fallen world to enter the true Promised Land. Though we do not cease to labor and witness here on earth, we set our hearts on the truth that our blessings will not come from Eden, but from the new Eden, the eternal rest that Jesus has prepared for us.

Blessed be the God and Father of our Lord Jesus Christ, who has
blessed us in Christ with every spiritual blessing in the heavenly places.
EPHESIANS 1:3

August 10

IN AUGUST 1722, Jonathan Edwards became an unordained supply preacher for a small Presbyterian church in New York City, though he was still two months shy of his nineteenth birthday. The church met at the corner of Wall Street and Broadway, in the present-day financial district. Edwards's time in Lower Manhattan was exhilarating, and a far cry from the quieter locales of his earlier years.

New York City had seven- to ten thousand residents at the time. The city brought Edwards into contact with many different cultures and even religions. Edwards had no trouble with the lively nature of the urban center, and seemed to come alive in it. He later wrote that his spiritual life thrived amidst the hustle and bustle of the city:

> I very frequently used to retire into a solitary place, on the banks of Hudson's River, at some distance from the city, for contemplation on divine things, and secret converse with God; and had many sweet hours there. Sometimes Mr. Smith and I walked there together, to converse of the things of God; and our conversation used much to turn on the advancement of Christ's kingdom in the world, and the glorious things that God would accomplish for his church in the latter days.[45]

Edwards enjoyed his eight months in New York, but found his pastoral work cut short when the small congregation—an offshoot of one of the city's leading Presbyterian churches—reunited with the original body. With this, Edwards left the city and did not reenter full-time pastoral ministry for several years. His time in New York provides an interesting contrast to his later work in Stockbridge on the frontier, and shows that the young theologian had a strong willingness to go wherever the Lord would have him labor. Today, like the young Jonathan Edwards, we need Christians to bring the light of Christ wherever they go—to their hometowns, to the suburbs, to the great cities of the world.

August 11

[Ephesians 2:6. "And made us to sit together in heavenly places."] . . . In places of heavenly honor and dignity, places above any place of earthly honor and trust. Believers sit in the place of priests unto God, and in the place of kings. They are in places of heavenly dominion and divine dignity. But it is in Christ, by virtue of their union with him, they are partakers of his honors and dominion. The devils are called in the Ephesians 6:12, "spiritual wickedness in heavenly places," ἐν ἐπουράιοις, the same word as here, because the devil had usurped God's throne, and reigned as God, and had divine honors paid him.

THE "BLANK BIBLE"

WE KNOW THE BIBLICAL principle that "the last will be first, and the first last" (Matthew 20:16). But life can seem so contrary to this truth that we struggle to hold it tightly. We feel powerless. In response, we can either despair or lash out, or try to grab on to what we feel should be coming to us. But this is a flawed strategy. Unlike Jesus, we cannot bring the Kingdom down from heaven on our own.

It's easy to forget that God has already given us everything we could want. In Christ, we have a title. We have a claim on the life to come. We "sit in the place of kings" through Christ. We are citizens of his Kingdom *now*. No one can take away our heavenly citizenship. We can never lose it. Christ has given it to us, and everything he gives is without limit and without cessation.

When we check our newsfeed or watch TV, we can feel so small, powerless, and discouraged. It's as if the world is on fire or has simply gone crazy. When our thoughts turn to our own circumstances, we may feel downcast about everything that seems lacking in our lives. But let us not lose heart. We must continually drive our thoughts upward to God—to "places of heavenly dominion and divine dignity," as Jonathan Edwards puts it. That realm is unshakable. We have a purchase there, and we are headed there. Soon Christ will overthrow Satan and restore all things. The first will be last; the last will be first.

[He] raised us up with him and seated us with him in the heavenly places in Christ Jesus. EPHESIANS 2:6

August 12

And so it is with respect to our exercises of love and gratitude to God. They are defectively corrupt and sinful, and might justly be odious and provoking to him, taken as they are upon the like account, and would be so, were it not that the sin and corruption of them is hid by Christ. God as it were don't see the odiousness and iniquity of them, and so accepts them for Christ's sake, which but of him would be worthy of his detestation.
THE "BLANK BIBLE"

EVERYTHING IN THE CHRISTIAN LIFE aims at our decreasing and God's increasing. More than any math equation or scientific theorem, we need to master this formula. The Christian life shines from many angles, but if we were to view it from afar and try to sum up its unique beauty, we would perhaps settle on a single word: *humility*. We are a humble people. We want to be humble; we are humbled by God. This is not unfairness on God's part; it is the right balancing of the universe. God must increase, we must decrease.

This matters not only for our sinful acts, but also for our good works. Even "our exercises of love and gratitude to God" fall short, as Jonathan Edwards avows. How true this is. We sometimes credit ourselves when we simply do as we should; but really, just how concentrated was that prayer time? How many times did our attention wander? Yes, we sat down to read the Scriptures, but why did our thoughts drift so easily to lesser things? Sure, we enjoyed fellowship with fellow believers, but why did we struggle with feelings of annoyance while conversing?

It is only the work of Christ that makes us acceptable in God's sight. There is nothing we can do that is pure and perfect. Even our best moments fall short of God's holy standard. This insight could lead us to self-pity, but it shouldn't. It should lead us to worship God all the more. For though we do not honor him as he deserves, he still shows us unceasing mercy and grace. He loves doing so. There is no room for pride in the Christian life. We are a humble people; he is a great God.

Whatever you do, in word or deed, do everything in the name of the Lord Jesus, giving thanks to God the Father through him.
COLOSSIANS 3:17

August 13

[First John 3:2–3. "We shall be like him, for we shall see him as he is. And every man that hath this hope in him purifieth himself, even as he is pure."] 'Tis as much as to say, As the perfect sight of Christ hereafter will make the saints like him in perfect holiness and glory, so a true faith in Christ, and hope of this future blessedness, with that knowledge of Christ from whence this faith and hope arises, will make men like Christ now in universal and increasing holiness and purity, will cause in them inclinations and endeavors after progress in holiness, and a coming nearer to that sinless perfection that is in Christ.

THE "BLANK BIBLE"

"DON'T BE SO HEAVENLY MINDED that you're of no earthly good." This saying has likely affected us more than we know, discouraging us from thinking about our eternal home, our blessed hope, our priceless inheritance. The image of absent-minded religious types, so entranced by the afterlife that they barely function, has influenced many people, including Christians. Because of such statements, we may even *fear* being heavenly minded.

But this statement is almost totally without merit. There is no greater catalyst for personal change than the hope of glory. You want to improve your eating habits? You wish to think about yourself less, and talk about yourself less? You want to start making better decisions? In sum, do you want to be of some "earthly good"? How can this all happen? The answer is obvious: Think much on Christ. Think of him perfectly obeying the Father in his incarnation. Think of him dying and rising from the tomb. Think of him ascending to the heavens. Think of him enthroned in majesty on high. Think of him splitting the skies in his apocalyptic return. Think of worshipping him with every believer from every age in the new heavens and new earth.

We can amend the pithy expression, then: "Be so heavenly minded that you're of some earthly good." Be so Christ-focused that you love your neighbor. Be so God-entranced that you care for others. The stereotypes are wrong. You can never think too much of God, too much of Jesus, and too much of heaven. Most of us do not come close to meditating to the extreme on divine things; most of us need to think much more about them. Be heavenly minded, and you'll definitely be of some earthly good.

Beloved, we are God's children now, and what we will be has not yet appeared; but we know that when he appears we shall be like him, because we shall see him as he is.   I JOHN 3:2

239

August 14

God is a prayer-hearing God. There is scarce anything that is more frequently asserted of God in Scripture than this, that he stands ready to hear prayer. Psalms 65:2, "O thou that hearest prayer, to thee shall all flesh come." 'Tis often said, if we seek him he will be found of us. 'Tis asserted, Psalms 34:10, that "they that seek the Lord shall not want any good thing."... [In] Psalms 86:4-5, God is said to be plenteous in mercy to all that call upon him; and [in] Psalms 145:18-19 the Lord is said to be nigh to all that call: "The Lord is nigh unto all them that call upon him, to all that call upon him in truth. He will fulfill the desire of them that fear him: he also will hear their cry, and will save them."

SERMONS AND DISCOURSES, 1739-1742

IT ISN'T HARD TO GET tripped up by speculations surrounding the Christian faith. Why does everything exist? Why does God allow sin in our world? One of the toughest questions is this: If God is sovereign, why do we need to pray? This last question has prompted many a late-night conversation.

We love to see intellectual and theological curiosity sparked. But the Bible, we note, spends far less time than your average college sophomore on speculative matters. God frankly does not offer us an extended philosophical treatise on the metaphysical workings of prayer. There are truths we can glean from Scripture, but the major message he communicates is this: *"Pray to me."* Prayer is appointed by God. He wants us to pray. As Jonathan Edwards summarizes, "God is a prayer-hearing God. . . . He stands ready to hear prayer."

This is the true mystery about prayer. God *wants* unholy beings like us to pray. He promises special blessings through our petitions; he will come close to us, and will "be plenteous in mercy." We have no right in ourselves to pray. We should not have access to the divine, and we should not draw any water from the eternal well. Nevertheless, in a miraculous display of grace, our great King doesn't bolt the doors to his Kingdom. Instead, he opens them wide, and calls to us to come and ask him for all we need. Don't get hung up on the tough questions. Pray. God loves when we do.

The LORD is near to all who call on him, to all who call on him in truth. PSALM 145:18-19

August 15

Resolved, not only to refrain from an air of dislike, fretfulness and anger in conversation, but to exhibit an air of love, cheerfulness and benignity.
LETTERS AND PERSONAL WRITINGS

WE SOMETIMES HEAR people say things like, "I would try that, but it's not part of my personality." It's true that we all have our own unique makeup; we're not all the same, and there is something to be said for understanding where we fall on the introvert/extrovert scale. For example, if we thrive in quiet settings by ourselves, we're probably not going to ask for a desk in the middle of an open-office floor plan.

But even as we reckon with who we are, we also need to seek personal growth. To that end, as we look over Jonathan Edwards's shoulder, we see him setting goals and pursuing his own development. He saw in himself a tendency for "an air of dislike, fretfulness and anger," and he swore to put off these attitudes. He wanted instead to radiate "love, cheerfulness and benignity." Reading accounts of his life, one finds evidence of both the melancholic and the cherubic in Edwards. He did not find it easy to choose gratitude over anxiety; he had to exert spiritual energy along these lines.

We have our own struggles. The key is not to excuse ourselves by thinking we cannot change, simply because we lean a certain way. We *can* change, and we want to work on our character day by day. We should not try to be someone else; that is not a good idea, and not what Edwards was after. But we want to know our tendencies, and where they cause problems, we want to correct them. The talkative should strive for more quietness; the meek should strive to speak up. The anxious should pray for peace; the laid-back should pray for a wake-up call. The fiercely critical should put on compassion, and the undiscerning should put on wisdom. The believer never settles for just okay, and never excuses a lack of improvement due to personality type. We work, we strive, and by God's grace we grow.

One of the Cretans, a prophet of their own, said, "Cretans are always liars, evil beasts, lazy gluttons." This testimony is true. Therefore rebuke them sharply, that they may be sound in the faith.   TITUS 1:12-13

August 16

Consider how happy those young persons must needs be that give up their youth to God and spend it in a strict walk in the ways of virtue and piety. This one thing, maybe, is enough to show that they are unspeakably happy that they live in a preparation for death; and then while they live, they live vastly more pleasantly. They have more comfort; their youth is pleasanter. They have better pleasures [of a] more excellent nature: heavenly and divine, solid and substantial—more exquisitely delighting. . . . The sweetest gratification of appetites [is theirs]. Outward enjoyments are vastly sweeter and better. . . . And their pleasures are such as will not die with youth. With respect to this life and its exercises and enjoyments, they shall not decay: their bloom and vigor will increase, perfected in glory.
SERMONS AND DISCOURSES, 1743-1758

I REMEMBER HEARING about a church youth group that decided to read through a book of Christian doctrine together instead of planning another round of silly games and "exciting events." One can imagine the fear and trembling the poor youth pastor might have felt; surely this could have been the moment of his pastoral undoing. But by all accounts, this large and thriving group loved reading biblical theology.

We underestimate our children. Though they're able to learn tough subjects in school like geometry, biology, and the football playbook, we assume they cannot handle matters of doctrine. At least that's how it often appears. After all, doesn't the common culture in many evangelical youth groups revolve around entertainment? Our students do need opportunities to run around, goof off, and breathe fresh air. Fun is good. But we're missing the boat if we send our kids to gatherings that provide only a thimbleful of Bible. We're setting them up to be picked off by clever unbelievers in college. If we haven't taught our students to engage with the tough questions of faith, it's not only *possible* they'll wander away from the church; it's *likely*.

Christian youth have unbelievable advantages before them. They taste the best things in life; "they have better pleasures . . . heavenly and divine, solid and substantial"; they may gratify their spiritual appetites like gluttons. Our children, as Jonathan Edwards lays out, do not burn their best years in adolescence, ascending to high-school nobility on the field, in the classroom, or with their peers. God willing, our children prepare early on for a long and fruitful walk with Christ. We set them up to do so when we take them through the deep waters of biblical teaching. Let us not ask too little of our children; in love and with good cheer, let us fill them full of sound doctrine and pray "their bloom and vigor will increase."

Teach us to number our days that we may get a heart of wisdom.
PSALM 90:12

August 17

LET'S TAKE AN HONEST, only-you-and-I-know-your-answer pop quiz. Which is easier to do when our pastors mess up and show they are human?

a. Pray for them
b. Criticize them

No one loves their pastor perfectly. Sometimes, in our haste to critique the pastor and other elders of the church, we overlook the fact that they are under spiritual attack from Satan. Pastors are like officers on the battlefield. They are in the thick of the action, leading the people of God, and thus the enemy would love nothing more than to take them out.

We need to pray regularly and earnestly for our pastors, and especially the chief expositors. We want them to minister as "a burning and a shining light," in Jonathan Edwards's arresting phrase. We want them to wax hot for God, and to zealously and affectionately help the sheep. Pastors are not self-sufficient Christians any more than we are. They have the weight of their congregations on their backs, in a sense, and so they need our prayers.

There are two kinds of pastors, and you can always spot them. The healthy ones stand out. They are loved by their members, cared for by their flocks, and they delight in pouring themselves out on behalf of the body. The discouraged shepherds, on the other hand, seem listless; they have little spring in their step; they preach less as an act of deliverance than as a duty of vocation. Take time today to pray for the pastors you know. Ask God to render them as burning and shining lights. They are not able to generate their own strength; they need the help of God and the fervent prayers of the people.

Brothers, pray for us, that the word of the Lord may speed ahead and be honored. 2 THESSALONIANS 3:1

August 18

God gives men great evidence of the truth of his word. . . . Pharaoh had many [kinds of] evidence. They that will not be convinced by the evidence are such as will not yield to the power of God's word. They that under the clear light of the gospel remain in unbelief [are as dark as Pharaoh]. [Many] men are [not] fully and effectually convinced of the truth of the doctrine. [They are] never thoroughly convinced of the fallen, miserable state of men by nature, [or] that Christ is the Son of God. They will not believe the threatenings [of God's word; they] remain unconvinced of the truth of the offers and promises [within it].

SERMONS AND DISCOURSES, 1743-1758

ONE THING A PRIDEFUL HUMAN HEART can do is make sin an intellectual matter. If we debate the nature of morality, we can stave off conviction of our own wrongdoing. This may be possible for unbelievers, but Christians mustn't blind themselves to the reality of indwelling sin. God, in his grace, has opened our eyes to see that depravity is not merely a concept; it is a reality. *Our* reality.

Thankfully, the Lord has given us abundant proof of the "fallen, miserable state of men by nature," in Jonathan Edwards's description. The piece of testimony that shuts the book on the matter is not somewhere far away, *out there*. Rather, it is our own hearts, *right here*, that show us we are sinners. So it is with every person who has inherited Adam's fallenness.

Praise God for his Word, and praise God for the fact that his teachings line up with the way things actually are. Christianity is not a wish-fulfillment exercise; we do not construct a philosophy in a dormitory, or a retreat center, and then wrestle it into being by an act of the will. Christianity tells us the truth in the Word, and Christianity opens our eyes to see the truth played out in the world. The Lord has made us realists—people who do business with the world as it really is. But as important as realism is, we need to see that we have hope, tremendous hope. We have the one great good thing in the cosmos, Jesus Christ, the Son of God, and all his "offers and promises."

> We also thank God constantly for this, that when you received the word
> of God, which you heard from us, you accepted it not as the word of men
> but as what it really is, the word of God. I THESSALONIANS 2:13

August 19

[Christ] did not say within himself, "Why should I undergo so much to save such vile miscreants that do so hate me, and are so cruel to their Savior? Why should I undergo so much for them that are such mortal enemies to me? Why should I expose my face to be spit on, my body to be torn and tormented for them that are so vile or base, as thus to treat me? . . . Jesus Christ did not say thus within himself, and so call for twelve legions of angels to deliver him out of their hands, or repel them by his own immediate power, as he might have done, and so rescued himself. But he patiently endured. His love stood this trial. He bore it all.
SERMONS AND DISCOURSES, 1734-1738

NOT LONG AGO, I read about a French philosopher who was enjoying a summer day at the beach. She had apparently come alone, but saw two children struggling against the surf. According to eyewitnesses, she dashed into the water, laboring to help them. In the course of this heroic effort, she was carried away by the sea and drowned.

We read stories like this and are deeply affected by them. There is nothing that so moves the human heart like self-sacrifice, even unto death. When people sacrifice themselves to help others, we are struck by their virtue. But how much greater is it to know that death is coming and yet not step back? At numerous points in his earthly life, Jesus could have "rescued himself," as Jonathan Edwards says. But while our Savior anticipated his coming sacrifice, he never flinched.

Never before (or since) has a man had such power at his fingertips but renounced it. The angels would have fallen on the Roman soldiers at Calvary. Fire could have rushed from the sky to consume the whole sordid scene. Jesus could have accessed the full fury of his divinity to overcome his executioners. But none of that happened. Jesus carried out the mission, bearing our sin and our shame. His example speaks to us, and exhorts us: Don't turn back. Don't give up. No matter the price, do not flinch.

For this reason the Father loves me, because I lay down my life that I may take it up again. No one takes it from me, but I lay it down of my own accord. I have authority to lay it down, and I have authority to take it up again. This charge I have received from my Father.
JOHN 10:17-18

August 20

"TO BE ABSENT FROM the body and to be present with the Lord" (2 Corinthians 5:8, NKJV). Few biblical teachings offer more comfort to the Christian than this—although the thought of "bodily absence" is not easy for us to comprehend. We live and move and spend our days as embodied people. Throughout our lives, we never leave our bodies. The body is truly our home, and there is no life we can imagine without it. Though we might occasionally wish for some tweaks and upgrades to our physical being, we nonetheless feel attached to it.

Upon dying, we will with full certainty leave our earthly bodies. In that moment, just a blink after we breathe our last, we will "go directly to heaven itself," as Jonathan Edwards writes. There is no intermediate state through which we must pass; Scripture knows nothing of this, nor of purgatory, where we stay for some time to have our sins purged. The thief on the cross heard the impossibly good news: "Today you will be with me in paradise" (Luke 23:43). Christ said this without qualification or contingency. The thief who had drowned himself in sin and suffering, and whose terrible existence led to his crucifixion, would that very day see God in heaven.

Like that thief, we have been sentenced to physical death due to our spiritual rebellion against God. We deserve nothing but pain and punishment and the bleakest of eternal destinies. But the thief's worst turn was his best, as it is with us. His evildoing brought him face to face with Jesus, as did ours. He offered no excuse that day, and neither shall we. Without knowing it, the thief made an appointment with God—just as God has made an appointment with us. Soon, we will be absent from the body and present with the Lord.

Between the throne and the four living creatures and among the elders I saw a Lamb standing, as though he had been slain.   REVELATION 5:6

August 21

In heaven, the spirits of just men made perfect do see him as he is. They behold his glory. They see the glory of his divine nature, consisting in all the glory of the Godhead, the beauty of all his perfections; his great majesty, almighty power, his infinite wisdom, holiness and grace, and they see the beauty of his glorified human nature, and the glory which the Father hath given him, as God-man and Mediator. . . . Now the saints, while in the body, see something of Christ's glory and love. . . . but when separated from the body, they see their glorious and loving Redeemer, as we see the sun when risen, and showing his whole disk above the horizon, by his direct beams, in a clear hemisphere, and with perfect day.

SERMONS AND DISCOURSES, 1743-1758

THERE IS A MOMENT in the movie *The Lord of the Rings: The Two Towers* that captures a little of the hope we possess as Christ's church. The fortress of Helm's Deep has nearly fallen into enemy hands; the orcs and goblins pound the door of the last stronghold, seconds away from overrunning the keep. In a last show of strength, Aragorn of Gondor and Théoden of Rohan decide they will ride out and meet their foes in a final stand. As they go, their friend Gimli looks out at the sky and says quietly, almost to himself, "The sun is rising."

When I watch this brave scene, I cannot help but think of the eternal destiny of the people of God. We presently see "something of Christ's glory and love," in the words of Jonathan Edwards. We are given by God all we can possibly take in, and more. But we live in a realm gone wrong. Some days, if we're honest, we struggle to gaze at our Savior. More than we would like, we live by faith the size of a mustard seed, with a vision of Jesus the size of a speck on the horizon.

But the sun is not long in its coming. Soon, it will reach its peak. The "direct beams" of the Son of God will stretch over all the eye can see. The "perfect day" will dawn and never fade. This news seems too good to be true, particularly in an age convulsed by disunity and wracked by wars and rumors of wars. The night at times seems to have overrun the light. But it is not so. No matter how dark things may appear, we cannot fail to remember that the Kingdom of God advances everywhere the gospel is preached and Christ is worshiped. Truly, the Son is risen. Truly, the sun is rising.

Yes, we are of good courage, and we would rather be away from the body and at home with the Lord. 2 CORINTHIANS 5:8

August 22

Resolved, never to do anything but duty; and then according to Ephesians 6:6-8, do it willingly and cheerfully "as unto the Lord, and not to man; knowing that whatever good thing any man doth, the same shall he receive of the Lord."
LETTERS AND PERSONAL WRITINGS

PLAYING LITTLE LEAGUE growing up, I remember the excitement in my Maine county about the Tommy Thompson trophy. Only one boy would get this award each year, for it signified the top baseball player in the region. Unless you threw in the sixties and cranked home runs over the fence, you knew you had no shot at the honor, but that did not diminish discussion about it.

It seems that Little League culture has changed. Today, there are many youth leagues where kids get trophies simply for participating. I'm happy for kids to have a positive experience in life, but one has to wonder about the message such a system communicates. If you show up, you're an all-star. You deserve to be celebrated. Such accolades may cultivate in young hearts the view that if we merely do what we should, we will gain recognition and renown.

We want to train our children to be like Jonathan Edwards—to do their "duty," regardless of whether they gain earthly honors for it. There will be times when we gain some thanks for what we do. There will be many more occasions when the work we do is thankless and anonymous, and no one sees but the Lord. Our daily faithfulness is not staked on a cultural concept; we do not make the mistake of thinking we deserve an award for doing what we should do. Yet it is also true that God loves it when his children work "willingly and cheerfully," seeking a better reward than a participation trophy. We quest after crowns and treasures in spiritual realms, knowing that silver and gold will fade, but what is done for the Lord will last forever.

Pursue righteousness, godliness, faith, love, steadfastness, gentleness. Fight the good fight of the faith. Take hold of the eternal life to which you were called.   1 TIMOTHY 6:11-12

August 23

The souls of true saints, when absent from the body, go to be with Jesus Christ, as they are brought into a most perfect conformity to, and union with him. Their spiritual conformity is begun while they are in the body; here beholding as in a glass, the glory of the Lord, they are changed into the same image: but when they come to see him as he is, in heaven, then they become like him, in another manner. . . . But while the saints are in the body, there is much remaining distance between Christ and them: there are remainders of alienation, and the vital union is very imperfect. . . . But when the soul leaves the body, all these clogs and hindrances shall be removed, every separating wall shall be broken down, and every impediment taken out of the way, and all distance shall cease.

SERMONS AND DISCOURSES, 1743-1758

WHEN HEAVEN COMES UP as a topic among Christians, it is not uncommon for the conversation to center on *reunion*. Good-hearted people express their desire to greet departed family members and friends again. But if we're not careful, we can make it seem as if the chief joy of the afterlife is a great gathering of the dearly departed in the heavenly fellowship hall.

Surely we will experience deep happiness in regaining fellowship with other deceased saints. But we must always take care that our interest in glory is not centered on humanity. Heaven is not a great place in any sense because of *us*. Heaven is a great place because God is there. Those absent from the body immediately go into the presence of Jesus Christ. Jonathan Edwards assures us that our "union with him" is complete. There, we "see him as he is." This is the greatest pleasure of eternity: We will worship the Lamb without ceasing.

We need not ignore the happy unity of heaven as we contemplate it. There is no isolated adoration of Christ in that place. God will gather all his people and "all distance shall cease" between us and him. No doubt the presence of loved ones will awaken delight in us we never thought possible. But Christ is the center of the saints' eternal worship. Christ is the point of heaven. It is reunion with him, granted through union with him, that we most desire.

We all, with unveiled face, beholding the glory of the Lord, are being transformed into the same image from one degree of glory to another.

2 CORINTHIANS 3:18

August 24

Departed souls of saints are with Christ, as they enjoy a glorious and immediate intercourse and converse with him. . . . And accordingly the souls of departed saints with Christ in heaven, shall have Christ as it were unbosomed unto them, manifesting those infinite riches of love towards them, that have been there from eternity: and they shall be enabled to express their love to him, in an infinitely better manner than ever they could while in the body. Thus they shall eat and drink abundantly, and swim in the ocean of love, and be eternally swallowed up in the infinitely bright, and infinitely mild and sweet beams of divine love; eternally receiving that light, eternally full of it, and eternally compassed round with it, and everlastingly reflecting it back again to the fountain of it.
SERMONS AND DISCOURSES, 1743-1758

WE OFTEN STRUGGLE to find our purpose as sojourners in this world. Knowing exactly what we are here on earth to do is not an easy question to answer. Are we here for survival? Do we exist for the indulgence of our lusts? Should we devote ourselves to "making the world a better place"—and what would that look like?

Scripture enters into this age-old conversation and gives us a weighty charge. We should think of ourselves as "vessel[s] for honorable use," as Paul teaches in 2 Timothy 2:20-21. Jonathan Edwards captured this principle in his own career, picturing believers as ones who receive "that light" of God, the sparkling of divine glory, and by a holy walk with Jesus reflect "it back again to the fountain of it." Thus, the point of human existence is not to labor for our own honor, but to receive divine light and reflect it back to heaven as an act of worship.

Our eternal vocation should inform the way we live today. It doesn't matter our precise role in the church or our exact calling in our daily lives. What matters is that we seek to receive the glory of God—wherever we find ourselves—and live in such a way that God sees in us a shining emblem of his holiness and love. We do not wait to glorify God in the heavenly places. We have this purpose, this calling, today.

You are my friends if you do what I command you. No longer do I call you servants, for the servant does not know what his master is doing; but I have called you friends, for all that I have heard from my Father I have made known to you. JOHN 15:14-15

August 25

This is the stream of Christ's delights, the river of his infinite pleasure; which he will make his saints to drink of with him; agreeable to Psalms 36:8–9, "They shall be abundantly satisfied with the fatness of thy house: thou shalt make them drink of the river of thy pleasures: for with thee is the fountain of life: in thy light shall we see light." The saints shall have pleasure, in partaking with Christ "in his pleasure," and shall see light "in his light." They shall partake with Christ of the same "river of pleasure"; shall drink of the same water of life; and of the "same new wine" in Christ's Father's kingdom (Matthew 26:29).

SERMONS AND DISCOURSES, 1743-1758

WE LIVE IN A FOODIE ERA. It's fun, really—restaurants seem to pop up everywhere, spanning the spectrum of global cuisine. On a given night, we can choose from any number of African, Caribbean, European, Asian, or American cuisines. Moreover, when we need a cup of coffee we have more options than any generation in human history could imagine. I always chuckle when asked which syrup I want in my drink—as if coffee needs a shot of raspberry to taste good.

When the Bible wants to engage us fully with the greatness of the afterlife, it invites us to a feast (Isaiah 25:6). It brings us to a holy meal, a great banquet, a spread overflowing with abundance of "fatness" and "new wine," as Jonathan Edwards points out. The afterlife does not appear in Scripture as a quiet, buttoned-down, abstemious affair. Life with God in the new heavens and new earth seems downright joyous. We will lose all obstacles to our worship and freely indulge in the fullness of God.

Heaven is no place for a joyless righteousness. Eternity is a land teeming with goodness. Jesus welcomes us to a feast there. He wants us to come and partake of his bounty. We cannot know the precise shape this aesthetic banquet will take. We can know that God intends for us to dine with him, to eat the sweetest theistic food there is, and to drink the purest drink we have ever tasted. God loves to bless his people, and we can be certain that the harvest of heaven will exceed any earthly banquet imaginable. No raspberry syrup necessary.

Father, I desire that they also, whom you have given me, may be with me where I am, to see my glory that you have given me before the foundation of the world. JOHN 17:24

August 26

When Christ instituted the Lord's Supper, and eat and drank with his disciples at his table (giving them therein a representation and pledge of their future feasting with him, and drinking new wine in his heavenly father's kingdom), he at that time led them in their praises to God, in that hymn that they sang. And so doubtless he leads his glorified disciples in heaven. David was the sweet psalmist of Israel, and led the great congregation of God's people, in their songs of praise. Herein, as well as in innumerable other things, he was a type of Christ, who is often spoken of in Scripture by the name of "David."
SERMONS AND DISCOURSES, 1743-1758

THE LORD'S SUPPER always caught my attention as a boy. Having come to faith, I understood the basic purpose of Communion: We ate the bread and drank the juice to remember the work of Christ on our behalf. With a tiny little cup of grape juice and a minuscule wafer, the church commemorated the greatest event in human history. The humility of the ceremony disguises the grandeur of what we celebrate.

But when you think about it, the plain nature of the Supper makes perfect sense. Christ did not lead his disciples into a ballroom to eat together before his crucifixion. He did not throw a lavish party to celebrate his homegoing. Instead, he hosted the most humble of feasts. The focus of the food he consecrated was not his eminence. Jesus instituted a spiritual meal that would point us back to his humiliation, his crucifixion—his *death*.

This sobering ceremony ultimately leads to praise. As Jonathan Edwards notes, Jesus led his disciples "in their praises to God." Communion is a serious ordinance. We must examine ourselves and not take the elements lightly. But Communion is also a victorious celebration. Jesus died for us. He defeated sin and Satan and death and hell. He led captivity captive, and he now "leads his glorified disciples in heaven." When we take the bread and the wine, we are not eating a meal that honors a noble defeat. We are eating a meal that celebrates a cosmic victory.

They shall hunger no more, neither thirst anymore; the sun shall not strike them, nor any scorching heat. For the Lamb in the midst of the throne will be their shepherd, and he will guide them to springs of living water, and God will wipe away every tear from their eyes.
REVELATION 7:16-17

August 27

Not only is each person of the Trinity concerned [in our redemption], but each person has his distinct part and, as it were, sustains a distinct character and charge in that affair. . . . All the difference between the Father and the other persons as to this matter is that the other two act as under another in what they do. But the Father acts as first and head of all. But yet each one may be said in some sort to sustain a distinct office. Each one has a distinct part to act, [and] stands in a distinct place and capacity, and sustains a distinct character in the affair of man's redemption, and has a distinct care and work that more especially belongs to him rather than to either of the other persons.
SERMONS AND DISCOURSES, 1743-1758

GROWING UP, it seemed that every basketball player wanted to be like Michael Jordan. They wore his jersey number (23) in youth sports; they bought his Air Jordan sneakers; and despite a distinct lack of Jordanesque ability, they shot the ball nearly as often as he did. There is something comical in watching a group of vertically challenged youngsters try to perform aerial leaps.

Nobody wants to be a mere "role player." Yet Jordan himself was part of a team on which far less gifted players were able to contribute. We can all fall prey to a *star* mentality. This is true in every sphere of life—church, business, school, or even the family. Whether we have the skills or not, we want the spotlight. We crave attention. In ways we may not even see, we hunger to get the glory.

How stunning to consider the difference between the desires of our narcissistic hearts and how the Father, Son, and Holy Spirit carry out the great work of redemption. Together, they share unity that nothing could dissolve and no one could break; yet each member of the Trinity "has a distinct part to act." First Corinthians 11:3 tells us that the Father is "the head" of the Son; John 15:26 informs us that both the Father and the Son send the Spirit to the church. The members of the Trinity carry out one inseparable work, but fill their own individual roles. The Father plans and leads, the Son creates and saves, the Spirit regenerates and indwells. In a world where everyone wants to be a star, the Godhead shows us that we find true glory in serving, and in filling our God-given roles.

> When the goodness and loving kindness of God our Savior appeared, he saved us, not because of works done by us in righteousness, but according to his own mercy, by the washing of regeneration and renewal of the Holy Spirit, whom he poured out on us richly through Jesus Christ our Savior, so that being justified by his grace we might become heirs according to the hope of eternal life.   TITUS 3:4-7

August 28

God's end in the creation of the world consists in these two things, viz. to communicate himself and to glorify himself. God created the world to communicate himself, not to receive anything. But such was the infinite goodness of God that it was his will to communicate himself, to communicate of his own glory and happiness; and he made the world to glorify himself, [as it is] fit that God should glorify himself. These two things ought [not] to be separated when we speak of God's end in the creation of the world, as the assembly of divines in speaking of the chief end for which man was created have judiciously united glorifying and enjoying {God}.
SERMONS AND DISCOURSES, 1743-1758

THE IMAGE MANY HAVE of God the Father is out of touch with biblical reality. In our sinful state, we might see the Father as wild and unpredictable. This common conception of God does not do justice to the divine truth. The Father is not uncontrolled and arbitrary; he created the world for a purpose. He is not the dread foe of happiness; he is the source and cause of it.

Jonathan Edwards argued that the Lord had two major purposes in bringing the world into existence. He wanted to "communicate" himself—that is, make himself known—and "glorify" himself, revealing his greatness. As it turns out, the two ends are complementary. By communicating himself, the Lord is glorified. What this means to Edwards—and it is very sophisticated reasoning and language, to be sure—is that God wants people to glorify him *by* enjoying him. These mutual purposes are "judiciously united" in historic Christian theology (as John Piper, for one, has argued).

This explosive thesis reframes both God and the Christian life. It marries obedience and happiness. It opens our eyes to see that the Father wants us to taste pleasure (Psalm 16:11). We can scarcely believe this idea when we first encounter it. So much of global religion revolves around duty—worship because it is right, not because it is joy-giving. But God is a different God from any other. He is the true God, and he is infinitely better and wiser than any false god the human mind has dreamed up. He doesn't separate holiness from happiness—he brings the two together. God is never more glorified by us than when we obey him for the purpose of tasting his pleasure.

You have put more joy in my heart than they have when their grain and wine abound. PSALM 4:7

August 29

JONATHAN EDWARDS preached thousands of sermons in his lifetime. Few of them drew more praise and more readers than "A Divine and Supernatural Light," which focused on the heart of the Christian faith. First preached in Northampton, this sermon became famous for its treatment of the "affectional" nature of Christianity. The faith is rational, Edwards argued, but it is also *more* than rational. Only those who embrace the gospel can truly know the things of God; there is no way to genuinely evaluate biblical religion but to experience it, to plunge all of one's being into the waters of God.

The theme of light recurs throughout Edwards's sermons and speaks to his aesthetic instincts. Just as physical light warms the body, so spiritual light warms the soul. But this divine and supernatural light does more than dazzle us; it changes the beholder, uniting heart, soul, and mind in one grand, overarching love for God:

> This light is such as effectually influences the inclination, and changes the nature of the soul. It assimilates the nature to the divine nature, and changes the soul into an image of the same glory that is beheld; 2 Corinthians 3:18, "But we all with open face beholding as in a glass the glory of the Lord, are changed into the same image, from glory to glory, even as by the Spirit of the Lord." This knowledge will wean from the world, and raise the inclination to heavenly things. It will turn the heart to God as the fountain of good, and to choose him for the only portion. This light, and this only, will bring the soul to a saving close with Christ. It conforms the heart to the gospel, mortifies its enmity and opposition against the scheme of salvation therein revealed: it causes the heart to embrace the joyful tidings, and entirely to adhere to, and acquiesce in the revelation of Christ as our Savior; it causes the whole soul to accord and symphonize with it, admitting it with entire credit and respect, cleaving to it with full inclination and affection. And it effectually disposes the soul to give up itself entirely to Christ.[46]

Interestingly, this sermon stems from Matthew 16:17, which makes no mention of light, but rather speaks of the need for divine revelation in the lives of true worshipers of God: "Blessed are you, Simon Bar-Jonah! For flesh and blood has not revealed this to you, but my Father who is in heaven." So it is with us. We are blessed. God has revealed himself to us. Our minds are captivated; our affections, our deepest appetites and instincts, now flow in a Godward direction. We are given "entirely to Christ."

August 30

The words of the Holy Scripture in the conclusion of our Bibles do manifestly hold forth thus much to us: that now the canon of the Scripture is finished, the established means of grace completed, and that no further revelation must be expected to be made to the church to the end of the world. The last book in our Bibles is the Revelation: not only placed last but was evidently written last, after all the other apostles were dead, after the destruction of Jerusalem, [and] after those events that Christ had foretold concerning the Jewish nation had had their fulfillment.
SERMONS AND DISCOURSES, 1743-1758

ONE OF THE MOST common refrains we hear from false teachers is this: *I have new revelation to give you.* The craftier ones may not say it so directly, but their message is the same. They may base their teaching on the Bible, but they weave in ideas that are not truly biblical. They twist the Scriptures, telling us that no one prior to them has properly understood it. And they tell us matters we've never heard, adding to the revelation of God.

If someone tells you they have a special revelation from God, the hair on the back of your neck should stand up. As Jonathan Edwards declares, "The canon of the Scripture is finished." The Spirit illumines Scripture, helping us understand and apply it. But "no further revelation must be expected" in our time. The book of Revelation completed the canon, and God ensured through history that his true followers received the letters and documents that were truly revelatory—from the Spirit, and not from men.

We don't need someone to give us a "deeper" encounter with God. There is no voice from God that will lead us to teach people some newer, richer way of meeting him. The way to draw near to God is to read his Word. With my whole heart I seek you, writes the psalmist in Psalm 199:10. How will his heart find God? He answers our question: "Let me not wander from your commandments!" The way to a deeper experience of God runs straight through the Bible. We meet the mind and will and goodness of God in the pages of the biblical text. The Spirit ministers to us as we read, and meditate, and soak up the Word. We do not need—or even want—new revelation as Christians. We do need, and want, more of God and more of his spiritual food.

> I warn everyone who hears the words of the prophecy of this book: if anyone adds to them, God will add to him the plagues described in this book, and if anyone takes away from the words of the book of this prophecy, God will take away his share in the tree of life and in the holy city, which are described in this book. REVELATION 22:18-19

August 31

If we compare the text with what is said elsewhere in this epistle, it confirms that not only all that are in a state of salvation do love God, but that they love God above the world. 'Tis said in the text, "This is the love of God, that we keep his commandments: and his commandments are not grievous. For whatsoever is born of God overcometh the world." By overcoming the world, the Apostle means overcoming worldly lusts or worldly affections. . . . And worldly affections are never overcome and subdued any other way than by heavenly affections' prevailing above them. The love of the world is not overcome but [by] the love of God prevailing above it, so as to set one at liberty.

SERMONS AND DISCOURSES, 1743-1758

THE WAY TO OVERCOME our lusts is not to grit our teeth, close our eyes, and shout, "Try harder!" The way to overcome our sinful appetites is to find something greater to love, and to pray that God will give us grace to do so. We need to stop our old patterns, and to exercise our will against sin. But that is not enough; we need to direct our interests, appetites, and affections *toward* something.

Jonathan Edwards lived in the eighteenth century, but he knew the natural temptations of the flesh. Humanity has always had to battle "worldly lusts." Sexual impurity—unclean thoughts, desires, and actions—are nothing new. They are as ancient as fallen human society. But in our visually oriented society today, with earlier standards of modesty and propriety forgotten, we recognize that we must fight with renewed vigor the temptation to lust.

To live a pure life, and to help our children and friends do so as well, we need wise habits. We need self-control. We need discipline. But more than anything, we need a big, all-consuming vision of a holy, loving, sin-destroying God before us. We need "heavenly affections," in other words. As we treasure God and devote ourselves to him, and pray often to him for help, he will purify us. Even the guiltiest among us, those who have become like a house without doors, may prevail over sin and temptation. In a world lost in lust, the church is a lighthouse, calling us all to put our evil desires to death and be clothed with the very fabric of Christ.

> If your right eye causes you to sin, tear it out and throw it away. For it is better that you lose one of your members than that your whole body be thrown into hell. MATTHEW 5:29

September

✝

September 1

September 1716: Jonathan Edwards begins college

AT THE AGE OF THIRTEEN, Jonathan Edwards left home in East Windsor, Connecticut, to begin classes at the Collegiate School of Connecticut (which later became Yale University). Though in Edwards's day the average age to begin college was sixteen, some younger students could enter the college if they had already learned the required languages. Edwards had learned Latin by age six, and he knew Greek and Hebrew by age twelve.

Edwards attended the branch of the school in Wethersfield, just ten miles from his family home. His principal tutor was his half cousin Elisha Williams. Williams was a gifted pedagogue who connected well with Edwards. Jonathan excelled in his studies, even as the school moved to the New Haven branch, where Timothy Cutler presided. Edwards earned both a baccalaureate and a master's degree, and was the school's top student throughout his tenure.

The young men who studied alongside Edwards did not impress him much. Then as now, too many students majored in foolishness while ignoring their studies. Edwards wrote his father a report of their shenanigans:

> Although these disturbances were so speedily quashed, yet they are succeeded by much worse, and greater, and I believe greater than ever were in the college before; they are occasioned by the discovery of some monstrous impieties, and acts of immorality lately committed in the college, particularly stealing of hens, geese, turkeys, pigs, meat, wood, etc., unseasonable night-walking, breaking people's windows, playing at cards, cursing, swearing, and damning, and using all manner of ill language, which never were at such a pitch in the college as they now are.[47]

Edwards did not suffer fools and foolishness, as one can see. Though he had to watch his habit of severity, Edwards had good reason to dislike this behavior. His peers, after all, were candidates for the ministry. The school was not a university in the modern sense; Yale was founded to train pastors. Edwards wanted his peers to pursue the Lord with sobriety and passion, and leave the silly stuff behind.

Pig-stealing aside, Edwards graduated with the terminal degree of his day, and went on to still greater intellectual heights. The course laid out for him by his father trained him to think critically and carefully in his studies, and set him up to become the leading pastor-theologian of his era. We do well to think about how we can support a learned pastorate in our time. Seminaries exist to strengthen the church; how can we strengthen such institutions?

September 2

"My peace I give unto you." Christ by calling it his peace signifies two things:

1. That it was his own, that which he had to give. . . . Silver and gold he had none: for while in his estate of humiliation he was poor. "The foxes had holes, and the birds of the air had nests: but the Son of man had not where to lay his head" (Luke 9:58). He had no earthly estate to leave to his disciples who were as it were his family: but he had peace to give them.

2. It was his peace that he gave them; as it was the same kind of peace which he himself enjoyed. The same excellent and divine peace which he ever had in God; and which he was about to receive in his exalted state in a vastly greater perfection and fullness: for the happiness Christ gives to his people, is a participation of his own happiness.

SERMONS AND DISCOURSES, 1743-1758

ALL JESUS HAD TO GIVE, when he came to the end of his life, was peace. In earthly terms, what a poor man! How different was our Savior from a child of the modern economy. We hear—and we should hear—that we need to save our money, budget wisely, and invest for the sake of our children and our retirement. All this is good. But if in the end you have nothing but the peace of God, then you and Jesus have a great deal in common.

We who scrape and press and hustle to make financial progress need these words. Though we should never cease to exercise fiscal wisdom, we should remember that the gifts of God are beyond worth. "Silver and gold," as Jonathan Edwards identifies, a sizable "earthly estate," a booming retirement account—Jesus had none of these. He chose to be poor for our sake, and he left nothing of material value behind. How unlike our Savior we are.

But Jesus actually knew wealth beyond compare. He gave to his disciples "the same kind of peace which he himself enjoyed." At all times, Jesus knew the Father, and lived accordingly. He never lost his mind worrying about the future. He didn't bicker and fight with his loved ones as his anxieties came to the surface. He had no bad habits that resulted from his need to cope with unending stress. Jesus knew his trials, but he lived in the "perfect peace" God promises to his faithful ones (Isaiah 26:3). More than any financial gift, this is God's inheritance for his chosen. The wondrous truth? We need not wait for it. All-surpassing peace is ours, now, *today.*

Peace I leave with you; my peace I give to you. Not as the world gives do I give to you. JOHN 14:27

September 3

Our Lord Jesus Christ has bequeathed true peace and comfort to his followers. Christ is called the "prince of peace" (Isaiah 9:6). And when he was born into the world, the angels on that joyful and wonderful occasion sang "Glory to God in the highest, on earth peace"; because of that peace which he should procure for and bestow on the children of men; peace with God, and peace one with another, and tranquility and peace within themselves: which last is especially the benefit spoken of in the text. This Christ has procured for his followers and laid a foundation for their enjoyment of, in that he has procured for them the other two, viz.: peace with God, and one with another.
SERMONS AND DISCOURSES, 1743-1758

HAVE YOU HAD the misfortune of spending time with a couple who constantly pick at each other? It's one of the most unpleasant experiences one can have. Some husbands and wives genuinely love each other and are committed to their marriage. But rather than working through conflict, and striving to understand their spouse, they operate in perpetual battle mode. No detail is too trivial, no moment too peaceful, for a fight.

The sadness of such a marriage stands apart from the peace that God gives his adopted children. Through the atoning death of Jesus, God cancels the debt we owe him. We give Christ all our sin, and he gives us all his righteousness. So God reconciles us to himself. But reconciliation cannot be contained. It seeps out of our relationship with God, and flows into our earthly relationships. God has made peace with us; we now make peace "one with another," writes Jonathan Edwards.

The Cross of Christ will revolutionize a marriage or a bitter heart. It will rescue and restore forgotten friendships and repair damaged bonds when we repent and confess our sins to one another. In our fallen state, we trap ourselves in patterns of enmity. But Christ springs the trap. He sends the Spirit to live inside of us, and the Spirit does not produce in us a heart of hatred, but one of love for the brethren. What strength and hope this gives us. We do not know for sure if all that is fractured will be restored before we go to be with God. But we do know that in Christ we possess all we could possibly need for reconciliation, for peace, and for the cessation of our personal battles.

In Christ Jesus you who once were far off have been brought near by the blood of Christ. EPHESIANS 2:13

September 4

Consider, your treatment of God is not only the same in kind but infinitely more heinous and aggravated. You take it very heinously when any of your fellow creatures treats you with contempt, who are but a worm of the dust, [much less than] a prince. . . and [yet] when your equal [treats you with contempt, you are enraged]; yea, when your superiors [are disrespectful of you, you are also aroused]. But how heinous, then, is it [for] the great Jehovah, who is infinitely above [you]?
SERMONS AND DISCOURSES, 1743-1758

LIFE IS FILLED with many small challenges. I often think about this when flying. However calm you try to be, you will likely find yourself challenged by the plane's uncommonly close quarters.

It isn't hard to become annoyed when trivial matters crop up. We feel offended; we feel wronged. But our sense of justice often malfunctions, doesn't it? We think a lot about our own problems, but we give very little thought to how much God puts up with, and how patient he is with us. When someone treats us "with contempt," tempers flare and Twitter accounts light up. But when we go a week without praying to God, or reading the Word, or pursuing what is excellent and edifying, we treat it like no big deal.

We need to call heaven and have our gravity restored. The Lord is "infinitely above" us, as Jonathan Edwards makes plain. Yes, we have to deal with many frustrations and annoyances in this earthly sojourn. But God constantly puts up with us. He shows incredible patience with wayward children like you and me. When a service professional tells us off, or the passenger in the next seat rudely claims every last inch of airplane real estate, we should exercise wisdom and self-control. We should also let our thoughts go to God, who so graciously loves us despite our wandering, fickle, selfish hearts. The battle for the armrest need not torpedo our spirituality; it can, if we will allow it, drive us to praise God.

Consider him who endured from sinners such hostility against himself, so that you may not grow weary or fainthearted.   HEBREWS 12:3

September 5

*Resolved, very much to exercise myself in this all my life long, viz. with the greatest openness
I am capable of, to declare my ways to God, and lay open my soul to him: all my sins,
temptations, difficulties, sorrows, fears, hopes, desires, and everything, and every circumstance.*
LETTERS AND PERSONAL WRITINGS

SELF-RELIANCE IS DEADLY. It may serve us well on a hike in the wilderness, but
in the spiritual realm, we must guard against going it alone. We need to "declare
[our] ways to God" and "lay open" our souls to him. This may come easily, or
it may not. But either way, we are not self-starting, self-driving machines. We
are needy creatures, made by God, filled with affections and cravings that only
God can satisfy.

The Lord wants us to lay our hearts bare before him, lifting up our "sins,
temptations, difficulties, sorrows" and more to him—not merely as an act of
confession, but to call down God's power, and make us strong in our weakness.
God knows our frailties better than we do. He fashions every trial so that we
will not trust in our own strength, but ask him for his. We may fool some of the
people some of the time, but we can never fool God. Everything about the life he
has designed nudges us in the direction of trusting him and seeking his strength.

We all have our moments when we think, *I need to handle this one myself.* But
we should resist the temptation to venture out in our own power. We should go
to the Lord with big challenges and small. We are not a self-dependent people.
We are a Spirit-indwelt people—which tells us everything we need to know about
how God wants us to live our lives.

> Say therefore to the people of Israel, "I am the LORD, and I will bring
> you out from under the burdens of the Egyptians, and I will deliver you
> from slavery to them, and I will redeem you with an outstretched arm
> and with great acts of judgment." EXODUS 6:6

September 6

The people of Christ are united one to another. This is a consequence of their union with Christ: he is their head of union. Having all so near a relation to one head, they all are necessarily nearly related one to another; having all one Father, they consequently become one family and are brethren one to another. Having one spiritual husband to whom they are lawfully espoused, it follows that they all together constitute one spouse of Christ, and consequently must be members one of another, as the Apostle says.

SERMONS AND DISCOURSES, 1743-1758

THERE IS NO SUCH THING as Lone Ranger Christianity. When we come to faith, we acknowledge that God is our King. Christ is our Lord. The Spirit is our strength. But the Trinitarian family has brought many others besides us into the overflow of its love. We gain membership in a body that spans the earth and all of history. Every believer is our brother or sister.

Tragically, some Christians believe they can worship God all by their lonesome. They say they don't need the church. Perhaps without realizing it, these folks deny the full effect of the work of Christ. The saving grace of God given to us through the ministry of Jesus not only knits us to God, but also to all God's children. Jesus is our "head of union," as Jonathan Edwards puts it. Jesus makes for himself a family from all the tribes and tongues and nations of the earth. Put differently, he doesn't marry a billion different spouses through the work of redemption. He takes for himself "one spouse" comprising the entirety of his blood-bought church (Ephesians 5:22-28).

We do not normally think of our spiritual fellowship in such striking terms. But far from requiring separation from others, our union with Christ brings us into fellowship with his entire body—that is, all other believers. Though our sins and lack of faithfulness to the Word present difficulties for unity, we must always remember how strong the bond is between Christians. The same force that knits us to Christ knits us to one another. We are "members one of another" (Romans 12:5, KJV) and always will be.

Now you are the body of Christ and individually members of it.

I CORINTHIANS 12:27

September 7

[God] knows everything past, [even] things a thousand years ago. [He also knows] everything to come, [even] a thousand years to come. [He knows] all the men that will be, [and] all that they will do, say, or think. This is more than all the rest: he perfectly knows himself. God is so great that we can't know but little of him.
SERMONS AND DISCOURSES, 1743-1758

SOME THEOLOGIANS ARGUE that God does not know everything. They argue that he is so committed to human liberty that he cannot know the future, nor does he foresee our actions. We should handle with care here. In granting mankind this extreme vision of freedom, we give up a great deal. If our concept of God does not include omniscience, we are dealing with a different "divine being" from the biblical one.

It is comforting beyond measure that God knows all things. He is omniscient. His knowledge and understanding face no limit or qualification. He perfectly comprehends both "everything past" and "everything to come." He knows everything about us, and we can hide no thought, no whispered word, no out-of-sight deed from him. We know "but little" of God, but he knows himself to the full. Divine omniscience undergirds the divine will. Because God knows all things, he is perfectly able to do all things well.

You and I don't know what's headed our way ten seconds from now, let alone a year from now, or twenty years in the distance. We have a hard enough time remembering what we ate for lunch yesterday, so finite is our memory. But the Lord has complete knowledge of what was, what is, and what is coming. He has planned every last step we will take. He knows the number of hairs on our heads. He knows, and he cares. He cares about forgetful, proud, straying creatures like us. Because he is God, and therefore omniscient, he is aware of all things and is bringing them to their rightful conclusion—including the destination of our souls.

Great is our Lord, and abundant in power; his understanding is beyond measure. PSALM 147:5

September 8

God is infinitely strong. [God] can do what he will; nothing is too hard; nothing is difficult or hard for him to do. [This] appears [in the] creation of the world: making things so great, making 'em out of nothing. All the men in the world can't make one grain of sand. . . . [God will] raise all the dead, overcoming all his enemies, great kings and their armies. [Meanwhile,] all the devils are held back by him.

SERMONS AND DISCOURSES, 1743-1758

WE CAN TRY TO DEFY the strength of God. We can shake our fist at him. But when it comes to divine omnipotence, there is one thing we cannot do: *Deny it.* Sure, we can try to dismantle the case for theism. But when a thunderstorm shakes an airplane like a twig, or a tornado touches down in the middle of a town, or ocean waves reach a hundred feet in height, we come into contact with the prospect of a power much greater than ours. What seems easy to debate in theory gets harder to deny in a terrifying moment.

Whether we want to admit God's infinite strength or not, we must reckon with the workings of our world, whose forces are so far beyond our power that we effectively have none. Every natural display of enormous power points us to a greater figure, one who is "infinitely strong." God made the world "out of nothing," using no preexisting materials. God raises the dead. God sends the world's most ferocious warriors to their graves with but a word. God holds "all the devils" back from his chosen. There is no limit to his strength.

Because God is God, we *want* him to have unlimited power. He is completely trustworthy, unlike what a skeptical culture urges us to believe. He uses his strength for good in every instance. He sweeps the earth of his enemies, and when the people of God suffer under threat of certain death, he sends his angels to protect them and give them victory. The book of Revelation is not God's best guess at the way things will turn out; it is sure and certain prophecy. It depends on the power of God for fulfillment. In every area, God is strong, infinitely strong, and he loves nothing more than to use his power to protect and propel his people.

I am God. . . . There is none who can deliver from my hand; I work, and who can turn it back? ISAIAH 43:12-13

September 9

He sees all you do, sees in the night, sees your heart, [and] remembers all. Here is encouragement to pray to God. [God] knows what you need, knows what is best for you. [He] can do all things for you, [and] can give you a new heart. No other can. Here is encouragement to go to Christ to save you[rself]. He is able, [for] he is God as well as man. He can save you from the devil: he takes the poor soul out of the mouth of the devil as a strong man comes and takes a lamb out of the mouth of a bear.

SERMONS AND DISCOURSES, 1743-1758

AS PORTRAYED REPEATEDLY in Scripture, the Lord is a warrior. He is not a toothless sovereign. We think of a text such as Isaiah 42:13:

> The LORD goes out like a mighty man,
>   like a man of war he stirs up his zeal;
> he cries out, he shouts aloud,
>   he shows himself mighty against his foes.

The world is not a neutral place. It is the site of a great war for souls between God and the devil. But the fight is not on equal terms. The Lord is awesome in strength, "mighty against his foes." When he joins the battle, the battle is over.

We need to remember this picture of God as we battle our flesh and oppose the devil. In some instances, we may feel trapped and bound. Sin may seem to have a hold over us. Perhaps we have fallen into a pattern of temptation, or failed to exercise self-control. Maybe we got together with some old friends and found ourselves in unedifying conversations that did not reflect our new nature. Or we acted in a crabby way to our kids, leaving them hurt and alone.

How thankful we are that God's nature has not changed. He is not a downgraded deity; he has not stopped being a "man of war," terrible in battle, victorious over the serpent. Jonathan Edwards is right: We need to "pray to God." He is a strong Savior and a mighty Lord. The Lord hears us when we pray, and he will act. He is able to take "a lamb out of the mouth of a bear." He will give us the power we need to overcome sin. He will do so for us because his own Son was the Lamb of God who died as a substitute sacrifice for us. He has not stopped helping us. "He cries out, he shouts aloud," and he comes to fight on our behalf.

The LORD is a warrior; the LORD is His name.   EXODUS 15:3, NASB

September 10

BY THE AUTUMN OF 1741, Jonathan Edwards had seen three separate seasons of revival—in 1734, 1740, and the summer of 1741. Nevertheless, skepticism persisted in New England to the degree that two parties emerged: the New Lights, who supported the no-holds-barred preaching of the gospel, and the Old Lights, who preferred the established rhythms of ministry over revival preaching.

Edwards defended the revival in his 1741 commencement speech at Yale. He showed great care describing neutral effects and definitive effects of a true work of God's Spirit. Above all, he said, wherever God moves, the love of God increases:

> Therefore when the Spirit that is at work amongst a people, tends
> this Way, and brings many of them to high and exalting Thoughts of
> the divine Being, and his glorious Perfections; and works in them an
> admiring, delightful Sense of the Excellency of Jesus Christ; representing
> Him as the chief among ten Thousands, altogether lovely, and makes him
> precious to the Soul; winning and drawing the Heart with those Motives
> and Incitements to Love, which the Apostle speaks of in that Passage of
> Scripture we are upon, *viz.* the wonderful, free Love of God in giving his
> only begotten Son to die for us, and the wonderful dying Love of Christ
> to us, who had no Love to him, but were his Enemies; as [1 John 5:9-10:]
> "In this was manifested the Love of God towards us, because that God
> sent his only begotten Son into the World, that we might live through
> him. Herein is Love; not that we loved God, but that he loved us, and
> sent his Son to be the Propitiation for our Sins.[48]

The address was later published with an impressively lengthy title: *The Distinguishing Marks of a Work of the Spirit of God, Applied to that Uncommon Operation that has lately Appeared on the Minds of Many of the People of This Land: With a Particular Consideration of the Extraordinary Circumstances with Which this Work Is Attended.* Edwards's considerations have helped Christians understand both personal conversion and the matter of revival. When someone professes faith in Christ, how should we handle this profession? What signs do we look for as proof of new birth?

Edwards's text identifies a raised affection for God, for Christ, and the convicting work of the Spirit in our hearts as the evidence of regeneration. Though we all face storms and controversies on earth, there is only peace for true believers when we meet the living God, and he imbues us with the distinguishing marks of a truly spiritual work.

September 11

Afflictions that are brought on men in this world are from the hand of God. Not only remotely from the constitution of the world, whereby it grows as naturally as briars and thorns, but there is a hand of God in [the] particular ordering. This is livelily represented; Job 5:6–7, "Although affliction cometh not forth of the dust, neither doth trouble spring out of the ground; yet man is born unto trouble, as the sparks fly upward." [The] ordering of God's wisdom [includes] the particular affliction, [its] nature, measure, time, continuance, [and] circumstances. [It is a matter of] his power—all in his hands—we ourselves [being] means [or] instruments, [God's] hand often remarkably appears [in our affairs at a] time unexpected, baffling [all our] endeavors [and our most carefully contrived] means. [Such an event] manifests remarkably the vanity of man's wisdom and power.

SERMONS AND DISCOURSES, 1743-1758

WE ALL WANT to plan our days according to "our most carefully contrived means." But life often doesn't cooperate. We head out, for example, on a long-anticipated vacation. Almost as soon as we do, the unexpected occurs, "baffling [all our] endeavors." The tickets cost more than we anticipated. The hotel room we selected online smells weird as soon we open the door. We sigh, and observe a moment of silence for our best-laid plans.

We would all like to believe that our lives will go according to our hopes. Sometimes things work in our favor, but no one can fully escape "afflictions," as Jonathan Edwards identifies them. God, in his wisdom, has ordained every-thing about our particular challenges: "nature, measure, time, continuance, [and] circumstances." Despite our best efforts to safeguard our days, God is pleased to expose the "vanity of man's wisdom and power." We can't orchestrate our lives; we can't even pull off the beach trip we planned.

Without God, the afflictions of life could cripple us or ignite us. We might rage against the world. With God, we know that we need to consider hardship a part of the sanctification process. We need not enjoy our afflictions, but we can approach them realistically and spiritually, knowing they will come and that God will use even the worst things to draw us closer to him (James 1:2-4). Our hope, after all, is not merely a great road trip, or a nice getaway. God is preparing us for an eternal weight of glory. That certainty is our best case scenario.

> All the inhabitants of the earth are accounted as nothing, and he
> does according to his will among the host of heaven and among the
> inhabitants of the earth; and none can stay his hand or say to him,
> "What have you done?" DANIEL 4:35

September 12

How the man is said to be happy whom God correcteth. [Happy is he] on whom God obtains
the end of chastisement, in correcting or rectifying his heart and behavior. There are two things:
turning from that which is evil or vain, and turning to that which is truly good.
SERMONS AND DISCOURSES, 1743-1758

AT ONE POINT in my inglorious athletic career, a coach called me out in front
of my peers. I was frustrated at not getting the drill right, and he addressed me
with some fervor. I wasn't one to clash with my coaches, but in the heat of the
moment, I answered him sharply. He looked at me, stunned, and then ordered
me off to the side to do push-ups. It was fitting punishment for my failure to
receive correction well. His manner wasn't perfect, but I've remembered that
lesson ever since.

We may not initially be thrilled when God corrects us. He does this in numerous ways: through the direct conviction of the Spirit after sin; through our spouse
or a friend encouraging us to repent; through the preaching of a sermon that
suddenly sends correction straight to the heart, like a heat-seeking missile. We
regularly need correction, much as we don't want to admit it; God frequently
sends correction, graciously choosing to give us what we need.

Jonathan Edwards is right: We should be "happy" when the Lord exposes
our failings. We need in that moment to do two things when conviction strikes:
We should turn from evil, and turn to good. The most practical way to effect
this two-part change is to confess our sin on the spot, and simultaneously ask
the Lord to give us the grace we need to choose righteousness from here on out.
Correction is going to come to us all. We should show gratitude to God that this
is so. The question before us is this: When correction comes, will we receive it
well, or fight it off?

For the moment all discipline seems painful rather than pleasant, but
later it yields the peaceful fruit of righteousness to those who have been
trained by it. HEBREWS 12:11

September 13

And that which makes the manifestation of the glory and love of God that is made by the gospel peculiarly joyful is the remarkable union of both those things with which that discovery of God that is made in the gospel is attended. God's glory is manifested in a work of love to us, and a work of most transcendent love; and God's love appears in such a manner as to be consistent with the glory of all his perfections, and not only so, but so as exceedingly to manifest the glory of every perfection. Such an union does unspeakably heighten the sweetness and joy of the manifestation.

SERMONS AND DISCOURSES, 1743-1758

THE JOY OF THE GOSPEL is twofold. First, we gain all things in Christ: forgiveness, peace, purpose, comfort, and a future hope chief among them. Once, we had nothing, and now we have everything. But this is not all we gain, or even the best part of our spiritual bounty. Gospel faith is the "discovery of God," as Jonathan Edwards elegantly phrases it. There was a time when we didn't know that this excellent being existed and ruled the world for his glory and our good; now we do.

It is the "discovery of God" that many people, even some Christians, need to make. When we share our faith with someone, or teach the chief duties and delights of the Christian life to believers, we should take care to make it clear that God is the greatest gift of all. We gain what we desperately need but cannot attain on our own. This is the wonderful truth. Forgiveness cleanses our hearts. Peace floods our soul. Purpose fills our days. All this happens through conversion, and all of it is a gift.

But we cannot separate the blessings of God from God himself. He is the chief joy of his people. He is the one who goes before us and stands behind us and sends out every one of the gifts we've addressed. Without him, there is no comfort, no future, no hope. It is the "union" of God and his kindnesses that pushes Christianity to an impossibly good level. Even if we received only God, this gift would be entirely worth it. Let's treasure the gift of God today.

God, who said, "Let light shine out of darkness," has shone in our
hearts to give the light of the knowledge of the glory of God in the face
of Jesus Christ. 2 CORINTHIANS 4:6

September 14

Conversion is an opening the eyes of the blind and causing light to shine out of darkness. And so, in every part of the work of sanctification, Christians, after they are become true Christians, may still complain that they are blind, exceeding blind; they may complain still of gross darkness, darkness that may be felt; and the light God gives 'em from time to time is like the shining of the light out of darkness when God said, "Let there be light" [Genesis 1:3]. And 'tis all an opening the eyes of the blind.

SERMONS AND DISCOURSES, 1739-1742

SOMETIMES WE FEEL like shipwrecked stragglers huddling on the beach. One wave pounds us, soaking every fiber of our clothing; then another wave rushes in; then another, and another. If we're not careful, we can feel this way regarding our status in the world. Everything seems bleak. We have no real hope. We sit by ourselves, having all but lost our distant hope of rescue. We feel cranky and defeated.

In such instances, we cannot see what God is doing. We feel as if we've gone blind—"exceeding blind," as Jonathan Edwards puts it. But this is not actually true. From nearly the first verse of the Bible, God has turned on the lights in a dark place. In fact, we could make a strong exegetical argument that light-giving has been God's chief activity since the creation of the world. He loves light; he is not indifferent to it. He takes no greater joy than to restore our sight, "opening the eyes of the blind." He wants to unveil his glory, and he gains much honor and happiness when we gaze on it.

This is the central business of our days: not bemoaning the darkness, real and awful as it is, but celebrating the radiance of the divine. Satan wants us to wear sunglasses all the time, but we will not consent. We have *seeing* to do. We have *glory* to behold. We have Christ's work of *redemption* to celebrate. There is one fact greater than all the darkness in the world. It is the eternal light, the holy beauty of God, who gives sight to the blind, that they may take in his wonders. Today, reject blindness. Choose this hour to truly *see*.

Arise, shine, for your light has come, and the glory of the LORD has risen upon you. ISAIAH 60:1

September 15

Though it be but a little that we can do, yet if we do anything for Christ in sincerity, there is no danger of its being ever forgotten. This was promised to Mary concerning that which she did to put respect upon Christ: that her act should be remembered and published so that, wherever the gospel should be preached throughout the whole [world], this that she did should be told for a memorial {of her}. And we see it fulfilled: we see how Christ has taken care that this act of hers should be recorded in the sacred records of the Word of God, to remain as long as the church remains and to be known everywhere where Christ's own name is known.
SERMONS AND DISCOURSES, 1739-1742

WE ALL CAN REMEMBER certain acts of kindness that others have done for us. This is especially true of the occasional above-and-beyond blessings we receive. I recall the time when my grandfather took me to my first Boston Red Sox game. I'm quite certain that I got almost no sleep the night before. The Sox won the game, and Tom Brunansky, a hard-hitting outfielder, gave me his autograph. I still remember it as one of the coolest days of my childhood.

But although we remember the highlights, the truth is we have forgotten, or have failed to realize, much of the good that has been done for us. For example, we remember almost nothing of the care our parents rendered to us in our early years. Waking up out of a dead sleep to help us; feeding us every day; giving us what we needed for success. These and so many other things we've frankly forgotten. But God has a perfect mind, and a perfect memory. He not only knows all he has done for us, but he never forgets what we have done for him.

There is, as Jonathan Edwards rightly sums up, "but a little that we can do" for God, even with all the force of heaven behind us. We are meager, meek creatures. We never serve our master as we should. Yet God rejoices in our small acts of faith and obedience. Mary anointed Christ with precious perfume (John 12:3), and her love was listed "in the sacred records of the Word of God." The Lord does not reprove his children when we try, however imperfectly, to honor him according to his Word. He is gentle and generous. He keeps record of our faithful deeds. He never forgets.

His master said to him, "Well done, good and faithful servant. You have been faithful over a little; I will set you over much. Enter into the joy of your master." MATTHEW 25:21

September 16

Christ and his church, like the bridegroom and bride, rejoice in each other, as in those that are the objects of each others' most tender and ardent love. The love of Christ to his church is altogether unparalleled: the height and depth and length and breadth of it pass knowledge: for he loved the church, and gave himself for it; and his love to her proved stronger than death. And on the other hand, she loves him with a supreme affection: nothing stands in competition with him in her heart: she loves him with all her heart: her whole soul is offered up to him in the flame of love.

SERMONS AND DISCOURSES, 1743-1758

THERE IS NO LOVE quite like the love of Christ for his bride. No one can equal it. No one can come close. Jesus loved the church with an everlasting love which is "altogether unparalleled" in history. Christ has no competitor in this regard. The "height and depth and length and breadth" of his active, overcoming, triumphant love transcend any known standard. If for no other reason than Christ's love for us, we should marvel and wonder and weep with joy for our Savior.

How different Christ's love is from any other love we might know. We may feel passion for our spouse, and affection for our kids and grandkids, and strong unity with our friends and fellow church members. But in none of these relationships will we offer spiritual atonement for sin. Our love cannot redeem anyone. It cannot buy anyone back from hell. Our love cannot pry the devil's claws off this world, deal him a death blow, and send him raging into the abyss. But the love of Christ can—and will.

So it is that the church offers its praise to Jesus. We feel "supreme affection" for our God. Nothing approaches or "stands in competition" with our love for the divine. The Lord does not need to prove himself today, to vindicate himself against human standards. The Father's gift to us of his Son is the once-for-all sign that God is love. No one can match him; no one can top him. We can never outlast or use up God's love. It is as real and as powerful today as it will be for all eternity.

Though you have not seen him, you love him. Though you do not now see him, you believe in him and rejoice with joy that is inexpressible and filled with glory, obtaining the outcome of your faith, the salvation of your souls. I PETER 1:8-9

September 17

Both the holiness and happiness of the Godhead consists in this love. As we have already proved, all creature holiness consists essentially and summarily in love to God and love to other creatures; so does the holiness of God consist in his love, especially in the perfect and intimate union and love there is between the Father and the Son.

WRITINGS ON THE TRINITY, GRACE, AND FAITH

WHAT BANDS DID YOU say you *loved* twenty or thirty years ago? Confronted with a list of our most-listened-to songs from our younger days, we might be inclined to suppress the document. We thought we loved that pop supergroup, or that death metal hair band, or that Top 40 sensation who turned out to be a one-hit wonder. For a season, we *thought* we loved that music, but it was not a love that lasted.

We are accustomed to this fleeting kind of love today. We may feel intense affection at the moment, and even declare our undying love for someone or something, only to forget all about it in a few months' time. We are fickle creatures. We do not think of love as coming with strong bonds and deep ties. But that is the nature of true love. True affection is both an act of the heart and of the will. Real love is grounded in "happiness," as Jonathan Edwards points out, but also in "holiness."

We don't get extra credit for loving God. He is an infinitely worthy being and we *should* love him. His perfections call forth our abiding affection. We reflect the very image of the holy Trinity when we love our Maker. The three persons love one another purely. Their love refines and focuses our love here and now. God is not a one-hit wonder. He is—and will be—the attention of the affection of all his people for eternity. Our love is not a gift we give to God. It is a sign that we know him, that he is making us holy, and that we have entered into a happiness this world cannot comprehend.

> The glory that you have given me I have given to them, that they may be one even as we are one, I in them and you in me, that they may become perfectly one, so that the world may know that you sent me and loved them even as you loved me. JOHN 17:22-23

September 18

There are these two things that God manifests himself by, and by which his designs are carried on, viz. his word and his works: the words of his mouth and the works of his hand. And the will of God must, and will surely be, fulfilled, and his name glorified by one or the other of these. By the one God makes known his will and proposes it, and exhibits motives to men's reason to influence them as moral agents to comply with the will of God. By the other God undertakes himself to fulfill his own will and obtain his own end, and therefore all things must be subdued to God by one or the other of these.

SERMONS AND DISCOURSES, 1743-1758

MANY PEOPLE SEEM to enjoy what we call *period pieces*. These television shows and films transport us to an earlier era, often one in which men and women interact in genteel and polite ways. So elaborate are the courtesies and manners that visiting the past in this way can be a shock to the system. People don't stare at their tiny phones, ignoring one another; they converse, they laugh, they treat their peers with respect.

Important as personal manners are, we have a much greater respect to pay. We have a God to obey. As Jonathan Edwards notes, God treats humanity as "moral agents." He calls us to honor him, for he is God. But in doing so, he doesn't seize every person in a vise grip. He "makes known his will and proposes it," and addresses our "reason" and "motives" to move us to savor him. Said more simply, God engages us with dignity. He made the human race by his own hand and continues to treat us with a courtesy we frankly do not deserve.

The Lord is not a background actor in a Victorian drama. He reigns and rules over all. Yet the way he usually engages mankind gets our attention. It shows us just how special human beings are. Even fallen, we are enchanted creatures, fashioned by God himself. The Lord treats us with a kindness we do not merit. In every way we have infinite reasons to trust him and go his way, wherever he may lead. The angels watch in awe. Ours is a drama worth not only viewing, but living.

You are the LORD, you alone. You have made heaven, the heaven of heavens, with all their host, the earth and all that is on it, the seas and all that is in them; and you preserve all of them; and the host of heaven worships you. NEHEMIAH 9:6

September 19

Resolved, always to do that, which I shall wish I had done when I see others do it.
LETTERS AND PERSONAL WRITINGS

ONE OF THE DUTIES of parents is training their children to do the right thing. Yet, if we're not careful, it's easy to slip into a mind-set in which we don't always *practice* what we *preach*. I noticed this in my own home recently. My children are sweet and listen well to instruction, but when we get back from a walk, they sometimes leave their Crocs in the middle of the steps. I wondered why—until I took a look at the location of my own shoes. Parental duty: failed.

We want to help our children to be like the young Jonathan Edwards: We want them to emulate the good actions of others. We are remarkably visual creatures; we learn what to do when we "see others do it," for both good and ill. So, even if we never open our mouths, we still leave a trail of behavior for others to emulate. We have a choice: we can either set a virtuous example, or a negative one. There really is no in-between option.

Christian parents often have very high standards. We are not merely raising and sheltering our children, trying to keep them generally headed toward adulthood. We're shaping precious, eternal souls every day. We're pointing our children toward heaven. We have eighteen years or so to nourish and cherish them directly, with the early years forming the time when the roots of a strong character are set. What a great task this is. It extends beyond fathers and mothers, in truth; every believer should hunt for righteous guides and follow them. People all around us are watching; let's give them a glimpse of the Godward life, one worthy of emulation.

Let no one despise you for your youth, but set the believers an example in speech, in conduct, in love, in faith, in purity.   I TIMOTHY 4:12

September 20

Christ gives peace to the most sinful and miserable [persons] that come to him; he heals the broken in heart and bindeth up their wounds. But 'tis impossible that they should have peace that continue in their sins. Isaiah 57:19–21, "I create the fruit of the lips; peace, peace to him that is far off, and to him that is nigh, and I will heal him. But the wicked are like the troubled [sea], when it cannot rest, whose waters cast up mire and dirt. There is no peace, saith my God, to the wicked." There is no peace between God and them, as they have the guilt of sin remaining on their souls and are under the dominion of sin. So God's indignation continually burns against them, and therefore there is reason why they should travail in pain all their days.

SERMONS AND DISCOURSES, 1743-1758

IN RECENT YEARS, Christians have begun to debate the role of human identity. A culture engulfed in sexual sin and narcissism has created many problems for the church. Some believers hear talk about "orientation" and wonder whether there is any part of themselves that is unchangeable. We're all tempted in some way to cling to our sinful past; we want there to be room for us to be a jealous Christian, a proud Christian, a lustful Christian, a gay Christian, a gluttonous Christian, an alcoholic Christian. But part of the fight against sin is knowing that we are acting against our "new nature" (Ephesians 4:22-24).

To call ourselves any kind of modified Christian weakens our fight against sin, because it tricks us into thinking we still have our old identity when the Bible says we don't. Canvassing a number of evil behaviors that characterize the unrighteous, the apostle Paul says, "Such were some of you" (1 Corinthians 6:9-11). We used to find our identity in our sins. Now we are new. The old nature pulls at us, to be sure, but we are not defined by it.

Christ does not redeem only part of our being. He redeems all of us. This doesn't mean we lose the temptation to unrighteousness. We will battle sin until we die. But we praise God even for the fight, for God will not allow us to rest easy in a state of unconfessed sin. He withholds his peace when we continually choose against him.

Jonathan Edwards's admonition is aimed at hearers who had never trusted Christ or turned from their wickedness. But his words apply to born-again believers as well. God never gives abiding peace to those who "continue in their sins." He will not cancel his forgiveness, nor void his grace. But we will surely feel uneasy when we wander away from him. When conviction dawns, we should treat it as a spiritual alarm, and run to Christ in repentance and full confession of sin. We are not part Christian, part devil. We are fully Christ's, and that means he continually calls us back to himself.

Whatever gain I had, I counted as loss for the sake of Christ. Indeed, I count everything as loss because of the surpassing worth of knowing Christ Jesus my Lord.   PHILIPPIANS 3:7-8

September 21

The human nature of Christ is yet in being. He still continues, and will continue to all eternity, to be both God and man. His whole human nature remains: not only his human soul, but also his human body. His dead body rose from the dead; and the same that was raised from the dead, is exalted and glorified at God's right hand; that which was dead, is now alive, and lives forevermore.

SERMONS AND DISCOURSES, 1743-1758

THE OLD TESTAMENT's central act is the Exodus. Through Moses, God delivers the Israelites from captivity, bringing them out of Egypt. Israel, however, does not enter a lasting rest. They must go on to battle many enemies from without, and the nation eventually collapses because of unrighteousness from within. Still, the Exodus stands in biblical history as a definitive event.

But the Exodus was not just a great act of leadership by Moses. It was not merely an indication that God protects his chosen ones. The Exodus points ahead to a greater deliverance, when Jesus Christ would die to free his people, his bride, from captivity. The Cross has made a way for us out of hell, the apocalyptic Egypt. But our journey out of darkness doesn't culminate in our present lives. We are saved, and we enjoy spiritual fellowship with the church. We await the final fulfillment of Christ's saving mission.

Jesus has gone ahead of us. He became like us in order to effect our salvation. The one who is both "God and man" brought God and humankind together. He is "raised from the dead" and ruling "at God's right hand," as Jonathan Edwards observes. We are traveling toward him. The Exodus continues. Not much longer, and we will be home for good. The one who passed through the waters of judgment has come out of them and "lives forevermore." So will we. Let us not lose heart, but keep walking, and never stop until we see the Promised Land, where we will live with God for eternity.

For freedom Christ has set us free; stand firm therefore, and do not submit again to a yoke of slavery. GALATIANS 5:1

September 22

The sun's so perpetually, for so many ages, sending forth his rays in such vast profusion, without any diminution of his light and heat, is a bright image of the all-sufficiency and everlastingness of God's bounty and goodness.
TYPOLOGICAL WRITINGS

THE SUN IS ABOUT 93 million miles from Earth. Yet, even though the sun is impossibly far away, we still cannot look directly at it for more than a second or two. We all remember the case of foolish kids from elementary school who defied the teacher's warning not to stare at the brilliant burning orb and came away yelping as a result. The sun's intensity is a given for many of us, but it never ceases to amaze me just how ferocious the sun's power is.

God is the sun of all Creation, sending forth rays of "bounty and goodness" to refresh his people. How we need the divine sun, and yet how often we act as if God has abandoned us. But he hasn't—not by a long shot. Just like the blazing furnace in the sky above us, God is the central reality of our daily existence. We are warmed physically by the sun; we are warmed spiritually by God.

Jonathan Edwards saw glimpses of holy truth in the created order, and so do we. Without God, we would have no light. We would have no bounty. We would have no goodness. Our God is all-sufficient and everlasting. How different he is from our own planet. His resources will never grow scarce. His stores of grace will never run out. He has inexhaustible gifts for those who love him. No person has occasioned the light of the sun; it doesn't rise each day because of a universal petition. God has appointed the sun to rise, and God has appointed a thousand good graces for his people.

Their voice goes out through all the earth, and their words to the end of the world. In them he has set a tent for the sun, which comes out like a bridegroom leaving his chamber, and, like a strong man, runs its course with joy. PSALM 19:4-5

September 23

The purity, beauty, sublimity and glory of the visible heavens as one views it in a calm and temperate air, when one is made more sensible of the height of them and of the beauty of their color, when there are here and [there] interposed little clouds, livelily denotes the exaltedness and purity of the blessedness of the heavenly inhabitants.
TYPOLOGICAL WRITINGS

WE SOMETIMES HEAR today that we should consider doing breathing exercises. When a stressful situation arises, we should take note of our inhaling and exhaling. Instead of taking shallow breaths, we should fill our lungs with air and slow down our heart rate. After reading about this practice in a magazine somewhere, I've tried doing it on occasion. Driving in rush-hour traffic, I've found, gives me regular opportunities to practice breathing deeply.

Breathing exercises can help us to manage our stress. We need not disdain such actions. But we should reject a vision of the body, and of our bodily processes, that offers us mastery over ourselves and our world. There is no pathway to lasting peace apart from God. Jonathan Edwards, a student of nature, reminds us that the "visible heavens" showcase the "exaltedness and purity" of the departed saints. We cannot apprehend pure rest here; we can find it only in heaven, where God dwells.

This world is an unruly place filled with turmoil and testing. Life is not fair. The sky regularly turns threatening and hostile, driving us inward. But there is a pure and lasting peace we may find. Knowing Jesus means that we have already discovered heavenly rest (Matthew 11:28-29). We care well for our body as believers, but our physical care flows from spiritual attention. We look up at the clouds and remember how tranquil heaven is. We are not there yet, but we are the redeemed of God. We can breathe in the fresh air of God's grace.

I will make a covenant of peace with them. It shall be an everlasting covenant with them. And I will set them in their land and multiply them, and will set my sanctuary in their midst forevermore.
EZEKIEL 37:26

September 24

When we travail up an hill 'tis against our natural tendency and inclination, which perpetually is to descend; and therefore we can't go on ascending without labor and difficulty. But there arises a pleasant prospect to pay us for our labor as we ascend, and as we continue our labor in ascending, still the pleasantness of the prospect grows. Just so is a man paid for his labor and self-denial in a Christian course.

TYPOLOGICAL WRITINGS

THERE IS NO KIND of effort quite like slip-sliding up a hill in cross-country skis. The entire time you're powering up the incline, you're sweating at a ridiculous level. Just when you think you're about to expire, you reach the top of the hill. Now, the delicious prospect of rushing downward beckons. We quickly forget the effort involved to reach the summit as the need for speed takes over.

Such endeavors, perspiration-laden or not, remind us of what Jonathan Edwards calls our "Christian course." We put in a great deal of effort to attack and conquer our sin. We push against the cursed gravity of a fallen order, straining to overcome trials and the tendency of things to fall apart in this realm. We preach the gospel and try to make disciples, hard as it is to engage people in meaningful spiritual conversation. Yes, we must all "travail up an hill."

But there is a "pleasant prospect" before us. We will not always fight the limitations of the earth. We will not forever take up our cross and follow Jesus, denying ourselves in order to honor God. The day is fast approaching when we will reach the top of the slope. We will cease striving. We will no longer have to fight the flesh. The climb will end. God will reward us for our labor, and we will enjoy the exhilaration of the ultimate glissade, our hearts flush and overflowing with happiness.

He said to all, "If anyone would come after me, let him deny himself and take up his cross daily and follow me." LUKE 9:23

September 25

We, in our fallen state, need garments to hide our nakedness (having lost our primitive glory) which were needless in our state of innocency. And whatsoever God has provided for mankind to clothe themselves with, seems to represent Jesus Christ and his righteousness: whether it be anything made of skin, as the coats of skins that God made our first parents represented the righteousness of Christ; or the fleeces of sheep do represent the righteousness of him who is the Lamb of God, and who was dumb as a sheep before his shearers.
TYPOLOGICAL WRITINGS

THERE IS NO SHAME quite like the shame of Adam and Eve. We read of their sin in Genesis 3 and cover our mouths in horror. They heard the very voice of God call them to obedience, to abstain from the fruit of the tree of the knowledge of good and evil, but they did not obey him. They listened, but not to God. They listened to the serpent and his antiwisdom. We should not think of ourselves as better than they were; we are Adam and Eve in our life's story, not the hero.

But if their shame was great, the righteousness of God in response was greater. The Lord himself slaughtered animals and made garments for the man and the woman. He provided them with warmth and comfort, even after their titanic act of disobedience. They abandoned God, but he did not abandon them. This act speaks to the ultimate clothing, the "righteousness of Christ," which God gives to all who will call upon him in repentance and faith.

The Lord himself provided the goats for Adam and Eve; the Lord himself has provided us with "the righteousness of him who is the Lamb of God," as Jonathan Edwards says. We lost our "primitive glory" in the Fall, the glory God gave to humankind before we trespassed. But though our loss was great, the weight of the second glorious gift far surpasses the first. We gain the very holiness of the Son of God himself. Even after our desecration of the will of God, he does not leave us alone, naked and without warmth. He gives the righteous robes of Christ to us, and never allows us to lose them.

In Christ God was reconciling the world to himself, not counting their trespasses against them, and entrusting to us the message of reconciliation. 2 CORINTHIANS 5:19

September 26

As the sun, by rising out of darkness and from under the earth raises the whole world with him, raises mankind out of their beds, and by his light as it were renews all things and fetches 'em up out of darkness, so Christ, rising from the grave and from a state of death, he as the first begotten from the dead, raises all his church with him; Christ the first fruits, and afterwards they that are Christ's at his coming. And as all the world is enlightened and brought out of darkness by the rising of the sun, so by Christ's rising we are begotten again to a living hope; and all our happiness and life and light and glory and the restitution of all things is from Christ rising from the dead, and is by his resurrection.
TYPOLOGICAL WRITINGS

WHAT WAS IT LIKE to be Lazarus? What went through his mind as he walked out of the tomb? We can only imagine what he must have thought. His final days were, no doubt, painful. He had no expectation of resurrection. He had descended, as every person must, into the depths. He had experienced the process of passing from life to death. He had seen his loved ones weep and thrash and wail as the light left his eyes. But now, his eyes beheld Jesus.

All hail Christ, the death killer! Just as the morning sun "renews" the "whole world" each day, so Christ brings us back from our sleeping, our eternal slumber. Jonathan Edwards saw the spiritual in the physical, and took great comfort from what he observed. So may we. We do not worship a God who only set up a working creation, thankful as we are for it. We worship a God who *breaks in* to our realm. We follow a Savior who *interrupts* our deathward spiral. He feels no need to stay apart and stand back. He enters our nightmare, he goes right to the door of the tomb, and he commands us to come forth.

It isn't Christ who must obey the world; it is the world, and everyone in it, who must obey *him*. We know in part what Lazarus experienced, for we too have tasted bitter, painful days. We have descended, day by awful day, into the depths. We have been without hope, with no one able to rescue us. But then Jesus came to the door of the tomb and summoned us. He called, "Come out!" and out we came. Today, we live as once-dead, now-alive people.

God, who said, "Let light shine out of darkness," has shone in our hearts to give the light of the knowledge of the glory of God in the face of Jesus Christ. 2 CORINTHIANS 4:6

September 27

When God began to make the world and put it into order and cause light to shine, it was a chaos, in a state of utter confusion, "without form and void, and darkness was upon the face thereof" [Genesis 1:2]. So commonly things are in a state of great confusion before God works some great and glorious work in the church and in the world, or in some particular part of the church or world, and oftentimes towards particular persons. . . . So we may expect it should be before the beginning of the glorious times of the church of God, and after this confusion, light will be the first thing that will appear—light, clearly to explain and defend the truth.
TYPOLOGICAL WRITINGS

GENERATIONS OF CHILDREN have grown up with Winnie-the-Pooh and his circle of friends. One of the indelible characters from these books is Eeyore. No matter how well things are going, the little gray donkey finds a way to inject gloom into the conversation. Eeyore spots the shadow in every sunbeam. His friends love him, and he loves them, but he has a hard time with life. He's not exactly a barrel of laughs to be around.

It is not hard to be an Eeyore. If we want to wallow in discouragement, we can find ample opportunity. It will gladly show up on our doorstep. It will crowd its way into our daily newsfeed. It will flood our social media accounts like a host virus and take them over. Discouragement spreads contagiously, and one cannot easily run it off. Before we know it, it has taken over our thoughts, and we're on our way to becoming bitter, wounded people.

We all need godly hope. The opposite of an Eeyore is not an Icarus, soaring up to the sun. We needn't pretend that evil doesn't exist. But we must remember, above all, the nature of the God we worship. He creates from "chaos," from "utter confusion" as Jonathan Edwards argues. He brings order where there is none, and causes "light to shine" in the shadows. He does this not merely in a make-your-day-a-little-brighter way. He is busy saving a people for himself. He is building his church through Christ. It is often when his people are at their lowest, as in the days before the Protestant Reformation, that he will strike suddenly, saving souls and growing his people in grace.

Lift your drooping hands and strengthen your weak knees, and make straight paths for your feet, so that what is lame may not be put out of joint but rather be healed. HEBREWS 12:12-13

September 28

Oh, how may angels stand, with pleased, delighted and charmed eyes, and look and look, with smiles of pleasure upon their lips, upon that soul that is holy; how may they hover over such a soul, to delight to behold such loveliness! How is it above all the heathen virtues, of a more light, bright and pure nature, more serene and calm, more peaceful and delightsome! What a sweet calmness, what a calm ecstasy, doth it bring to the soul! How doth it make the soul love itself; how doth it make the pure invisible world love it; yea, how doth God love it and delight in it; how do even the whole creation, the sun, the fields and trees love a humble holiness.
THE "MISCELLANIES"

"LET'S BE TOLERANT AND FAIR." We hear this plea from various corners of society today. Our senses begin to tingle, for our culture has a rocky relationship with actual tolerance. We *aspire* to give all views a place at the table, but the human heart is naturally set to believe in right and wrong. Even if we reject Christian morality, in other words, we will still cling to some sort of ethical framework. In our day, people often reject biblical ethics, but simply replace them with a secular version that includes tolerance and fairness.

But few people actually practice these principles—in part because these unreligious "values" have no real grounding. We say that we should tolerate people, but why, if we're not accountable to any supreme being for our conduct? Small wonder that many people abandon these guidelines when the fur starts flying. By contrast, Christians are called to a far nobler standard. We are called to be surpassingly *holy*—that is, set apart for good. God wants us to reflect the moral excellence and ethical purity of his own nature. Our set-apart God desires a set-apart people.

Holiness is not relative; it has a foundation, one found in the heavens, where God dwells. It stands "above all the heathen virtues," writes Jonathan Edwards, by which he means non-Christian standards. For this reason, spiritual purity is rare and precious, akin to jewels we spend decades trying to find in mines and shafts below the earth. The common stones of tolerance and fairness are coveted by many today, but when people see true holiness, they stop and stare. Holiness has a unique beauty that no one can deny, for it reflects the very nature of God. It is our possession, and it is our daily calling.

A highway shall be there, and it shall be called the Way of Holiness;
the unclean shall not pass over it. ISAIAH 35:8

September 29

ONE CANNOT HELP BUT marvel at the dogged example of Jonathan Edwards. Getting fired is terribly difficult for anyone, but the unpleasantness for Edwards was compounded by his fame. When he lost his pastorate in Northampton in 1750, the news traveled across the American colonies, and across the ocean, as well.

But Edwards did not shrink back or lose himself in self-pity. He picked up stakes and moved his sizable family to the frontier of western New England. In Stockbridge, he preached in a much humbler context and did the day-to-day tasks of a missionary. He sought to evangelize the Native Americans in the town, he preached the Word, he sought to strengthen the church. He also found time to write, and enjoyed his most fruitful literary years. He wrote books on theology and philosophy, and longed to complete two more (that, sadly, went unfinished). These two works, *The Harmony of the Old and New Testament*, and *A History of the Work of Redemption*, cover God's fulfillment of his designs in all of church history and display how Christ fulfilled the promises of God.

Edwards enjoyed his season in Stockbridge, and he balked when the call came. His letter to the trustees from the College of New Jersey is remarkable for its candor and pathos:

> The chief difficulty in my mind, in the way of accepting this important and arduous office, are these two: first my own defects, unfitting me for such an undertaking, many of which are generally known; besides other, which my own heart is conscious to. I have a constitution in many respects peculiar unhappy, attended with flaccid solids, vapid, sizy and scarce fluids, and a low tide of spirits; often occasioning a kind of childish weakness and contemptibleness of speech, presence, and demeanor; with a disagreeable dullness and stiffness, much unfitting me for conversation, but more especially for the government of a college. This poorness of constitution makes me shrink at the thoughts of taking upon me, in the decline of life, such a new and great business, attended with such a multiplicity of cares, and requiring such a degree of activity, alertness and spirit of government; especially as succeeding one, so remarkably well qualified in these respects, giving occasion to everyone to remark the wide difference.[49]

One can see that Edwards had no grand leadership ambitions. He did not mince words about his infelicities, or his sense that he was "in the decline of life." But as he soon learned, following our big and wise God means not following a "normal" course of affairs. God may well see fit to disturb our quietness, and give us a task we never imagined. If that is the case, we can know that we're in good company.

September 30

The pleasure of religion raises one clear above laughter and rather tends to make the face to shine than screw it into a grimace; though when it is at its height it begets a sweet, inexpressibly joyful smile, as we know only a smile is begotten by the great pleasure of dear friends' society.
THE "MISCELLANIES"

HIGH SCHOOL SUPERLATIVES, looking back, were a doozy. Who came up with the idea that high schoolers should rank one another, anyway? Don't teenagers already have enough insecurity to face down—do we really need to publish a list of the most attractive and accomplished among us? Academic excellence is one thing; that makes some sense. But best hair? nicest smile?

Thankfully, winning these awards—or not—means little to our personal development. But our yearbook awards do get one thing right: There is something about a smile. We all enjoy a smile. When a baby smiles, even the stoniest heart softens. On a date, when the ice cream we've purchased yields a smile, it's like fireworks of the soul. But there is a much richer kind of smile—one that stems from the deepest satisfaction and thankfulness. This is the kind that breaks out on our faces when we hear the truth of God and remember how good it is.

This smile is not merely a passing grin. It is more what Jonathan Edwards calls a "sweet, inexpressibly joyful smile" that we cannot hold back, so transported are we by God and his grace. This is the kind of smile you see on the face of a believer whose joy is beyond this world. This is the sort of smile you glimpse as a faithful believer readies for eternity. This is the type of smile that emerges when Christians who have nothing in common serve one another out of genuine love. This expression of pure joy is the best version of a smile.

These things I have spoken to you, that my joy may be in you, and that your joy may be full. JOHN 15:11

October

✝

October 1

Every atom in the universe is managed by Christ so as to be most to the advantage of the Christian, every particle of air or every ray of the sun; so that he in the other world, when he comes to see it, shall sit and enjoy all this vast inheritance with surprising, amazing joy. And how is it possible for a man to possess anything more than so as shall be most to his advantage? And then besides this, the Christian shall have everything managed just according to his will; for his will shall so be lost in the will of God, that he had rather have it according to God's will than any way in the world.

THE "MISCELLANIES"

WE SOMETIMES HEAR stories about celebrities and their "super agents"—the professionals who arrange the deals and windfalls with all the commas and zeroes in them. They scheme and calculate and plan to get their clients as much money as humanly possible. The top agents obsess over the performers they work with, thinking of little else. Life is about gain; they are about gain.

The average Christian does not have a stylist. We do not have an in-home chef. We do not have a publicist, and not a whole lot to publicize if we did: *Jennifer Smith went to Target today; it was an exciting trip; she used her Red Card, and saved $3.07 on paper towels and pasta.* But here is what we do have: a God who loves us and is bending all things to our good. Jonathan Edwards puts it beautifully: "Every atom in the universe is managed by Christ so as to be most to the advantage of the Christian." This is a breathtaking truth.

God blesses us in untold ways here on earth, to be sure; gain in earthly terms is not necessarily evil. But the Lord's focus, the "advantage" that he is storing up, is the heavenly reward that awaits us. Because of this, divine management of the Christian life involves not merely peaceful days, but also challenging trials. When we persevere, God gets the glory and we gain eternal rewards. When we press on, when we fight through, whatever our lot, we can know this: God is ordering every second, every "particle of air," for our good and his renown.

I know that you can do all things, and that no purpose of yours can be thwarted. JOB 42:2

October 2

October 2, 1758: Sarah Edwards dies of dysentery in Philadelphia

THROUGHOUT HER LIFE, Sarah Edwards spent many nights at home with her husband and children. The Edwardses kept company about town and had a wide social circle, but they preferred being together as a family over conducting a whirl of activity. For this reason, Jonathan and Sarah were very close. Sarah loved her husband very much, and saw herself as his helpmate. She faced many challenges throughout her life with Jonathan, but she knew from his preaching and her own stout faith to look to the Lord when clouds covered the sun.

How strange, then, that the Edwardses died apart from each other. Sarah was not with Jonathan when he died in Princeton, New Jersey, in March 1758. On April 3, she wrote to her daughter Esther:

> What shall I say? A holy and good God has covered us with a dark cloud. O that we may kiss the rod, and lay our hands on our mouths! The Lord has done it. He has made me adore His goodness that we had him so long. But my God lives; and He has my heart. O what a legacy my husband, and your father, has left to us! We are all given to God: and there I am and love to be.
> Your ever affectionate mother,
> Sarah Edwards[50]

This was a terrible time for the Edwards clan. Esther herself never read these words. She died on April 7, leaving two tiny children as orphans. Her husband, Aaron Burr, Sr., had died the previous September while serving as president of the College of New Jersey (now Princeton University).

Without Jonathan's leadership, Sarah determined to care for little Sally Burr and Aaron Burr Jr. A grieving grandmother, Sarah made the difficult journey to Philadelphia in the fall of 1758 to retrieve the children. There she became ill from dysentery, and she died just a few days shy of her beloved husband's birthday. She had raised eleven children, loved Jonathan as his wife for more than three decades, and pointed many to Christ by her gracious, godly example.

To the end, Sarah stayed fixed on God. Though her husband died suddenly, she did not lash out at the Lord, but confessed of her Savior: "He has my heart." This was the only bond stronger for her than that which she shared with Jonathan. May it be so for us. May we love those around us in deed and in truth, but may we love God much, much more.

October 3

Now some may say, why could not God, of his mercy, pardon the injury only upon repentance without other satisfaction, without doing himself any hurt? I also ask, why could not he of his mercy pardon without repentance? For the same reason he could not pardon with repentance without satisfaction. For all the repentance man is capable of is no repentance at all; or which is the same thing, it is as little as none in comparison of the greatness of the injury, for it cannot bear any proportion to it. . . . Wherefore, we are not forgiven now because our repentance makes any satisfaction, but because thereby we reject the sin and receive the satisfaction already made.

THE "MISCELLANIES"

ONE OF THE MOST POWERFUL acts one can witness is a person rejecting sin. We were not made as beasts, after all. We are not animals, mere slaves to our appetites. God created us and made us for himself. Though we have fallen from the Lord, from the lofty heights of Eden, we have tremendous dignity and worth. We were not made for this fallen earth; we were made for heaven.

As believers, by the "mercy" of God, we "reject the sin" that beckons to us. This is not a virtuous act that we provide for ourselves; all our forgiveness and all our standing with God comes from his kindness. But his mercy is an enabling mercy. When tempted, we have the power to turn away from evil. It has no hold over us. Clearly, God wants sin to suffer defeat to the fullest possible extent. He meets the perfect demands of his justice through the blood of Christ—so he achieves "satisfaction," as Jonathan Edwards puts it. God forgives us through "repentance," offering "pardon" to the penitent. And he gives us the ability to scorn unrighteousness. Sin is not merely wounded on our behalf; it is routed. Put to *flight*.

We have the opportunity today to show a watching world that God is vindicated and Satan is cast down. Let us not manage our iniquity today, moving it around from one account to the next, trimming a bit here and there. Let us own the power of Calvary. Let us glorify God by rejecting the sin that seeks to entangle and choke us. All around us, people give in to their lusts and base appetites. But we are not spiritual animals. God has redeemed us, and God has freed us from the power of sin. We are conquerors.

The God of peace will soon crush Satan under your feet. The grace of our Lord Jesus Christ be with you. ROMANS 16:20

October 4

HAPPINESS IS THE END OF THE CREATION, as appears by this, because the creation had as good not be, as not rejoice in its being. For certainly it was the goodness of the Creator that moved him to create; and how can we conceive of another end proposed by goodness, than that he might delight in seeing the creatures he made rejoice in that being that he has given them? It appears also by this, because the end of the creation is that the creation might glorify him. Now what is glorifying God, but a rejoicing at that glory he has displayed? An understanding of the perfections of God, merely, cannot be the end of the creation; for he had as good not understand it, as see it and not be at all moved with joy at the sight.
THE "MISCELLANIES"

GOD DID NOT MAKE the cosmos as an infomercial. His goal was not merely to convey a momentary "understanding of the perfections of God." Christianity is a living drama. We are plunged into the story of redemption that God has been weaving from the beginning of time. God wants participants, not spectators.

Neither does the Lord want us to merely gain information about him. True, he gives us able minds to know him, and the human mind is a beautiful, God-made thing. But the Lord wants more: He wants our hearts and minds to work together such that we comprehend him rightly, we see him as he truly is through his Word, and are thus "moved with joy at the sight," as Jonathan Edwards sums it up. This is what God desires. He wants worshipers. He wants men and women who will enter fully into this great work and fill their roles with joy.

Happiness is the end of the creation. When we find happiness in the Lord, we find what our hearts have yearned for all our days. This informs what we do on a daily basis. We take in truth—not for its own sake, not to win a theology Quiz Bowl, but to throw wood on the fire of our worship. As we study God, we savor him, and we do not leash our affections. We see God, and the sight of him intoxicates us. This is true in our daily pursuit of the Lord, and this is true in congregational worship. Are we happy? This is what God wants. This is what he gives us.

These things I have spoken to you, that my joy may be in you, and that your joy may be full. JOHN 15:11

October 5

JONATHAN EDWARDS came into the world as a son of the Puritans. He was born to New England spiritual royalty—his father, Timothy Edwards, served as an eminent minister in East Windsor, Connecticut, while his mother, Esther Stoddard Edwards, was the daughter of Solomon Stoddard, a man revered in the seventeenth and eighteenth centuries as a preacher and revivalist.

Jonathan grew up in a home filled with women. He had four older sisters and eventually would have six younger ones, as well. Of Timothy Edwards, it was said that he had "sixty feet of daughters," for all ten were strikingly tall, as was Jonathan. Remarkably for that day and age, all eleven children survived childhood.

Edwards was born into a time of considerable societal instability and conflict. During his youth, the Protestant British, the Catholic French, and the Native Americans fought for control of North America. Just three months after Jonathan was born, Native Americans attacked the nearby town of Deerfield and killed several of Edwards's extended family members, carrying the rest to captivity in Canada. Though we might have an image of a serene, undisturbed New England in Edwards's day, the combative nature of the era shaped young Jonathan and trained him to prepare for eternity.

Jonathan grew up with affectionate yet strict parents in the Puritan style. Letters from Timothy's brief time as a military chaplain during Queen Anne's War reveal a father who cared for his children and spiritually led them. Timothy's example served Jonathan well as both a pastor and a father, and in the providence of God, set Jonathan up to become the leading theological leader of not only his eminent family, but of the American tradition. We may not have an ancestral history like Jonathan's, but we can all do our part to strengthen Christian homes. We need more families like the one in which Edwards was reared.

October 6

We are the highest affected with the lowest excellencies; we have the easiest and greatest delight in things that in themselves are least delightful; things that are less beautiful and amiable in themselves, strike much quicker and deeper in with the sense and propension and constitution of the mind than things that have in themselves the highest excellence, most charming beauty and exquisite sweetness. Yea, we can hardly bring ourselves to be in any measure pleased with the beauty, or to taste any sweetness at all, in things that are infinitely the greatest excellencies.
THE "MISCELLANIES"

To FUNCTION AS HUMAN BEINGS, we don't have to enjoy what might be called *high culture.* Listening to classical music is not a necessary duty. But if we pay attention to our society, we can observe a steady downward pull toward the low and the base. Gravity seems to exert pressure not only on our vertical leap, but also on our souls. We choose what is easily consumed rather than that which requires thought, attention, and concentration.

The Fall not only left us as sinners, but has lowered our gaze and affected our appetites. We do not run toward the excellent, the complex, and the beautiful; rather, as Jonathan Edwards observes, "We are the highest affected with the lowest excellencies." In Adam, our affections have grown dull. We stare listlessly at screens, when a realm of real beauty lies just inches away; we send our video-game characters on grand adventures while our own lives languish; we consume silly, pointless media instead of pursuing things of "the highest excellence."

Conversion saves our souls. It also saves our senses. It reenchants the world. We come out of the waters of judgment, washed by the blood of Christ, to find the "greatest excellencies" all around us. The natural order teems with the beauty of God; the Word unfolds to us the mind, will, and heart of the Lord. Salvation does not remove us from this realm; it plunges us more deeply into this place and urges us to plunder our surroundings for God's honor. Our hearts will not find contentment in lesser pursuits; God's work in us means that we have a ferocious hunger for him—and for all true excellency, all true beauty, and all virtuous pleasure.

As a deer pants for flowing streams, so pants my soul for you, O God.
PSALM 42:1

October 7

Christ and his church rejoice in each other's beauty. The church rejoices in Christ's divine beauty and glory. She as it were sweetly solaces herself in the light of the glory of the Sun of Righteousness; and the saints say one to another, as in Isaiah 2:5, "O house of Jacob, come ye, let us walk in the light of the Lord."... And Christ delights and rejoices in the beauty of the church, the beauty which he hath put upon her: her Christian graces are "ornaments of great price in his sight" (1 Peter 3:4). And he is spoken of as "greatly desiring her beauty" (Psalms 45:11).

SERMONS AND DISCOURSES, 1743-1758

MY HEART BREAKS whenever I hear a young woman say that her father never told her she was precious. A father doesn't have to tell his daughter that she looks like a supermodel. (Our worth is not based on our appearance, contrary to what our secular culture encourages us to believe.) But every father has the privilege—and responsibility—of helping his daughter know that God made her beautiful just the way she is.

We will not all be beautiful in the eyes of the world; but a true, spiritual beauty is the inheritance of every Christian. Through Christ, we become lovely in the eyes of God. He washes us, and purifies us, and clothes us in his own holy garments (Ezekiel 16:9-13). He cherishes us, and showers us with affection.

We were not made to win beauty contests. We were made to display the living perfections of God. The church is the bride of Christ, and the object of his attention. He "delights and rejoices in" our beauty, which is *his* beauty, as Jonathan Edwards notes. We have a higher and richer union than this world can afford; with Christ, we have *spiritual* union, a bond that transcends physical and earthly connections. We may not have grown up with affirmation from our parents. How tragic this is—but how gracious is God. We now know the mystery the angels long to look into: We are the beloved of our Savior. We are precious in his sight.

Many waters cannot quench love, neither can floods drown it.
SONG OF SOLOMON 8:7

October 8

Thus also, when the believer receives Christ by faith, he receives him as a safeguard and shelter from the wrath of God and eternal torments, and defense from all the harms and dangers which he fears. . . . Wherefore, the dispositions of soul which Christ looks at in his spouse are a sweet reliance and confidence in him, a humble trust in him as her only rock of defence, whither she may flee. And Christ will not receive those as the objects of his salvation who trust to themselves, their own strength or worthiness, but those alone who entirely rely on him.
THE "MISCELLANIES"

AMERICAN INTELLECTUAL HISTORY is in some ways a great contest between two erudite New Englanders: Ralph Waldo Emerson and Jonathan Edwards. In 1841, Emerson published his famous essay on self-reliance, which opens with the admonition, "*Ne te quaesiveris extra*," or, "Do not seek for things outside of yourself."[51] Self-reliance, Emerson contended, is the essence of true humanity. One does not trust outside authorities; one listens to the inner voice, and follows one's own instincts. That is the essence of human flourishing.

Few people today would know to cite Emerson for these thoughts, but this worldview clearly conflicts with that of Jonathan Edwards, who writes, "Christ will not receive those . . . who trust to themselves, their own strength or worthiness" but only "those alone who entirely rely on him."

The problem with Emerson's argument is simply this: As fallen and fallible humans, we cannot trust ourselves. We are not God. We make terrible and tragic mistakes. We commit great ungainly blunders. We bruise feelings and blow up friendships. We can barely balance the checkbook, let alone unerringly guide our own souls to self-realization. We need a rescuer. Trusting "thyself" has not brought lasting happiness; it has not even brought temporal happiness. We need Christ. Today, let us graciously resist wisdom that in truth is unwise. Let us cry out to God and rely entirely on him.

Before I was afflicted I went astray, but now I keep your word. You are good and do good; teach me your statutes. PSALM 119:67-68

October 9

DAVID BRAINERD WAS a light that blazed for a short time and then was extinguished. After studying at Yale, and showing great "New Light" enthusiasm—he once denounced his tutor for having no more knowledge of Christ than a chair—Brainerd served as a missionary to the Native Americans in and around New Jersey from 1743 to 1746. Born with weak health, and prone to overwork, he fell ill with tuberculosis. After staying on the field as long as he could, he ended up in the Edwardses' home in May 1747.

During his convalescence, Brainerd grew very close to Jerusha Edwards, Jonathan and Sarah's second eldest child. After Brainerd's strength increased, Jerusha traveled with him to Boston, but he again became unwell and returned to Northampton. He would never travel again, nor preach the gospel. Before Brainerd died, he spoke some of his last words to Jerusha, telling her he was greatly comforted that they would be united in the afterlife, worshiping the Lord together. The two had a special bond and are buried side by side in Northampton.

Jonathan Edwards memorialized Brainerd in a stem-winder of a sermon entitled "True Saints, When Absent from the Body, Are Present with the Lord," based on 2 Corinthians 5:8. Edwards began the sermon by speaking of the apostle Paul:

> The Apostle in this place is giving a reason why he went on with so much boldness and immovable steadfastness, through such labors, sufferings and dangers of his life, in the service of his Lord; for which his enemies, the false teachers among the Corinthians, sometimes reproached him, as being beside himself, and driven on by a kind of madness. In the latter part of the preceding chapter, the Apostle informs the Christian Corinthians, that the reason why he did thus, was, that he firmly believed the promises that Christ had made to his faithful servants of a glorious future eternal reward, and knew that these present afflictions were light, and but for a moment, in comparison of that far more exceeding and eternal weight of glory. The same discourse is continued in this chapter; wherein the Apostle further insists on the reason he had given of his constancy in suffering, and exposing himself to death in the work of the ministry, even the more happy state he expected after death.[52]

David Brainerd did not preach the gospel for long, but his example has inspired countless missionaries to heed the call of Christ, travel to the ends of the earth, and if necessary die in service to the Kingdom. What a legacy from a faithful Christian man.

October 10

The redemption by Christ is particularly wonderful upon this account, inasmuch as the justice of God is not only appeased to those who have an interest in him, but stands up for them; is not only not an enemy but a friend, every whit as much as mercy. Justice demands adoption and glorification, and importunes as much for it, as ever it did before for misery; in every respect that it is against the wicked, it is as much for the godly.

THE "MISCELLANIES"

IT IS A WORLD-SHAKING experience to have someone stand up for us. I once heard a man named Robert Lewis tell about his son being bullied. When Lewis learned about it, he didn't go on the warpath. Instead, he called a meeting with his son and the bullies. Lewis stood up for his son, telling the other boys that they were not to harm him any longer. This example of fatherly courage has never left my memory.

Without Christ, we have no one to help us. Jesus is the holy man, the warrior King, who does not withhold his assistance. He "stands up" for his church, as Jonathan Edwards spells out. He is an enemy to the enemy of his people; he is a friend to the friendless. Jesus is not only willing to spend time with the bright and the beautiful. He also goes to the destitute, the unpopular, and the desperate. A strong Savior, he lifts them out of the depths; he adopts them as his own by his death and resurrection, and he glorifies them by calling them to dwell with him in heavenly places.

We must sometimes wait for justice. Christ has not *completed* his deliverance of his people. But do not misunderstand him or underestimate him. Jesus is a warrior. The Father sent him to do violence to the kingdom of darkness, and he will fulfill the mission. He has gone to war on our behalf, and he will engage the devil once more. He will not defeat his foes with chariots or guns or cannons or planes. He will defeat his enemies with a word. What hope, and what encouragement to action, this is for us.

> From his mouth comes a sharp sword with which to strike down the nations, and he will rule them with a rod of iron. He will tread the winepress of the fury of the wrath of God the Almighty.
>
> REVELATION 19:15

October 11

The greatness, distance and motion of this great universe, has almost an omnipotent power upon the imagination; the blood will even be chilled with the vast idea. But the greatness of vast expanse, immense distance, prodigious bulk and rapid motion, is but a little, trivial and childish greatness in comparison of the noble, refined, exalted, divine, spiritual greatnesses. Yea, these are but the shadows of greatness and are worthless, except as they conduce to true and real greatness and excellency, and manifest the power and wisdom of God.
THE "MISCELLANIES"

SECULAR SCIENTISTS do very well for themselves writing popular books about "the wonder of the universe." It is a strange thing, this brand of wonder, for it begins in nothingness and terminates in nothingness. There can be no order, no rhythm, no design to being that has no intelligence behind it. Secular "wonder" ends up being little more than interplanetary sightseeing. It's there; we see it; it looks remarkable; then the show's over.

God intends for this "great universe," as Jonathan Edwards labels it, to impress us. God did not make a snow globe. He made "greatness of vast expanse" that exercises nearly "omnipotent power upon the imagination." But the cosmos is not an end unto itself. When we investigate it, we are witnessing "but the shadows of greatness," the dust trail of the magnificent being who made all we see and study.

Do not believe the secular myth that the universe came from nothing and is headed to nothing. There is a "vast expanse" beyond us because God is beyond us. There is "immense distance" in front of us because there is no limit to the divine being. There is "prodigious bulk" to observe because God is omnipresent, greater than we can measure. There is "rapid motion" in every millisecond because God is a being of action. The true story of all our exploration is not what *appears* wondrous to us in our telescope. The true story is about the one who *is* wondrous, and who made whole galaxies to dazzle us with his "power and wisdom."

The voice of the LORD is over the waters; the God of glory thunders,
the LORD, over many waters. The voice of the LORD is powerful; the
voice of the LORD is full of majesty. PSALM 29:3-4

October 12

When we say that all men by nature are altogether depraved and corrupted, and without the least grain of true holiness, children of wrath, nothing else can truly be intended but that every man is so of himself, as he is of nature. Nothing else is belonging to us but sin and misery, as we are in Adam; nothing but misery belongs to us according to the first covenant, that we are all under in our first state; and when we are born, nothing else is in us according to the first constitution of things. . . . What he has given him now is according to a new and extraordinary way; 'tis being born again.

THE "MISCELLANIES"

MANY PEOPLE HAVE an interest in "where are they now?" stories. That pop singer who once dominated the music business now sells hot peppers by the sea. The linebacker who ruled the middle of the field now carries mail in the suburbs. The classmate who barely said a word in class now has an online business selling handbags, and is a millionaire. We are fascinated by those who have everything, and lose it; and those who have nothing, but gain a great deal.

As Christians, we fall in the second category, praise God. We came into the world without any spiritual goodness to commend us to the Lord. Whatever our material circumstances, Jonathan Edwards reminds us that every last one of us truly gets only spiritual "sin and misery" from our ancestors. There is no way that parents can fail to pass on a "depraved and corrupted" nature to their children. Our families might know prosperity, or we might know poverty, but every child inherits only sin from Mom and Dad. It cannot be otherwise, much as our parents might want to break the curse for their kids.

How good it is to know that God overcomes our "first state." He gives us a second birth through the Holy Spirit. The way to hell is old and common; the way to God is "new and extraordinary." We have nothing from birth, but God gives us everything in Christ. It doesn't matter much which career we enter, or what level of success we achieve in our vocation. The key matter for believers is not where we have been. It is who we are in Christ, and what he enables us to be, today and every day.

He who did not spare his own Son but gave him up for us all, how will he not also with him graciously give us all things? ROMANS 8:32

October 13

This is one way whereby the future happiness of saints is increased: happiness receives all its relish from a sense of the contrary; if it were not for this, joy would be dull and flat. Now this sense is obtained by a reflection on the miseries of this life, and looking on the torments of the damned. Wherefore, the greater the afflictions of this life were, the more sweet, caeteris paribus, will the heavenly happiness be.

THE "MISCELLANIES"

WE NEED NOT FIND joy in bad circumstances. We should actively despise illness, disunity, conflict, death, and the other evils of a fallen world. Scripture never encourages us to think of the bitter fruits of darkness as good. Indeed, we should pray against these woes. We should seek happy, prosperous lives for our families. We should desire good for our congregations. We should exult when sickness departs and health dawns.

While there is no inherent good in what Jonathan Edwards calls "the miseries of this life," it is profitable for Christians to contemplate them. This will not prove difficult for us; after all, we must all face trials. God does not withhold adversity from any believer. One way our earthly difficulties benefit us is this: They remind us how "sweet" God's blessings are. Without any challenges, we would not know how joyous joy is, or how happy happiness is. This is true not only of temporary afflictions, but even of hell itself. How glorious is heaven by contrast!

Some Christians will undergo terrible challenges here on earth. Whether this is true for us or not, we may know that the pain we taste here will only amplify the "heavenly happiness" we will soon enjoy. This does not lead us to give thanks for sickness, unemployment, conflict, or death. It does lead us to give thanks to God, who uses even the worst things to give us the best things. Affliction may seem unending; but truly, the night will not last long. The morning is coming, and it will be all the sweeter for our suffering.

If the tent that is our earthly home is destroyed, we have a building from God, a house not made with hands, eternal in the heavens.

2 CORINTHIANS 5:1

October 14

The saints in heaven will doubtless eternally exercise themselves in contemplation; they will not want employ this way. . . . The object of their thought shall be the glory of God; which they shall contemplate in the creation in general, in the wonderful make of it, particularly of the highest heavens, and in the wonders of God's providence. . . . They shall employ themselves in singing God's praise, or expressing their thoughts to God and Christ, and also to one another; and in going from one part of heaven to another, to behold the glories of God shining in the various parts of it.

THE "MISCELLANIES"

HEAVEN IS VEILED FROM US while we're on earth. This is not because God is unkind, or that he wants to leave heaven to our imagination. It is because the glories of heaven exceed our capacities for understanding and experience. The apostle Paul voiced this reality when he spoke of being caught up to "the third heaven" (2 Corinthians 12:2). There he received "visions and revelations of the Lord," and heard what "cannot be told, which man may not utter" (2 Corinthians 12:1, 4).

The Bible pulls back the curtain only a little on the blessed afterlife. But what we see in passages such as Revelation 21 gives us much insight, as much as God intends for us to have. Just as our lives on earth are about Christ, our eternal lives in heaven will center on Christ, on "singing God's praise," as Jonathan Edwards tells us, and in rapturously gazing on "the glories of God shining" all throughout the realm where our Maker dwells.

The focus of heaven is not us. And it is not the things of earth—though theologians debate how much the new heavens and new earth will resemble the present ones. The focus of heaven is "the glory of God." We read this and nod—but there is a great roar of thunder in those words. We have learned about eternity in the Word of God, and we know what God wants us to know. But until our translation to eternity, we will have only hints of a greater reality. Much that we will soon understand and experience cannot be told, and we cannot utter. We cannot help but be an eager people, awaiting the fullness of glory.

If then you have been raised with Christ, seek the things that are above, where Christ is, seated at the right hand of God. Set your minds on things that are above, not on things that are on earth. For you have died, and your life is hidden with Christ in God. When Christ who is your life appears, then you also will appear with him in glory.

COLOSSIANS 3:1-4

October 15

I used to think sometimes with myself, if such doctrines as those of the Trinity and decrees are true, yet what need was there of revealing of them in the gospel? what good do they do towards the advancing [of] holiness? But now I don't wonder at all at their being revealed, for such doctrines as these are glorious inlets into the knowledge and view of the spiritual world, and the contemplation of supreme things; the knowledge of which I have experienced how much it contributes to the betterment of the heart.

THE "MISCELLANIES"

IT IS HARD TO DISCOVER the spiritual realm. It is everywhere around us, but we cannot find a physical doorway into it. The way into the knowledge of God is the Word of God. The Word of God not only gives us revelation about spiritual beings, like angels and demons, it also allows us to traverse what Jonathan Edwards calls "glorious inlets" into the Godhead. We learn the very foundation of reality in Scripture: Father, Son, and Spirit. Knowledge of our three-in-one God promises to transform both our faith and our practice.

God is three persons, but God is one. We don't hop between gods in our prayers. We pray to one God. Unlike the pagans of old, we do not believe that our lives depend on the clash between warring deities. We need not fear that the sea god's quarrel with the sun god will submarine our life goals. The three persons of the Godhead are not clashing Titans; they are loving colaborers.

All around us, people pick and choose their spirituality. They think they can select a spiritual reality for themselves, and then direct their worship and needs accordingly. But we know this isn't so. We love the Father, the Son, and the Holy Spirit. We believe in unity in diversity because we find it in the Godhead. Some will tell us that our love of the Trinity is foolish, but we have left our foolish speculations behind. The Trinity is fact. The Trinity is truth. The Trinity gives us a foundation to stand on, and a loving, authoritative God to worship. Let us study the Trinity.

May the grace of the Lord Jesus Christ, and the love of God, and the fellowship of the Holy Spirit be with you all.

2 CORINTHIANS 13:14, NIV

October 16

We see that the narrower the capacity, the more simple must the beauty be to please. Thus in the proportion of sounds, the birds and brute creatures are most delighted with simple music, and in the proportion confined to a few notes. So little children are not able to perceive the sweetness of very complex tunes, where respect is to be had to the proportion of a great many notes together in order to perceive the sweetness of the tune. Then perhaps we shall be able fully and easily to apprehend the beauty, where respect is to be had to thousands of different ratios at once to make up the harmony. Such kind of beauties, when fully perceived, are far the sweetest.
THE "MISCELLANIES"

THE BATTLE OVER CHRISTMAS music is the true culture war of our time. Here is the center of the debate: Can we listen to our favorite songs before December? I know purists on both sides. Personally, I try to resist playing such pieces before the season really kicks off. But there are certain tracks I cannot help but play—they are simply too beautiful. This is true of Handel's *Messiah*. Composed in 1741, when Jonathan Edwards was at the peak of his vocation, the *Messiah* seems to me one of the greatest musical accomplishments of all time.

Whatever one's precise opinions about the proper beginning of the Christmas season, to hear an orchestra at the height of its performance exhilarates the mind and moves the soul. This is especially true of "very complex tunes." Most of us do not have a carefully trained ear to appreciate "a great many notes together." But in heaven, Edwards suggests, we will hear "thousands of different ratios" and so listen to symphonic worship in perfect harmony.

A love for classical music is not a necessity for the Christian faith. But Edwards's point is worth considering. The Trinity itself directs us to appreciate complexity—a complexity we would not have thought possible. A piece that brings many voices and instruments into harmony speaks to a richness, a depth of experience that transcends the power of even many voices singing one note together. Whatever our exact aesthetic interests in the afterlife, we can know that the praise of Christ in song will exceed by far anything we have heard on earth. Let us prepare ourselves to exalt God. Let us now, whether as professionals or amateurs, sing praise to God—in season or out.

Be filled with the Spirit, addressing one another in psalms and hymns and spiritual songs, singing and making melody to the Lord with your heart, giving thanks always and for everything to God the Father in the name of our Lord Jesus Christ. EPHESIANS 5:18-20

October 17

October 17–19, 1740: George Whitefield preaches in Northampton

JONATHAN EDWARDS never ceased to desire fresh visitations of the Spirit among his people. By 1740, he had already seen one major outbreak of revival in Northampton. But he yearned for a new work of God to visit his community. The opportunity came when the young evangelist George Whitefield—then only twenty-five years old—made his second journey to the American colonies.

Whitefield, a reformed Anglican preacher, is widely considered one of the greatest preachers in history. Converted while at Oxford, Whitefield had a great hunger for God, and he soon joined what was derisively called the Holy Club, formed by John and Charles Wesley. The three friends prayed, studied Scripture, and considered how to serve the Lord. After Whitefield was denied numerous Anglican pulpits due to his "enthusiasm," he resolved to preach in the open air to thousands of people at a time—and scores were converted.

Edwards followed Whitefield's ministry closely, as he did with all newsworthy religious developments. After Whitefield contacted Edwards to ask for a preaching date, Edwards replied enthusiastically: "I have a great desire, if it may be the will of God, that such a blessing as attends your person and labors may descend on this town, and may enter mine own house, and that I may receive it in my own soul."[53] In mid-October, Whitefield came to Northampton and preached four sermons that had a major effect on the church. Edwards reportedly wept while hearing Christ so powerfully proclaimed. As the two men shared time together, Edwards took the opportunity to give Whitefield some counsel, urging him not to denounce ministers in towns he had not visited. One red-hot preacher advising another.

Later, Edwards shared some of the fruit of the visit with Whitefield: "I have reason to think that a considerable number of young people, some of them children, have already been savingly brought home to Christ. I hope salvation has come to this house since you was in it, with respect to one, if not more, of my children."[54] After hearing Whitefield speak, Edwards adopted a freer style of his own in the pulpit. He preached with fewer notes and extemporized more.

This altered style soon bore striking fruit when Edwards took the pulpit in tiny Enfield, Connecticut (now Massachusetts) to preach "Sinners in the Hands of an Angry God." In more ways than one, Whitefield had an effect on Edwards, though the two men spent just three days together. Although scarcely acquainted, these sons of thunder helped change the spiritual character of the American colonies, forever stamping the culture with an evangelical seal. Who knows what God may do through our own Christ-centered friendships?

October 18

The best, most beautiful, and most perfect way that we have of expressing a sweet concord of mind to each other, is by music. When I would form in my mind an idea of a society in the highest degree happy, I think of them as expressing their love, their joy, and the inward concord and harmony and spiritual beauty of their souls by sweetly singing to each other.
THE "MISCELLANIES"

ONE OF THE SNEAKY SIGNS of spiritual and congregational health is singing. What we sing about—and listen to—we in some way celebrate. We don't sing merely to convey information; rather, we sing about what we value highly, what we aspire to, what we *desire*. It is worth looking around Sunday worship in your congregation, and observing how many people are barely producing noise. If our buildings are so big, why is our singing often so tame?

Some might respond that they actually do the church a favor by staying quiet. This may be true. For others, the musical accompaniment approaches a level best described as "raucous," so singers feel like peasants before Alexander the Great: better to surrender than resist. But lifting our voices to God in song is not biblically optional. The people who love God produce music "expressing their love, their joy" and the "concord" found in God, as Jonathan Edwards notes.

The church needs to find its voice again. We need to sing to God and to one another. We should not outsource the musical worship of God to professionals. Praising God is too important for that. God did not instruct us in the New Testament to tap only the operatically gifted to lift their voices. He wants the whole congregation to sing. It has always been so. Do not quiet your voice. Lift it up to God. No more tepid singing, please.

I will sing to the LORD as long as I live; I will sing praise to my God while I have being. PSALM 104:33

October 19

We see how great love the human nature is capable of, not only to God but fellow creatures. How greatly are we inclined to the other sex! Nor doth an exalted and fervent love to God hinder this, but only refines and purifies it. God has created the human nature to love fellow creatures, which he wisely has principally turned to the other sex; and the more exalted the nature is, the greater love of that kind that is laudable is it susceptive of. . . . Therefore when we feel love to anyone of the other sex, 'tis a good way to think of the love of Christ to an holy and beautiful soul.

THE "MISCELLANIES"

ONE OF THE MOST HUMOROUS cultural vignettes of recent years was a news story about a young Olympic skier named David Wise. This gifted young man had shot to the top of his sport, but he had also done something more noteworthy in our contemporary culture: He had gotten married and had children before turning twenty-four. In their profile, NBC News labeled his path an "alternative lifestyle." Many responded to this humorous tag, but compared to many men his age, Wise stands out among his peers.

Jonathan Edwards is right: Our hearts are "capable of" great capacities of "love" for God and man. For many people, this means an inclination to the "other sex." For his glory, God made the man to desire the woman, and the woman to become a helper to the man (Genesis 2:18-25). In his common grace, the Lord gives humanity the gift of drawing near to one member of the opposite sex in marriage. He intends this union to bring delight, happiness, and refinement to both spouses.

Getting married at a young age seems weird, even transgressive, today. But nothing could be further from the truth. It is normal and natural for many young men and women to enter into marriage. It is a beautiful thing when we feel "greatly" pulled to the opposite sex. We should do our part to recover a marriage culture in the church, to celebrate youthful unions, and to hold out mature older couples as examples of purity and honor. Marriage is not weird; it is natural. It points beyond our own bond to a much more glorious one: the marriage of Christ and his church. This is no "alternative lifestyle"; this is the plan of God, the grand outcome of history.

> "Therefore a man shall leave his father and mother and hold fast to his
> wife, and the two shall become one flesh." This mystery is profound,
> and I am saying that it refers to Christ and the church.
> EPHESIANS 5:31-32

October 20

[W]hen we pray for grace for the sake of Christ, we should intend thereby to desire God to remember that 'twill be to his Son's joy and happiness; for the bestowment of God's grace upon us was the joy that was set before him, the reward he expected, that made him cheerfully subject himself to such torments. Our happiness was a thing he really desired, and made an agreement with God about, by which he was to undertake great labors . . . and the more of us obtain grace, and the more grace and happiness we obtain, the more pleasure and glory doth he enjoy. And therefore 'tis for his sake we may ask of God, for our grace is his joy.

THE "MISCELLANIES"

GOD IS CONSPIRING to make you happy today. In order to be sad and downcast, you will have to work against God. This doesn't mean that everything in your day will come up roses; it doesn't mean that clouds will avoid you, songbirds will accompany you on your errands, and people will pay only nice-but-nonintrusive compliments to you. Following God right now may involve twists and turns you never anticipated. But whatever your course, God desires your "happiness" and "pleasure," as Jonathan Edwards reminds us here.

If God had not intended to make us full of grace, and thus surpassingly happy, he would not have given us Jesus. Jesus is a terrible gift if you're trying to drench people in misery. The pleasures of Christ are not small and insignificant; they are explosive and great. What a salvation he won on our behalf. He took on the very wrath of his Father against our sin, and exhausted it at the Cross. He willingly underwent terrible "torments" in order to remake and renew us. As great as the cost of our deliverance was, even greater is the happiness it yields, for all this work is Christ's work, and Christ's accomplishment.

With a foundation like this, no wonder Paul tells the Corinthians, "Finally, brothers, rejoice" (2 Corinthians 13:11). He says this after two letters of correction and rebuke. Nonetheless, despite the weakness of this people, they *must* rejoice. They are the people to whom God has given his Son. They can do nothing other than rejoice. So it is with us. God is actively conspiring to make us happy in the Son. The question is: Will we rejoice?

> Though the fig tree should not blossom, nor fruit be on the vines,
> the produce of the olive fail and the fields yield no food, the flock
> be cut off from the fold and there be no herd in the stalls, yet I will
> rejoice in the LORD; I will take joy in the God of my salvation.
>
> HABAKKUK 3:17-18

October 21

The saints whom we shall so ardently love loving others as well as ourselves, will be so far from raising jealousy in us, that it would raise jealousy if they did not. For their love of other saints is so much for the same things, and is so much the same principle, that 'tis equivalent to love to ourselves; it will be only the love to us multiplied. We shall not be jealous of those that are higher in glory, not only because we shall love them most, and because they will be most humble, but because they will love us most; because the highest will be the holiest, and the most holy will love holiness best, and they that love holiness best will love the saints best.
THE "MISCELLANIES"

WHAT A POISON JEALOUSY IS! There may be no sin that is harder to confess, and harder to detect, than this one. Other sins dump us onto a pile of shame; we have a hard time hiding a touchy temper, a foul mouth, or a narcissistic spirit. Gluttony creates its own obvious results; drunkenness leaves us dissolute and undone; lust creates habits that godly believers can spot right away—among them, restless eyes and unwise conversations.

But jealousy is a silent killer. We can have envy swelling like a balloon near to bursting in our hearts, and no one may be aware. Anytime we hear the name of the person we hate—for jealousy *is* hatred—we may bridle, but no one may see it. When talking with a person whose status or achievements we covet, we can twist the conversational knife without the other person necessarily knowing it. What a danger, a poison, jealousy is to the soul.

As a longtime pastor, revivalist, family man, and author, Jonathan Edwards faced plenty of jealousy in his day. Gifted and accomplished people usually do. He no doubt had his struggles to handle others' jealousy well, but he tried throughout his life to lift his gaze. He thought much of heaven, as we have seen, and that brought comfort to his soul. There, he writes, "we shall not be jealous of those that are higher in glory," for God will perfect our love. Seeing the "most holy," he argues, will thus make us most happy. Whatever shape heavenly interaction takes, we can know that jealousy will no longer plague us. Until that marvelous day, let us not poison ourselves. Let us fight envy, looking to God—and to no other—for our security and worth.

When men in the camp were jealous of Moses and Aaron, the holy one of the LORD, the earth opened and swallowed up Dathan, and covered the company of Abiram. PSALM 106:16-17

October 22

[Job 19:25. "For I know that my redeemer lives."] Job mentions this because he is about to express his hope of what would be after he was dead. He should die, and the worms should destroy his body, but his redeemer lived. And hence he hoped that he would redeem his body from the power of the grave. The resurrection of the body, and that glorification of the whole person that will then be, is especially called "redemption" in the New Testament. And because his redeemer lived, he hoped that though he died, he should live again by his redemption, for in that he lives, we shall live also.

THE "BLANK BIBLE"

DEATH IS A PROBLEM that will not go away. Without eternal hope, death hangs above our heads like a murderous cloud. We can distract ourselves for a time, and act as if death doesn't loom over us. We can drown out the prospect of death in worldly things, or at least try to. We can explain death away, viewing it as nothingness, or the end of being, and nothing more. But in reality, we know to the core of our souls that there is no solution to death.

That is, except one. Jesus Christ performs the miracle of miracles. He overcomes death—but more than this, he uses death to give us life. Christ turns the worst possible thing that can happen to us into the best possible thing. That which we rightly fear, we rightly dread, we rightly *hate*, becomes the very passageway to glory. There is one who died but who rose from "the power of the grave." This single instance births everlasting hope in us; a hope so strong that nothing can overcome it.

Of course, we must still suffer the effects of the Fall. Coming to faith does not mean that we instantaneously escape the consequences of sin, whether Adam's or our own. Unless Christ returns first, we will die. Our bodies will age and break down, and then our earthly life will leave us. We may face great pain in the terminal process. We may have to endure hardship before we depart this earth. But our hope is Job's hope. Our confidence is Job's confidence. Because Christ our Redeemer lives, "we shall live also." Our chief problem has become the gateway to our chief hope.

If we have been united with him in a death like his, we shall certainly be united with him in a resurrection like his. ROMANS 6:5

October 23

The being of God may be argued from the desirableness and need of it thus: we see in all nature everywhere that great necessities are supplied. We should be miserably off without some light in the night, and we have the moon and stars; in Egypt and India they are very much without rain, and they have the floods of Ganges and Nilus and great dews; in Greenland the sun's rays are exceeding oblique, and he is above the horizon so much the longer to make it up.
THE "MISCELLANIES"

YOU CAN TELL what our hearts long for by our screen savers. Perhaps they show coastal vistas, with people lounging by azure pools. Or maybe they reveal windswept cliffs and craggy hills, the kind a certain kind of tourist loves to scale. They could also show charming towns, filled with picture-perfect shops selling the best bread imaginable. One way or another, we are drawn to a vision of serenity.

But no place on earth knows pure calmness. People in every place, however appealing, have what Jonathan Edwards calls "great necessities," and beyond this, serious challenges. He points to countries that suffer drought, or floods, or a lack of light; we can extend the point, and acknowledge crippled economies, natural disasters, and troubled politics in the places we yearn to visit. Nowhere is without need; nowhere is without trouble of some kind.

By his grace, the Lord at once wants us to know both satisfaction and deprivation. We *should* want to visit lovely destinations. But we must also know that we cannot find lasting serenity or fulfillment without God. We, too, have huge, gaping needs. More than any psychological matter, we need the Lord. It is right that we observe the places and peoples of this world and see how they lack essential elements. But we must turn from there to ourselves. We need God. Thankfully, we have him today, whatever the screen saver shows, whether a vacation beckons us or not.

The young lions suffer want and hunger; but those who seek the LORD lack no good thing. PSALM 34:10

October 24

Fall 1722: Jonathan Edwards begins writing his "Resolutions"

DURING HIS TIME in New York City, Jonathan Edwards undertook the practice of writing spiritual resolutions that he would follow. He likely did this as an outflow of his conversion experience the year before, to help him maintain a disciplined spiritual life.

We should carefully delineate Edwards's spiritual resolutions from a legalistic perspective of faith. In penning his seventy resolutions over a year's time, Edwards was not establishing an extrabiblical standard for himself that he thought would grant him extra favor with God. Instead, the young man was capturing what he believed to be the essence of vital, warm-hearted piety, and nailing it to the wall of his heart so that he would not lose his zeal for God.

In his introduction to this body of material, Edwards asks the Lord for his help in walking "holily":

> Being sensible that I am unable to do anything without God's help,
> I do humbly entreat him by his grace to enable me to keep these
> Resolutions, so far as they are agreeable to his will, for Christ's sake.
> Remember to read over these Resolutions once a week.[55]

Edwards knew that he could not obey and please the Lord without divine aid. The resolutions are a stirring glimpse into the larger engine of the young man's grace-powered holiness. It was God's kindness, and nothing else, that would enable Edwards to "keep these Resolutions." The goal, as Resolution 63 identifies, was to be "a complete Christian," by which Edwards meant a mature, well-rounded man of God. His zeal for God and zest for discipline inspired him, and continues to inspire us, to greater growth in God. We do not necessarily need to write our own resolutions. But we would do well to emulate Edwards's tenacious pursuit of the Lord.

October 25

When Christ hung dying upon the cross, he was doing that that was the most wonderful act of love that ever was; and the posture that he died in was very suitable to signify his free and great [love]: he died with his arms spread open, as being ready to embrace all that would come to him. He was lift up [upon the] cross above the earth with his arms thus open, and there he made an offer of his love to the world. . . . By this love he drew men to him, as he says, "If I be lift up from the earth, I will draw [all men] unto me" [John 12:32].
THE "MISCELLANIES"

WE SEE THE TWO FATES of humanity when we study the Cross of Christ. No starker picture could ever be drawn. Here is love at its apex, "the most wonderful act of love that ever was," as Jonathan Edwards declares. Yet God painted this perfect portrait of love on a canvas of destruction. The Son of God stretches out his arms, welcoming all who repent of sin and trust in his name, even as his arms are held fast by nails.

The dying Christ is the victorious Christ, and his victory is love. Love triumphs over judgment and death. The church sees this scarlet truth when we fix our gaze on Calvary. But not everyone does. In the nineteenth century, for example, Albert Schweitzer argued in *The Quest of the Historical Jesus* that Christ "lays hold of the wheel of the world to set it moving on that last revolution," but that this wheel "crushes Him." Liberal Protestantism did not see victory in the death of Christ—certainly not victory over our own iniquities.

Jesus did not die as a monument to his cause. He did not die to inspire us to go out and live sacrificial lives for positive causes. Jesus died as an act of love. His act of love was not weak, but strong. From the moment he offered himself up as a blood sacrifice for sin, Jesus has drawn sinners to himself. So many gurus, so many thinkers, have come and gone, and their accolades and ideas are forgotten. But the love of Christ endures. Knowing this truth, let us persevere in faith. Jesus has drawn us; Jesus will draw many more besides.

I, when I am lifted up from the earth, will draw all people to myself.
JOHN 12:32

October 26

But because God does everything beautifully, he brings about this their happiness which he
determined, in an excellent manner. . . . For there are these two propensities in the divine
nature: to communicate goodness absolutely to that which now is nothing, and to communicate
goodness to that which is beautiful and holy. . . . He has a propensity to reward holiness, but
he gives it on purpose that he may reward it; because he loves the creature, and loves to reward,
and therefore gives it something that he may reward.
THE "MISCELLANIES"

WE HAD A FAMILY TRADITION when I was growing up. At the end of the school
year, we all went out for sundaes, which were a rare treat. The ice cream shop in
our small town had maybe five or ten flavors, and their sundaes were pretty basic
as well. But because we rarely went out for ice cream, I remember those sundaes
like they were a precious commodity.

The very nature of a reward traces back to God and Christianity. If God were
not involved in our daily existence, the universe would be a cold and ungenerous
place. There would be no motivation for showing kindness to others; no need
to extend ourselves and sacrifice precious resources for others. But with God,
we live in a warm Kingdom under the rule of a gracious sovereign. The very
character of God activates such blessings. God is love, and love, by definition,
acts in generosity. God "loves the creature," Jonathan Edwards assures us, "and
loves to reward."

We do not deserve rewards for holiness. The character traits that occasion
God's favor are qualities that the Holy Spirit produces in us (Galatians 5:22-23).
But because God is God, he finds great pleasure in bestowing blessings on his
children for obedience. In our day, we don't need to discover some elaborate new
way to please God. We need only to obey God. Doing so is the right thing to
do; doing so means we will gain something better than any treat this world can
offer, no matter how delicious.

> The LORD repay you for what you have done, and a full reward be given
> you by the LORD, the God of Israel, under whose wings you have come
> to take refuge! RUTH 2:12

October 27

[T]he very end of Christ's dying for sin, was that the glory of God's jealousy, holiness and justice might be consistent with this grace; that while God thus manifested his mercy, we might not conceive any unworthy thoughts of God with respect to his majesty and authority and justice, as we should be in danger to do if grace was offered absolutely: we should not know what a great evil sin was, and how dreadful a thing it is to offend an infinite majesty, and how holy and jealous God is. Seeing therefore that this is the end of Christ's coming, that we might be sensible of this, though we are saved and all sin forgiven; it seems therefore necessary that we should be made sensible of it, in order to our being brought into a state of salvation.
THE "MISCELLANIES"

THE GOOD NEWS of the gospel can sound to some ears like *freedom to sin.* "I am totally forgiven by God! Nothing and no one can remove me from him? Awesome! Now I can do whatever I want, right?" Not quite. Jonathan Edwards encourages us to see that the very design of the gospel counters our tendency to treat grace cheaply. Even as our mouths hang open at the totality of our redemption, we also see "how dreadful a thing it is to offend" the Lord.

But our hearts can grow dull to even the most sparkling biblical teachings. What if we had committed a crime, a terrible one, in a spasm of stupidity and evil? What if we found ourselves on death row, only to receive notice that a family member or a friend had stepped in and died in our place? Would we not spend the rest of our days thinking about that act? No doubt it would motivate us to live differently, to never forget the sacrifice that gave us a future.

This is what Christ has done for us. But he not only saved our earthly lives; he gave us eternal life by his grace. We are cleansed, but our redemption could not have come at a greater price. Nothing could grant us more hope, peace, and purity than the perfect salvation Christ accomplished. How, then, can you and I take the grace of God for granted? We think of Paul's words in Romans 6, just after he unfolded the mystery of Christ's imputed righteousness: "What shall we say then? Are we to continue in sin that grace may abound? By no means! How can we who died to sin still live in it?" (Romans 6:1-2). Are we free in Christ? Absolutely. Are we free to do whatever we please, even sinning against the Lord, thinking that it doesn't matter? Absolutely not.

Cleanse your hands, you sinners, and purify your hearts, you double-minded. JAMES 4:8

October 28

April-October 1738: Jonathan Edwards preaches a sermon series called Charity and Its Fruits

By the late 1730s, Jonathan Edwards began to realize that the effects of the revival of 1734–1735 had waned. Though Edwards and the Northampton revival had drawn international attention, and more importantly had sparked outbreaks of gospel awakening throughout the colonies and beyond, the people of Northampton were slipping back into their old ways of bickering, not taking church seriously, and neglecting the spiritual disciplines. To counteract this, Edwards preached several series of sermons aimed at fanning the flames of revival.

"Heaven a World of Charity or Love," the capstone sermon of the sixteen-part series later published under the title *Charity and Its Fruits,* is perhaps Edwards's greatest sermonic achievement. It shows the same literary craftmanship as "Sinners in the Hands of an Angry God," Edwards's more famous sermon. "Heaven," however, is as nourishing and heartening as "Sinners" is discomfiting. Few messages in Christian history capture the boundless nature of divine love better than Edwards does here:

> *Love in heaven is always mutual.* It is always met with answerable returns of love; with returns that are proportioned to its exercise. Such returns, love always seeks; and just in proportion as any person is beloved, in the proportion is his love desired and prized. And in heaven this desire of love, or this fondness for being loved, will never fail of being satisfied. No inhabitants of that blessed world will ever be grieved with the thought that they are slighted by those that they love, or that their love is not fully and fondly returned.
>
> As the saints will love God with an inconceivable ardency of heart, and to the utmost of their capacity, so they will know that he has loved them from all eternity, and still loves them, and will continue to love them forever. And God will then gloriously manifest himself to them, and they shall know that all that happiness and glory which they are possessed of, are the fruits of his love. And with the same ardor and fervency will the saints love the Lord Jesus Christ; and their love will be accepted; and they shall know that he has loved them with a faithful, yea, even with a dying love. They shall then be more sensible than now they are, what great love it manifested in Christ that he should lay down his life for them; and then will Christ open to their view the great fountain of love in his heart for them, beyond all that they ever saw before. Hereby the love of the saints to God and

Christ, is seen to be reciprocated, and that declaration fulfilled, "I love them that love me." And though the love of God to them cannot properly be called the return of love, because he loved them first, yet the sight of his love will fill them with joy, and admiration, and love to him.[56]

Charity and Its Fruits, an extended meditation on 1 Corinthians 13, wasn't published until after Edwards's death. Over the years, it has been reprinted many times and has drawn many to ponder God's love—and to meet the God who *is* love.

October 29

That is our great encouragement, that God has declared from heaven that Christ is his beloved Son, in whom he is well pleased; and we have confidence that seeing it is so, and we are in him, that he will be well pleased with us for his excellency's and righteousness' sake. I think we are plainly taught this doctrine, Ephesians 1:6, "He hath made us accepted in the Beloved," where we are plainly taught this, that we are accepted and beloved because we are in him who is beloved. . . . Seeing we are clothed with him who is so beautiful, and for his beauty with which we are clothed, are we accepted and loved.

THE "MISCELLANIES"

ON MY LUNCH BREAKS, I sometimes read about athletes. Recently I heard about a player who makes more than $200 million from his team and more than $200 million from a shoe company. This player is worth close to half a billion dollars. All for running up and down the court, bouncing a ball.

It could go without saying that the teeming majority of humanity will not possess such wealth. I, for one, have never made a penny from sports. Why, then, am I so interested in them? I suppose I like sports for the same reason that many people like theater groups or knitting circles: belonging. We were not made for isolation. We were not made to find sufficiency in ourselves or grant ourselves the status we seek so strongly. We were made for God, and for membership in his body. Initially, he accepted Adam and Eve as they were; but they rebelled against him, and in them we all fell, and now we wander the earth, questing after what we've lost.

In Christ, we find it. In Christ, the Father is "well pleased with us," as Jonathan Edwards sums it up. There is no loftier position we could find. There is no stronger security, no richer acceptance. Why do we try to find our identity in lesser things, knowing we never will? We do not need riches. We do not need the approval of our peers. We do not need lofty titles. We do not need lots of "followers" on digital platforms. We need to be clothed in Christ, and we are. Poor or otherwise, we have acceptance from God. We have a family. What we always wanted, we now possess.

In the way of your testimonies I delight as much as in all riches.
PSALM 119:14

October 30

That humiliation is grace it appears, because Christ says, "Blessed are the poor in spirit, for theirs is the kingdom of heaven" [Matthew 5:3]. Now we can understand nothing by the poor in spirit, but those that see their own poverty; that are emptied of themselves; that see they are wretched, and miserable, and poor, and blind and naked; that see that in themselves they are nothing. . . . 'Tis God's manner to give special discoveries of his glory and grace after brokenness of spirit, not only at first conversion but through the whole Christian course.

THE "MISCELLANIES"

"GOSPEL WAKEFULNESS." My friend Jared Wilson coined this phrase to summarize how God grants his people "special discoveries of his glory and grace," as Jonathan Edwards puts it. In these moments—or seasons—we gain a special sense of God's nearness, his kindness, his goodness. Perhaps we have slept spiritually for a time; perhaps our affections have ebbed. Then God, praise his name, wakes us up. He shows us how great his gospel truly is.

There is no special sequence of events that leads to these "special discoveries." Surely, suffering can heighten our apprehension of the grace of God. A friend calls us out for a pattern of sin. We get dumped after a long relationship we thought was going well. The church that offered us a job rescinds it. The circumstances will vary, but the point remains the same: Our "humiliation" can lead to a fresh awareness of "poverty" in spirit. We're not so high and mighty as we thought. We need the Lord in a desperate way.

An earlier generation used to sing about the need to "count your blessings— name them one by one." Sometimes, though, we go to count our blessings, and we can name only one. Such times seem lean, and may well be. But they also may be prime locations for "gospel wakefulness," for freshly searching out the jaw-dropping fact that the infinite God has elected, regenerated, and glorified us. It turns out one blessing is all we truly need.

I pray that the sharing of your faith may become effective for the full knowledge of every good thing that is in us for the sake of Christ.

PHILEMON 1:6

October 31

THE PREACHER WHO later became famous—or infamous, if you prefer—for the image of sinners dangling over hell "by a single thread" had a lifelong interest in spiders. When he was twenty, Jonathan Edwards sent his "Spider Letter" to an unnamed official whom historians have identified as the Honorable Paul Dudley, a judge. Dudley had been a classmate at Harvard of Jonathan's father, Timothy, and was a fellow of the Royal Society of London (over which Isaac Newton presided).

The letter shows Edwards's intellectual precocity and love for the created order. He must have gotten very close indeed to spiders to observe their "flying in the air."

> And this, Sir, is the way of spiders' working. This is the way of their going
> from one thing to another at a distance, and this is the way of their flying
> in the air. And although I can say I am certain of it, I don't desire that the
> truth of it should be received upon my word, though I could bring others
> to testify to it to whom I have shewn it, and who have looked on with
> admiration: But everyone's eyes who will take the pains to observe will
> make them equally sure of it; only those who would make experiment
> must take notice that it is not every sort of spider that is a flying spider,
> for those spiders that keep in houses are a quite different sort, as also
> those that keep in the ground, and those [that] keep in swamps upon
> the ground amongst the bogs, and those that keep in hollow trees and
> rotten logs; but those spiders that keep on branches of trees and shrubs
> are the flying spiders. They delight most in walnut trees, and are that sort
> of spiders that make those curious, network, polygonal webs that are so
> frequently to be seen in the latter end of the year. There are more of this
> sort of spider by far than of any other.[57]

Though Edwards's observations were not published by the Royal Society of London, they did become famous in later years. Showing that he adored Creation, but did not see it as an end unto itself, when he submitted his observations to the world's premier scientific organization, he concluded with a poetic celebration of the Maker:

> Hence [there] is reason to admire at the wisdom of the Creator, and
> to be convinced that it is exercised about such little things in this
> wonderful contrivance of annually carrying off and burying the
> corruption and nauseousness of the air, of which flying insects are little
> collections, in the bottom of the ocean where it will do no harm.[58]

November

†

November 1

The sum of all that Christ purchased is the Holy Ghost. God is he of whom the purchase is made, God is the purchase and the price, and God is the thing purchased: God is the Alpha and the Omega in this work. . . . Therefore the Holy Ghost that believers have, here is said to be the earnest of the inheritance, or purchased possession [Ephesians 1:14]. The earnest is some of the same given beforehand; the purchased possession is only a fullness of that Spirit.
THE "MISCELLANIES"

MANY CHRISTIANS FEEL confused about the Holy Spirit. They know biblical language about being "filled" with the "Holy Ghost," as Jonathan Edwards identifies him, but they know little of how this works. They may read Ephesians 5:18 and come away discouraged because of this: "Do not get drunk with wine, for that is debauchery, but be filled with the Spirit," the next step of which is to sing. Are we all a bunch of believers walking around on spiritual fumes?

It's actually good that we feel discomfort with this idea. Nobody wants to play the ecclesial role of the guy who drives everywhere with his gas gauge on E. We want a full tank; we want to hit on all cylinders. The most literal translation of "be filled with the Spirit" is "be being kept filled." The Greek verb is in the passive tense. The workings of this process are admittedly a little mysterious, but the takeaway is plain enough: God gives us his Spirit, and we walk in the Spirit's power.

The concept here is similar to our salvation. God has saved us, but we must also walk in a manner worthy of our calling. God has given us all "fullness of that Spirit" who resides in every Christian, and yet we must also produce fruit in keeping with our Spirit-given repentance (Matthew 3:8). Should we pray for more of the Holy Ghost, then? Yes, we should. But we should not think the answer to this prayer means we will suddenly levitate. The answer to this prayer means that God's grace will continue to do its work in us: We will hate sin, and we will love our Savior. Spirit-filling is not a matter of how we feel. It is a matter of how we live, today and every day.

As for me, I am filled with power, with the Spirit of the LORD, and
with justice and might, to declare to Jacob his transgression and to
Israel his sin. MICAH 3:8

November 2

'Tis part of God's sovereignty, that he may if he pleases bring afflictions upon an innocent creature if he compensates it with equal good; for affliction with equal good to balance it is just equivalent to an indifference. And if God is not obliged to bestow good upon the creature, but may leave it in the state of indifference, why mayn't he order that for the creature that is perfectly equivalent to it? God may therefore bring many and great afflictions upon the godly, as he intends to bestow upon them an infinitely greater good, and designs them as a means of a far greater good, though all their sins are satisfied for.
THE "MISCELLANIES"

THE DISCIPLES DIDN'T know what they were asking for. As the Gospel of Mark records, the boldness of their question outran their character: "James and John, the sons of Zebedee, came up to [Jesus] and said to him, 'Teacher, we want you to do for us whatever we ask of you.' And he said to them, 'What do you want me to do for you?' And they said to him, 'Grant us to sit, one at your right hand and one at your left, in your glory'" (Mark 10:35-37). The understated answer from the Son of God: "You do not know what you are asking" (Mark 10:38).

The disciples wanted the good stuff from the Kingdom of God—the perks of leadership. But they had no inkling of the cost of Christ-exalting leadership. They construed faith in Christ as a path to earthly gain much like any other—you work your way up the ranks, you prove yourself, you get close to the boss, and you secure a seat at the table—or in this case, a seat at the right and left hand of God. James and John, the "sons of thunder," were requesting the very throne of Christ for themselves.

Yet even as Jesus avoided signing them up for divine prerogatives, he indicated that they would indeed follow his course (Mark 10:39-40). It turned out that the Father had willed a similar fate for these men. To use Jonathan Edwards's terminology, the Father would indeed "bestow upon them an infinitely greater good" than anything they could imagine. But as with all God's people, this greater good would come through serious risks and a weighty cost. There is indeed a way to heavenly advancement, just as our natural minds might think. But it is not the way of glory; it is the way of the Cross.

This light momentary affliction is preparing for us an eternal weight of glory beyond all comparison, as we look not to the things that are seen but to the things that are unseen. For the things that are seen are transient, but the things that are unseen are eternal. 2 CORINTHIANS 4:17-18

November 3

When he feels those motions he knows what they be, and he sees that it would be utterly incongruous for him to have them, that God should give them to him, if he did not accept of him. This is that seal and that earnest of the Spirit that we read of; this is that white stone and new name, which no man knows but he that receives it [Revelation 2:17]. Thus the Spirit of God bears witness together with our spirits, that we are the children of God, Romans 8:16.
THE "MISCELLANIES"

THE FIRST AND ONLY time in the Bible that Jesus addresses his Father as *Abba*, essentially meaning "beloved Father," comes just before his ghastly death. Mark 14:36 records his Gethsemane prayer: "Abba, Father, all things are possible for you. Remove this cup from me. Yet not what I will, but what you will." The Father does not remove the cup. Instead, he bids his Son to drink it to the last drop.

Because the Son lifted the wrath of God to his lips, we too can address God as *Abba*. We may not know Aramaic, but Romans 8:15 teaches us that we possess the privilege of intimate access even now: "For you did not receive the spirit of slavery to fall back into fear, but you have received the Spirit of adoption as sons, by whom we cry, 'Abba! Father!'" The context of our crying out to the beloved Father is not one of suffering, but opportunity. Through the faithfulness of Jesus, we now speak to God with joy, where once we could approach him only in fear.

All this is through the Holy Spirit, who is God's "seal," his personal pledge and guarantee of our redemption. "The Spirit of God," Jonathan Edwards teaches, "bears witness . . . that we are the children of God." In our flesh, we may doubt this. But even if we weaken, we have an abiding witness. The Spirit overwhelms our fears. The Spirit picks us off the ground, where we lie in a misbegotten state of fright. The Spirit is like the king's adjutant who goes outside the castle, outside the kingdom, and brings the one who ran off in fear into the king's throne room. We are that one.

Beat your plowshares into swords, and your pruning hooks into spears;
let the weak say, "I am a warrior." JOEL 3:10

November 4

Why should we suppose that God would make any promises of spiritual and eternal blessings to that which has no goodness in it? Why should he promise his grace to a seeking of it that is not right, or to those that don't truly seek it? . . . For the proper means of obtaining grace is seeking of it truly, with a love and appetite to it, and desire of it, and sense of its excellency and worthiness, and a seeking of it of God through Christ; and to such as seek it thus, God has faithfully promised that he will bestow it.

THE "MISCELLANIES"

THE ANCIENT GREEKS and Romans told tales of mighty warriors and heroic voyages. These adventurous souls had what some have called *glory hunger*: setting out to make a name for themselves, to prove their mettle in battle and exploration. They defied death and beat the odds, caring far more for risk than for safety.

The Christian heart also has a "glory hunger." But we do not seek it for ourselves. As Jonathan Edwards suggests, we have a "love and appetite" for grace. We are like pointer hounds on a fox hunt—we pick up the scent for the Spirit of God, and we follow eagerly. No Christian should have an indifferent posture regarding God's goodness and God's fame. This is our heartbeat.

We cannot glorify God by sitting on our hands. The gospel is what I call *risky*, meaning it summons us to a life of doxological (God-honoring) action. We may not know exactly how best to undertake such a quest. But we can trust that if we commit ourselves to seeking the glory of God, he will put us to work. God does not want to dampen down our fire; he wants us to carry the fire into all the world. This is not work for a select few. Every Christian is called to get in the game and to seek the grace of God in their own lives and the lives of others. Some appetites need dampening; Christian glory hunger should increase still more.

You are a chosen race, a royal priesthood, a holy nation, a people for his own possession, that you may proclaim the excellencies of him who called you out of darkness into his marvelous light.   I PETER 2:9

November 5

The exaltation of some in glory above others, will be so far from diminishing anything of the perfect happiness and joy of the rest that are inferior, that they will be the happier for it. Such will be the union of all of them, that they will be partakers of each other's glory and happiness. 1 Corinthians 12:26, "If one of the members be honored, all the members rejoice with it."
THE "MISCELLANIES"

ONE OF MY SEMINARY professors once shared a story that hit me hard. He said that when you're young and someone gives you the opportunity to preach, even to just a handful of people, the opportunity feels so weighty that you joyfully exclaim, "Why *me*, God?" But as you get older, and you go along in your career, and you see others getting opportunities you want, the question changes. It becomes cloudier: "Why *not me*, God?"

Our hearts, in truth, are never far from envy and bitterness. If we're honest about our thought life, we face regular temptations to despise others and embrace self-pity. To fight this awful tendency, we must think much of the life to come. In eternity, we will not mentally stab and hurt one another, tearing each other down in a passive-aggressive fit of envy. In heaven, we will "be partakers of each other's glory and happiness," as Jonathan Edwards argues. There will be no place for man-centered thinking; our minds and souls will focus on God and his awesomeness.

Some will very likely receive greater rewards than others in the age to come. Our pursuit of God on this earth matters, and the Lord rewards the faithful. In keeping "the rules of the Lord," the psalmist says, "there is great reward" (Psalm 19:10-11). Hebrews 11:6 teaches the same principle: "Without faith it is impossible to please him, for whoever would draw near to God must believe that he exists and that he rewards those who seek him." The bond of our union in glory will be so strong, so thick, so unopposable, that we will revel in the rewarding of faithful believers in eternity. Whatever our circumstances, may this truth cause us to cry out in humble joy, "Why *us*, Lord?"

> If one member suffers, all suffer together; if one member is honored, all rejoice together. I CORINTHIANS 12:26

November 6

Sorrow and grief for sin is a duty, because we are not capable of having so perfect views of these things, but that a right sense of the odiousness and folly of sin will necessarily cause grief. A sense of the great evil of sin is good, absolutely considered; but grief for sin is so, only in a certain presupposed state and circumstances.

THE "MISCELLANIES"

IT IS GOOD AND RIGHT to feel sorrow over our sin. Jonathan Edwards goes so far as to call this approach to iniquity "a duty," and he is right. We think of the instruction of Paul to the Ephesian church: "Do not grieve the Holy Spirit of God, by whom you were sealed for the day of redemption" (Ephesians 4:30). Paul wrote these words to a redeemed people. Though saved, the Ephesians had to take care that they did not deeply upset the Spirit by their sin.

We should not feel despair in our sin, because God's grace covers us. But that doesn't mean we don't feel genuine remorse, and even grief. Even as born-again believers, we still have a serious capacity to do damage to others. One heated conversation can yield a caustic remark that plays in the mind for months. One subtle put-down can leave a struggling friend in a tailspin. One foolish choice on a business trip—the kind people make all the time in their folly—can blow up a home. Before sin takes hold, we must fight it. Part of our battle involves grieving over the evils we commit.

Christians think a lot about the lavish grace of God. But while avoiding moroseness and obsessive self-examination, we never relinquish in our minds "a sense of the great evil of sin." We don't want to camp out there, but we do want to think afresh about the horrible character of transgression, and the horrific consequences of depravity. There is no "undo" button for our foul deeds. Do not linger for days in despair over your moral failings. Instead, confess them freely to God. Let us not grieve the Spirit.

The Israelites separated themselves from all foreigners and stood
and confessed their sins and the iniquities of their fathers.
NEHEMIAH 9:2

November 7

So it is represented in the Scripture, that we are washed from our filthiness in Christ's blood; whereas, although the blood of Christ washes us from our guilt, yet 'tis the Spirit of Christ that washes from the pollution and stain of sin. But however, the blood of Christ washes also from the filth of sin, as it purchases sanctification; it makes way for it by satisfying, and purchases it by merit. As the sacrifices under the law typified Christ's sacrifice, not only as a satisfaction but as meritorious obedience, they are called a sweet savor upon both those accounts; and therefore we find obedience compared with sacrifice, Psalms 40:6 ff.
THE "MISCELLANIES"

THE WAGES OF SIN IS DEATH. To be perfectly just, God the Father must punish sin, and punish it fully. His holy character would fail if he did not do so. Though some wish to sand away God's edges, we should give thanks to him that he does not relax his standards of righteousness. Any sin is a sin against God. And because God is an infinite God, any sin against him is an infinite offense. This means he must exact infinite justice against it.

But there is a way out of this situation for fallen creatures like us. The Lord is not only perfectly just, he is perfectly merciful as well. He will pardon the guilty if sacrifice is made. But not just any sacrifice—an infinitely holy God requires an infinitely perfect and pure offering for sin. Outside of this, the wicked have no hope. Scripture teaches that Christ made this very sacrifice. His holy blood washed our unholy hearts clean "from the pollution and stain of sin," making us spotless in the sight of God. Jonathan Edwards contends that Christ's blood purifies also "the filth of sin," meaning we are fully made new. No taint or stench of unrighteousness remains for the children of God. All this the law promised through the sacrifices of bulls and goats, and Christ brought to fulfillment by his substitutionary death, the meeting of all the law's holy demands.

We may remember our past and *feel* filthy. We may close our eyes and be able to recall to mind terrible things. But if we have confessed these sins to God and trusted Christ for forgiveness, we are not what we feel. We are not filthy. We are washed by the blood of Jesus. This is not a car-wash kind of cleansing; this is a once-and-for-all work of the Son of God.

Such were some of you. But you were washed, you were sanctified, you were justified in the name of the Lord Jesus Christ and by the Spirit of our God. I CORINTHIANS 6:11

November 8

[Unless] a man has a discovery of the glory and excellency and loveliness of God as well as his terrible greatness, will not in this world make a man leave off quarreling and objecting. They will neither be freed from a disposition to quarrel, nor indeed will it convince 'em that they are every way justly dealt with. . . . The sight of the awful greatness of God, gives [a man] a sense of the proportion between his sins and a very great punishment, provided he were but convinced that the blame was altogether from and in himself.

THE "MISCELLANIES"

WHEN TALKING WITH a tough-as-nails unbeliever, we sometimes think, *This person is closed to rational conversation. I can pray for him or her, but I've gone as far in conversation as I can go.* People really can become hardened to the things of God. First Timothy 4:2 speaks of those whose "consciences are seared." Such individuals have denied God for so long that they are lost in a haze of unbelief.

Some folks who fit this profile have a "disposition to quarrel." Jonathan Edwards faced such foes in his Northampton congregation. These people may have quick minds and faster tongues; they may be able to wiggle out of any conviction and create confusion in the face of certainty. But please don't misunderstand: These quarrelers cannot actually tweak the moral fabric of the universe. They cannot overturn God's wisdom and refute his truth. But tragically they can trick themselves into thinking they've gotten the better of us, and of God.

We may find there are no arguments we can offer to such people to convert them. Nothing satisfies their intellectual objections and their hearts' settled hostility toward God. They are not merely separated from God by a few stray considerations; they hate him (Romans 3:10-18). Only the Lord can awaken such people. Only a vision of "the awful greatness of God" can convince the hard-hearted. In a moment of frustration when engaging such people, we might be tempted to think, *Only God can save them.* And we'd be right. Only he *can* save them. Only he can take the quarreler, the one running from God and fighting back all the way, and make that person a trophy of grace. He can—and he does.

If anyone teaches a different doctrine and does not agree with the sound words of our Lord Jesus Christ and the teaching that accords with godliness, he is puffed up with conceit and understands nothing. He has an unhealthy craving for controversy and for quarrels about words, which produce envy, dissension, slander, evil suspicions. I TIMOTHY 6:3-4

November 9

The freedom of gospel grace is ordinarily explained thus, that the blessing is bestowed only for accepting. But 'tis sometimes in the Word of God expressed by its being bestowed only for seeking or asking: "Seek, and ye shall find; ask, and [ye shall] receive; knock, and it shall be opened unto you" [Matthew 7:7]. There is both a seeking and accepting implied in the nature of faith.

THE "MISCELLANIES"

GOD REWARDS THOSE who seek, ask, and knock. This teaching by Jesus pushes against our natural hesitancy regarding God. We might think that he blesses those who sit tight, stay quiet, and don't disturb him. But it isn't that way. The Lord wants us to venture toward him. He wants us to ask him for mercy and grace. He wants us to disturb his peace and lift up our requests to him.

Some Christians struggle with the assertive nature of true Christianity. They import a faulty understanding into their doctrine of God, thinking of the Lord as a majestic king whom none dare approach or address. But we cannot say it strongly enough: That is not the character of the biblical God. He gives "blessing," Jonathan Edwards asserts, both from "seeking and accepting." He is the King of kings, and none can sum up his grandeur, but he is a king unlike any other. This King gives blessings freely, which we are right to accept when they come in his good time. But this King also wants his subjects to come to him, to seek him, to knock on his castle door.

God sometimes withholds blessings from us because of our sin, or sometimes simply for his good pleasure. But we mustn't miss this thread of biblical teaching: Sometimes God withholds blessings from us *because we do not ask* (James 4:2). In the simplest of terms, we fail to receive because we fail to pray. Prayer requires trust and love; sometimes we falter in our trust, and wane in our love. The message of Christ rings in our ears: *Come to me. You will not be bothering me. You will not annoy me. Knock, and I will open the door; pray, and I will hear your prayers, and answer.*

Hannah prayed and said, "My heart exults in the LORD; my horn is exalted in the LORD. My mouth derides my enemies, because I rejoice in your salvation. I SAMUEL 2:1

November 10

'Tis no wonder that none can tell how sweetly the fruit of the Tree of Life is but those that have tasted; no wonder that none know that the Lord is gracious so well as they that have tasted and seen. Believers have had those exercises of soul towards spiritual things that are very well represented to tasting: they have tasted of the bread of life by faith [John 6:35], they have drunk of the water of life [John 4:14], they have tasted of the wine and milk that Christ has given [John 2, 1 Peter 2:2–3]. 'Tis these only that can testify from their own knowledge that the judgments of God are sweeter than the honey and the honeycomb.

SERMONS AND DISCOURSES, 1723-1729

OURS IS A TIME when "virtual reality" is hot. If you go to a high-tech trade show, for example, you can put on a massive helmet that looks a bit like a technological wastebasket, and you can "travel" to another place. True reality, on the other hand, requires no special equipment and can be accessed at any time. All we need is faith in God to gain access to his Kingdom and see things as they really are.

In the Kingdom of God, we live in true reality, for we see things as God sees them. The Holy Spirit enables us not only to view the world from God's perspective, but also to *taste* "of the bread of life by faith," as Jonathan Edwards puts it. This is a feast no VR device can simulate. Furthermore, Edwards writes, we are invited to drink of the "water of life" and consume the delicious "wine and milk that Christ has given." What a rebuke this sensory spread is to our impoverished understanding of Christianity. God has invited us to his table. He has filled our plates, and our cups, to overflowing with joys "sweeter than . . . honey," better than any meal a five-star chef can create.

But this tasting does not happen only for us when we convert to Christ. We taste the holy bread, water, and food every day as we feast on the goodness of God in his Word. People might think they want "virtual reality." There is no way, however, to improve on the Kingdom of God, in which we truly see, truly taste, and truly live.

> Jesus said to them, "I am the bread of life; whoever comes to me shall not hunger, and whoever believes in me shall never thirst."
>
> JOHN 6:35

November 11

November 11, 1723: Jonathan Edwards becomes the pastor of a small church in Bolton, Connecticut

IN APRIL 1723, after the small New York City Presbyterian congregation that Jonathan Edwards had pastored for eight months reunited with a larger congregation in the city, Edwards moved back to his hometown of East Windsor, Connecticut. There, his father, Timothy, recommended that he take the pastorate of a newly formed church in the small town of Bolton, which had recently been settled by residents of Windsor and East Windsor. On November 11, barely a month after his twentieth birthday, Jonathan agreed to become their pastor.

Despite his vaunted reputation in our day, Edwards did not travel an easy path to pastoral leadership. He struggled with impatience, as many young men do, and he had no love lost for tiny Bolton, especially coming on the heels of his big-city experience. In one of his Bolton sermons, titled "Nothing upon Earth can Represent the Glories of Heaven," he lingered at length on a description of the heavenly city. One wonders if his mind was drawn to the topic in part because he longed to be elsewhere:

> Here we have a metaphorical description or visionary representation of
> the city of God, that Zion that stands on the Mount of God, so often
> spoken of in the holy Scriptures, in the Old Testament prophecies; that
> Jerusalem which is the mother of us all, that city spoken of, Hebrews
> 12:22–24; that Mount Zion, that city of the living God, that heavenly
> Jerusalem, where there are an innumerable company of angels, where
> there are the general assembly of the church, of the firstborn which are
> written in heaven. . . . Here is the end of all the labors of the Christian;
> here is our Father's house, here is the end of the race.[59]

Not long after he preached this sermon, Edwards left Bolton to become a tutor (equivalent to a professor today) at Yale.

Edwards's early pastoral work, at Bolton as in New York City, readied him to communicate dense and arresting biblical images to needy and sometimes distracted people. For the rest of his career, he attempted to put into language the glories of biblical Christianity. It wasn't easy to be a pastor, Edwards saw, but the hard work was worth it. He used these kinds of situations to train his mind to love the world less and to yearn for heaven more, a discipline that will benefit every Christian.

November 12

The child of God doth as it were see and feel the truth of divine things even intuitively; that is, they see so much of religion, that they plainly discern that it must needs be the offspring of God. They can feel such a power and kind of omnipotency in Christianity, and taste such a sweetness, and see such wisdom, such an excellent harmony in the gospel, as carry their own light with them, and powerfully do enforce and conquer the assent and necessitates their minds to receive it as proceeding from God, and as the certain truth. They bring so much of the image of God with them, that it is plain beyond question that they are from him.
SERMONS AND DISCOURSES, 1723-1729

JONATHAN EDWARDS'S MIND was primed to search out the deepest things of existence. Yet though he studied and worked and polished and debated, devoting thirteen hours a day to his vocation, he stubbornly resisted any notion of Christianity that reduced it to mental matters alone. There is a bit of irony here, in that one of the church's most brilliant thinkers helps us to see, by way of carefully reasoned sermons and documents, that the Christian faith is not only about thinking.

Human beings are complex and wondrous creatures, able not only to reason, but also to desire, and to *feel*. Those of us who adore sound doctrine and work to promote it everywhere we can should not back away from this contention. If we were not made to *feel* the truth, we would not love it. We would only contemplate it and then—*click!*—receive it as fact. But this is a far, far cry from the Bible's depiction of how we trust in Jesus.

We must never sever our experience from our doctrine; truly, our doctrine must shape our experience. But let not us pulverize our hearts. We are right to feel "a power and kind of omnipotency in Christianity." Our faith does not sit gently on us, lighter than a feather. It ripples through our being, a holy and surging life force. We taste the "sweetness" of Christ and feel delighted. We know we are created in the "image of God," but when we open ourselves to embrace this principle, we feel caught up to the clouds. We were made to think, made to desire, made to *feel* in the image of God.

Deep calls to deep at the roar of your waterfalls; all your breakers and your waves have gone over me. PSALM 42:7

November 13

['Tis] not the hearing of elegant descriptions of a beautiful face that can ever make a person have a sense of the sweetness and amiableness of the beauty; 'tis not the slight notion of beauty by hearsay that causes love to burn in the heart: but it is the sight of the eye. One glance of the eye doth more than all the most particular descriptions that can be given. Thus unbelievers know nothing about spiritual beauty but by hearsay; but to the godly, God has given a glance, opened to the immediate view of their minds, and there breaks in upon their souls such a heavenly sweetness, such a sense of the amiableness, as wonderfully affects the heart, and even transforms it.
SERMONS AND DISCOURSES, 1723-1729

IT IS ONE OF THE SADDEST things we can encounter. When we talk to people about the gospel and ask them where they stand with God, they reply that they prayed a prayer asking Jesus into their heart years ago, so they're good. They know the Lord. Yes, they might not go to church all the time, and no, they don't necessarily follow all the rules of "organized religion," but they still believe in Jesus. I have heard this kind of response many times.

Here is the saddest part of all: When they mention Jesus, there is no light in their eyes. There is no joy in their tone. There is no excitement at meeting someone else who adores Christ above all else. The reason for this lack of response is, typically, because many people say they love him, but have never actually met him. They may have prayed a prayer or walked an aisle, but they've never truly met the Savior. The truth, in the end, does nothing for them. It does not create worship; it ends up creating hostility, for Christ's rightful claim to rulership of all things can only frustrate our human pride and self-sufficiency. So it is for those who hear the gospel—and perhaps even respond to it in some outward way—but never repent and trust Christ.

How different it is when we meet other born-again believers. How their eyes light up when we mention the wonders of Jesus to them. They do not operate by what Jonathan Edwards calls "hearsay," some lesson they heard in the past that failed to grip them. They see Christ directly. He has redeemed their lives from the pit at great price. They have seen his mercy at work in their lives. More than any technical breakdown, writes Edwards, "one glance of the eye doth more than all the most particular descriptions that can be given." We are those who know, and see, the indescribable one.

One thing have I asked of the LORD, that will I seek after: that I may dwell in the house of the LORD all the days of my life, to gaze upon the beauty of the LORD and to inquire in his temple. PSALM 27:4

November 14

Religion sweetens temporal delights and pleasures. . . . And as we have already said, the temporal delights of the Christian are much sweeter than the earthly pleasures of the wicked, because they are taken with moderation; so also because they are taken in their own season and, in other respects, right manner. Every[thing] is most beautiful and most pleasant in its season. Snow is not beautiful in summer, or rain in harvest. Ecclesiastes 3:11, "He hath made everything beautiful in his time."

SERMONS AND DISCOURSES, 1723-1729

No ONE IS IMMUNE to the deadly thought: *If I could just have what I want, then I would be unendingly satisfied.* But here is the strange fact: Some people *do* get what they want. They reach the point in life where they can indulge their appetites and desires seemingly without ceasing. Yet these same people often live lives of quiet misery. They think that earthly pleasures will free them; in actuality, they trap them.

In the estimation of Jonathan Edwards, Christians should be no strangers to pleasure. But we also treat "temporal delights" differently than unbelievers. The major difference stems from nothing other than "moderation," which involves forgoing fullness of satisfaction in order to enjoy pleasure all the more.

Many people face the temptation of immoderation. This is a common phenomenon in prosperous societies like ours. In contrast to most people in most eras of history, we have too much food—or to put it more precisely, we *eat* too much, and now suffer from a host of ailments and diseases related to overconsumption. The church would do well to recover the practice of moderation. Neither the glutton nor the miser will live the pleasant life God intends for us to have. The wise pleasure-seeker will take all things in "right manner," and everything "in its season."

> There is an evil that I have seen under the sun, and it lies heavy on mankind: a man to whom God gives wealth, possessions, and honor, so that he lacks nothing of all that he desires, yet God does not give him power to enjoy them, but a stranger enjoys them. This is vanity; it is a grievous evil. ECCLESIASTES 6:1-2

November 15

'Tis impossible that anyone should see anything that appears to him excellent and not behold it with pleasure, and it's impossible to be affected with the mercy and love of God, and his willingness to be merciful to us and love us, and not be affected with pleasure at the thoughts of [it]; but this is the very affection that begets true repentance. How much soever of a paradox it may seem, it is true that repentance is a sweet sorrow, so that the more of this sorrow, the more pleasure. Especially do great delights ensue and follow it.

SERMONS AND DISCOURSE, 1723-1729

THERE ARE TWO WORDS that can clear away hostility, remove a root of bitterness, and renew broken relationships: *I'm sorry*. We can add two more: *Forgive me*. Of all the contributions to the good of humanity, Christianity has made few more important than the apology. Owning our wrongdoing and making it plain is not something we teach little kids simply to minimize playground spats and lunchroom intrigues. Confession and repentance are at the core of strong character and a thriving faith.

In a world without God, there would be no reason to apologize. When the strong dominate the weak—not as a moral duty, but as a law of nature—there is no motivation for the strong to apologize. They can (and, one could argue, *should*) wreak havoc, claw their way to the top of the heap, and do whatever is necessary to stay there. If we are merely highly evolved animals, I suppose we could *choose* to apologize, but we need not do so based on any moral imperative. But if God exists, and we need his forgiveness, and part of why we need his forgiveness is because of how we damage and defeat one another, then we have every reason to apologize. We *must* apologize.

Saying, "I'm sorry, please forgive me," will do more than thousands of hours of explanations, reasons, and play-by-play breakdowns. As Jonathan Edwards submits, "repentance is a sweet sorrow"—and the "more of this sorrow, the more pleasure." Despite what our stubborn hearts may say, "great delights" come when we repent of our wrongs. It is a paradox, this joy-through-sorrow. But it is more than this; it is a door to healing, to wholeness, and to love.

Do you presume on the riches of his kindness and forbearance and patience, not knowing that God's kindness is meant to lead you to repentance? ROMANS 2:4

November 16

'Tis a great pleasure for an intelligent and rational being to be excellent. . . . The believer may rejoice, and does rejoice, to see the image of God upon their souls, to see the likeness of his dear Jesus. The saints in heaven, who have all remainders of pride taken away, do yet rejoice to see themselves made excellent by God and appearing beautiful with holiness. And if it be a great pleasure to see excellent things, it must be a sweet consideration to think that God of his grace has made me excellent and lovely.

SERMONS AND DISCOURSES, 1723-1729

WE SOMETIMES HEAR maxims like this in evangelical circles: "I'm a beautiful mess, and God loves me just like that." We understand the sentiment and cheerfully affirm that our Father helps those who cannot help themselves. This is a key part of the heart of the Christian faith. But this one teaching will not suffice to capture the full sweep of God's intention for his beloved. God not only loves the unlovely; he makes the unlovely lovely.

Let us take care that our doctrine of salvation includes the doctrine of sanctification. Growing in holiness is not only the duty of the believer; it is our privilege. We are looking ahead to a future time when, as Jonathan Edwards writes, we will fully "be excellent," thus "appearing beautiful with holiness." God is going to complete what he has started. How richly encouraging this is for faltering creatures like us.

But we should not underplay the present work of God in our souls. We are even *now* being changed into the "likeness of [our] dear Jesus." We are a butterfly in chrysalis. God is giving us, and all his people, a roaring, rushing desire for conformity to the very character of Christ. Yes, God receives us just as we are. But there is a second miracle like unto it: Christ makes us just as he is. This process does not end until our ultimate glorification, but neither does it stall out following our conversion. We may be a "beautiful mess," as some say. But God loves the business of cleaning us up, and he will not lay aside the task until he is finished.

He who was seated on the throne said, "Behold, I am making all things new." Also he said, "Write this down, for these words are trustworthy and true." REVELATION 21:5

November 17

The pleasures of doing well are very sweet to the godly. We must take heed that we do not confound the pleasure of the proud man, who is lifted up because he thinks he of his own ability does better than others, and of the Christian, who rejoices in the grace of God that enables him to obey him and do good works. 'Tis essential to a Christian that it be his delight and pleasure to obey God and do well. The wicked loves to act basely, but the Christian loves to act rationally and excellently. 'Tis their delight to imitate God and live [like] Jesus, and act like a rational creature.

SERMONS AND DISCOURSES, 1723-1729

NOBODY SINS by accident. In other words, there is no class of virtuous humanity out there who steps into evil like one mistakenly splashes into a puddle. We may not be aware of all the iniquitous deeds we do—we surely are not—but at our sinful core "the wicked loves to act basely," as Jonathan Edwards judges the matter.

When we love evil, we love that which does not love us back. Evil does us no good; it offers us no aid; it secures for us nothing happy. Evil may speak soothingly to us, lulling us to sleep, so that we drift off, thinking we are safe. But when we awake, we see that our house has been plundered, and we've been robbed of all we have. The wicked love to act basely, but they are traveling down a spiral and they don't know it.

What a contrast we have in the transforming grace of God. He not only *compels* us to do what we should, and what will beget lasting peace, but he also gives us redeemed affections. We "delight to imitate God" and to "obey God and do well." Evil will never, in any way, shape, or form truly help and comfort us. But as we discover through the gift of God's love, God loves us back. We end up at his feet, miserable and dejected, desperate for his kindness, worn out by our quest for depravity. In throwing ourselves on him, we wake up and see that the shelter to which we have come is a palace, and we have been elevated to the court of the king.

If you love me, you will keep my commandments. JOHN 14:15

November 18

The godly man takes unspeakable delight in thinking that God, the governor of the world and the most excellent Being, loves him and is his friend. What delight do men take sometimes in the love of their fellow creatures, that they think ['em excellent]. And can we be so foolish as to think that there is any comparison between this and the delight that the godly take in thinking that God is their friend, yea, that he loves them with a very great love, has given himself to them, and the like?
SERMONS AND DISCOURSES, 1723-1729

I'VE HEARD A GOOD NUMBER of messages calling students to the mission field. I am grateful for this, and I know that the Lord uses oratory to send workers to unreached peoples. But I do sometimes compare the excitement of the call to the on-the-ground experience of the missionary (or church planter, or church revitalizer). If we're not careful, our anticipation can outpace our commitment.

It is good to draw up plans, raise support, and speak with passion about what you see the Lord calling you to do. But then you go—you leave your familiar comforts. You leave family and friends. You sacrifice a great deal—in practice, not merely in theory. You land on "the field," as it is called, and you may labor for months, years, possibly even decades before seeing anyone come to faith in Jesus. The rousing message that once inspired you now seems distant; the dream, the noble glory of the call, seems to have faded.

In these kinds of settings, we must return to first principles, namely this: God is our "friend," as Jonathan Edwards notes. He, "the most excellent Being," has taken notice of us, his lowly creatures. He rejoices in us "with a very great love," and not a distant love, as with a far-off relative, but a self-giving, presently felt love. We must reconcile ourselves to hardship in this life: Depending on what God calls us to do, we may not see an explosive response to the gospel, such as in the book of Acts. We may walk the path of Jeremiah. We may have precious few friends at our sides as we follow the Lord. If we have God, though, we have the only friend we need.

> I will make you to this people a fortified wall of bronze; they will fight against you, but they shall not prevail over you, for I am with you to save you and deliver you, declares the LORD. JEREMIAH 15:20

November 19

If we should do what in us lies to live peaceably with all men, we must forgive one another. If anything is done wherein we think another to blame, we ought to forgive and bury [it] in oblivion, and not to suffer all love to be broken on the account and hatred to prevail, if something is done whereby we are wronged and injured; and not only to forgive upon their manifestation of repentance and upon their acknowledgment, but although they should continue obstinate, and should finally persist in what they had done, we ought so far to forgive, or nevertheless to retain a hearty good will and readiness to do any kindness from the heart, so as to be neighborly towards him and peaceable with him.

SERMONS AND DISCOURSES, 1723-1729

IT IS HARD NOT TO hold on to anger. It has a way of persisting, of sticking close, of hanging around. As Christians, we know that forgiveness, once granted, has no "fine print" that allows us to stay mad. We know the truth, but sometimes we still want to hold on to our anger. But when we forgive, we must hold nothing back. We must forgive in full.

It isn't that we turn a blind eye to what has happened. In many cases, it is impossible to completely forget what has happened. But Christians are called to a higher standard and never more so than when we are called to forgive and keep on forgiving. The father in the parable of the Prodigal Son models this heart attitude (Luke 15:11-32). The younger son has indulged his lusts repeatedly, bringing much shame to his eminent father. But when the son returns home in a cloud of misery, his father doesn't seize on the opportunity to shame him to exact the price of his injured pride. He throws a banquet for the repentant prodigal.

Jonathan Edwards has it right: As far as we have been wronged, "we ought so far to forgive" when repentance comes. Christians do not offer partial reconciliation to others, for Christ has not offered partial reconciliation to us. We have the chance to show the world the unique power of divine forgiveness when we are wronged, and to make things fully right with our would-be enemies. When we resolve matters, it isn't with a qualification. Because of the magnitude of God's grace, we are freed from clinging to hurt or lingering in pain. As far as we are wronged, when reconciliation emerges, we ought so far to forgive.

Put on then, as God's chosen ones, holy and beloved, compassionate hearts, kindness, humility, meekness, and patience, bearing with one another and, if one has a complaint against another, forgiving each other; as the Lord has forgiven you, so you also must forgive.

COLOSSIANS 3:12-13

November 20

Let the mouths of God's people be filled with his praises for saving them from sin. Sinners have great reason to bless God for his restraining them from sin, that he has not suffered them to be much worse than they be: for God don't owe them his restraining grace. But God's people have much more reason to bless his name, that he has not only given them restraining, but sanctifying, grace. . . . Wherefore praise the Lord whilst you have any being, and declare the wondrous things that God hath done for you.
SERMONS AND DISCOURSES, 1723-1729

SEVERAL YEARS AGO, I was playing a video game with a friend. As the game loaded, the game-maker's logo came up, and a little voice said "Question everything!" That rebellious little message accomplished its purpose. As you can tell, it got into my brain and never left. But as I thought about this subversive slogan, I soon realized that if I were called to "question everything," I should question this little admonition as well. I should question the skeptics; I should doubt the doubters.

We should not question God. We should seek to understand truth. Further, we should praise him for giving us grace of all kinds. One type that we don't think about much is what Jonathan Edwards calls "restraining grace." This form of benevolent action on God's part means "he has not suffered them to be much worse than they be." Instead of allowing us to indulge the fullness of our human depravity, God has in all sorts of cases, visible and invisible, stopped our evil designs. Praise God for his restraining grace.

Grace is so great that it calls for all our attention. We love sanctifying grace, for it means we grow in godliness. But we mustn't lose sight of restraining grace. In a world that beckons us toward wickedness, that wants us to pull things apart at the seams, and that urges us not to trust authority but to hate it, God wades in. He stops so much of the evil we could perform. Instead of questioning God and his Word, we should praise him at all times and in all seasons.

When Samuel saw Saul, the LORD told him, "Here is the man of whom I spoke to you! He it is who shall restrain my people."
I SAMUEL 9:17

November 21

God oftentimes makes use of men's own experience to convince that they are helpless in themselves. When they first set out in seeking salvation, it may be they thought it an easy thing to be converted. They thought they should presently bring themselves to repent of their sins and believe in Christ, and accordingly they strove in their own strength with hopes of success; but they were disappointed. And so God suffers 'em to go on striving to open their own eyes and mend their own hearts, but they find no success. . . . They can see nothing at all; it is all Egyptian darkness for all. They have been striving to make themselves better, but they are as hard as ever. . . . So God suffers 'em to strive in their own strength till they give out, till they come to despair of helping themselves. The prodigal son, he first strove to fill his belly with the husks which the swine did eat, but when he despaired of being helped that way, then he came to himself and entertained thoughts of returning to his father's house (Luke 15:16–17).
SERMONS AND DISCOURSES, 1730-1733

THERE IS ALMOST NO WORD we detest more than this one: *helpless*. We want to be anything but helpless. It makes sense to protect ourselves, after all. So we troubleshoot every area of life—the car has the emergency blanket, the house has fire insurance, the kids have their bike helmets on. If we're not careful, though, we can mistake basic physical readiness for spiritual fitness—a common mistake of our faltering hearts. Because things are generally in order around us, we think that our souls must be secure as well. But apart from Jesus, all our efforts at self-preservation are nothing more than dust in the wind.

As fallen human beings, we don't need little bits of life betterment; we need radical deliverance from our sin. In the words of Jonathan Edwards, as we "go on striving to open [our] own eyes and mend [our] own hearts, . . . [we] can see nothing at all; it is all Egyptian darkness." Spiritually, our hearts are twisted and turned away from God. We strive to improve ourselves, to sand down our faults and play up our virtues, but our strength inevitably fails.

As Christians, we are freed by grace to know and come to terms with our circumstances. We know that we have no sufficiency in ourselves for life and godliness. We need Jesus, and we need him to the uttermost. Our response, then, is not to try to make ourselves *seem* sufficient, but to live in Christ's empowering grace, pointing others to the strength he gives. Ultimately, all remedies will fail, except one: *Jesus*.

He was longing to be fed with the pods that the pigs ate, and no one gave him anything. But when he came to himself, he said, "How many of my father's hired servants have more than enough bread, but I perish here with hunger!" LUKE 15:16-17

November 22

Psalms 144:5. "Bow thy heavens, O Lord, and come down." This was never so remarkably fulfilled as in the incarnation of Jesus Christ, when heaven and earth were as it were brought together. Heaven itself was as it were made to bow that it might be united to the earth. God did as it were come down and bring heaven with him. He not only came down to the earth, but he brought heaven down with him to men and for men. It was a more strange and wonderful thing. But this will be more remarkably fulfilled still by Christ's second coming, when he will indeed bring all heaven down with him, viz. all the inhabitants of heaven.
THE "BLANK BIBLE"

DO YOU WANT TO LEARN about heaven? There are many books that purport to share an insider's version of the afterlife, telling us what it feels like to go to heaven and what we can expect in eternity. These visions allegedly assure us that heaven is real. *It's not imaginary! I went there. Trust me.*

I'm always happy to hear that people are interested in heaven. The afterlife is something we all should think about far more often than we probably do. But with respect to our celestial tourist authors, we know someone who not only *went* to heaven, but who "brought heaven down with him" as Jonathan Edwards observes. In the life and ministry of Jesus Christ, eternity broke into this world. Christ's miracles testify to his divinity, but they do not serve merely as testimony They also show that everyone who follows Jesus enters a different world. We not only swear allegiance to the true King, but we enter his spiritual Kingdom, where the world is made right and the glory of God shines undimmed.

We await the full dawning of God's Kingdom on this earth. Soon, the Lord will remake this place, and it will become the new Jerusalem. The glory of God will cover the earth. There yet remains the fulfillment of the promise of new heavens and a new earth (Isaiah 65:17). We're not there yet; but the Word of God opens our eyes to see that we need not wait around for heaven to show up. Do we want proof that heaven is real? Let us look to Christ. He went there. Let us trust the Word.

He who descended is the one who also ascended far above all the heavens, that he might fill all things. EPHESIANS 4:10

November 23

Resolved, never to allow the least measure of any fretting uneasiness at my father or mother. Resolved to suffer no effects of it, so much as in the least alteration of speech, or motion of my eye: and to be especially careful of it, with respect to any of our family.
LETTERS AND PERSONAL WRITINGS

THE OBEDIENCE OF CHILDREN sometimes seems like a lost cause today. I was at the neighborhood pool with my kids when I heard a mother say to her three-year-old: "Honey, come get your sandwich." The child did not budge. Then the mom switched tactics: "Sweetie, Mommy really wants you to eat it. Please come." The young boy remained immovable. So Mommy tried again: "Honey, we need to leave soon! Come eat." I don't need to tell you how "Honey" responded (or didn't).

Obedience is no small matter. Too often, however, parents don't require it, even in evangelical circles. We talk a lot about loving our kids today, and about showing affection to our offspring more than previous generations did; and yet one could argue that we actually do not love our kids as we should. Training them to obey authority not only prepares them for adulthood, it also prepares them to do well as Christians. God is our ultimate Father, and obedience to him is not optional.

Even when Jonathan Edwards was nearly twenty years old, he resolved to honor his parents. He did not mean this in an end-of-the-day kind of way; he was not attempting to follow them only in the broad strokes of their counsel. He wanted to convey a surpassingly sweet spirit, to not produce "the least alteration of speech" when asked to help them. He saw no disconnect between the status of his heart and the cast of his eye; he had evidently learned that rolling his eyes would undermine any verbal commitment to obedience. In a child-centered age, we must take care that we do not set up our children for failure. Children need to obey their parents; children need to learn to obey God.

Children, obey your parents in everything, for this pleases the Lord.
COLOSSIANS 3:20

November 24

[T]here must be these following things in order to a right trust in God. . . . There must [be]
a lively sense of our need of him, and the insufficiency of all other confidences. If we see not
our great and perishing need of help and relief, we shall never come to God for relief, because
we shall think we can do without him; and except we see that nothing else is sufficient to
afford us help but God alone, we neglect to come to God, and seek something else [in which]
to put our confidence. Such is man's natural enmity against God, that he had rather trust in
anything in the world, than God.

SERMONS AND DISCOURSES, 1720-1723

WE HAVE ALL MADE splendid discoveries in an attic or basement. Perhaps it was finding a precious family heirloom in a steamer trunk. Or maybe you found some blackmail-worthy photographs of your father or mother in their color-clashing, wild-haired younger days. Every once in a while, someone will find a priceless possession in a forgotten location. I once heard about the discovery of a world-renowned Picasso painting, worth millions of dollars, that turned up in the course of spring cleaning. (There you have it—do your spring cleaning!)

There is nothing we could ever find, though, that exceeds the value of our trust in God. This is the one discovery on this planet most needful for us. Yet as we look around, so few of our neighbors seem to esteem God. Their lack of interest in the divine bleeds over into their lives. They think that possessions, or family, a coveted job title, or a bunch of traveling, will give them what they most want. Some people would rather "trust in anything in the world," Jonathan Edwards summarizes, than trust in God. The one thing we need most is the one thing we often refuse.

The true Christian is one whose sense of dependency on God is alive and awake. Whether in dramatic circumstances or the quiet moments of life, we find that "all other confidences" fail. Nothing apart from God will meet our "great and perishing need of help and relief," Edwards avows. Unbelievers would rather trust in anything but God; believers would rather trust in God than anything. Our faith is not merely an insurance policy for eternity. If we are truly in Christ, we will daily trust God, daily cling to him, daily feel our "lively sense" of his total sufficiency and our insufficiency. Nothing is better than to have only God, to have made the discovery that exceeds all others.

Some trust in chariots and some in horses, but we trust in the name of the LORD our God. PSALM 20:7

November 25

[T]here must be these following things in order to a right trust in God. . . . There must be a firm belief of his all-sufficiency. After we have seen our need and necessity, that we are poor, wretched, blind, and naked, and stand in great need of help, the next thing is to see where the help is to be had: we must see who is able to help us, before we shall come to him for help. After we have seen our own insufficiency, and the insufficiency of everything else but God; after we have seen that there is nothing else to take hold of, but we must take hold on God or perish, then we must see God's all-sufficiency, and that there is enough in him for us. We must believe his almighty power, that he is able to do everything for us that we need to have done.
SERMONS AND DISCOURSES, 1720-1723

SOME WILL EXPERIENCE physically what is true for all of us spiritually: We have only one hope of rescue. Not long ago, the news showed people being pulled from flood waters in various storm-soaked areas of America. In most cases, those who were being helped did not have many options from which to choose. They didn't select their deliverer ahead of time or negotiate the terms of their rescue. They gratefully, tearfully reached out to strong arms that pulled them from the floodwaters and away from almost certain death.

In a spiritual sense, the same is true for every Christian. God does not partner with other people or organizations to bring salvation to completion. He does all the saving himself, and he unveils himself to the repentant as their only sufficient Savior. Many others may offer their assistance, to be sure. We hear from spiritualists that we need to get in touch with the universe. We hear from community-changers that we must do all the good we can. We hear from different religious groups that we must perform certain rituals to be made right. Only Christianity begins in the radical "all-sufficiency" of an almighty God, as Jonathan Edwards terms it.

Without Christ, we are all abandoned on a rooftop in a flood and without a boat. Spiritually, "there is nothing else to take hold of," and in truth, no one even looking for us. The hour grows late, and night falls. The waters rise, with no help in sight, and no means to summon it. Then, suddenly, out of the darkness our Rescuer comes. He is mighty to save us (Isaiah 63:1). Day by day, trial by trial, he is all we need.

Let not the flood sweep over me, or the deep swallow me up, or
the pit close its mouth over me. PSALM 69:15

November 26

[T]here must be these following things in order to a right trust in God. . . . There must be a firm belief of God's merciful nature, and that he is willing to help us and do for us: a trusting in God is a trusting in his mercy and goodness. Many are kept from trusting in God, because they think they have committed so much sin that there is not mercy in God enough for them. He therefore must be sensible, that there is mercy enough, as well as power enough, [to] save the most vile returning sinner.

SERMONS AND DISCOURSES, 1720-1723

THERE IS PERHAPS no stranger thought than this: I cannot confess my sin to God because I would be ashamed. The thinking behind such a notion is off-target in the extreme. God already sees everything we do, knows everything we think, hears everything we say. There is nothing we can hide from him. We can try to shield our wickedness from others, but we cannot keep God from seeing every bit of our shamefulness.

What wondrous words, then, are these: No one has "committed so much sin that there is not mercy in God enough for them." Jonathan Edwards dealt with many pastoral cases in his long career. He saw and heard of horrible misdeeds. But he never met a sinner who could hide from God, or whose sin exceeded God's forgiving reach. There is no such fallen being. Every last one of us lies bare before the eyes of God. Yet though the Lord sees all vileness, he waits to hear confession. He waits, poised and ready to forgive.

This matters not only for non-Christians, but for converts to Christ, as well. We must never think there is a category called "secret sin." There are sins that we *think* are secret, but they are not. God sees them all. Still, in Scripture, he never encourages people to wait to come to him until they have things worked out and tidied up. The one and only way we gain cleansing and healing and standing with God is to release ourselves from the delusion of secrecy and embrace the freeing mercy of Jesus. God's goodness never runs out, never runs dry. If there is repentance, "there is mercy enough" for us.

The LORD passed before him and proclaimed, "The LORD, the LORD,
a God merciful and gracious, slow to anger, and abounding in steadfast
love and faithfulness. EXODUS 34:6

November 27

[T]here must be these following things in order to a right trust in God. . . . A firm belief of God's truth and faithfulness to his promises: there is no trusting in God without a firm belief of the Word of God, and the revelation he has made concerning himself, especially his gracious promises. As men will not trust men, except they think them faithful to their trusts, so they will never trust God till he sees His faithfulness. It is a contradiction to suppose that a man can quietly and sweetly commit himself, soul and body, forever into His hands, when he at the same time questions whether He will be true to his trust.
SERMONS AND DISCOURSES, 1720-1723

FANDOM IN MODERN times approaches unbelievable levels. I remember when I was in seminary that a few friends drove through the night to watch a game, and then drove back in the early morning. And one of them had to preach the next day. We've all heard a pastor speak who didn't get enough sleep; he mixes up his words, and generally isn't as sharp as he would like. I can only imagine what a fourteen-hour day in the car would do for a sermon!

Many folks have no difficulty understanding commitment to a team, a program, or a university. But for some mysterious reason, they face great and grave obstacles in committing to God, and the people of God. These challenges, in fact, seem insurmountable, even as these same people profess to know the living God. When we see an all-encompassing willingness to follow one's hobby, but a desultory spirit regarding biblical religion, we are witnessing a lack of the kind of commitment that following Christ entails.

We do not go halfway with the Lord. We either trust God and follow him as our sovereign Savior, or we do not. A half-in, half-out attitude places us in eternal jeopardy. Only those who have a "right trust in God," a total commitment of heart, soul, body, and spirit will escape hell and enter heaven. As Jonathan Edwards suggests, the one who "questions whether" God will prove true lacks settled confidence in the divine. God never encourages us as believers to go back on our trust, and to slacken our faith. He seeks to fan our faith into a flame. This is what true Christianity means: a whole-soul seeking after God. We are not perfect, not by a long shot; but we are *committed*, born again to a living hope.

Not everyone who says to me, "Lord, Lord," will enter the kingdom of heaven, but the one who does the will of my Father who is in heaven.
MATTHEW 7:21

November 28

[T]here must be these following things in order to a right trust in God. . . . A love to God: there is no such thing as trusting in God, as long as we are enemies to him and hate him; it is not possible we should come to God, and sweetly repose our souls upon him, as long as we have an aversion and antipathy to him, as we all naturally [do]. As soon as we come into this world, and look behind us upon him that has just made us, we fly from him as we would from a mortal enemy, and instead of trusting in him continue to run with all our might from him, till he discovers his excellency and loveliness to us, and powerfully changes us and causes us to love him: then we shall venture quietly to rely upon him, and rest in him.

SERMONS AND DISCOURSES, 1720-1723

WE SEE THE SAD HEADLINES every day—stories of divorce and familial breakdown. "How could this happen?" we sigh to ourselves. But all who are married know how it can happen. One of the main ways that couples break apart is by failing to stay together. I don't mean they stop living at the same address, but they fail to actively love each other. They take their covenant for granted and are surprised when it withers away over time.

True Christians, as Jonathan Edwards points out, seek every day "to rely upon" God, and "rest in him." We may say we love Jesus, but we *show* our love for Jesus by making him the one from whom we seek comfort and support. It would be strange to say that we love someone with whom we spend very little time, never consult, and never turn to in times of trouble. So it is with God. If we say we love him, then others should be able to *observe* the expression of this deep-seated affection in our daily practice.

Let us never leave our first love. Let us cling to him. We have no reason to avoid God, and every reason to run to him and throw ourselves at his feet. He has opened our eyes to his "excellency and loveliness." Love for many today is an emotion they may have felt in childhood, before the bloom came off the rose. But not so for Christians. Love is our resident state of being, for God's love never leaves us as orphans, and we who are loved never cease to return his covenantal affection. We rely upon it; we rest in it.

We have come to know and to believe the love that God has for us. God is love, and whoever abides in love abides in God, and God abides in him. I JOHN 4:16

November 29

[T]here must be these following things in order to a right trust in God. . . . A hope in him, that he will bestow his mercy on us: neither can we be said to trust in God, except we hope that he will bestow upon us what we trust in him for. How can we trust in God for that we don't believe, nor hope that he will ever bestow upon us what we trust in him for? Therefore, when once we are come to this hope, arising from this belief of, and love to God, there remains nothing but to [trust in him].

SERMONS AND DISCOURSES, 1720-1723

As CHRISTIANS, we are not gambling eternity on Jesus Christ, hoping against hope that things will turn out in the end. Though all around us, people approach death with uncertainty, convinced that no one can know for sure how things will end up, that is not the perspective or the spirit of biblical Christianity.

We think, for example, of the apostle John's words on the significance of faith: "I write these things to you who believe in the name of the Son of God, that you may *know* that you have eternal life" (1 John 5:13, italics added). What a priceless verse this is. Here John connects belief and knowledge, but not mere informational know-how; rather, knowledge that is tested by fire and solid as titanium. If you believe in Jesus, you may *know* that you will live with God for eternity.

So we see how closely connected *knowing* is to *hoping*. We are not on a celestial hot-air balloon ride, aspiring somehow to find the grand resting place in the skies. Because we have placed our faith in Jesus Christ, we now have a settled confidence—hope born of knowledge—that "he will bestow upon us what we trust in him for," as Jonathan Edwards sums it up. We hope, not from a vague desire for things to turn out well, but because we *know* the living God. He has made himself known to us. Now we trust him, confident to the fullest degree that he will do what he has promised.

See what kind of love the Father has given to us, that we should be called children of God; and so we are.   1 JOHN 3:1

November 30

[T]here must be these following things in order to a right trust in God. . . . A rest and satisfaction in the soul, arising from such a belief of, love to, and hope in God. The sight of his great necessity and danger makes him restless and uneasy: when he sees danger all around him, and destruction every minute ready to take hold of him, and sees nothing that he can trust to, he must needs be very restless and in a very uneasy state. But, when he sees a God that can save him, and stands ready, and is very willing to do it, and besides that has given his word and oath that he will do it, if he will depend upon Him; when he sees that God is excellent and lovely, and worthy to be trusted and depended on: he then hopes in God, and places his dependence there, and so no more fears those evils that he was in danger of before. There follows a rest, satisfaction, and repose in the soul, relying upon God; this rest in God, and satisfaction from believing in him, loving of him, and hoping in him, is that trust that we speak of.

SERMONS AND DISCOURSES, 1720-1723

EVERY CHRISTIAN should have an unshakable faith. I don't mean that we can remove all trouble from our lives, for we surely cannot. God sends us trials by which to grow our dependence on him (James 1). Our faith is only hell proof because of God. He takes us from what Jonathan Edwards calls "a very uneasy state," when nothing is certain except the promise of judgment, and he gives "repose in the soul" through the Holy Spirit.

The faith that God grants to believers is as strong as the ocean tide. No one can turn it back. No one can quell true faith. No one can squelch it or stamp it out. We think of martyrs from Christian history and see such strength of conviction in them. In the second century, a slave girl named Blandina suffered torment upon torment when she was stretched on a rack and set upon by ferocious animals. Yet she did not relinquish her faith in the face of physical trauma. Even as she suffered horrible torture, she encouraged her fellow Christians to remain strong in the Lord.

When we read of narratives like Blandina's, we cannot help but wonder if we have opened our heart to God as fully as we should. Do we weaken ourselves? Do we believe that the faith God gives is smaller than it truly is? Today, we can return to the core reality of our divinely granted trust in God. As Christians, we have unshakable faith and invincible hope because God has granted us these things. Whether we are called to the most ordinary existence or a martyr's early death, our God is strong—strong for us, and strong in us.

Faith is the assurance of things hoped for, the conviction of things not seen. For by it the people of old received their commendation.

HEBREWS 11:1-2

December

✝

December 1

JONATHAN EDWARDS DID NOT shy away from airing his views, or engaging those who disagreed with him. Over the course of his many years of ministry, he worked on a lengthy response to the Arminian theology that influenced many in his day. While he was on the missionary frontier in Stockbridge, he published *A Careful and Strict Inquiry into the Modern Prevailing Notions of that Freedom of Will, Which Is Supposed to Be Essential to Moral Agency, Virtue, and Vice, Reward and Punishment, Praise and Blame.* (That title would probably not fly with a publisher today.)

Freedom of the Will is a dense and complex book. The text is indeed careful and strict, making the argument that a world without a sovereign God determining the future, and thus the actions of moral agents, collapses into absurdity:

> If that first act of the will, which determines and fixes the subsequent
> acts, be not free, none of the following acts, which are determined by it,
> can be free. If we suppose there are five acts in the train, the fifth and last
> determined by the fourth, and the fourth by the third, the third by the
> second, and the second by the first; if the first is not determined by the
> will, and so not free, then none of them are truly determined by the will:
> that is, that each of them are as they are, and not otherwise, is not first
> owing to the will, but to the determination of the first in the series, which
> is not dependent on the will, and is that which the will has no hand in the
> determination of. And this being that which decides what the rest shall be,
> and determines their existence; therefore the first determination of their
> existence is not from the will.[60]

Edwards sought to reconcile God's sovereignty and human responsibility—a view that has come to be known as "compatibilism." Freedom, as Edwards defines it, does not mean "doing whatever you want," but essentially "acting according to one's nature." Though some have argued that Edwards teaches what philosophers call *determinism*, it would be more accurate to describe his teaching as a doctrine of *moral necessity*—that is, we have the natural ability to obey God, but the moral inability to do so. This idea neatly sums up Edwards's overall argument about why sinners do not come to Christ outside of a work of God. We *could* come to God, but we don't want to, for in Adam we have fallen. We are free, in other words, to follow our nature, but our nature does not incline toward God.

Freedom of the Will deserves a closer reading. It is a deep and difficult text, but its careful distinctions and biblical grounding have helped many believers work their way through difficult questions about our freedom and God's sovereignty.

December 2

I used to pray five times a day in secret, and to spend much time in religious talk with other boys; and used to meet with them to pray together. I experienced I know not what kind of delight in religion. My mind was much engaged in it, and had much self-righteous pleasure; and it was my delight to abound in religious duties. I, with some of my schoolmates joined together, and built a booth in a swamp, in a very secret and retired place, for a place of prayer. And besides, I had particular secret places of my own in the woods, where I used to retire by myself; and used to be from time to time much affected. My affections seemed to be lively and easily moved, and I seemed to be in my element, when engaged in religious duties.

LETTERS AND PERSONAL WRITINGS

OUR IMAGE OF CHILDREN today is often skewed. We say they need maximum play time, and we should entertain them at church. If we want to engage children, we need to use gross-out humor and extreme silliness, or else their tiny little attention spans will wander and we will lose them for the Kingdom.

Children are fun and sometimes silly. But we should not underestimate them—especially the children of our churches. They have deep spiritual capacities waiting to be unlocked. We see this in the spiritual experience of Jonathan Edwards. Even before his conversion, he took the things of God very seriously. He essentially "played" church and pantomimed religion. He learned under devout parents who trained him to know the Bible, and to live rightly. His father and mother—Timothy and Esther Edwards—raised him as a spiritual being first and foremost. It wasn't until later that young Jonathan finally came to Christ. But his father and mother had already laid a very strong theological and practical foundation for him.

This development was not one-sided. Young Jonathan took pleasure in learning and in trying to emulate his godly parents. His example encourages us to approach our children with great spiritual earnestness and seriousness. We want them to gain a taste for divine wisdom while they live in our homes. We want them to see that following Jesus is better than anything else. Even those who are not parents have a great opportunity to come alongside families and show children that Christianity is not merely a matter of household priority, but also a personal and corporate joy. Childhood is not a wasted time before life really kicks in; childhood is when we should learn to revere and love God.

> Be careful to obey all these words that I command you, that it may go well with you and with your children after you forever, when you do what is good and right in the sight of the LORD your God.
>
> DEUTERONOMY 12:28

December 3

From my childhood up, my mind had been wont to be full of objections against the doctrine of God's sovereignty, in choosing whom he would to eternal life, and rejecting whom he pleased; leaving them eternally to perish, and be everlastingly tormented in hell. It used to appear like a horrible doctrine to me. But I remember the time very well, when I seemed to be convinced, and fully satisfied, as to this sovereignty of God, and his justice in thus eternally disposing of men, according to his sovereign pleasure. But never could give an account, how, or by what means, I was thus convinced; not in the least imagining, in the time of it, nor a long time after, that there was any extraordinary influence of God's Spirit in it: but only that now I saw further, and my reason apprehended the justice and reasonableness of it.

LETTERS AND PERSONAL WRITINGS

BEFORE JONATHAN EDWARDS launched into ministry, he entertained persistent doubts about the character of God—doubts that centered on the Lord's election of some to eternal life and others to eternal damnation (Romans 9). Though he grew up under a father who preached this doctrine and trained him to trust it, Edwards had a quiet insubordinate streak, and God's sovereignty in salvation seemed "a horrible doctrine" to him.

This is a striking part of Edwards's past. The man associated in history with preaching the sovereign will of God once struggled to affirm it at all. His example shows us that many believers grapple with the fullest dimensions of God's ownership and rulership of all things. There may be no tougher biblical matter to reckon with than the reality of divine choosing. Why does God choose some, and not others? How is this just? Frail and finite creatures like us may hit turbulence when we encounter this concept. Surely, there has been a great and sprawling conversation over the centuries on this matter; more than a few theologians and pastors have backed away from it and have emphasized other elements of the biblical witness instead.

But Edwards's doubts did not persist forever. As he studied the Word, there came a time when he understood the "justice and reasonableness" of the divine will. What was formerly a horrid principle became a comforting one. We all come to a fork in the theological road: either God is completely in charge of all things, or he is not. Though it may seem scary to trust a God who is so big that he fixes eternal destinies, we must in the end ask, "How could a being who is truly God not control all things?" Either God is limited in his power or he is not; either God is perfect in all his ways, including election and reprobation, or he is not. These are hard questions we all face. But if we will submit ourselves to the Word, God will help us greatly to trust him and rest in his all-wise providence.

> [Election] depends not on human will or exertion, but on God, who has mercy. For the Scripture says to Pharaoh, "For this very purpose I have raised you up, that I might show my power in you, and that my name might be proclaimed in all the earth." So then he has mercy on whomever he wills, and he hardens whomever he wills.
>
> ROMANS 9:16-18

December 4

And there has been a wonderful alteration in my mind, with respect to the doctrine of God's sovereignty, from that day to this; so that I scarce ever have found so much as the rising of an objection against God's sovereignty, in the most absolute sense, in showing mercy on whom he will show mercy, and hardening and eternally damning whom he will. . . . I have oftentimes since that first conviction, had quite another kind of sense of God's sovereignty, than I had then. I have often since, not only had a conviction, but a delightful conviction. The doctrine of God's sovereignty has very often appeared, an exceeding pleasant, bright and sweet doctrine to me: and absolute sovereignty is what I love to ascribe to God. But my first conviction was not with this.

LETTERS AND PERSONAL WRITINGS

THE ALL-ENCOMPASSING sovereignty of God can seem overwhelming. Even when we've long trusted God for our eternal deliverance, we may find ourselves at the outer limits of our comprehension when confronted with the problem of evil and the nature of human freedom. *Yes, God is all-good and all-wise,* we might think, *but how do we understand human agency in relationship to his almighty power?*

Jonathan Edwards was certainly no stranger to such complex matters. For years, he bucked against the teaching of his father, and hardened himself against the "absolute sovereignty" of God. But over time, as he studied God's Word, he gained trust in the divine. For the rest of his days, he not only assented to God's total oversight of all things, but found it "an exceeding pleasant, bright and sweet doctrine."

Scripture gives us a great example of such learning in the example of Job. Job did not take a graduate-level class in philosophy to understand the will of God, or to embrace the rulership of God. He went through deep waters, and cried out to God in the midst of great pain. The closing chapters of the book of Job offer some of the Lord's strongest statements about his sovereignty (Job 38-41). Taken along with what the apostle Paul writes in the book of Romans, the essential idea is this: God is God. He owns all the rights. He does all things well. He deserves our absolute trust. We will not rest by questioning God or by running from him; we will rest when we cease doubting God and walk with him. As simple as this lesson might seem, it can take a lifetime to learn.

"I will make all my goodness pass before you and will proclaim before you my name 'The LORD.' And I will be gracious to whom I will be gracious, and will show mercy on whom I will show mercy."
EXODUS 33:19

December 5

And found, from time to time, an inward sweetness, that used, as it were, to carry me away in my contemplations; in what I know not how to express otherwise, than by a calm, sweet abstraction of soul from all the concerns of this world; and a kind of vision, or fixed ideas and imaginations, of being alone in the mountains, or some solitary wilderness, far from all mankind, sweetly conversing with Christ, and wrapt and swallowed up in God. The sense I had of divine things, would often of a sudden as it were, kindle up a sweet burning in my heart; an ardor of my soul, that I know not how to express.

LETTERS AND PERSONAL WRITINGS

MANY CHRISTIANS TODAY seem to fall into one of two camps: Either we experience a regular stream of spiritual ecstasies, or we never do. One side is in danger of making faith into a constant parade of the spectacular; the other is in danger of draining faith of its supernatural power. In truth, the normal Christian life is rather ordinary, yet filled with everyday glory.

This was true for Jonathan Edwards. Most of his time was taken up with the regular work of the ministry and the common rhythms of family life. As a man entranced by God, he did not float above the ground; he laughed with his children at dinner, talked with his wife about a troubling matter in the church, and did the grunt work that any believer in any vocation must do. But Edwards also had certain times when the "sweetness" of holy love washed over him. Many years later, C. S. Lewis gave voice to his own version of these experiences, which he called "pure Northernness."[61] These were numinous encounters—deep experiences with the wonder of the divine.

For his part, Edwards felt such closeness with God when alone. He loved to walk and ride his horse in the wilderness. When by himself, he would pray, sing songs to God, and meditate on spiritual truths. Edwards never suggests that there is a way to activate a special sense of closeness with God. But his example commends solitary, set-apart seeking after God. Life is busy for us, as it was for Edwards, the pastor, husband, and father of eleven. We may feel as if we do not have space for such closeness with God. But we do. In the ordinary pursuit of the Lord, we may rest assured there is everyday glory. There is the presence of God with us. He never leaves us. He never forsakes us.

My soul longs, yes, faints for the courts of the LORD; my heart and flesh sing for joy to the living God. PSALM 84:2

December 6

My sense of divine things seemed gradually to increase. . . . My longings after God and holiness, were much increased. Pure and humble, holy and heavenly Christianity, appeared exceeding amiable to me. I felt in me a burning desire to be in everything a complete Christian; and conformed to the blessed image of Christ: and that I might live in all things, according to the pure, sweet and blessed rules of the gospel. I had an eager thirsting after progress in these things. My longings after it, put me upon pursuing and pressing after them. It was my continual strife day and night, and constant inquiry, how I should be more holy, and live more holily, and more becoming a child of God, and disciple of Christ.

LETTERS AND PERSONAL WRITINGS

NOT LONG AGO, I came across the true story of two twins who were separated at birth and adopted by different families. Both boys were named James by their adoptive parents. Both became police officers. Both married women named Linda. The names of each man's son: James Alan and James Allan. Both had a dog named Toy. Both divorced their wives and remarried women named Betty.

Just as we cannot make this stuff up, we also cannot accidentally go to heaven. None of us will die and a moment later find ourselves in the realm of glory, stunned by the strangeness of our eternal destiny. To see God, we must strive after him. Jonathan Edwards was a passionate man, but it was not until his twenties that he set his face like a flint to "live more holily." He wrote seventy resolutions for himself, kept a diary of his spiritual progress, and devoted himself to pursue God.

We may not write any resolutions, and we may not keep a spiritual diary. But every believer can seek the Lord. Every Christian can advance in holiness. No one is irretrievably stuck. No one is unable to "be more holy." Further, no true child of God will grow in godliness by accident. We must thirst after God. We must pray for more of him. We want to be like Jacob, and not let God go until he blesses us; we want to be like the importunate widow, and keep going to the judge for aid (Luke 18:1-8). God will not delay long. He will bless his people, he will meet our needs through his Spirit, and he help us to be more holy. This is no coincidence; this is the promise of God spoken over his church.

> In a certain city there was a judge who neither feared God nor respected man. And there was a widow in that city who kept coming to him and saying, "Give me justice against my adversary." For a while he refused, but afterward he said to himself, "Though I neither fear God nor respect man, yet because this widow keeps bothering me, I will give her justice, so that she will not beat me down by her continual coming." LUKE 18:2-5

December 7

She had an excellent way of governing her children: she knew how to make them regard and obey her cheerfully without loud, angry words, or heavy blows. . . . And when she had occasion to reprove and rebuke, she would do it in few words, without heat and noise, with all calmness and gentleness of mind. And in her directions or reproofs, in any matters of importance, she would address herself to the reason of her children, that they might not only know her inclination and will, but at the same time, be convinced of the reasonableness of it. She need speak but once; she was cheerfully obeyed; murmuring and answering again was not known among them.
SAMUEL HOPKINS, "A Short Sketch of Mrs. Edwards's Life and Character"

THE BEAUTY OF A MOTHER'S LOVE for her children is wondrous to behold. Recently, I read the story of a mother in Texas who gave her own life to save the life of her child. Trapped by severe flooding, the woman had had to abandon her car. Soon, the waters rose so high that she and her child were floating along as the woman tried desperately to keep the child's head above water. Rescuers arrived on the scene just as the mother's strength gave out. She drowned, but saved the life of her three-year-old child.

This moving story reminds us of the world-defying nature of motherly love. Few instincts are stronger in this world than the love of a mom for her kids. By all accounts, Sarah Edwards—wife of Jonathan Edwards—was an excellent mother. She had eleven children and a very busy husband, but Sarah exhibited a gracious spirit and "had an excellent way of governing her children," according to Samuel Hopkins, one of Edwards's students. Jonathan and Sarah taught their children to obey their authority, and did not tolerate "murmuring and answering again."

Many young women grow up today without much guidance about mothering. We live in a permissive age, and so many parents neglect to care for their children—to love them—by wisely leading and disciplining them. Sarah Edwards provides a model of such investment. Her first priority was loving the Lord, then supporting her husband, and then training her children in the ways of godliness. She served faithfully, often thanklessly, and left to her family and to history a strong example of godly femininity. Motherhood owes not to the invention of any one society or group; motherhood was created by God to display his glory through the care and nurture of children. May the Lord raise up many like Sarah Edwards in our day; women who do not fear the world, women for whom service to God is not drudgery, but delight.

Hear, my son, your father's instruction, and forsake not your mother's teaching, for they are a graceful garland for your head and pendants for your neck. PROVERBS 1:8-9

December 8

Every Christian family ought to be as it were a little church, consecrated to Christ, and wholly influenced and governed by his rules. And family education and order are some of the chief of the means of grace. If these fail, all other means are like to prove ineffectual. If these are duly maintained, all the means of grace will be like to prosper and be successful. . . . And let children obey their parents, and yield to their instructions, and submit to their orders, as they would inherit a blessing and not a curse. For we have reason to think from many things in the Word of God, that nothing has a greater tendency to bring a curse on persons, in this world, and on all their temporal concerns, than an undutiful, unsubmissive, disorderly behavior in children towards their parents.
SERMONS AND DISCOURSES, 1743-1758

THE CHRISTIAN FAMILY IS, as Jonathan Edwards says, a "little church," a place where God is exalted and Christian doctrine and character are formed. The head of a family is the husband and father; he is effectively the pastor of the home, responsible for leading his loved ones to know and worship the Lord. To the father, and also to the mother, the children owe obedience; they must "yield to their instructions" and not live unsubmissive to their parents.

Every child will submit to something or to someone. Our fallen culture urges our children to follow and obey its wayward morals. The doctrine of anti-obedience taught at every turn by a secular order is in truth far more authoritarian than any Christian practice. We follow a God who is authoritative in full, to be sure, but who is loving, compassionate, and fatherly. The god of this world, who seeks the allegiance of every sinner, is unloving, hateful, and an absentee father. He entices sinners to follow him, promising them acceptance, but then destroys them. He offers no heaven, only hell.

If we do not train our children, we may know that the world will. All around us are pedagogues and leaders and intellectual influencers who would undo the Christian training and teaching we give to our kids. We cannot save our progeny on our own. Only God can snatch them from the hand of the evil one. But we can do a great deal to exalt God in our home, and to lovingly rear our children to understand that "his rules" prosper us and Satan's ways weaken us. We want our children to learn wisdom from the earliest years, to obey authority from their youngest days, to see that holiness is a gift and disobedience a curse. All this formation begins in the home, the place where God is exalted.

Fathers, do not provoke your children to anger, but bring them up in
the discipline and instruction of the Lord. EPHESIANS 6:4

December 9

Let me now . . . repeat and earnestly press the counsel, which I have often urged on heads of families here, while I was their pastor, to great painfulness, in teaching, warning and directing their children; bringing them up in the nurture and admonition of the Lord; beginning early, where there is yet opportunity; and maintaining a constant diligence in labors of this kind: remembering that, as you would not have all your instructions and counsels ineffectual, there must be government as well as instructions, which must be maintained with an even hand, and steady resolution; as a guard to the religion and morals of the family, and the support of its good order. Take heed that it ben't with any of you as it was with Eli of old, who reproved his children, but restrained them not; and that by this means you do not bring the like curse on your families, as he did on his.

SERMONS AND DISCOURSES, 1743-1758

"YOU HAVE YOUR HANDS FULL, DON'T YOU?" I can't tell you how many times I've heard these words as a young father. People see me taking my three children to dinner when my wife is visiting family and think that I deserve pity. I appreciate their concern, but I'm not suffering. I'm living the good life! Children are not a curse. They are a blessing from God, and I rejoice at the little ones God has given my wife and me.

Fatherhood is hard work and always has been. Like Jonathan Edwards, pastors have always had to rally fathers to their tasks, and reproach them for their failures. Every father must acknowledge his sins and weaknesses. But praise God, the Lord does not leave us in the depths. He lifts us up. He calls us to be "heads of families" in Edwards's language, meaning we occupy an impossibly noble position. We are the authority in our homes. We are responsible for the spiritual and physical well-being of our wives and children. We must maintain "constant diligence" in leading, providing for, and protecting our loved ones.

Such a high calling depends on "an even hand, and steady resolution." We must invest in our marriages, for it was Adam, not Eve, who was called to "hold fast" to his wife (Genesis 2:24). We must invest in our children, spend time with them, and restrain them from evil. Acting in compassionate firmness, we cannot spare the rod when it comes to discipline for wrongdoing; the father who does not punish wrong "hates" his offspring, according to Proverbs 13:24. Most of all, we are free to delight in our children, to love them without limit, to enjoy them without guilt. As fathers, our hands may be full, but they are full of blessing.

> These words that I command you today shall be on your heart. You shall teach them diligently to your children, and shall talk of them when you sit in your house, and when you walk by the way, and when you lie down, and when you rise. DEUTERONOMY 6:6-7

December 10

December 1748: Jonathan Edwards completes An Account of the Life of the Late Reverend Mr. David Brainerd

DAVID BRAINERD was an unusual man who had shown an unusual devotion to the mission of God. When Brainerd sought a time of recuperation at the home of Jonathan Edwards, the two men found common ground in their intense spirituality and unstinting devotion to the Lord. After Brainerd died in October 1747, Edwards decided to publish Brainerd's diary.

Edwards was not the first to do so, however; portions of the diary had already gone to print. But Edwards putting his valuable imprimatur on a document meant that it had the potential to go farther and wider than a normal book. After some fairly significant editing on Edwards's part, the book debuted in 1749. *An Account of the Life of the Late Reverend Mr. David Brainerd* found an audience right from the start. It directly contributed to the missionary calling of figures such as John Wesley, William Carey (who took the Bible and Brainerd's diary with him to India, and called the latter his "second Bible"), and Adoniram Judson. All the way into the twentieth century, leaders such as Jim Elliot and John Piper cited Brainerd as a significant influence on their lives. The book has never gone out of print, which is a remarkable achievement.

Edwards took pains to show that his subject was not perfect. Like anyone, he had real weaknesses, including a strong temper and a disposition to excessive work. The pastor nonetheless commended the diary to readers because

> notwithstanding all these imperfections, I am persuaded, every pious
> and judicious reader will acknowledge that what is here set before him
> is indeed a remarkable instance of true and eminent Christian piety in
> heart and practice; tending greatly to confirm the reality of vital religion
> and the power of godliness, most worthy of imitation, and many ways
> tending to the spiritual benefit of the careful observer.[62]

The life of David Brainerd is a powerful reminder to all Christians that our lives need not end in accolades, worldly renown, or even spiritual "success" to count. Sometimes, God will take even humble faithfulness to him and amplify it many, many times over. So it was with David Brainerd, and so it may be with us, should the Lord allow.

December 11

Doubtless there was some influence that natural temper had in the religious exercises and experiences of Mr. Brainerd, as there most apparently was in the exercise of devout David, and the apostles Peter, John, and Paul: There was undoubtedly very often some influence of his natural disposition to dejection in his religious mourning, some mixture of melancholy with truly godly sorrow and real Christian humility, and some mixture of the natural fire of youth with his holy zeal for God, and some influence of natural principles mixed with grace in various other respects, as it ever was and ever will be with the saints while on this side heaven.
THE LIFE OF DAVID BRAINERD

BY SOME COUNTS, out of every ten missionaries leaving home to go preach the gospel to unreached peoples, just one or two are men. This is a tragedy. Men and women can and should serve the Lord as missionaries across the world. We have no quota for either sex. But men today seem especially susceptible to being drawn off the field to pursue lesser things: sports, video games, controversies, an easy and unchallenging existence.

Jonathan Edwards had his faults, but he was determined to make his life count for God. So too was his younger friend David Brainerd, a man who gave up many things in order to preach the gospel to Indian tribes in the Northeast. Brainerd drove himself so relentlessly to preach the gospel that his body gave out and he died at a young age. Though Edwards and other counselors urged Brainerd to pace himself, the young man had "the natural fire of youth" and a "holy zeal for God," as Edwards put it in commending the missionary's now-famous diary. As restless as Brainerd was for the glory of God to spread over the earth, nothing could dampen his spirit.

In a comfortable age, we need to give young men a doxological vision for their lives. We want them to be less like their bleary-eyed peers who refuse to grow up, and more like the men of old who exuded holy fire for God. If the church is to be strong, we need young men to step into eldership positions (1 Timothy 2). If our missions enterprise is to thrive and not languish, we need men to lead in this calling, like Paul, the original missionary and church planter. We do not need fewer godly men with righteous ambition and holy energy; we need more, many more, to emulate Brainerd and Edwards and William Carey and Adoniram Judson and C. T. Studd and Eric Liddell, men who lost their lives in order to gain them.

When I was a child, I spoke like a child, I thought like a child, I reasoned like a child. When I became a man, I gave up childish ways.

I CORINTHIANS 13:11

December 12

Lord's Day, May 13. Rose early: Felt very poorly after my long journey, and after being wet and fatigued. Was very melancholy; have scarce ever seen such a gloomy morning in my life; there appeared to be no Sabbath; the children were all at play; I a stranger in the wilderness, and knew not where to go; and all circumstances seemed to conspire to render my affairs dark and discouraging. . . . Yet he was pleased to support my sinking soul, amidst all my sorrows; so that I never entertained any thought of quitting my business among the poor Indians; but was comforted to think that death would ere long set me free from these distresses. . . . Went and preached, first to the Irish and then to the Indians: And in the evening, was a little comforted; my soul seemed to rest on God and take courage. Oh, that the Lord would be my support and comforter in an evil world!

THE LIFE OF DAVID BRAINERD

DAVID BRAINERD, the famous missionary to native tribes in the Northeast, knew great joys and sorrows in his work. He was an emotionally turbulent man, and could veer back and forth between extremes. Despite his frailty, Brainerd persevered in his calling as a missionary. For long stretches of time, he saw little fruit from his work. Over the course of several years, however, he watched as God saved numerous men and women through Brainerd's preaching of the gospel.

His diary, edited by Jonathan Edwards, gives us a long look at the missionary's on-the-ground experience. He lived among a pagan people who had no natural inclination to follow Christ. He preached, and preached some more, but his words often fell on stony ground. He lived in hardship, often sleeping in freezing conditions, with little to warm and nourish him. With these difficult circumstances, it is little wonder that he took comfort in the thought "that death would ere long set me free from these distresses." Brainerd might not be the first candidate we would choose to write the modern-day missionary e-mail update. That much is certain.

Most believers are not called to Brainerd's work. But all believers are called to take up their cross and follow Christ, the first missionary. There is only one Christ, and there is one baptism in his name. We all must shoulder the splintered wood of the Cross. We all must deny ourselves. We all must walk after Jesus in holiness and fullness of commitment. We need more Christians of this kind, just as we need more missionaries like David Brainerd, figures who courageously live out the costly implications of the way of Christ.

The Son of Man is going to come with his angels in the glory of his
Father, and then he will repay each person according to what he has done.
MATTHEW 16:27

December 13

And in prayer I was exceedingly enlarged, and my soul was as much drawn out as ever I remember it to have been in my life, or near. I was in such anguish, and pleaded with so much earnestness and importunity, that when I rose from my knees I felt extremely weak and overcome; I could scarcely walk straight, my joints were loosed, the sweat ran down my face and body, and nature seemed as if it would dissolve. So far as I could judge, I was wholly free from selfish ends in my fervent supplications for the poor Indians. I knew they were met together to worship devils, and not God; and this made me cry earnestly, that God would now appear and help me in my attempts to break up this idolatrous meeting.

THE LIFE OF DAVID BRAINERD

WE ALL KNOW CHILDREN who find it very hard to give up their early dependence on milk. You can scarcely blame them; God ordered it that they would receive their core nourishment from milk, and it is the only diet they knew for a good long while. But some children love to nurse long past their earliest days.

It's not hard for Christians to prefer milk—spiritual milk—as well. But the Bible urges us onward: we are to hunger after "solid food" (Hebrews 5:12-14). We should want truth. We should crave sound doctrine. As we mature and grow, God gives us more biblical desires. Instead of focusing solely on ourselves, we desire to bless others. We want their salvation; we yearn for their spiritual good.

In missionary David Brainerd's praying ministry, detailed in his well-known diary, we see what a deep concern for the unsaved looks like. Brainerd never did anything dispassionately, but his love for the lost was nothing less than fierce. He was "in such anguish" for them, and prayed so hard that he "felt extremely weak and overcome" afterward. He lived near Native American tribes and could hear them gathering "to worship devils," and hated that this was so. Brainerd's efforts appear unusual, but in truth, every believer should pray earnestly and searchingly for the conversion of the lost. Let us love the truth, the meat of God's good Word. Then, let us be like David Brainerd and a long line of godly intercessors, and "cry earnestly" for friends, family members, and people all over the world to come to Christ.

Brothers, my heart's desire and prayer to God for them is that they may be saved. ROMANS 10:1

December 14

The beams of this spiritual Sun don't only refresh but restore the souls of believers. Thus it is said that the Sun of righteousness [shall arise] with healing [in his wings]. These beams heal the souls of believers. As we often see that when the trees or plants of the earth are wounded, the beams of the sun will heal the wound and by degrees restore the plant, so the sweet beams of the Sun of righteousness heal the wounds of believers' souls. When they have been wounded by sin and have labored under the pain of wounds of conscience, the rays of this Sun heal the wounds of conscience. When they have been wounded by temptation and made to fall to their hurt, those benign beams, when they come to shine on the wounded soul, restore and heal the hurt that has been received.

SERMONS AND DISCOURSES, 1739-1742

JONATHAN EDWARDS KNEW of what he spoke. During the 1740s, he suffered "wounds" to his soul while pastoring in Northampton, where he tried to bring about changes in the church such that only true believers in Christ could join the congregation and take Communion. But things went badly for him. Members of his own extended family publicly opposed him, slandering his motives and stirring up dissension among the people, leading to Edwards's eventual dismissal in 1750.

Even before this awful conclusion, Edwards had "been wounded by sin" and felt "the pain of wounds of conscience." He tasted the bitter fruit of this world, and he knew he needed regular refreshment. The modern answer to this need is typically physical; if we're struggling, we need some "me time," perhaps on a beach somewhere. Going to the beach is great, but Edwards knew he needed stronger medicine. He needed spiritual healing.

The care that every believer receives from God is not distant, but is given by God himself. The Lord does not give his people a feelings boost; he ministers his own presence to them, reminding them of his truth, his compassion, his restoring grace. We will all face hurts we do not deserve. Friends we thought were steadfast will leave us. Family members will grow embittered against us. We may lose a position unjustly. But even in the worst circumstances, the fact that we have divine help lifts us above the seas, and keeps us from sinking into the depths.

O LORD, you have brought up my soul from Sheol; you restored me to life from among those who go down to the pit. PSALM 30:3

December 15

The sick soul by these beams is restored, as plants that have grown in shady and cold places appear sickly and languishing, if the shade be removed and the sunbeams come to shine down upon them, will revive and flourish; or as the clear shining of the sun after the rain. The beams of this Sun heal of the mortal poison of the fiery serpent, as the children of Israel were healed by looking on the brazen serpent in the wilderness. . . . The soul of a convert is raised from the dead by the shining of the beams of this Sun, as we see the rays of the sun in the spring revives the grass and herbs as it were from the dead and causes a resurrection of them from the dust, making 'em to spring out of the ground with new life.
SERMONS AND DISCOURSES, 1739-1742

NO ONE CAN ARGUE WITH HEALING. When we witness it, it stops us cold. I recently saw a video of deaf people who received aural technology that allowed them to hear for the first time. Initially, as the technicians tested the device, I felt dispirited as nothing registered on the faces of the individuals. But then, in a flash, they could hear. A little baby suddenly looked up at his mother, as he heard the sound of her voice. It is impossible to capture in words the power of such moments.

God is in the miracle-performing business. He loves to raise the souls of converts "from the dead" as Jonathan Edwards says; he rejoices to see his children "revive and flourish." The whole drift of Christianity is upward; God wants to elevate us, to lift us up, to cleanse and restore us. We sometimes hear that the lost cannot have faith in Christ unless they see a miracle. But every born-again believer testifies to the supernatural character of Christianity. We break down; we fall apart; we languish. God builds up; God restores; God revives.

We need to bring this principle into every aspect of our lives. Perhaps our first love has grown cold. We have prayed to God for years to help us in some way, but he has not answered our prayer as we desire. Maybe we are beginning to drift from him; maybe trust is weakening. The daily grind of life may be wearing us down in a way that almost no one can see, but we know is happening. Whatever situation we face, God is a reviving God. He loves to heal and restore. Let us listen to his voice, and go to his Word to hear him speak afresh.

He answered them, "Go and tell John what you have seen and heard:
the blind receive their sight, the lame walk, lepers are cleansed, and
the deaf hear, the dead are raised up, the poor have good news preached
to them. LUKE 7:22

December 16

It seems to be a thing in itself fit and desirable, that the glorious perfections of God should be known, and the operations and expressions of them seen by other beings besides himself. If it be fit that God's power and wisdom, etc., should be exercised and expressed in some effects, and not lie eternally dormant, then it seems proper that these exercises should appear, and not be totally hidden and unknown. . . . As God's perfections are things in themselves excellent, so the expression of them in their proper acts and fruits is excellent, and the knowledge of these excellent perfections, and of these glorious expressions of them, is an excellent thing, the existence of which is in itself valuable and desirable. 'Tis a thing infinitely good in itself that God's glory should be known by a glorious society of created beings.

ETHICAL WRITINGS

IT IS SAD that churches sometimes feel as if they must justify their existence by pointing to their programs, achievements, and numbers. It isn't wrong to be active as a congregation and to seek the upbuilding of the body through various means. But churches should communicate, in every way they can, that simply by meeting to worship the living God each week, they are doing something intrinsically valuable. Worship is an activity that needs no justification or enhancement.

Our inherently glorious God has always desired that a righteous people would worship him. His glory should not "lie eternally dormant" as Jonathan Edwards suggests. His "glorious perfections" should be made known to all. The highest good in the cosmos comes when we delight in God's intrinsic, undeniable excellence—when we "consent" to it, admire it, and even revel in it. This is why God's people gather each Sunday: We are the "glorious society of created beings" who see and treasure the greatness of our King.

Christianity is not a spectator sporting event, with only a handful of gifted souls selected for service while the rest of us watch from the grandstands. We are a "kingdom of priests," all with a role to play in "proclaim[ing] the excellencies of him who called [us] out of darkness into his marvelous light" (1 Peter 2:9). Anywhere we savor God, and seek to honor him by our corporate witness, he is honored. Our churches need not seek to impress the watching world. We need only dedicate ourselves to the awesome task given to us by God: to celebrate him, enjoy his grace, and know his glory. Such worship is not only good; it is *infinitely* good.

> You shall eat in plenty and be satisfied, and praise the name of the LORD your God, who has dealt wondrously with you. And my people shall never again be put to shame. JOEL 2:26

December 17

If such a preservation of the church of God, from the beginning of the world hitherto, attended with such circumstances, is not sufficient to show a divine hand in favor of it, what can be devised that would be sufficient? But if this be from the divine hand, then God owns the church, and owns her religion, and owns that revelation and those scriptures on which she is built; and so it will follow, that their religion is the true religion, or God's religion, and the scriptures, which they make their rule, are his word.

A HISTORY OF THE WORK OF REDEMPTION

"THE GRASS WITHERS, the flower fades, but the word of our God will stand forever" (Isaiah 40:8). So too will the people of God stand forever. As long as the gospel is preached, God will not fail to have followers in his name. Throughout human history, the church has prevailed despite fearsome odds. From a human perspective, there have been high times and low times, but God has never abandoned his cause. His Kingdom is not without its King.

In an unfinished book titled *A History of the Work of Redemption*, Jonathan Edwards traces God's work in human history. He shows that God has carried out the "preservation of the church" from the very beginning, and he will prosecute this great aim all the way until the end. We think of the many difficulties the people of God have faced. Waves of persecution in the church's first three centuries, leading to many martyrs. The raising up of Augustine in North Africa out of a pagan background. A medieval period that saw the gospel light dimmed but never extinguished. A remnant of the true church existing through the Lollards, the ministry of Jan Hus, Jansenism, and the writings of William Tyndale. The Protestant Reformation filling the world with light as Luther, Calvin, Zwingli, and the early Baptists preached the gospel of grace and recovered the primacy of the all-sufficient Word of God.

Yes, God has been faithful in every season to preserve his true people. The "divine hand" not only authored the Scriptures in speaking through holy men; the divine hand has guided history and strengthened the witness of the church. The divine hand is not aged or arthritic. God is still shepherding the affairs of this world to their rightful conclusion. He will never allow his church to die out. The Word of God stands forever. Even today, in our quiet devotion to God, he is bringing his will to pass, and his plans to completion.

> Go on up to a high mountain, O Zion, herald of good news; lift up
> your voice with strength, O Jerusalem, herald of good news; lift it up,
> fear not; say to the cities of Judah, "Behold your God!" ISAIAH 40:9

December 18

In the midst of these complicated labors . . . [Edwards] found at home one who was in every sense a help mate for him, one who made their common dwelling the abode of order and neatness, of peace and comfort, of harmony and love, to all its inmates, and of kindness and hospitality to the friend, the visitant, and the stranger.

THE WORKS OF PRESIDENT EDWARDS

HOME ISN'T MEANT to be a disaster zone. It is meant to be a haven, a little fore-taste of heaven. Because God has such great intentions for marriage, and for the families created by marriage, we may know with certainty that the enemy targets every Christian marriage and wants every parent to fail in their duties and respon-sibilities. We sometimes treat the family as if it is a plane on autopilot, humming along, when in truth it is a garden that needs continual tending.

Jonathan and Sarah Edwards fought for their marriage. As two sinners liv-ing in close quarters with each other, they encountered many obstacles in life. Sometimes we hear that if we can just find a mate who is "compatible" with us, we will taste the unending bliss of wedded union. But this is not possible in a fallen world. We might share a good number of interests—if so, that is wonderful. But as humans, we are inherently selfish. We find it easier, many times, to fight rather than listen. We don't want to compromise, even on unsubstantial matters. Almost nothing exposes sin more than marriage.

We have to work at marriage. We cannot assume that all will be peace and tranquility. We see in the Edwardses' example that they sought to live out biblical roles in the home: Jonathan acted as the head of his family, the leader, and Sarah served as his "help mate." The Edwardses lived according to the Word of God in their home, honoring the Puritan vision of marriage as a display of the love of Christ and his church (Ephesians 5:22-33; Genesis 2:16-25). But they did not merely believe certain texts; they put them into practice and contended for their marriage. They tried hard to kill sin together and forgive one another. The result was a hard-won place of "kindness and hospitality." The Edwards home was not a warzone. It was a haven, as ours can be.

Enjoy life with the wife whom you love, all the days of your vain life
that he has given you under the sun, because that is your portion in life
and in your toil at which you toil under the sun. ECCLESIASTES 9:9

December 19

THE POPULAR IMAGE OF Jonathan Edwards as an authoritarian minister does not stand up to the facts. In truth, Edwards waited for decades to change the aspect of his Northampton church that most troubled him: the Communion policy. He wished to change it so that no one living in open sin would take the Lord's Supper and therefore drink judgment on themselves (1 Corinthians 11:29).

Along these same lines, Edwards sought in 1748 to tighten up the church's standards of membership. Under Solomon Stoddard's leadership, new members were asked to formally assent to basic orthodoxy, show that they lived a generally moral life, and not be involved in any major scandal. Stoddard believed that if he could get people into the church, he could see them converted, in part through the Lord's Supper.

Edwards had harbored concerns about this policy for years. It was not until 1748, however, that he sought to institute changes. He began by asking for a "credible profession" of conversion, and when a young man sought to join the church, Edwards asked him to draw up a statement giving testimony to his salvation. Initially, the young man agreed, but he later backed away after word got out about the new membership standards.

Later, a young woman sought to join the church, and she assented to the matter of writing up a profession account. The committee that oversaw the church— Edwards wanted a council of elders to help him lead the flock, but instead had a committee—rejected the young woman's application by a vote of fifteen to three.[63] Edwards was in trouble. Nothing seemed to be working for him. Earlier in 1748, he had taken up his pen to try to persuade others of his views, arguing that "it is both evident by the Word of God, and also granted on all hands, that none ought to be admitted as members of the visible church of Christ but visible and professing saints, or visible and professing Christians."[64] But though Edwards's arguments would convince many in later generations, his own flock bristled.

Edwards had run into a buzz saw. The Northampton congregation did not think lightly of his new policy. Many members, after all, would be implicated for a lack of vibrant faith, were Edwards's new standards to take effect. The simple truth is this: Jonathan Edwards presided over a congregation that had grown, in part, from lax membership practices, including not restricting membership to only conversion-professing believers.

As 1748 closed, Edwards's standing at Northampton was in peril. We take a warning from his example: Though God and his love are fixed and steadfast, this world is an unstable place. We should not fear this truth, but neither should we close our eyes to it.

December 20

God is the host; 'tis he that makes the provision and invites the guests. And sinners are the invited guests. Believers are those that accept of the invitation. And Jesus Christ, with his benefits that he purchased by his obedience and death, and which he communicates by his Spirit, is the entertainment. This is the meat and drink. Christ gives himself for the life of the world. He is slain that we may as it were eat his flesh and drink his blood, as the sacrifices of old were slain and then that which was not burnt was eaten. Thus considered, God the Father is the host and Christ is the entertainment. Believers, as they live a life of faith, they do as it were feed upon Christ Jesus; they live upon him; he is their daily bread.

SERMONS AND DISCOURSES, 1723-1729

JESUS CHRIST SAID many things that bothered people; but nothing quite like his self-identification as the "bread" of his people. "I am the living bread that came down from heaven. If anyone eats of this bread, he will live forever. And the bread that I will give for the life of the world is my flesh" (John 6:51). John's Gospel tells us that "many of his disciples turned back and no longer walked with him" (John 6:66) after this surprising and misunderstood statement.

In our time, public relations experts might take Jesus aside and try to smooth out his message. But Jesus' words were well-chosen. He was declaring that he was not around merely to affirm religious rituals and teach some pleasant truths. Rather, he was the exclusive savior of the world; he was the manna in the desert. Only he could give life; only he could sustain that which is truly spiritual. Jonathan Edwards gets at the heart of Christ's meaning: Believers must "feed upon Christ Jesus." Through faith in Christ, we live. He is our "daily bread."

The gift of Christ comes not in harmless little packets delivered to us each day. The gift of Christ is represented in Scripture as a feast, and we are not held back from his sustenance. We gain strength through our Savior in our present circumstances. Yet the Bible also points ahead to an appointed time when all the people of God will gather in the age to come. John foreshadows that day: "The angel said to me, 'Write this: Blessed are those who are invited to the marriage supper of the Lamb.' And he said to me, 'These are the true words of God'" (Revelation 19:9). We live now by the grace of Christ Jesus; we will soon join him at his table as his spotless bride. As we depend on him today, and follow him now, let us not forget what is coming for the people of God.

Come, everyone who thirsts, come to the waters; and he who has no money, come, buy and eat! Come, buy wine and milk without money and without price. ISAIAH 55:1

December 21

Feasts are made upon joyful occasions and for the manifestations of joy. Ecclesiastes 10:19,
"A feast is made for laughter." Christians, in the participation and communion of gospel
benefits, have joy unspeakable and full of glory, a sweeter delight than any this world affords.
We are invited in that forecited place, Isaiah 55:1–2, to come, that our souls may delight
themselves in fatness. When the prodigal son returned, they killed the fatted calf and made a
feast, and sang and danced and made merry; which represents the joy there [is] in a sinner,
and concerning him, when he comes to Christ.
SERMONS AND DISCOURSES, 1723-1729

IT IS A STRANGE THING indeed to have fine taste. A television comedy some years ago featured characters who had a Finer Things Club, and they stood apart from the crowd as they discussed literature, drank tea, and cultivated social graces. It's true that some pursue "finer things" out of snobbery. But one wonders if there is something missing from culture—even evangelical culture—that makes little place for beauty and sophistication.

The Bible understands and promotes pleasure. It doesn't look down its nose at finer things. Through the prophet Isaiah, the Lord asks his people, "Why do you spend your money for that which is not bread, and your labor for that which does not satisfy? Listen diligently to me, and eat what is good, and delight yourselves in rich food" (Isaiah 55:2). The point of this passage is not ultimately physical, but spiritual. The Lord wants his covenant people to know that, in him, they have blessings beyond compare. The promises of false gods will not satisfy. They give crumbs, not bread; we work strenuously to sample their goods, only to find them disgusting.

Not so with Christ. God, the author of pleasure, invites us to a holy banquet table, a place where we have "joy unspeakable," in Jonathan Edwards's exegetical vision. This is not a place to go for a subsistence meal. God has "killed the fatted calf and made a feast," and invited all to come. The wonder of this meal is amplified beyond anything we can experience in this world, because the very provision of the guests is the holy Son of the host. Jesus Christ *is* our feast. He is our joy. He is our laughter. We do not need the world's bread, nor do we need its fancy clubs. We need only this table, this delight, this Christ.

You have put more joy in my heart than they have when their grain and wine abound. PSALM 4:7

December 22

And it also tends to peace, as it fixes the aim of the soul to a certain end; so that the soul is no longer distracted and drawn contrary ways by opposite ends to be sought, and opposite portions to be obtained, and many masters of contrary wills and commands to be served; but the heart is fixed in the choice of one certain, sufficient, and unfailing good: and the soul's aim at this, and hope of it, is like an anchor to it that keeps it steadfast, that it should no more be driven to and fro by every wind.

SERMONS AND DISCOURSES, 1743-1758

ONE OF THE MOST stunning life turnarounds I've heard happened to British philosopher C. E. M. Joad. Joad was a gifted speaker who advocated pacifism in his earlier days; he spoke against Britain's opposition to Hitler early in the 1930s. He became head of the philosophy department at Birkbeck College in London and published more than one hundred well-received books, becoming a trusted voice on the BBC show *The Brains Trust*. Joad had a strong interest in paranormal activity and promoted it even as he lived an on-the-go life, giving speeches, traveling all over England, and enjoying his celebrity.

But then it all came crashing down. Despite his considerable earnings, Joad loved to hop aboard trains without paying. He was caught in 1948, and fined two British pounds. But the national news knocked Joad's star from the sky. The BBC dismissed him, his hopes for further social advancement cratered, and he suffered a severe blow to his health. Once sailing high, Joad now crumpled in a heap. But his strange story had not ended. In despair, he read some works of C. S. Lewis, and decided to return to the Anglican Church of his birth. Just a few years later, in 1953, Joad died and his narrative concluded.

Joad's unusual story fits well with Jonathan Edwards's description of the unconverted soul. Before Christ makes us his own, we are "driven to and fro by every wind"; we are restless, rootless, some folks even turning frenetic. Not having Christ, in sum, can make us half-crazy. Not every unbeliever lives in this way, but a good number do. If we just keep ourselves busy enough, goes the thinking, we'll stave off the darkness. But this is not so. Only Christ can "anchor" the soul, and fix us "to a certain end."

Blessed are those servants whom the master finds awake when he
comes. Truly, I say to you, he will dress himself for service and have
them recline at table, and he will come and serve them.   LUKE 12:37

December 23

[T]he Scripture also speaks of Christian practice as a distinguishing and sure evidence of grace to persons' own consciences. This is very plain in 1 John 2:3: "Hereby we do know that we know him, if we keep his commandments." And the testimony of our consciences, with respect to our good deeds, is spoken of as that which may give us assurance of our own godliness; "My little children, let us not love in word, neither in tongue, but in deed . . . and in truth. And hereby we know that we are of the truth, and shall assure our hearts before him" (1 John 3:18–19).
RELIGIOUS AFFECTIONS, 1746

"How DO I HAVE assurance that I am a Christian?" We can go several directions with such a query. First, our ground of assurance is always and only the finished work of Christ. Like the Israelites who looked on the bronze serpent and lived, we have looked on Christ and been born again. Our trust and hope and righteousness are found in him.

A second major part of assurance is what Jonathan Edwards calls our "Christian practice." James 1:22 is helpful here: "Be doers of the word, and not hearers only, deceiving yourselves." But the clincher comes from James 2:

> Someone will say, "You have faith and I have works." Show me your
> faith apart from your works, and I will show you my faith by my works.
> You believe that God is one; you do well. Even the demons believe—
> and shudder! . . . You see that a person is justified by works and not
> by faith alone. And in the same way was not also Rahab the prostitute
> justified by works when she received the messengers and sent them out
> by another way? For as the body apart from the spirit is dead, so also
> faith apart from works is dead.   JAMES 2:18-19, 24-26

God intends for born-again Christians to minister assurance to themselves by producing works of righteousness. Every single time we follow Scripture, we witness to ourselves by the Spirit's power that we are saved, that we do not live as the world lives, and that Christ has claimed us. Assurance comes from trusting Christ first and foremost. It comes secondarily from obeying him. Doing as God commands not only pleases him, but also helps us live righteous lives.

> Do not present your members to sin as instruments for unrighteousness,
> but present yourselves to God as those who have been brought from
> death to life, and your members to God as instruments for righteousness.
> ROMANS 6:13

December 24

Though you are a great way off from us, yet you are not out of our minds: I am full of concern for you, often think of you, and often pray for you. Though you are at so great a distance from us, and from all your relations, yet this is a comfort to us, that the same God that is here, is also at Onohquaga; and that though you are out of our sight and out of our reach, you are always in God's hands, who is infinitely gracious; and we can go to him, and commit you to his care and mercy. . . . We hope that God will preserve your life and health, and return you to Stockbridge again in safety; but always remember that life is uncertain: you know not how soon you must die, and therefore had need to be always ready.

LETTERS AND PERSONAL WRITINGS

"Though you are out of our sight and out of our reach, you are always in God's hands." So wrote Jonathan Edwards to his daughter Esther in 1753. Just a few years later, Edwards uttered similar words when he left for Princeton. Pained by his departure, going only because he thought the will of God summoned him, he left his home, and then turned and said, "I commit you to God."[65]

His conviction that his family was not his own shines through both statements. Ultimately, Edwards could do nothing to keep Esther from harm, just as he could not ensure his loved ones' safety as he took up residence in Princeton. The truth is, at the time of his letter to Esther, she had less than five years to live, and so did he. He could not carry her into eternity; he could not ferry his wife and children across the river Jordan. Only God could.

So it is for every child of God. No earthly person or institution can ensure our safety. But though this sounds foreboding, we who are in Christ are right where we want to be. Like Esther, we are "always in God's hands." No one can snatch us away. Nothing can happen to derail the will of God for our lives. Life is uncertain, and we don't know how long we have on this earth. But though we could not be any less certain about our earthly future, we cannot be any *more* certain about our heavenly home. We will go there, sooner or later. We will cross the river Jordan, as a host of other saints have done before us. We stand now on the stormy banks of the river, but we see the other side. We are not drifting. We are not in danger. We are always in God's hands.

> My sheep hear my voice, and I know them, and they follow me. I give
> them eternal life, and they will never perish, and no one will snatch
> them out of my hand. My Father, who has given them to me, is greater
> than all, and no one is able to snatch them out of the Father's hand.
> JOHN 10:27-29

December 25

Jonathan Edwards's last words: "Trust in God, and you need not fear."

JONATHAN EDWARDS'S FINAL pronouncement comes with some irony for those who read "Sinners in the Hands of an Angry God" in high school under the oversight of a disapproving teacher. Isn't Edwards the wig-wearing theologian who told everyone how awful they were, and how much trouble they're in?

In truth, Edwards was a theologian of comfort just as he was a theologian of warning. He labored to craft sermons that would lift his people out of the slough of despond. He tried valiantly to awaken joyful affections for God in the members of his congregation. The work he prayed for and strategized over and wrote much about was not a project of damnation, but of salvation, of revival, of awakened sinners. Edwards was not a judge, after all; he was a preacher. He preached every chance he got, everywhere he could, to everyone who would listen (and could stay awake).

Edwards's final words capture the mission of his life and the heartbeat of his theology. He yearned for fellow image-bearers not to trust in themselves, but to look to Jesus for their rescue. Only the blood of Christ can atone for our sin; only faith in the atoning sacrifice can pardon the guilty. Faith, Edwards knew, was the enemy of fear. Christians who humbly repent of their sin and place their faith in Christ have nothing at all to fear. Edwards gave us this assurance with his dying breath. His words, now found only on a printed page or a computer screen, summon us to live like he lived, and die like he died.

If we trust in God, we need not fear.

Trust in the LORD with all your heart, and do not lean on your own understanding. PROVERBS 3:5

December 26

Resolved, when I feel pain, to think of the pains of martyrdom, and of hell.
LETTERS AND PERSONAL WRITINGS

THERE ARE MANY FASCINATING aspects of evangelical culture. One of them is the "unspoken" prayer request, usually shared during public prayer meetings or other such set-aside time. When a person shares an unspoken request, the room grows quiet. Everyone immediately does two things at once: They try not to puzzle out what the request actually is, even as they puzzle out what the request might be.

A prayer meeting—and corporate prayer in general—is a glorious enterprise. Yet if we are not attentive to biblical priorities, our intercessory focus can turn inward. We have all been in gatherings where a dozen requests came to the surface and about half were for physical ailments. We don't mock such requests—in fact, we *should* pray for God to heal our fragile bodies. But we don't want to lose sight of the bigger picture. Jonathan Edwards knew this temptation as we all do, and committed himself to "think of the pains of martyrdom" when injured. He did not want to disappear into his own troubles; he wanted a wider perspective on pain.

Pain can drive us into a darkened tunnel. But we should not let it. When we feel pain, we should pray for relief and share this request with others. But we also need to remember that brothers and sisters around the globe suffer far more than we do. We are not, most of us, paying a great cost for our faith. Some in other parts of the world are paying the ultimate price. They are imprisoned, persecuted, and pursued unto death for confessing Christ. Our pain is not insignificant. We do not pretend it doesn't exist. But there is greater suffering than our own. Keeping this in mind helps us to keep others in view and to pray for the flourishing of all the saints, whether their requests are spoken or not.

In this you rejoice, though now for a little while, if necessary, you have been grieved by various trials. I PETER 1:6

December 27

FEW MATTERS IN Jonathan Edwards's life and ministry proved more controversial than the revival he helped to lead. His main opponent was Charles Chauncy, pastor of Old South Church in Boston and a titanic figure in New England Protestant circles. Chauncy led the charge of the so-called Old Lights and carried on a multi-year debate with Edwards about the legitimacy of what we now call the First Great Awakening.

After the publication of Edwards's *Distinguishing Marks*, which followed his *Faithful Narrative of a Surprising Work of God* (1737), Chauncy took to arms. He published *Seasonable Thoughts on the State of Religion in New England* in the fall of 1743. Chauncy's basic proposition was this: "The plain truth is an *enlightened mind*, and not *raised affections*, ought always to be the guide of those who call themselves men; and this, in the affairs of religion, as well as other things."[66]

Edwards disagreed strongly with Chauncy's proposition. The affections were not by nature beastly; they could be directed toward beastly things, but God created the inmost appetites and desires of humanity for the direct experience of his love and delight. Edwards worked for several years to respond to Chauncy's hammer blow, and finally explained his doctrine in his *Treatise on Religious Affections* (1746):

> True religion, in great part, consists in holy affections.
> We see that the Apostle, in observing and remarking the operations and exercises of religion, in the Christians he wrote to, wherein their religion appeared to be true and of the right kind, when it had its greatest trial of what sort it was, being tried by persecution as gold is tried in the fire, and when their religion not only proved true, but was most pure, and cleansed from its dross and mixtures of that which was not true, and when religion appeared in them most in its genuine excellency and native beauty, and was found to praise, and honor, and glory; he singles out the religious affections of love and joy, that were then in exercise in them: these are the exercises of religion he takes notice of, wherein their religion did thus appear true and pure, and in its proper glory.[67]

The treatise is packed with argument and deserves a full reading on its own merits. It established Edwards as the figure in Christian history who most linked the heart to the mind. The differences between Edwards and Chauncy still exist today; evangelicals are regularly mocked for their passion by mainstream media. But God has given his church too much joy for his people to fret over their branding.

True religion does consist, in great part, in holy affections.

December 28

IN THE COURSE OF DEFENDING the place of religious affections in the life of the believer, Jonathan Edwards took pains to distinguish true signs of a genuinely divine work from neutral ones. He listed twelve, six of which we will cover today, and all of which help us think through the fiber and character of true Christian faith.

Here in summary form, with brief explanations, are the first six of the twelve signs that do not prove (or disprove) that affections are gracious, with brief explanations.

1. **Powerful—very great—affections are no proof that they are gracious.** (In other words, we may feel the power of genuine spirituality but not know the Lord.)
2. **That the affections have great effects on the body is no proof that they are gracious.** (The body can be affected without a true work occurring.)
3. **Talking much of the things of religion—being fluent and fervent—is no guarantee that they are gracious.** (Talking about spiritual things is no sure sign that God has moved in a sinful heart.)
4. **We have the capacity to excite affections by our own contrivance.** (This realm is not only influenced by God, but by Satan and his demons, who have power over unbelievers; so we should not assume any religious inclination is automatically from God.)
5. **That the affections come with texts of Scripture cannot forswear that they are holy.** (Edwards's point is that even the devil can know, and quote, Scripture.)
6. **That there is an appearance of love in the affections does not mean they are necessarily from God.** (It may well be the case that we *seem* to love God, and give outward evidence of the same, but do not.)[68]

These careful comments give us clarity as we take stock of our own faith. It is no sure sign of saving faith to have emotion toward God. Our faith is not grounded in our feelings, or in any part of *us*. Our faith is grounded only in Christ. Knowing Christ produces great joy and opens up our hearts to the full range of emotions. But we must always remember: It is not our faith that saves us. It is Christ and Christ alone.

December 29

IN YESTERDAY'S ENTRY, we listed the first six signs that neither prove (nor disprove) that affections are gracious, that God has salvifically come upon a person or a group. Today, we list in summary form the final six of these neutral signs.

1. **A person may at once experience religious affections of many kinds but not know the Lord.** (People can have all manner of responses happening at once, but this does not necessarily mean they are converted.)

2. **One may feel comforts and joys after a seeming awakening but not know true comfort in God.** (Mere relief over the idea of pardon does not equal being born again, for without definite trust in Christ we have no hope.)

3. **A person's disposition to spend much time in religion does not guarantee the presence of regeneration.** (One thinks of people like Martin Luther before his conversion, who was exceedingly religious, but did not know Christ.)

4. **Being inclined to praise and glorify God verbally does not mean the affections are righteous.** (False teachers will regularly give outward praise to God. See 2 Peter.)

5. **A person's exceeding confidence in being born again does not signal that he or she necessarily is.** (Simply because a person expresses unshakable confidence of being born again does not mean that person is born again.)

6. **The outward manifestations of seeming conversion may make other Christians think that one is converted but not be grounded in internal change.** (We may think a person is converted when no saving work has come to pass.)[69]

These comments encourage us to think carefully when helping professing Christians process their experiences. We are not looking for people who merely do the right things, as Jonathan Edwards makes clear. To be considered a Christian, a person cannot possess only the trappings of religion. He or she must have a whole-souled love of God as he reveals himself in Scripture. We do not try to dampen the affections of a professing believer; we do, however, strive to help him or her see that it is God who is the end of the Christian faith, and nothing else besides.

December 30

IN HIS EFFORT to defend the authenticity of the revivals, Jonathan Edwards listed twelve signs that showed evidence of "truly gracious affections." Where these emerged, God had likely worked in a majestic, converting way on individuals or groups of the lost. No one but God could know the state of the heart for certain, but these signs—taken together—pointed to the ministry of the divine.

Here are summaries of the first six of the positive signs.

1. Affections arise from those influences and operations on the heart that are "spiritual, supernatural, and divine." (Conversion is fundamentally a miracle.)
2. Affections are objectively grounded in the "transcendently excellent and amiable nature of divine things, as they are in themselves" (and not in self-interest). (It is the love of God, and not the mere desire to take care of oneself, that drives us to the Almighty.)
3. Affections are rooted in "the loveliness of the moral excellency of divine things." (The root of the love of God is praise for his holiness, his moral perfection, and perfect character.)
4. Affections "arise from the mind's being enlightened, rightly and spiritually to understand or apprehend divine things." (The Spirit drives us to the Word, and not fundamentally to impressions or mystical glosses.)
5. Affections are "attended with a reasonable and spiritual conviction of the judgment, of the reality and certainty of divine things." (Gospel faith creates conviction. When we know God, we no longer drift on a doctrinal sea, for we have found harbor in Christ Jesus.)
6. Affections are attended with "evangelical humiliation." (True Christianity does not create spiritual pride, but rather leads us, over the entirety of our lives, to see how needy we are, and how great Christ is.)[70]

These observations by Jonathan Edwards remind us that Christianity is not a club, a social gathering, or one viable spiritual path among many. Christianity is the truth; it is grounded in God; it is discovered in his Word; it tends to the humiliation of the sinner and the exaltation of the divine. So may it be in our lives today!

December 31

IN DEFENDING the revivals of the 1730s and 1740s, Jonathan Edwards listed twelve signs that gave heartening evidence of the Lord's activity in needy hearts and a desperate people. What follows are summaries of the last six of the positive signs, all of which deserve careful meditation and biblical confirmation.

1. **Holy affections bring about "a change of nature."** (We gain nothing less than a new nature, a new state of being, through regeneration.)
2. **The convert exhibits the "lamblike, dovelike spirit and temper of Jesus Christ."** (God breeds meekness and gentleness in unruly, angry hearts.)
3. **True spirituality "soften[s] the heart" and brings about "tenderness of spirit."** (If unbelief is marked by hardness of heart, conversion is marked by softness of heart to the truth.)
4. **There is "beautiful symmetry and proportion" in the character of a convert.** (Joy mixes with godly sorrow in the lives of believers.)
5. **Conversion yields a great "spiritual appetite and longing of soul" after spiritual things.** (There is an insatiable longing for God, and the things of God, in the hearts of believers, which does not go away in this life.)
6. **True righteousness breeds tangible, visible effects.** (There is a consistency and abiding interest in holiness that contrasts with those who have not tasted salvation.)[71]

These final signs direct us to the biblical reality that a good tree bears good fruit (Matthew 7:17-18). We have labored all year long to know the Lord. As the Spirit of God takes the people of God deeper into the Word of God, we will exhibit the character of God by the grace of God. Like Jonathan Edwards, our guide over these months, we are not perfect people. We are imperfect people praying for more holiness, more love, and more of Christ. The good news is this: All that we need, we have. All of God is ours. He has made us his own. No one can take us away from him.

We are always in God's hands.

Acknowledgments

I am grateful to the Lord for this opportunity to write. In eternity, I anticipate thanking Jonathan Edwards for allowing me to be his coauthor of six books now (and counting).

My wife, Bethany, was a tremendous support during this project. My son and two daughters were sweet and encouraging, offering me little notes, prayers, and occasional tackles upon my returning home. I love this precious family with all that I have.

My research assistants at Midwestern Baptist Theological Seminary in Kansas City, Missouri, deserve special thanks for their excellent work: Austin Burgard, Brandon Freeman, Ronni Kurtz, Sam Parkison, Jake Rainwater, and Tyler Sykora. All of these men took my MDiv elective course on Jonathan Edwards, "Theology and Life of Jonathan Edwards," and excelled in it. Students of this fiber are why I love teaching. Amid trials on every side, they give me tremendous hope for the future of Christ's church.

Erik Wolgemuth, my literary agent, helped in myriad ways throughout the project, and first connected me with Jon Farrar of Tyndale House Publishers. This book was Jon's idea, and though it took a little while to gestate, I loved this idea from the first, and enjoyed writing the book all the way through. To get to write alongside one of history's greatest minds is an inestimable gift. Thank you, Jon.

Thanks go out, as well, to Rick Holland, pastor of Mission Road Bible Church in Kansas City, for his friendship, prayers, and suggestions during my writing.

Finally, this book is dedicated to Dr. Jason Allen, president of Midwestern Seminary and a dear friend of mine. He has made it a joy for me to serve the churches of the Southern Baptist Convention by training future generations of pastor-theologians, missionaries, and ministry workers. Jason is a leader of the highest caliber, a watchman on the wall, and I am grateful for his friendship and leadership.

Resources

INTRODUCTION TO JONATHAN EDWARDS:
Owen Strachan and Douglas Sweeney, *The Essential Jonathan Edwards: An Introduction to the Life and Teaching of America's Greatest Theologian* (Moody, 2018).

AN INTENSIVE THEOLOGICAL ENGAGEMENT WITH JONATHAN EDWARDS:
John Piper, *Desiring God* (Multnomah, 2011).

ADVANCED READING ON JONATHAN EDWARDS:
George M. Marsden, *Jonathan Edwards: A Life* (Yale University Press, 2003).

TO READ JONATHAN EDWARDS HIMSELF:
Visit edwards.yale.edu, the official website of the Jonathan Edwards Center at Yale University, which provides free and searchable access to all the Works of Jonathan Edwards. (The print volumes, twenty-five in number, are well worth buying for bibliophiles and Edwards enthusiasts.)

Source Information for Epigraphs

Jonathan Edwards, *An Account of the Life of the Late Reverend Mr. David Brainerd* (Boston: D. Henchman, 1749), 121.

Jonathan Edwards, *The Works of Jonathan Edwards, Volume 1, Freedom of the Will*, ed. Paul Ramsey (New Haven, Yale University Press, 1957), 133, 278, 283, 285-286, 288.

Jonathan Edwards, *The Works of Jonathan Edwards, Volume 2, Religious Affections*, ed. Paul Ramsey (New Haven, Yale University Press, 1959), 108, 124-125, 200, 242, 250, 252-253, 257-258, 319-320, 324, 394, 420-421.

Jonathan Edwards, *The Works of Jonathan Edwards, Volume 4, The Great Awakening*, ed. C. C. Goen (New Haven, Yale University Press, 1972), 331, 337-340, 344, 381, 404-406, 518-519.

Jonathan Edwards, *The Works of Jonathan Edwards, Volume 7, The Life of David Brainerd*, ed. Norman Pettit (New Haven, Yale University Press, 1984), 95-96, 249-250, 261-262.

Jonathan Edwards, *The Works of Jonathan Edwards, Volume 8, Ethical Writings*, ed. Paul Ramsey (New Haven, Yale University Press, 1989), 430-432, 531, 554, 559, 560. Italics in the original.

Jonathan Edwards, *The Works of Jonathan Edwards, Volume 9, A History of the Work of Redemption*, ed. John F. Wilson (New Haven, Yale University Press, 1989), 449.

Jonathan Edwards, *The Works of Jonathan Edwards, Volume 10, Sermons and Discourses 1720-1723*, ed. Wilson H. Kimnach (New Haven, Yale University Press, 1992), 455-456.

Jonathan Edwards, *The Works of Jonathan Edwards, Volume 11, Typological Writings*, eds. Wallace E. Anderson, Mason I. Lowance, Jr., and David H. Watters (New Haven, Yale University Press, 1993), 54, 56, 58, 63, 66, 74-75.

Jonathan Edwards, *The Works of Jonathan Edwards, Volume 13, The "Miscellanies," a-500*, ed. Thomas A. Schafer (New Haven, Yale University Press, 1994), 163, 175-176, 184-185, 188, 199-200, 218-221, 224, 245-246, 286, 295-296, 328-329, 331-332, 345-346, 348, 375-376, 390, 395-396, 433-434, 447-448, 453-457, 474, 477-478, 482, 496-497, 511, 538.

Jonathan Edwards, *The Works of Jonathan Edwards, Volume 14, Sermons and Discourses: 1723-1729*, ed. Kenneth P. Minkema (New Haven, Yale University Press, 1997), 76-80, 103-109, 126-127, 171-172, 281-282, 287.

Jonathan Edwards, *The Works of Jonathan Edwards, Volume 16, Letters and Personal Writings*, ed. George S. Claghorn (New Haven, Yale University Press, 1998), 65, 66, 80-81, 88, 91-94, 109-110, 249-250, 289, 358, 416-417, 419, 577-580, 666-667, 730, 753-758, 790-793, 795.

Jonathan Edwards, *The Works of Jonathan Edwards, Volume 17, Sermons and Discourses, 1730-1733*, ed. Mark Valeri (New Haven, Yale University Press, 1999), 64, 65, 71, 85, 97-98, 117, 118-119, 128-129, 135, 138, 157, 166-167, 170, 171, 194-195, 202-205, 208, 213-214, 215, 225, 254-259, 261, 273, 279-280, 288, 294-295, 327-328, 343, 346, 376, 379, 380, 396-397, 413, 414, 417, 423, 424, 431-433, 443-444.

Jonathan Edwards, *The Works of Jonathan Edwards, Volume 19, Sermons and Discourses, 1734-1738*, ed. M. X. Lesser (New Haven, Yale University Press, 2001), 41, 43, 64-65, 70, 89-90, 112, 125, 129, 131, 140, 150-151, 214, 248, 250, 265, 270, 310, 311, 380-381, 383-384, 387, 389, 393, 396, 400-401, 447, 456, 460, 462-463, 477, 484, 504, 505, 511, 565-566, 567, 570, 573, 578, 584-586, 593, 594.

Jonathan Edwards, *The Works of Jonathan Edwards, Volume 20, The "Miscellanies," 833-1152*, ed. Amy Plantinga Pauw (New Haven, Yale University Press, 2002), 52-53, 57, 71-72.

Jonathan Edwards, *The Works of Jonathan Edwards, Volume 21, Writings on the Trinity, Grace, and Faith*, ed. Sang Hyun Lee (New Haven, Yale University Press, 2003), 113, 186-187.

Jonathan Edwards, *The Works of Jonathan Edwards, Volume 22, Sermons and Discourses, 1739-1742*, eds. Harry S. Stout and Nathan O. Hatch (New Haven, Yale University Press, 2003), 56-57, 91-92, 93, 95, 101-102, 142, 172-173, 191, 215, 392, 410-412, 415-416, 530, 531-532.

Jonathan Edwards, *The Works of Jonathan Edwards, Volume 23, The "Miscellanies,"* 1153-1360, ed. Douglas A. Sweeney (New Haven, Yale University Press, 2004), 73, 84, 94, 230, 347, 350, 382, 394-395, 409.

Jonathan Edwards, *The Works of Jonathan Edwards, Volume 24, The "Blank Bible,"* ed. Stephen J. Stein (New Haven, Yale University Press, 2006), 216, 251, 267, 281, 281-282, 440, 478-479, 539, 854, 931-932, 950-951, 1019-1020, 1037-1038, 1078, 1092, 1096, 1117-1118, 1189.

Jonathan Edwards, *The Works of Jonathan Edwards, Volume 25, Sermons and Discourses,* 1743-1758, ed. Wilson H. Kimnach (New Haven, Yale University Press, 2006), 101-102, 108-110, 116-119, 144-146, 180-181, 210, 212, 227-236, 242-243, 290-292, 484-485, 520-521, 539, 542, 544, 550, 562, 585-586, 643-645, 648-650, 705.

Jonathan Edwards, *The Works of Jonathan Edwards, Volume 40, Autobiographical and Biographical Documents,* ed. Jonathan Edwards Center; http://edwards.yale.edu/archive?path=aHR0cDovL2Vkd2FyZHMueWFsZS5lZHUvY2dpLWJpbi9uZXdkwaGlsby9zZWxlY3QucGw/d2plby4zOA==.

Samuel Hopkins, *The Life and Character of the Late Reverend Mr. Jonathan Edwards, President of the College at New Jersey* (Boston: S. Kneeland, 1765), 95.

Sereno E. Dwight, *The Works of President Edwards: With a Memoir of His Life, Volume 1* (New York: S. Converse, 1829), 127.

Notes

1. Quoted in Elisabeth D. Dodds, *Marriage to a Difficult Man: The Uncommon Union of Jonathan and Sarah Edwards* (Laurel, MS: Audubon Press, 2005), 15.
2. Sereno E. Dwight, *The Works of President Edwards: With a Memoir of His Life*, Vol. 1 (New York: S. Converse, 1829), 114-115.
3. George M. Marsden, *Jonathan Edwards: A Life* (New Haven: Yale University Press, 2003), 21–22.
4. "Memoirs of Jonathan Edwards," in *Jonathan Edwards*, Henry Rogers, Sereno E. Dwight, The Works of Jonathan Edwards, Vol. 1 (London: William Ball, 1839), ccxxviii.
5. Dodds, *Marriage to a Difficult Man*, 62.
6. Ibid., 63.
7. *The Works of Jonathan Edwards*, Vol. 8, *Ethical Writings*, ed. Paul Ramsey (New Haven: Yale University Press, 1989), 560. Italics in the original.
8. Ibid., 554, italics in the original.
9. Ibid., 559, italics in the original.
10. Solomon Stoddard, *The Safety of Appearing at the Day of Judgment, in the Righteousness of Christ, Opened and Applied* (Northampton, MA: Thomas M. Pomroy, 1804), 12.
11. "The Journal of Esther Edwards Burr," *Historia Obscura*, archived May 13, 2013, by Aya Katz; www.historiaobscura.com/tag/absent-mother.
12. Ibid.
13. Ibid.
14. From a letter written by Esther Edwards Burr to her father, Jonathan Edwards, archived in *Works of Jonathan Edwards*, Vol. 1, Christian Classics Ethereal Library, http://www.ccel.org/e/edwards/works1.i.xxiv.html.
15. *The Works of Jonathan Edwards*, Vol. 16, *Letters and Personal Writings*, ed. George S. Claghorn (New Haven: Yale University Press, 1998), 249–250.
16. Acts 17:28, NIV
17. Samuel Hopkins, comp., *Memoirs of the Late Reverend Jonathan Edwards, A.M.* (London: James Black, 1815).
18. Marsden, *Jonathan Edwards: A Life*, 491.
19. *The Works of Jonathan Edwards*, Vol. 8, 531, italics in the original.
20. *The Works of Jonathan Edwards*, Vol. 16, 65.
21. Ibid., 66.

22. *The Works of Jonathan Edwards*, Vol. 1, ed. Edward Hickman (Edinburgh: The Banner of Truth Trust, 1974), 224.

23. Marsden, *Jonathan Edwards: A Life*, 293.

24. *The Works of Jonathan Edwards*, Vol. 4, *The Great Awakening*, ed. C. C. Goen (New Haven: Yale University Press, 1972), 147–148.

25. *The Works of Jonathan Edwards*, Vol. 19, *Sermons and Discourses*, 1734-1738, ed. M. X. Lesser (New Haven: Yale University Press, 2001), 158.

26. *The Works of Jonathan Edwards*, Vol. 4, 150.

27. Tiffany Owens, "Walking through fire," *WORLD*, February 21, 2014, https://world.wng .org/authors/tiffany_owens.

28. Jonathan Edwards, "Youth Is Like a Flower That Is Cut Down," in *Sermons and Discourses, 1739–1742*, ed. Harry S. Stout, Nathan O. Hatch, and Kyle P. Farley, *The Works of Jonathan Edwards*, Vol. 22 (New Haven: Yale University Press, 2003), 336.

29. Ibid., 336-337.

30. Joseph Campbell, *The Hero with a Thousand Faces*, Bollingen Series XVII, third edition (Novato, CA: New World Library, 2008), 23.

31. Jonathan Edwards, "Doctrine of Original Sin Defended," in *The Works of President Edwards*, ninth edition, vol. 2 (New York: Leavitt & Allen, 1857), 323.

32. Marsden, *Jonathan Edwards: A Life*, 258.

33. Samuel Sewall, *The Selling of Joseph: A Memorial* (Boston: Bartholomew Green and John Allen, 1700), 1.

34. *The Works of Jonathan Edwards*, Vol. 16, 786.

35. Jonathan Edwards [Jr.], *The Injustice and Impolicy of the Slave Trade: And of the Slavery of the Africans* (Newburyport, MA: Charles Whipple, 1834), 17.

36. Ibid., 29.

37. Jonathan Edwards, "Narrative of Surprising Conversions," Nov. 6, 1736, in *The Works of President Edwards* in Four Volumes, reprint edition, vol. 3 (New York: Leavitt & Allen, 1851), 270.

38. Marsden, *Jonathan Edwards: A Life*, 343.

39. Jonathan Edwards, *The Works of Jonathan Edwards*, Vol. 25, *Sermons and Discourses*, 1743-1758, ed. Wilson H. Kimnach (New Haven: Yale University Press, 2006), 488.

40. *The Works of Jonathan Edwards*, Vol. 22, 410.

41. Jonathan Edwards, *The Works of Jonathan Edwards*, Vol. 17, *Sermons and Discourses*, 1730-1733, ed. Mark Valeri (New Haven, Yale University Press, 1999), 206.

42. *The Works of Jonathan Edwards*, Vol. 16, 792. ·

43. *The Works of Jonathan Edwards*, Vol. 12, 482.

44. *The Sermons of Jonathan Edwards: A Reader*, Wilson H. Kimnach, Kenneth P. Minkema, and Douglas A. Sweeney, eds. (New Haven: Yale University Press, 1999), 110.

45. *The Works of Jonathan Edwards*, Vol. 16, 797.

46. *The Works of Jonathan Edwards*, Vol. 17, 424.

47. *A Jonathan Edwards Reader*, John E. Smith, Harry S. Stout, and Kenneth P. Minkema, eds. (New Haven: Yale University Press, 1995), xxvii.

48. Jonathan Edwards, *The Distinguishing Marks of a Work of the Spirit of God* (Boston: S. Kneeland and T. Green, 1741), 54.

49. *The Works of Jonathan Edwards*, Vol. 16, 726.

50. *The Works of Jonathan Edwards*, Banner of Truth edition, vol. 1 (Edinburgh: Banner of Truth, 1974), clxxix.

51. Ralph Waldo Emerson, "Self-Reliance" (1841), in *Self-Reliance and Other Essays*, ed. Stanley Appelbaum, Dover thrift edition (Mineola, NY: Dover, 1993), 19.

52. *The Works of Jonathan Edwards*, Vol. 25, 225.

53. *The Works of Jonathan Edwards*, Vol. 16, 80.

54. Ibid., 87.

55. Ibid., 753.

56. Jonathan Edwards, *Charity and Its Fruits* (New York: Robert Carter & Brothers, 1854), 485-486.

57. *The Works of Jonathan Edwards*, Vol. 6, 166-167.

58. Ibid., 168.

59. *The Works of Jonathan Edwards*, Vol. 14, 137.

60. Jonathan Edwards, "Inquiry into the Freedom of the Will," in *The Works of President Edwards in Four Volumes*, reprint edition, vol. 2 (New York: Leavitt, Trow, 1844), 21-22.

61. C. S. Lewis, *Surprised by Joy: The Shape of My Early Life* (New York: Harcourt Brace, 1955), 69.

62. *The Works of Jonathan Edwards*, Vol. 7, 96.

63. Marsden, *Jonathan Edwards: A Life*, 347.

64. *The Works of Jonathan Edwards*, Vol. 12, 182.

65. Marsden, *Jonathan Edwards: A Life*, 491.

66. Ibid., 281.

67. *The Works of Jonathan Edwards*, Vol. 2, 95.

68. Adapted from Jonathan Edwards, *A Treatise Concerning Religious Affections* (New York: Leavitt, Trow, 1845), 22-35.

69. Ibid., 35-57.

70. Ibid., 65-137.

71. Ibid., 155-182.

Scripture Index

407

Topical Index

411

About the Author

OWEN STRACHAN is associate professor of Christian theology at Midwestern Baptist Theological Seminary and serves as a senior fellow of the Council on Biblical Manhood and Womanhood. In addition to being a contributing writer for the Gospel Coalition, he has written for *The Atlantic*, the *Washington Post*, OnFaith, *First Things, Christianity Today, The Federalist*, and the *Scottish Bulletin of Evangelical Theology*. Owen also regularly speaks to media outlets, including Fox News, the *Hugh Hewitt Show*, and the *Eric Metaxas Show*, and works as a research fellow of the Ethics and Religious Liberty Commission of the Southern Baptist Convention. He is married and is the father of three children.